Explaining Economic Policy Failure

Studies of the East Asian Institute,
Columbia University

Explaining Economic Policy Failure

Japan in the 1969–1971 International Monetary Crisis

Robert C. Angel

Columbia University Press New York

Columbia University Press
New York Oxford

Library of Congress Cataloging-in-Publication Data
Angel, Robert Charles, 1943–
Explaining economic policy failure : Japan in the 1969–71
international monetary crisis / Robert C. Angel.
p. cm. — (Studies of the East Asian Institute, Columbia
University)
Includes bibliographical references and index.
ISBN 978-0-231-07440-7
1. Monetary policy—Japan—History—20th century. 2. Monetary
policy—United States—History—20th century. 3. Japan—Foreign
economic relations—United States—History—20th century. 4. United
States—Foreign economic relations—Japan—History—20th century.
5. Japan—Economic conditions—1945–1989. 6. Japan—Economic
policy—1945–1989. 7. International finance—History—20th century.
I. Title. II. Series: Studies of the East Asian Institute.
HG1275.A54 1991
332.4'952—dc20 90-27196
CIP

Casebound editions of Columbia University Press books are Smyth-
sewn and printed on permanent and durable acid-free paper

Printed in the United States of America

To James William Morley

Studies of the East Asian Institute, Columbia University

The East Asian Institute is Columbia University's center for research, publication, and teaching on modern East Asia. The Studies of the East Asian Institute were inaugurated in 1962 to bring to a wider public the results of significant new research on modern and contemporary East Asia.

Contents

Preface

Mikio Mizuta, Japan's embattled minister of finance, led a group of senior international monetary officials aboard a regularly scheduled Pan American flight bound for Washington, D.C., on Wednesday afternoon, December 15, 1971. There, after a day of preliminary bilateral discussions, he and his subordinates joined counterparts from the world's largest industrialized market-economy nations in the spacious and elaborately decorated halls of the Smithsonian Institution's castle on the Mall for a final round of negotiations that settled Japan's most serious postwar international crisis and assured Mizuta a place in Japanese diplomatic history.

Two days of discussion, bluster, threats, and pleas in and around the Smithsonian's castle ended Saturday afternoon, December 18th, with the unexpected arrival of U.S. President Richard Nixon. Nixon congratulated the assembled officials on their efforts and immediately informed a large multinational crowd of journalists that the Group of Ten finally had reached agreement on a new global system of fixed exchange rates, an accomplishment he compared to that of the Bretton Woods Conference of 1944.[1] The 1971 "Smithsonian Agreement" would disappoint Nixon's high expectations, but it did end a long period of intense conflict between the United States and her major trading partners over appropriate rates of exchange. Mizuta had agreed, with Tokyo's approval, to a 16.88 percent up-valuation of the yen against the U.S. dollar as part of the final settlement, relieving months of international pressure and uncertainty. The newly established system of fixed exchange rates was certain to bolster global confidence in the international monetary system, slow defensive and speculative purchases of Japan's yen and attending inflow of unwelcome U.S. dollars, and silence the drumbeat of journalistic speculation.

Still, Mizuta and his entourage feared public criticism of their marathon negotiating effort as they began the long trip home from Dulles International Airport. For two decades Japan's international monetary experts had insisted publicly and privately that any change in the yen's parity would have disastrous consequences for the domestic economy, consequences far more serious than those of the periodic slowdowns imposed when the rate of economic growth bumped up against the "balance-of-payments ceiling." The government was pledged to resist foreign pressure to change the yen's parity at all cost, and had predicted—with West Germany's postwar experience as supporting evidence—that an initial adjustment would only encourage demands for further change. This considered, the Japanese public and communications media might well conclude their representatives had been defeated by international adversaries behind the thick walls of the Smithsonian. And to make matters worse, some members of the negotiating team were inclined to agree.

The international crisis that finally forced Japan's delegation to adjust the yen's parity in late 1971 had been brewing for more than two years. President Nixon's electrifying earlier announcement on Sunday evening, August 15, 1971 (Monday morning, August 16, Japan time), of the administration's decision to suspend the dollar's convertibility into gold and to impose a 10 percent surcharge on all dutiable imports had raised the critical temperature considerably. But the crisis had actually begun for Japan in 1969, when other global trading-system members began to protest Japan's growing propensity to run a surplus in the current account of her international balance of payments, and thereby to accumulate foreign currency reserves at a rate that further endangered the stability of the international monetary system.

Japan by late 1969 had moved, in the opinion of most international observers, from "deficit-prone" to "surplus-prone" international economic status, a change that under the rules of the Bretton Woods system required a fundamental reordering of Tokyo's international economic priorities. Japanese authorities, however, were far less optimistic about their own situation. They accepted the accuracy of monthly statistical reports showing ever-higher Japanese surpluses, and agreed with European and American near-term predictions (confirmed by their own confidential official forecasts) that the upward trend was likely to continue. But official Japanese opinion differed with the prevailing international assessment of Japan's long-term balance-of-payments prospects.

Ministry of Finance (MOF) officials responsible for management of Japan's international monetary affairs had struggled for decades against foreign exchange scarcity, devising and implementing strategies that maximized export earnings and minimized expenditures on imports. They had been forced every few years to recommend the imposition of politically unwelcome growth-dampening measures, once prolonged domestic economic growth had stimulated imports and reduced the growth of exports to the point that foreign exchange reserves declined to unhealthy levels. For them, Japan's newly acquired wealth was a welcome but temporary windfall, nothing more than an unusually high point in the familiar up-and-down postwar pattern. Long experience with deficits had conditioned them to resist any hasty response to foreign grumbling that might later threaten Japan's ability to pay her own way in the world once the balance-of-payments situation returned to their conception of "normal." Foreign currency reserves considered an embarrassment today, MOF international monetary officials reasoned, later would be welcomed as insulation against "balance-of-payments ceiling" crises yet to come.

In addition to the bothersome current account surplus, Japan's international economic officials were increasingly concerned from late 1969 onward with the stability of the international monetary system. Confidence in the U.S. guarantee to maintain the convertibility of the dollar into gold—the cornerstone of the postwar arrangements—had declined to the extent that holders of dollars throughout the world were exchanging them for other currencies expected to increase in value, creating an alarming outflow of U.S. dollars into other countries. By 1969 demands from all points of the compass for fundamental systemic reform had increased in volume and intensity from background murmur to roar. Most disturbing for Japan, such calls usually included proposals for a major realignment of the world's exchange rates.

No country felt more dependent than Japan upon the international economy, and upon a reliable, predictable international monetary system to link her traders and investors to the world. The tremors that shook the system during the late 1960s were measured and analyzed as carefully as the high-Richter-scale earthquakes that rattled Tokyo's new skyscrapers. Foreign proposals for international monetary reform throughout 1969 and 1970 generated alarming articles in Japan's daily and weekly press, especially when Japan's growing international surpluses were identified as a major cause of the problem. But Japan's representatives, fearing a loss of international economic competitiveness, continued to oppose meaningful reform of the Bretton Woods system. They insisted that IMF rules placed responsibility for recovery of equilibrium squarely upon the shoulders of deficit countries, which, including the United States, should apply the politically unpalatable domestic economic belt-tightening measures necessary to reduce imports and expand exports.

Tokyo did respond to increasingly severe foreign criticism with proposals for liberalization of restrictions on imports and foreign investment in the Japanese economy, easily reversible technical adjustments designed to slow the accumulation of foreign reserves, and with international public relations and lobbying programs intended to maintain the status quo by weakening foreign pressure for change at its source. They refused, however, even to consider any adjustment in the fixed Y 360 = $1 parity of the yen. It took the shock of the Nixon administration's August 15, 1971 announcement to change their minds, and then only after nearly two weeks of intense internal debate.

History has proved the "stand fast" judgment of Japan's international monetary officials to be far off the mark on this fundamentally important issue. Their delay had serious negative economic consequences at home, and even more serious and enduring political consequences for Japan in the international arena. Japan's international accounts continued to register embarrassing surpluses, and her manufactured exports remained concentrated in a few politically sensitive product areas, a pattern that incited domestic anti-Japan business and trade union pressure on the national governments of her most important trading partners. Confidence in the Bretton Woods system continued to deteriorate until marginal, then fundamental, changes became unavoidable, in part the result of what European and American observers began to characterize as Japan's selfish and short-sighted international economic behavior. After more than two years of resistance, Japan in late 1971 was forced by irresistible foreign pressure to abandon the misguided policy of maintaining the fixed Y 360 = $1 exchange rate and to begin to implement the policy measures inevitably required to adapt her economy to changes in the international economic environment.

Japan's response to fundamental change in her relationship with the international economic environment within the context of a disintegrating international monetary system during the late 1960s and early 1970s has proved an interesting subject for study first because of the great importance of the issue. Japan's high standard of living depends upon solid trade and investment relationships with other nations whose economies can supplement her inadequate supplies of foodstuffs, primary products, and semiprocessed goods and absorb her manufactured exports. The government takes very seriously its responsibility for maintaining an effective relationship with the world economy. And its discharge of that responsibility is monitored carefully by Japan's business community, communications media, and public. Assessment of their handling of this task is a key factor in the government's overall performance rating.

Therefore, unease over anything as fundamental to Japan's relationship with the world economy as the international monetary system was considered important by the whole nation. It was, in fact, the most important international challenge Japan had faced since the end of World War II, and all of Japan was interested in the outcome. Hardly a day went by, especially during 1971, that an article about the international monetary crisis wasn't front-page news. Television news broadcasts and even entertainment programs were drenched with discussion of the issue. The public may not have understood all of the technical detail, but they believed the yen's exchange rate was of direct and immediate importance to their own economic interests and expected their government to do something about it.

Japan has been shielded from military threats of crisis intensity since World War II, so there has been no opportunity to study her postwar response to such a challenge. Although economic rather than diplo-military, the 1969–1971 international monetary crisis was the closest Japan had come to a serious threat to her overall well-being since the end of the war. Since the policy-making system has changed little since the early 1970s, analysis of Japan's response to the 1971 international monetary crisis provides clues to how the system might respond to similar international crises, including diplo-military challenges, if and when they occur in the future.

Another interesting feature of Japan's response to the 1969–1971 international monetary crisis is the "general," rather than "specific" nature of the challenge. Our best economic policy-making studies of Japan to date have focused upon the government's handling of issues related to particular sectors of the economy such as textiles, automobiles, computers, or agricultural products. These specific issues provide important insights into Japan's policy processes, but by their nature are of greater importance for some sectors of the business community and government than for others. This limits the scope of attention and involvement of governmental and private-sector actors. The international monetary crisis, in contrast, was important—and was understood to be important—to all sectors of Japan's economy and public. Since any change, especially a change in the parity of the yen, was expected to affect the overall business environment, even groups and individuals not involved in foreign trade or investment were concerned. This more general interest broadened the scope of potential policy process participants.

Yet another interesting aspect of the 1969–1971 international monetary crisis was its relatively long time period, first surfacing in a serious way in 1969, and intensifying throughout 1970 and 1971. Most high-intensity issues quickly come and go, leaving policymakers with little time to respond, and analysts with little material to study. This issue provided both in abundance. It went through several levels of intensity, beginning with a routine phase during much of 1969 and 1970. Sudden growth in international account surpluses created a "protracted crisis" environment during the early part of 1971, which escalated into "intense crisis" with the August 15 announcement of the suspension of U.S. dollar convertibility into gold and imposition of the 10–percent surcharge on dutiable U.S. imports. Protracted crisis then characterized conditions between the float of the yen on August 27 and the Smithsonian settlement in mid-December.

The Japanese government's handling of international monetary affairs during the late 1960s and early 1970s was neither an economic nor a political success, and this is yet another interesting feature of this particular issue. Most English-language material, scholarly and journalistic, presents a very positive image of Japan's economic policy machinery and its operation. This trend is hardly surprising—only appropriate—considering Japan's remarkable record of economic achievement in the modern period, particularly after World War II. Foreign scholars and popular writers have focused more of their efforts on explaining Japan's economic successes than on instances of failure.

While there is no reason to question the widespread assumption of the overall positive impact of the government's economic policies, this pattern of research has led to the accumulation of literature that presents the English-language student with a somewhat unbalanced overall interpretation of the economic functions of Japan's government. A study that takes as its focus an issue on which the performance of Japan's economic policy machinery has been judged less than a success should provide some balance. That the issue selected was as important to Japan—and to the rest of the world—as the 1971 international monetary crisis should make it even more useful.

A final point of interest is the importance of U.S. pressure for the outcome of Japan's policy formulation and implementation processes. Foreign pressure in one form or another is an inevitable component of any negotiation that attempts to resolve international conflict, be it subtle manipulation of eyebrow or conspicuous movement of the instruments of war. Nothing is unique about Japan and the United States pressuring each other in some fashion to achieve their own objectives. Yet Japan's international policy processes seem to rely more heavily on "foreign pressure" *(gai-atsu)* than do those of other countries, especially in her relations with the United States, a phenomenon that has not gone unnoticed in Washington.

The Textile Wrangle by I. M. Destler, Haruhiro Fukui, and Hideo Sato, perhaps the best English-language sectoral study of the politics of postwar U.S.-Japan economic relations, includes material on the role of *gai-atsu* in the resolution of the 1969–1971 conflict over textile trade.[2] Their work provides an interesting point of comparison, especially since the natures of the issues under consideration were so different. The textile issue was a typical sectoral problem, and one on which it would be difficult for the fabled "neutral observer"—let alone anyone in Japan—to feel much sympathy for the American position. The 1971 international monetary issue, on the other hand, was general rather than sectoral, and provided an area of disagreement upon which the angels themselves may have experienced difficulty in choosing sides.

In this study I focus on the formulation and implementation of Japan's overall international monetary "policy" during the period, as Raymond Bauer has used the term, rather than on routine actions or tactical decisions, to identify and explain the interaction of those factors that produced Japan's official response to the shift from deficit- to surplus-prone balance-of-payments status and the change in her international monetary environment during the late 1960s and early 1970s.[3] Important policy process participants include five categories of individuals and institutions: elected officials and political parties; career bureaucratic officials and government ministries; businessmen and representatives of business interest groups; international monetary experts outside government; and the communications media and general public. Following the general pattern suggested in the bureaucratic politics literature, I went in search of answers to four general questions:[4]

1. *Who were the most important individual and institutional participants in the policymaking process, and what determined their access?* Government participants—both politicians and bureaucrats—could be expected to become involved on the strength of their official positions. Yet a list of responsible elected and appointed officials taken from a government organization chart likely would include some nonparticipants while excluding important actors. Private individuals, for example, might have obtained access on the basis of their reputation for expertise, as representatives of some private interest or as members of the communications media.

2. *What were the stands, or positions, of each participant, and how were they determined?* Given the sensitive nature of the issue, some participants likely expressed positions in public quite different from their actual opinions or from the positions they pressed during private policy discussions. Also, given the long time period, the stands of significant policy participants might well have changed. The individual's organizational affiliation, his personal background, his perceptions of the international economic situation and of the Japanese domestic economy's well-being, as well as the other concerned individuals with whom he came in contact, all were considered possible determinants of policy "stands," or positions.

3. *What were the relative levels of influence and the sources of that influence?* Which individual and organizational participants were most important in determining policy response to the burgeoning surpluses, and what made them important? Possible determinants

of influence include formal authority, control over the allocation of important resources, information or expertise, bargaining skills, and prior relationships with other influential individuals. Influence or power is difficult to measure precisely. But reasonable estimates can be made by comparing the individual's own opinion of his influence with that of the opinions of others around him, and by comparing the number of times that his "stand," or position, coincided with the final policy outcome.

4. *How did the various participants' positions, influence, and their actions combine to determine the outcome of the policy process?* Put another way, how did Japan respond to the change in her international monetary environment brought about by the shift from deficit- to surplus-prone balance-of-payments status during the late 1960s and early 1970s?

The scholarly and popular literature on the remarkable performance of Japan's economy during the modern period gives a great deal of credit to the government's economic policy role. Often mentioned as explanations for their success are: a highly qualified and motivated government bureaucracy; a minimum of "political interference" in important economic decision making; a preference for bottom-to-top flows of policy initiatives rather than the more dictatorial top-down model thought to characterize other systems; a "consensus" style of decision making that strives to include all actors with a potential interest in the issue under consideration; and a remarkable ability to promote cooperation among groups with diverse interests. In light of all this, what happened to international monetary affairs during 1971?

I began the search for information with which to answer the above questions in the United States, with a review of public accounts of events published during the period available, especially back issues of Japan's major national newspapers, weekly economic news magazines, and scholarly monographs and periodicals. These sources provided a chronology of the more important events, some speculative reports of behind-the-scenes discussions (which generated specific questions for personal interviews) and a sense of the problem as it was felt in Japan at the time.

During the 1975–1976 academic year, with generous support from the Fulbright-Hayes Program and the Social Science Research Council, I visited Tokyo armed with an outline of events to comb that part of the public record not available in the United States. I added a few detailed accounts of events published some years later by individual participants and informed observers. Those accounts provided more detail and helped to clarify official and unofficial positions of the policy participants. To these I added information from the government record, including transcripts of parliamentary debates on the floor of the Upper and Lower House and relevant parliamentary committees. Some unpublished records of government agencies and private institutions also were made available during my 1975–1976 stay in Tokyo, but access to such documents was very limited, and those made available obviously were carefully selected. Such a response was not unexpected since the government's handling of the 1969–1971 international monetary crisis was still a sensitive topic of conversation among current and former Japanese government officials more than five years after the event.

The final source of information came from over fifty personal interviews with virtually all of the central participants. A list of interviews appears in the Appendix, but many were granted with the understanding that the information provided would not be directly attributed to the source. During each interview I attempted to clarify the positions attributed to each participant in the public record, the nature of the unpublished negotiations on important points, the reasons behind each participant's stand, and each participant's opinion of his own behavior, the behavior of other participants, and of the policy performance of the Japanese system as a whole.

None of the participants refused to be interviewed. Most interviewees were cooperative, and many seemed genuinely interested in explaining what they believed actually happened. But all participants were reluctant to discuss certain sensitive aspects of the subject. It was easier to confirm noncontroversial information already available in the public record than it was to fill in certain critical details. The interviewees were without exception highly professional, experienced individuals, unlikely to be finagled into revealing much more than they thought appropriate to an eager foreign researcher, even when tempted with the possibility of avenging wounds from old policy battles in print.

It would be difficult to conjure up a group better suited to play the villains in an academic piece than the Nixon-Connally-Volcker combo. And indeed I initially selected this topic because it seemed ideally suited to demonstrate how Washington's economic nationalism, ignorance of Japan, disinterest in foreign economic relations, and lack of in-house expertise on Japan can combine to produce intense political friction in the U.S.-Japan economic relationship. But by the end of the information collection phase of the study I could no longer sustain the belief that Japan's response would have been significantly different, or that the adjustment process would have been smoother, if only Washington had been more patient, better informed about Japan, or had made their intentions clearer before the infamous "Nixon shocks."

The Nixon administration certainly was insensitive in its dealings with Japan on this and other issues, and it was by no means overstaffed with officials who could call themselves Japan experts in public without embarrassment. But these factors and overall American treatment of Japan were not the most—or even the second-most—important determinants of the outcomes of Japan's policy processes.

Ministry of Finance officials responsible for international monetary affairs maintained tight control of the issue throughout the period of the study, and they adamantly opposed any change in the fixed Y 360=$1 parity of the yen. Confident of their ability to manage international pressure for change through Japan's system of effective foreign exchange controls and intense international public relations and lobbying campaigns, they ignored mounting evidence of "fundamental disequilibrium" and growing international hostility toward economic Japan. Instead they focused all of their energies on maintaining the fixed exchange rate, and even failed to develop internal contingency plans with which to cope with international monetary developments of the sort initiated by President Nixon on August 15, 1971.

Potential competitors for influence over this important issue, including other governmental ministries and agencies, Japan's business community, independent international monetary "experts," the communications media, and general public opinion were effectively excluded by the highly technical, sensitive, and secretive nature of international monetary affairs. And in contrast to more sector-specific issues, this issue's more general nature discouraged formation of private-sector pressure groups in opposition to established policy.

Even top-level political actors were isolated from Japan's international monetary policy processes. The Liberal Democratic party cabinet under Prime Minister Eisaku Sato was responsible under the postwar constitution for oversight and integration of the work of each ministry and agency of the national bureaucracy, and was also institutionally positioned to order a re-examination of policy if they had wished. But Sato and his cabinet avoided involvement for all of the above reasons, and because of Japan's tradition of "political noninterference" in the work of the bureaucracy. This tradition of political noninterference ususally is identified as a positive attribute of Japan's policy-making processes. But Japan's handling of international monetary affairs between 1969 and 1971 demonstrates that it also weakens supraministerial coordination of policy, which makes it difficult for Japan to respond promptly and effectively to changes in her international environment.

Lacking effective central political coordination of the separate bureaucratic fiefdoms, Japan's system is inclined to rely on foreign pressure *(gai-atsu)* to resolve internal policy disputes far more than is healthy either for Japan or for Japan's relationships with the sources of that pressure. For issues of true national importance with significance broader than the domain of a single ministry and its officials, the responsibility of Japan's political leadership for the national interest becomes more than an ideological nicety. Their active participation is required to avoid policy errors that inevitably arise from bureaucratic "localitis" and "tunnel vision," and to avoid increasingly unwelcome doses of *gai-atsu.* Although undesirable, such external pressure is likely to substitute for effective supraministerial policy coordination for the foreseeable future, with increasingly unfortunate consequences for Japan's international relations.

I gratefully acknowledge the support, encouragmeent, and perseverance of numerous individuals and organizations during the long preparation of this manuscript. Professors Gerald Curtis, Herbert Passin, Andrew Nathan, and Hugh Patrick of Columbia University, John Campbell of the University of Michigan, T. J. Pempel of Cornell, Yoshitaro Kato of Japan's Institute of Local Government, Edward Lincoln of the Brookings Institution, and anonymous Columbia University Press reviewers read all or parts of the draft and made valuable suggestions for revision. The final product benefited gretly from their comments and criticism. Professor James W. Morley of Columbia's Department of Political Science and often director of the East Asian Institute, first suggested the subject of the study. Special thanks is due him for many years of unwavering support, encouragement, helpful criticism, and his personal example as teacher and scholar.

The Fulbright-Hays Program, the Social Science Research Council, the East Asian Institute of Columbia University, and the Institute of International Relations of the University of South Carolina all granted generous financial support. Columbia's East Asian Institute provided a year of administrative support and the opportunity to work in a most stimulating environment. The Department of Government and International Studies at the University of South Carolina granted partial release from teaching responsibilities during the fall term of 1986. In Japan, the National Diet Library, the Archives Section of the Ministry of Finance, and Keidanren offered research facilities and access to some of their files and reference materials. The project would have been inconceivable without this institutional support, for which I am deeply grateful.

While few named are likely to agree with my conclusions, many individuals in Japan and the United States gave freely of their time, information, and advice in the hope of improving American understanding of economic and political Japan and U.S.-Japan relations. Especially helpful in Japan were Messrs. Takashi Hosomi, Iichiro Hatoyama, and Toyoo Gyohten of the Ministry of Finance, Yasushi Hara of Asahi Shimbun, and Masaya Ichikawa of Voice of America. Professors Takafusa Nakamura and Motoo Kaji of Tokyo University provided early advice on the general approach, and introductions to government officials, politicians, and businessmen. From beginning to end, Mr. Hiroshi Ando of Asahi Shimbun critiqued my approach, provided alternative interpretations of events, arranged invaluable personal introductions, and provided additional reference material. In Washington, Mr. Richard Lawrence of the Journal of Commerce and Mr. Rich Thomas of *Newsweek* recalled Washington's response to the crisis from the economic journalist's perspective, rounded up additional unpublished materials, and arranged meetings around town with other observers and participants.

Ms. Tamio Togasaki of Columbia's Japan Documentation Center and Ms. Miwa Kai of the Columbia University East Asian Library both made valuable suggestions during the preliminary search in Japanese source materials. Messrs. Key Kobayashi, Thadeus Ohta, and Hisao Matsumoto of the Library of Congress facilitated access to their vast collection, and suggested many additional Japanese language sources. Mr. Azusa Tanaka of the National Diet Library arranged convenient use of his library facilities, and also suggested new paths of inquiry. At the University of South Carolina, Ms. Sudah Retan searched out and confirmed statistical data. Ms. Michelle Fox provided general research assistance without complaint during the hectic final stage of the project, checked footnotes, designed, and then created the statistical tables. Ms. Kate Wittenberg, Mr. Leslie Bialler, and the highly professional staff of the Columbia University Press all were most helpful, encouraging, and patient with an inexperienced author. Mr. Roy Thomas of New York City provided far more than copy editing. His blue and red pencils exposed inconsistencies, clarified murky passages, and made the manuscript far more readable. Mr. David Fischer of Columbia, South Carolina, created the index promptly and with good humor. To all I express my sincere thanks.

A special expression of gratitude goes to my wife, Junko T. Angel, without whom the project would have been impossible even to consider. For more than twenty-five years, through thick and thin, she has been an unwavering source of advice, encouragement, and support, accepting without complaint the familial adjustments required, and rejecting flatly even credible excuses for failure to complete the manuscript. Finally, loving thanks to our children, Lisa and Andrew, for enduring the missed vacations, weekends, and evenings of normal family life.

1. The Rise and Decline of the Bretton Woods System

International Monetary Relations

Trade and investment among nations requires agreement on how the value of one national currency is expressed in the values of others. The gold standard handled this potentially disruptive problem throughout much of the latter half of the nineteenth and the beginning of the twentieth centuries. Currencies of all major trading countries were denominated in gold. Gold was coined and circulated by most countries, and any other currency—paper or metal—was guaranteed convertible into gold by the issuing government. Traders receiving payment for exported goods in a foreign currency either received gold or were able to exchange that foreign currency for their own, or for gold, at a highly predictable rate. International reliability and predictability were the gold standard's main advantages as an international monetary regime.[1]

The late nineteenth- and early twentieth-century gold standard also provided international trading nations, at least in theory, with impartial automatic or market pressure toward international balance-of-payments equilibrium. Imbalances were settled with transfers of gold from deficit to surplus countries. The transfer of gold from countries that tended to import more than they exported reduced their total money supply, deflating domestic and export price levels. The resulting price advantage in foreign markets tended to increase the deficit-prone countries' exports, moving them toward equilibrium. In contrast, the money supplies of surplus countries that received the gold expanded, driving up domestic and export prices, moving them in the opposite direction, also toward international equilibrium.

This international reliability and predictability came, however, at the cost of considerable domestic economic dislocation. Richard Cooper emphasized this domestic economic cost during a conference at the Brookings Institution held to discuss proposals to revive the gold standard during the first term of the Reagan presidency. He argued: "The one feature the gold standard did secure was stability of exchange rates among major currencies, except for those that remained on silver. Under the gold standard, price stability and other domestic objectives were, when necessary, relinquished to preserve stability in exchange rates."[2] The gold standard could provide international reliability and stability only when the central governments of trading nations could resist political demands for change generated by its harsh domestic economic consequences.

World War I forced temporary suspension of the gold standard mechanism as belligerent nations tightened national control of their economies to direct all available economic resources toward military preparedness. Imports and exports were tightly controlled and nearly all foreign accounts were frozen by the combatants. But the international predictability and stability of the prewar gold standard were not forgotten after the end of the war as the nations of Europe struggled to reconstruct their national economies and the international economic relationships so important to that effort.

Great Britain announced convertibility of her pound into gold in 1925 and the French franc followed in 1926, but both at unrealistic rates of exchange. Great Britain returned the pound to its prewar rate, considerably overvalued, while France moved in the opposite direction, pegging the franc at one-fifth its prewar rate, grossly undervaluing it on world markets.[3] Such unrealistic conversion values, combined with the declining willingness of national governments to subordinate domestic economic objectives to those of international balance required to maintain the gold standard, threatened the system's long-term survival.[4]

The gold standard adopted during the interwar period was more complex than its pre-WWI predecessor. In order to conserve gold stocks and reduce the domestic destabilizing impact of international flows, the governments of the participating countries suspended the coining of gold and called privately held monetary gold into their central banks.[5] It was the central banks, then, that during the interwar period transferred gold when necessary at a fixed price in response to international balance-of-payments imbalances.

Participating countries also included the gold-backed currencies of other countries in their official reserves. The U.S. dollar, for example, was accepted by other countries and held as part of their reserves with the understanding that the United States government would honor its commitment to exchange those dollars for gold upon demand.

Exchange rates instability was the inevitable result of divergent national economic interests and the inability of the governments of the major trading nations to impose the domestic political discipline required to make the system work. The disadvantages of international cooperation and system maintenance gradually came to outweigh the perceived advantages, as noted by Ragnar Nurkse in a late League of Nations publication: "The fate of the gold exchange standard was sealed when France decided in 1928 to take nothing but gold in settlement of the enormous surplus accruing to her from the repatriation of capital and from the current balance of payments. The French gold imports certainly aggravated the pressure of deflation in the rest of the world and especially in London."[6]

Participating nations one after another abandoned convertibility during the late 1920s, and even Great Britain, the system's strongest supporter, was forced to withdraw by 1931. In June and July of 1933 the League of Nations sponsored the World Monetary and Economic Conference, a multilateral exploration of means to develop an alternative that would stabilize exchange rates. This extensive effort ended in failure.[7]

The world depression encouraged beleaguered governments during the 1930s to implement competitive devaluations intended to increase sales of their exports at the expense of their trading partners, a trend that created even more exchange rate turbulence. Restrictive trade policies, higher and higher tariffs, and import restrictions worsened the situation. The international monetary system was in total disarray by the outbreak of World War II.

Political and military considerations overshadowed international economic concerns during the second world war, just as they had during the first. Germany's minister for economic affairs and president of the Reichsbank, Dr. Walther Funk, proposed a new plan for postwar European international monetary relations in 1940 that included Germany at the core of an "intelligent division of labour between the various European countries."[8] Funk's proposal inspired little support in the rest of the world and was ignored by Great Britain and the United States. It was clear that alternative measures would have to be ready for implementation once the war ended.

The 1944 Bretton Woods Conference

At the invitation of the United States, official representatives of 44 countries and a special representative from Denmark met at the Mount Washington Hotel in Bretton Woods, New Hampshire on July 1, 1944, to complete negotiations on the final shape of the postwar international monetary system. Their accomplishments were remarkable considering the political and economic sensitivity of the issues involved and the diverse national interests represented, even with Germany, Italy, and Japan excluded.

The group's task was simplified from the outset by two important factors. First, all agreed that what preceded 1944 was not worth saving. The bitter experience of competitive devaluations, protective tariffs, and the international depression was fresh in the minds of all participants. Germany's wartime economic policies and behavior also provided the external threat so supportive of internal cohesion and cooperation, and a convenient bad national example to which all could refer. So in 1944 there was no in-place system with the support of an intense minority that could complicate or delay the negotiations.

A second factor promoting the success of the Bretton Woods conferees was that discussion during the latter stages of the negotiations was restricted almost entirely to two plans presented by the two most important international economic powers—one from the United States, largely the work of then Assistant to the Secretary of the Treasury Harry Dexter White and his staff at Treasury; the other from Great Britain and developed by John Maynard Keynes. With the United States expecting postwar international surpluses and Great Britain expecting deficits, the differences of interests and opinions between them conveniently expressed the most critical points of disagreement about the structure of the postwar system.[9]

Keynes' plan naturally reflected his perception of Great Britain's national economic interests at the end of hostilities. The war had deprived Britain of any near-term hope of generating exports sufficient to pay for the imports required for postwar reconstruction, and Keynes' proposal naturally emphasized access to international credit for reconstructing nations. Keynes hoped to maintain freedom of action for member countries and to prevent the proposed Fund from interfering in the domestic economic policies of participating nations. U.S. representatives, on the other hand, hoped to institute tighter Fund control over member nations.[10]

Keynes' plan went through several drafts prior to the Bretton Woods Conference. The fourth version, circulated in early 1942, contained the main points.[11] The centerpiece was to be an International Clearing Union.

> The proposal is to establish a Currency Union, here designated an International Clearing Union, based on international bank-money, called (let us say) bancor, fixed (but not unalterably) in terms of gold and accepted as the equivalent of gold by the British Commonwealth and the United States and all members of the Union for the purpose of settling international balances. The Central Banks of all member-States (and also of non-members) would keep accounts with the International Clearing Union through which they would be entitled to settle their exchange balances with one another at their par value defined in terms of bancor.[12]

The Union was to be controlled by a board with members appointed by the member states. Like a supranational bank, the International Clearing Union would loan funds to those countries whose imports temporarily exceeded their exports, and accept surplus funds as deposits from those countries whose exports exceeded their imports. Since each country in surplus would have corresponding deficits in other countries exactly equal to the amount of their surplus, the system would always stay in overall balance, and credits would be available to finance the deficits of heavy importers because their credits would be deposited with the Clearing Union.

Of course, overall balance would not be enough. The system had to include rules that would prevent member countries from running either chronic deficits or surpluses. To accomplish this, Keynes' plan suggested that each country be assigned a "quota," a figure proportional to the foreign trade of that country during three years prior to the war, which would define the amount that each country could borrow from the Clearing Union during a deficit period and also their responsibilities as their borrowing reached certain levels of their total quota.

Interesting in hindsight, Keynes' plan included a proposal unattractive at the time to his American counterparts but which they might well have welcomed twenty years later, that would have required creditor nations, as well as debtor nations, to pay a 1 percent fee on the amount their account was out of balance with the Clearing Union. Although there was no limit fixed in the plan upon the creditor nation's surplus with the Union, since such a limit would automatically result in overall imbalance, this inclusion of the one-percent charge on surplus accounts would have distributed responsibility for the maintenance of overall international monetary system balance more fairly among both debtor and creditor nations, a feature the U.S. government might have found useful in years to come.

Harry Dexter White's American plan also went through several drafts during the early 1940s, and was published on July 10, 1943, as the position of the international monetary experts in the Department of Treasury.[13] White's plan proposed the formation of "The International Stabilization Fund of the United and Associated Nations." The "Fund" was to be made up of contributions by member countries in gold, their own currencies, and their government securities, amounting to around $5 billion. Each national member's "quota" for contribution was to be determined by a complex formula that would depend upon their gold and foreign currency holdings, foreign trade, and national income. The fund was to have its own monetary unit, called "Unitas," with its value linked to gold. But "Unitas" was a far cry from the international currency, "bancor," proposed by Keynes. In fact, a previous version of the White plan went to some lengths to explain that a new international currency was an unnecessary addition to the scheme that would only simplify economic research.[14]

Changes in exchange rates, initially based on the rates prevailing on July 1, 1943, with exceptions for obvious distortions, were to be the business of the Fund. After agreement on their initial value,

> Changes in the exchange value of the currency of a member country shall be considered only when essential to the correction of fundamental disequilibrium in its balance of payments, and shall be made only with the approval of three-fourths of the member votes including the representative of the country concerned.[15]

White's Stabilization Fund too was to be run by a board of directors, one from each participating country, with each Director's vote weighted according to the size of the quota of the country he represented. Decisions, except where agreed different, were to be made by majority vote. The board was to appoint a managing director and an executive committee. Once the Fund was established and financed by contributions from each of the member countries, any country in balance-of-payments difficulty was to be allowed to buy the foreign exchange needed to settle its international debts from the Fund with its own currency, provided that such transactions did not bring the Fund's total holdings of the purchasing country's currency to over 100 percent of its national quota (50 percent during the first year of operation).

Compared with Keynes' plan, White's, first of all, was of much smaller scale. The total resources to be made available to member countries under the Stabilization Fund's quotas were to be much smaller than the sources of "credit" envisioned for Keynes' Clearing Union. Also, White's plan had no provision to increase the total amount of international liquidity as foreign trade expanded after the end of the war. In addition, the White plan foresaw a much more important role for the international institution in the establishment of each country's exchange rate than had Keynes.' Rates were not to be changed by member countries without the consent of the Fund. This caution reflected the U.S. position as the most likely creditor nation after the end of the war, with fears that indiscriminate devaluations might be made by deficit-prone countries.

The final versions of each proposal clearly represented the relatively near-term economic interests of the proposing nation as they were understood by each side at the time. Had U.S. Treasury officials known that the United States was destined to become deficit- rather than surplus-inclined by the late 1960s, their response to some of the points in Keynes' proposal may have been different. Richard Gardner comments in the preface to the new edition of his impressive 1956 study *Sterling-Dollar Diplomacy:* "If the United States had accepted the Clearing Union and used it to cope with the financial problems of the postwar period rather than the Marshall Plan and other postwar aid programs, it would have accumulated some $30 billion in unconditional liquidity—enough to finance virtually all the US deficits in the 1950s and 1960s."[16]

After comparing notes, British and American representatives agreed to meet between September 15 and October 9, 1943, in Washington to bring their positions into closer agreement. Keynes led the British delegation and White the American. These Washington negotiations and subsequent exchanges of drafts resulted in the

Anglo-American Joint Statement, a final draft of which was published the following April. During these talks Keynes agreed to work within the American "Stabilization Fund" framework, suggesting that it be called an "International Monetary Fund" in January 1944.[17]

Although agreement even between the two major actors was far from complete, the United States issued invitations to the governments of 44 countries and a representative from Denmark to attend the final conference after one more preliminary conference in Georgia that June. Each delegate arrived at Bretton Woods at the beginning of July 1944 with 1,200 pages of proposals and amendments. The time suggested for completion of the final negotiations was twenty days.

Detailed records of the official and unofficial meetings were not kept, but at the end of three weeks a document considered sufficiently specific to present to the governments of the various participants for ratification, and yet ratifiable, was agreed upon.[18] This Bretton Woods Agreement created two new international organizations: the International Bank for Reconstruction and Development (to be known as the World Bank), which would provide loans for the reconstruction of European economies damaged by the war, and the International Monetary Fund, the organization of interest here. As stated in its Articles of Agreement, the IMF proposed to promote:

1. International monetary cooperation
2. Domestic economic growth and employment in member countries through expanded international trade
3. Exchange rate stability
4. The elimination of foreign exchange restrictions
5. The financing of temporary international deficits for member countries
6. International balance-of-payments equilibrium among member countries[19]

Each country was assigned a quota by the Committee on Quotas during the conference, chaired by Fred M. Vinson, later secretary of the treasury. Agreement on the size of the quotas was reached through a complex formula devised by the Treasury Department that took into account each country's GNP, total reserves, and share of world trade, with a final round of political haggling at Bretton Woods. The total of all 45 countries' quotas was to be $8.8 billion, including $1.2 billion from the USSR, which participated in the conference but failed to join the IMF. The U.S. share was $2.75 billion, roughly one-third of the total, and that of the United Kingdom $1.3 billion. The quotas defined each country's contribution to the international currency pool, its voting strength in IMF decisions, and the amount available to it for borrowing when imports exceeded exports. Quotas were to be reviewed every five years.

Par values for each currency were to be set in terms of gold or the U.S. dollar, which in turn was pegged to gold at $35 per ounce. These values were to be maintained within a margin of plus or minus 1 percent. Rules were established that allowed member countries to change their currency's par value in cases of "fundamental disequilibrium"—a term far more political than economic, and therefore never clearly defined—after consultation with the Fund. After discussions among the member countries, initial par values for 32 countries were published by the Fund on December 18, 1946.[20] The remainder of the Agreement's twenty Articles defined the working relationship between the member governments and the Fund, spelled out member countries' obligations, and went into some detail about the administrative apparatus that would manage this new overseer of the Free World's monetary system.

Just before the deadline for ratification, on December 27, 1946, the seemingly impossible task of establishing an International Monetary Fund was completed when 29 countries representing over 80 percent of the total Fund quota signed the Agreement. Fund operations then were free to begin on March 1, 1947.

Strengths and Weaknesses of the Bretton Woods System

The international monetary system established at Bretton Woods began operation in 1946. Keynes, White, and their colleagues had given the world's trading nations a system far more suited to the postwar political and economic environment than any of its predecessors. Margaret Garritsen de Vries, official IMF historian, has summarized the accomplishments of the Fund, and concludes that during the 1950s it had accomplished its three primary objectives: establishment of par values for all exchange rates, removal of exchange restrictions, and establishment of currency convertibility.[21] It provided in surprising measure the combination of stability, predictability, and flexibility required to enable world trade to adapt to the domestic economic and political change that occurred at different rates around the world.

In spite of its remarkable accomplishments, the system was not without weaknesses, however, and as a contributing factor of the causes of the international monetary crisis Japan faced during the late 1960s and early 1970s, these weaknesses must necessarily be the focus of this study. In *The International Monetary System, 1945–1976,* a comprehensive survey of postwar international monetary affairs seen from the staff of the Federal Reserve Board, Robert Solomon has identified three general systemic weaknesses: a lack of means to expand world reserves at a rate appropriate for the growth of world trade; a vaguely defined balance-of-payments adjustment process; and difficulty dealing with "large disequilibrating capital flows."[22]

The liquidity problem—creation of worldwide reserves adequate to finance the expanding volume of international trade—and its relationship to the U.S. balance of payments had been identified at least as early as October 1959 by Robert Triffin in testimony before the Joint Economic Committee of Congress in terms of what became the famous "Triffin dilemma": "a) if the United States corrected its persistent deficits, the growth of world reserves could not be fed adequately by gold production at $35 an ounce; but that b) if our deficits continued, our foreign liabilities would far exceed our ability to convert them into gold upon demand, and bring about a gold and dollar crisis."[23]

The significance of the international liquidity problem for this study lies in its impact on the international response to the growing U.S. deficit. Although continuing U.S. deficits concerned other nations, they realized that the system required this inflow of liquidity to support its expansion. This need dampened concern and criticism abroad and at home during the 1950s and early 1960s of the growing American deficit problem, since any serious effort to stanch the flow of U.S. dollars into the system would also force agreement on the design and implementation of a more systematic source of liquidity.

The exchange rate adjustment issue inspired yet another source of classic tension between national and global objectives during the Bretton Woods Conference. The conferees hoped to design a system that would prevent wild exchange rate fluctuation like that of the interwar period. But they also realized that some rate adjustment was required to allow member nations to adapt over the years to internal and external economic changes. The solution was a *stable,* rather than a *fixed,* exchange rate system.

This still left two problems of high political sensitivity: location of responsibility for exchange rate changes, and agreement on the conditions under which such changes should be made. Keynes, fearing U.S. impatience with Britain's ability to meet her financial obligations during postwar reconstruction, pressed for national autonomy with a minimum of international interference in each member nation's economic policies, including the exchange rate. White, on the other hand, reflecting the interests of a surplus nation perhaps too confident of its own economic future, was more concerned with whether or not member nations would meet their obligations under the new international system, and the potential financial liability for the United States should they refuse. Joseph Gold notes that in the April 1942 version of his proposal White even gave the new institution the right to determine exchange rates. But "since then there has never been a disposition to empower the Fund to compel a change in the exchange rate of a currency. Under Article IV of the Second Amendment, however, the Fund may conclude that a change in, or the immobility of, the exchange rate for a member's currency is inconsistent with its obligations under Article IV."[24]

At the end of the conference the Articles of the Fund stated that changes in exchange rates were appropriate under conditions of "fundamental disequilibrium," a vague term that seems to make sense, but that the conferees were either unable or politically unwilling to define. John Williamson has commented that "Although never formally defined, and therefore a target for much critical academic comment, there was never much doubt what this concept meant: a situation in which a country could not expect to achieve basic balance over the cycle as a whole without deflating output from full capacity or restricting trade or payments for balance of payments reasons."[25] So, fundamental disequilibrium may have been more obvious than the academic literature implies. But that has not saved government officials with international monetary responsibility from the arduous task of explaining time and again why conditions in their nation do not represent what we all understand to be "fundamental disequilibrium."

A related weakness of the Bretton Woods system was the disproportionate responsibility for maintenance of equilibrium placed on deficit nations. The Bretton Woods agreement included no effective source of institutionalized pressure on surplus nations to assume responsibility for maintenance of international balance. Even Keynes' relatively mild proposal mentioned above for a 1 percent surcharge on surplus countries had been rejected.

This systemic weakness was unimportant as long as the United States remained the overwhelmingly dominant member of the international system, and American balance-of-payments outflows were judged beneficial by all parties. U.S. officials could respond to dips in American accounts with lectures to their deficit nations counterparts, such as Japan, on the need to be more thrifty and more aggressive in international trade in order to pay their international bills. The situation changed, however, once the surpluses shifted to other member nations who found remedial action politically difficult.

The Bretton Woods System During the 1950s and 1960s: From Dollar Shortage to Dollar Glut

In spite of some inevitable long-term weaknesses, the Bretton Woods Agreement did produce a system that allowed most nations to pursue their postwar domestic economic objectives with a minimum of international interference for nearly twenty-five years. But problems of adjustment and liquidity, together with rapid postwar change in relations among the major economic powers, gradually combined to produce insuperable problems. Within fifteen years of the initial agreement the international monetary system was under severe strain from a number of sources, most of which were related to the U.S. dollar.

Early Postwar Dollar Shortage. The war effort strengthened, rather than weakened, the American industrial base. This was in sharp contrast to immediate postwar conditions in the major European trading nations and Japan. For several years, demand from those nations for American industrial products seemed unlimited as they struggled to repair war damage and bring their standards of living back to prewar levels. This demand, in turn, created strong demand abroad for the dollars needed to pay for American goods, making the U.S. dollar the world's strongest currency by far during the early postwar years. Thus was born the early postwar "dollar shortage."

The dampening impact of the dollar shortage on European and

Japanese postwar redevelopment efforts became more of a concern for American policymakers as their growing perception of an international communist threat heightened the political, as well as the economic, importance of the economic recovery of Western Europe and Japan. The Marshall Plan, announced in 1948, was part of the American effort to bridge the gap. Between 1948 and 1952 $16 billion in unsecured funds flowed through its programs from the United States to European countries. In addition, the United States encouraged large-scale devaluations of the other major currencies against the dollar and gold in order to increase the competitiveness of their exports abroad and reduce the costs of their imports.[26]

As the only currency guaranteed freely convertible into gold or other currencies during this early period, the U.S. dollar soon became the "key currency" of the international monetary system. The U.S. dollar, in Triffin's words, "had unwittingly acquired the poisoned 'privilege' of being used overwhelmingly as the universally acceptable 'parallel' currency against which every other country sold or redeemed its own national currency in the exchange markets."[27] Other countries began to use the dollar freely as a medium of exchange in their international transactions, as the medium with which they intervened to stabilize the parity of their own currency within the plus or minus 1 percent required by the International Monetary Fund's rules, and as part of their official reserves in place of gold. Great Britain, whose currency had played a similar prewar role, made a final effort to restore sterling to its prewar prominence in the world monetary order with announcement of full convertibility in 1947. The market, however, met the British move with a speculative attack on the pound so severe that it forced suspension of convertibility within a few weeks.[28] The 1947 effort only deepened British international debt and left the U.S. dollar with no competition for Triffin's "poisoned privilege."

American efforts to provide other countries with dollars adequate to finance their purchases of U.S. goods in the 1940s and early 1950s proved most effective. Even though the United States ran healthy trade surpluses in most years, outflows of foreign aid, military spending, and investment dollars created net outflows throughout the 1950s for every year except 1957. News of the deficits was welcomed at home and abroad for some time, helping to limit, as they did, the dollar shortage.[29] International confidence in the U.S. guarantee of the convertibility of the dollar into gold remained strong. Other nations were willing to add the system's

Table 1
Year-end Values of Major Western Currencies 1950–1970
(Expressed in U.S. Dollars)

	United Kingdom (Pound)	*West Germany (DM)*	*France (Franc)*	*Canada (Dollar)*
1950	2.801	—	.2850	.9696
1951	2.805	—	.2850	.9878
1952	2.814	—	.2850	1.0430
1953	2.820	—	.2875	1.0330
1954	2.820	.2355	.2863	1.0380
1955	2.806	.2384	.2863	1.0370
1956	2.812	.2488	.2863	1.0460
1957	2.810	.2383	.2863	1.0620
1958	2.811	.2395	.2388	1.0450
1959	2.818	.2399	.2044	1.0580
1960	2.818	.2398	.2042	1.0540
1961	2.817	.2519	.2042	1.0180
1962	2.818	.2510	.2041	.9580
1963	2.806	.2518	.2041	.9290
1964	2.801	.2519	.2042	.9320
1965	2.806	.2517	.2042	.9320
1966	2.805	.2519	.2042	.9320
1967	2.802	.2519	.2042	.9330
1968	2.409	.2517	.2032	.9320
1969	2.397	.2713	.2020	.9310
1970	2.406	.2754	.1816	.9840

Source: Standard and Poor Statistical Index, 1984.

"key currency" to their official reserves without complaint. And, as Triffin and others have indicated, any reduction in supplies of American dollars abroad would have required system participants to devise a new source of liquidity.

Continued Dollar Outflow Intensifies International Monetary Unease. The postwar economic reconstruction of Europe—with the exception of the United Kingdom—and Japan reduced their import dependence on the United States and increased the competitiveness of their exports in world markets. The change was gradual but steady. By the late 1950s the Europeans were no longer as eager to accept unlimited amounts of U.S. dollars in settlement of American obligations as they had been during their period of recovery. The widely publicized decline in American gold reserves intensified concern abroad about American willingness and ability to maintain the commitment to exchange U.S. dollars into gold at $35 per ounce upon demand, the cornerstone of the whole system. U.S. gold stocks had declined by more than $5 billion between 1958 and 1960, compared with a total reduction of only $1.7 billion during the previous seven years.[30]

By 1960, a presidential election year, the "gold flow" was a popular subject of political discussion as U.S. gold stocks continued to decline through payment of international obligations. Demand for gold suddenly drove the price on the London market to $40 an ounce for a short time at the end of October, splashing international monetary affairs onto the front pages of even American newspapers, and inspiring presidential candidate John F. Kennedy to declare during an October 31 campaign speech that as president he would take all measures necessary to defend the dollar-gold exchange rate at $35 per ounce.[31]

Pressure on the system continued during the Kennedy Administration and intensified throughout the 1960s. European governments, especially the French, had become more confident and willing to press their own interests in their dealings with the United States. They complained of the unfair advantage the "key currency" role of the dollar afforded the United States, charging that only American domestic economic policies were unrestrained by international economic considerations, and that American corporations were buying European assets with dollars of increasingly dubious value. There were no credible suggestions, however, that the U.S. dollar be devalued, either from Europe or the United States. Rather, the demand was for incremental adjustment within the international monetary system as it had evolved since Bretton Woods: more conservative domestic economic policies, reductions in U.S. foreign investment, and a review of American foreign aid and military spending.

Palliative Measures. International efforts were made during the 1960s to stabilize the system, especially to increase confidence in the U.S. dollar. In addition to formalization of the Gold Pool in 1961, the Basle Arrangement of 1961 of the Bank for International Settlements provided informal, secret agreements among its participants to support each other's currencies when under speculative attack.[32] In 1962 the General Arrangements to Borrow were arranged among the ten largest members of the IMF. This arrangement provided guarantees of loans to any country whose currency came under fire, should its borrowing rights in the IMF be insufficient to dampen that pressure.[33] Currency swap arrangements among the major countries also were arranged for the same reason.[34]

At home, the Kennedy administration confirmed the new president's campaign pledge to maintain the dollar's convertibility into gold at the $35 per ounce rate, and took additional measures to reduce the flow of U.S. dollars and gold abroad, including promotion of foreign tourism and investment in the United States, cuts in the foreign aid budget, export promotion efforts, and the "Kennedy Round" of tariff reduction negotiations. "Roosa Bonds," named for Robert Roosa, then under secretary of the treasury for monetary affairs, were sold to countries such as Germany that were dependent upon the United States for military support. Paying no interest, but guaranteed convertible upon expiration at the same rate of exchange at which they were purchased, these bonds were issued in order to raise public confidence in the dollar.[35]

The Crisis Intensifies. International monetary shakiness intensified during the Johnson administration. Only the most optimistic officials continued to believe that stability could be achieved without major changes in the way the system was managed. The combined cost of the Great Society social welfare programs and the Vietnam War created domestic deficits in Washington that further eroded national confidence in the dollar, and led the international monetary system toward an even more serious crisis in the mid-1960s. As conflict in Southeast Asia escalated, European countries pointed to U.S. deficits and complained that the United States was using its privileged international monetary position to finance an unjust war.

The Johnson administration attempted to counter the outflow of dollars with voluntary restraints on American investment abroad in early 1965, mandatory capital controls at the beginning of 1968, and finally tax-enhancing and government expenditure-reducing measures at the end of June 1968. But dollars continued to flow from the United States to countries with stronger currencies, eroding the credibility of the U.S. commitment to maintain the dollar's convertibility and the stability of the overall system.

Domestic economic problems and growing international deficits combined to leave Great Britain vulnerable to attack in 1967. In spite of strong official denials of plans for a devaluation of sterling, the pressure increased, primarily from the French. Great Britain ultimately was forced to devalue again in November 1967, and the British adjustment was taken as further evidence of overall systemic instability, encouraging nervous foreign holders of dollars to exchange them for gold. Repeated announcements from Gold Pool participants of their intention to support the $35 an ounce rate had little impact in the market, and gold flowed from the pool in a river. By March 1968 the situation was impossible to sustain. After a hectic day of trading, the market was closed on March 15 and a two-tier system was created under which gold would find its own price level in a free market in one tier, and official transactions would be carried out at $35 an ounce in the other.[36]

The finance ministers of the ten major countries held emergency meetings in Bonn in late November 1968 to discuss countermeasures but failed to reach agreement. Private-sector market participants were confident in their predictions of the direction of eventual adjustment which stimulated huge swings of speculative short-term capital from one currency to another, with the U.S. dollar, the West German mark, the French franc, and the Japanese yen receiving the most attention.

Dramatic student and labor demonstrations against a background of domestic economic strain and unemployment produced a sense of crisis in France during 1968. This, in turn, stimulated speculation about the future of the franc and frantic flights from francs to other currencies, especially the German mark. In spite of the firm official denials of any plans for a devaluation, France was forced by the intensity of the attack to bolster her declining foreign currency reserves through activation of swap arrangements, IMF borrowings, and even the sale of gold. Even after President de Gaulle's resignation, the new French government of Georges Pompidou announced its firm intention to maintain the parity of the franc and instituted strict anti-inflationary policies to help reduce the outflow of funds. Their efforts proved ineffective, however, and on August 10, 1969, the franc was devalued by 11.11 percent, a figure even higher than pessimistic international opinion had expected.[37]

West Germany became the reluctant recipient of much of the funds flowing from France in anticipation of an up-valuation of the mark. Pressure was particularly intense in November 1968 during the meeting of the Group of Ten in Bonn and continued throughout

1969. West German economic authorities stuck by their commitment to maintain the mark's parity, however, arguing that the imbalance was created by the domestic economic policies of the United States and other nations. General elections scheduled for the end of September 1969 made the situation even more sensitive politically.

In spite of their effort, the Germans were forced by speculative pressure to close the exchange on September 25, just before the election. They notified IMF authorities that they would allow the mark to float once the exchange opened on the 29th, the first day of the Fund's annual meeting, held that year in Washington, D.C. The dramatic international announcement, made by Managing Director Pierre-Paul Schweitzer during his opening address, further shook confidence in the system, especially since the float occurred after repeated German assurances that they intended to maintain their parity. The German move left only the U.S. dollar and the Japanese yen in the speculative spotlight for the time being.

Adjustment Reform Efforts Fail. By the late 1960s, in light of the creation of Special Drawing Rights and the huge outflow of U.S. dollars, reform efforts had shifted from concern over whether or not the international monetary system could generate liquidity adequate to finance expanding international trade to the more difficult exchange rate adjustment problem.

As noted above, the Bretton Woods conferees drafted an agreement that supplied the world with *stable,* not *fixed* rates of exchange. But they left the exchange rate adjustment procedures rather vague. Each nation was free to define "fundamental disequilibrium" to suit its immediate economic and political needs. Changes in rates of exchange, especially for the larger countries, became increasingly difficult in lieu of strong, institutionalized rules of the game. The parity adjustments that did occur were traumatic events, each worse than the last, preceded by destabilizing flows of short-term speculative capital that weakened confidence in the international monetary system, created domestic economic problems, and generated domestic political problems for the governments finally forced to change their parities. Exchange rate adjustment by the end of the 1960s, as noted by Margaret de Vries, was made even more difficult by the spectacular growth of the Eurocurrency market, funds beyond the control of any government, the multinationalization of large corporations, the growing number of large banks with foreign branches, and even—ironically—the success of postwar efforts to liberalize government controls over capital and foreign exchange.[38]

The tension surrounding the changes in the parities of the franc and mark provided a sense of greater urgency for the ongoing discussion of methods to improve exchange rate flexibility. For years academic and government economists had been proposing rules changes that would increase exchange rate flexibility. They recognized that it was often politically difficult for governments to approach the IMF with requests for agreement to make a change in their parity, and that for various reasons such changes were often put off, especially by the larger countries, until market pressures had grown to a point that sudden, destabilizing adjustments became unavoidable. Supporters of reform suggested that a revision of the rules which would provide for more gradual, or automatic, adjustment in response to fundamental changes in the international environment, or a country's domestic economy, would help to avoid destabilizing rate changes and improve the overall stability of the system.

Two methods were most frequently mentioned: a widening of the band of plus-or-minus fluctuation that was allowed a currency from its fixed parity under the provisions of the IMF Articles of Agreement; and, a "crawling peg" system that would allow the parity of each currency to be moved up or down by a specified percentage of its value during a specified period of time in response to market forces.[39] The sense of impending crisis that overhung international money markets during the late 1960s brought these discussions of the need for greater exchange rate flexibility out of the lecture hall into the IMF boardroom.

At the suggestion of Managing Director Schweitzer, the IMF executive directors began to discuss possible methods of introducing more exchange rate flexibility in January 1969. Between January 15 and March 10 ten top-secret meetings of the executive directors were held at IMF headquarters in Washington to discuss proposals for wider margins, crawling pegs, and a system of dual parities, one for trade and one for capital transactions. The subject became the focus of more public discussion during the annual IMF meeting at the end of September. The 1969 annual meeting agreed after some debate that the Fund should continue to study the proposals. By August 12, 1970, this diverse group of staff and executive directors had painfully crafted a report entitled "The Role of Exchange Rates in the Adjustment of International Payments" for presentation to the Fund's board of governors at the September annual meeting.[40]

Although the report contained only modest proposals to reduce the "rigidity" of the system while maintaining its basic stability, and in spite of the heightened concern during the annual meeting over the system's future caused by the recent French and German experiences and the May 31 Canadian announcement of a float, the IMF governors rejected the report's conclusions in Copenhagen and opposed any further consideration of methods to increase exchange rate flexibility. Japan's representative, Finance Minister Takeo Fukuda, was among the proposal's strongest opponents.

It is unlikely that any of the modest reforms proposed in 1970 by themselves would have corrected the growing lopsidedness of the international monetary system, even if they had been immediately agreed upon and implemented. But if approved they would have become an important step toward an eventual international settlement of the problem within the framework of the Bretton Woods system that would have made radical unilateral action by the United States less likely. Their rejection itself increased speculation that the system was basically unstable and it was only a matter of time before more dramatic action would be taken.

The gold crisis, destabilizing parity changes for the British pound, the French franc, and the West German mark between 1967 and 1969, as well as concern over the continuing hemorrhaging of the American dollar all proved inadequate to force meaningful international monetary reform on a reluctant community of nations. Short-term funds continued to flow into West Germany; the international economic position of the United States and confidence in the dollar continued to deteriorate; and Japan, the only major country other than the United States to avoid a parity change since the setting of the current rate in the late 1940s, stoutly resisted any suggestion of an up-valuation, in spite of large and increasing international surpluses, making the yen an increasingly attractive target for international speculation.

U.S. Domestic Economic Performance Intensifies the Crisis

After more than five years of the relatively free-spending Johnson administration, the November 1968 victory of the more conserva-

Table 2
Selected U.S. Economic Indicators, 1960–1973

	Consumer Price Inflation *	*Wholesale Price Inflation* *	*GNP Growth* *	*Unemployment Rate*	*Fed. Reserve Disc. Rate*
1960	1.5	0.5	4.1	5.5	3.53
1961	0.7	−0.2	3.2	6.7	3.00
1962	1.2	0.0	7.7	5.5	3.00
1963	1.6	−0.1	5.4	5.7	3.23
1964	1.2	0.4	7.1	5.2	3.55
1965	1.9	3.4	8.3	4.5	4.04
1966	3.4	1.7	9.5	3.8	4.50
1967	3.0	1.0	5.9	3.8	4.19
1968	4.7	2.8	8.9	3.6	5.17
1969	6.1	4.8	7.6	3.5	5.87
1970	5.5	2.2	5.0	4.9	4.95
1971	3.4	4.0	8.0	5.9	4.88
1972	3.4	6.5	9.4	5.6	4.50
1973	8.8	18.2	11.5	4.9	6.44

Source: President's Council of Economic Advisers, *Annual Report*, February 1974
* Percent Change from Preceding Year

tive Richard Nixon raised public expectations for a return to higher economic growth, lower inflation, and perhaps even a tolerable level of unemployment. With a keen sense of their sources of electoral support and the electorate's expectations, Nixon and his political advisers realized that their economic policy of "gradualism" had to show fairly immediate results if that confidence was to be repeated at the polls in 1970 and 1972.

The disappointing 5.8 percent rise in the consumer price index during the first half of 1969 was easily blamed on the free-spending policies of the previous administration. And during late 1969 there was still time to predict confidently that the Federal Reserve Board's clampdown on the money supply would soon achieve results. But during the second half of 1969 inflation continued to rise at about the same rate as during the first, in spite of higher interest rates and unemployment and sluggish GNP growth. Excuses became more difficult to make as the months went by. Even conservative economic commentators with sympathy for the Republican administration began to suggest publicly that the Federal Reserve Board might be overdoing its dose of monetary castor oil.

The first half of 1970 proved even worse. Consumer prices rose at an annualized rate of about 6 percent, unemployment stood at 4.7 percent in June (1.3 percent above its June 1969 level, meaning that another million Americans were out of work) and inflation-adjusted GNP was dropping at an annual rate of over 3 percent.[41] After nearly two years in office it became politically impossible for the Nixon administration to continue to blame the nation's economic performance on its Democratic predecessors. By mid-1970 Washington's confidence in its domestic economic game plan began to waver, and splits appeared within the ranks of the president's senior economic advisers in and out of government.

The dramatic bankruptcy of the Penn Central Railroad in mid-1970 and the costly two-month United Auto Workers' strike against General Motors later in the year heightened public discontent. Campaigning under the banner of "Nixonomics," the Democratic party dealt the Republicans a heavy blow in the November 1970 midterm elections, picking up more than ten seats in the House of Representatives. This electoral setback inspired a sudden conversion to a public profession of the Keynesian economic faith by President Nixon himself, and renewed calls from his conservative economic advisers for consideration of an "incomes policy," a proposal flatly rejected by Nixon before and after his election. The first half of the following year brought even worse inflation and unemployment and ever-widening public discontent with the administration's ability to solve the economic problems they had been elected to tackle.

The international economic arena provided no relief for the praise-starved group of economic reformers. After some improvement during the first half of 1970 over the disappointing 1969 performance, American international economic accounts began to trend downward once again in the latter half of 1970, with the slope steepening during the last quarter of the year. After three quarters of surplus performance in 1970, the current account once again registered a $166 million deficit between October and December, and the official reserves transactions balance for the year was $9.8 billion in deficit, compared with a $2.7 billion surplus in 1969, reflecting a heavy loss of U.S. dollars to the Eurodollar market. Although the United States had been able to maintain its traditional surplus in the purchase and sale of goods and services to other countries, that balance too began a decline in the third quarter of 1970, a trend that was to continue throughout the period of this study. And, as Washington eased monetary conditions in the latter

Table 3
U.S. Global Economic Balances, 1960–1973

	Global Trade Account	*Global Current Account*	*Gold Reserves*
1960	4,892	1,801	17,800
1961	5,571	3,069	16,950
1962	4,521	2,456	16,060
1963	5,224	3,199	15,600
1964	6,801	5,783	15,470
1965	4,951	4,306	14,060
1966	3,817	2,320	13,230
1967	3,800	2,051	12,060
1968	635	−443	10,890
1969	593	−1,050	11,860
1970	2,176	416	11,070
1971	−2,698	−2,790	11,080
1972	−6,912	−8,353	10,490
1973	−653	334	11,650

Source: President's Council of Economic Advisers, *Annual Report,* February 1974
Note: Unit U.S. $1 million

half of 1970 in response to the dismal performance of the domestic economy, both the current situation and the outlook for the future on the international side became more and more depressing.

The Exchange Rate Option. With little hope for near-term improvement in the U.S. economy sufficient to renew international faith in the value of the dollar and a dramatic improvement in the international economic performance, attention within the U.S. international monetary policy community began to turn toward exchange rate adjustment. A change in the dollar's exchange rate could not be made easily. At home, President Nixon had campaigned on a promise to strengthen, not weaken, the international position of the dollar. It would be difficult politically to explain to the public and their elected representatives why anything called a devaluation would be a step in that direction. Furthermore, any change in the dollar price of gold would, under U.S. law, require the approval of Congress, a measure that administration political strategists considered at the time difficult to achieve.

With the U.S. dollar still the key currency of the Bretton Woods system, there were international as well as domestic difficulties with a dollar parity change. European countries and Japan were expected to resist such a move if only because it would reduce the international competitiveness of their goods. A unilateral American parity change could simply result in equivalent countervailing parity changes on their part, leaving the situation essentially as it was before. If done in a clumsy fashion, the resulting international monetary turbulence could prove more damaging to all concerned than the current disequilibrium.

In spite of those domestic and international political difficulties, U.S. government officials with international monetary responsibility began to exchange memoranda concerning the pros and cons of exchange rate adjustment for the dollar at least as early as January of 1971. William B. Dale, the U.S. executive director of the International Monetary Fund since November 1962, circulated a secret memorandum (since declassified under the Freedom of Information Act) among Treasury Department officials in late January entitled "Exchange Rate Realignment and Related Matters." In it Dale presented "some essential elements of a scenario which would be aimed at accomplishing a major realignment of exchange rates while still observing certain of the unavoidable constraints on possible action by the United States and taking account of what may be legally and practically feasible in the existing international monetary system."[42] The Dale scenario included a suspension of the dollar's convertibility into gold just before the annual meeting of the IMF later in the year, a closing of the U.S. exchange markets for a short period, and intensive international negotiations that would result in "a major realignment of exchange rates which could be called either an appreciation of other rates relative to the dollar or a depreciation of the dollar relative to other currencies, depending on one's taste and one's national affiliation."[43]

Dale concluded:

> It is obvious that the negotiating problems would be of a truly extraordinary degree of difficulty and complexity; that technical and policy "spinoffs" from the main propositions briefly put forward above could be major; and that—at least in the short term—financial markets everywhere would be in an uproar. The question is: Can a gradual (or fast) disintegration of the free world's economic and financial system be evaded by any less ambitious proposal?[44]

In late February 1971 George Willis, a seasoned Treasury Department international monetary professional, wrote a "confidential, for limited distribution" memorandum for Under Secretary

Paul Volcker on the worsening international economic position of the United States, the continuing flow of U.S. dollars into Europe, and declining American gold stocks.[45] In contrast to the Dale memo, Willis' does not propose any particular course of action. But it does mention the possibility of adverse international reaction to a U.S. decision to suspend the convertibility of gold, implying that this option was being considered actively in private early in 1971 within U.S. official circles.

Michael Bradfield, assistant general counsel of the Treasury Department, even prepared a complex legal analysis of the Treasury secretary's authority to initiate action to change the dollar's international parity, including mention of the Emergency Banking Act's provision that during national emergencies declared by the president the secretary "has authority to regulate or prohibit any transactions in foreign exchange, transfers of credit or payments by, through or to any banking institution," mentioning that it might be important when the decision about how to deal with the international problem finally was made.[46]

Congressional concern over international economic affairs intensified during early 1971 in response to burgeoning balance-of-payments deficits and import competition in the American market. The Joint Economic Committee (JEC), for example, issued a report coauthored by Senator Charles Percy and Congressman Blackburn on March 29 in which they argued that the United States could no longer afford to ignore the balance of payments or to impose its international monetary will on the rest of the world. They suggested that American monetary officials should listen more carefully to the opinions of their counterparts from other countries and make more of an effort to coordinate domestic and international economic policies. But foreign countries, in the opinion of the two JEC members, should also consider exchange rate adjustment if they felt that their dollar holdings were accumulating to unacceptable levels.[47] The JEC report's concerns were echoed a few days later in a *New York Times* editorial on the increasingly serious problem of excessive dollar holdings by foreign countries and resulting U.S. deficits. The *Times* suggested that other countries consider currency realignment and also supported the idea of greater exchange rate flexibility.[48]

These public suggestions that a change in the parity of the U.S. dollar might be in order, of course, further weakened the confidence of foreign and domestic holders of dollars in its future. Again in early April dollars began to flow out of the United States into Western Europe at an even more alarming rate. By April 3 the situation became so serious that the Treasury Department felt compelled to issue an unusual public explanation. They labeled the flows essentially short-term, insisted that the government had no interest in a change in exchange rate policy, and added that Treasury believed parity adjustments by other countries were not called for at that time.[49]

This reaction led to the charge from abroad, and even from critics at home, that the Nixon administration was following a policy of "benign neglect" in its dealings with the rest of the world, ignoring the U.S. deficit situation with the expectation that other countries would take their own countermeasures once they tired of accumulating U.S. dollars of questionable future value. Treasury Secretary John Connally's rejection of the policy of "benign neglect" later in the month at a meeting of the U.S. Chamber of Commerce was taken with a grain of salt at home and abroad, and by the end of April European calls for U.S. action were reported from government officials in West Germany and France.[50] Also, by April the more sophisticated U.S. communications media had begun to explain the complexities of a dollar devaluation and its effect on the U.S. economy and the international monetary system to an increasingly uneasy American public.

The situation had not improved by the time trade statistics for the first quarter of 1971 were released in late April. Department of Commerce Assistant Secretary Passer announced on April 27 that the American trade surplus in March had declined to $245.4 million, bringing the 1971 first quarter current account surplus to only $431 million. Passer said that the Commerce Department feared that the U.S. trade surplus would disappear for 1971 under existing international economic conditions.[51] This was gloomy news indeed since the United States had depended upon the trade surplus to help balance the rest of the international accounts during the 1950s and 1960s. Such dark prospects in Washington made the West German economic crisis the following month even more difficult to manage.

The Deutsche Mark Crisis and Its Aftermath. May brought yet another international monetary crisis. Against a background of tight monetary conditions in West Germany and easing monetary policy in the United States, a report released in late April by a respected

West German research institute recommending a deutsche mark float triggered an enormous speculative surge of U.S. dollars into German money markets. Just one day after assuring their public and the world that the situation was under control, the German government was forced on May 5 to close the official exchange markets. Austria, Belgium, Luxembourg, the Netherlands, Portugal, and Switzerland immediately followed suit. On May 9 the government announced that it would reopen the market the following morning with a floating mark. The German decision to deal with their international monetary predicament through exchange rate policy, of course, intensified public speculation at home and abroad that Japan would be the next country forced to take similar action, and that the time was not far off.[52]

In spite of official statements by Treasury Secretary John Connally, the Nixon administration's leading spokesman since his appointment in March, that the German crisis had not changed the position of the United States on the dollar, U.S. Congressional leaders began to intensify their pressure on the executive branch for some corrective action—pressure that was directly related to Japan. Senator Jacob Javits and Congressman Henry Reuss introduced a Joint Resolution on March 12 urging President Nixon to call an international conference at which the whole Bretton Woods system could be reviewed, including the question of parities. Javits urged Japan specifically to consider a revaluation of the yen during a speech on the Senate floor the same day.[53]

Senator Abraham Ribicoff, chairman of the Subcommittee on International Trade of the Senate Finance Committee, also began a series of highly publicized hearings on the international economic situation on May 18 at which administration officials and American businessmen were invited to testify. Many of the witnesses were sharply critical of Japan's foreign economic policy as a whole, and of the undervalued yen in particular.[54] On the opening day of the Ribicoff hearings, Secretary Connally amazed the audience by expressing his personal opinion that the Japanese yen was undervalued. His qualification that at present no official U.S. countermeasures were required was small comfort to jittery Japanese government officials. The same message was taken to Tokyo by members of the American delegation of the Third U.S.-Japan Parliamentary Exchange Program, led by Senate Minority Leader Hugh Scott, whose members urged the Japanese government to consider a revaluation of the yen as a solution to their problem.[55]

With Secretary Connally's Congressional testimony of May 18 fresh in mind, Assistant Secretary of State for Economic Affairs Philip Trezise increased the pressure on Japan for a more meaningful response during a press conference in Tokyo on May 24. Trezise said that it was his personal opinion also that the yen was undervalued. He added that the question of whether or not Japan should more rapidly liberalize trade and investment was an issue quite apart from that of the parity of the yen, a suggestion interpreted by some Japanese observers to imply that the United States would press Japan to revalue with or without a successful liberalization effort. In the tinderbox atmosphere of late May 1971 the Trezise statement dominated Japanese headlines for some time, even generating an angry personal response from Prime Minister Sato himself, while State and Treasury Department official denials of any change in U.S. policy went almost unnoticed.[56]

Since the sudden acceleration in Japan's accumulation of balance-of-payments surpluses and foreign currency reserves in the late 1960s, the United States and other trading nations had encouraged the Government of Japan to take measures to stabilize its "fundamental disequilibrium." Japan's international monetary officials consistently rejected such categorization, argued that any surpluses were only prolonged upsides of an inevitably cyclical pattern, and, above all, stood in support of maintenance of the international monetary status quo, especially fixed exchange rates. The events of May, however, persuaded even Japan's rigid officials that something had to be done.

2. Japan in the Postwar World Economy

Japan's economic and political systems faced two enormous challenges during the early postwar years. The first was basic economic reconstruction: the struggle to provide food, clothing, shelter, employment, and a glimmer of hope to a war-weary population. The second challenge emerged during the mid-1950s: the opportunity to move beyond restoration of Japan's prewar level of prosperity to achieve unprecedented national economic growth, success at which would support a heretofore undreamed of Japanese standard of living comparable to that enjoyed by the Western industrialized democracies, an accomplishment adequate to quench the bitterness of Japan's wartime defeat.

The manner in which the nation responded to both challenges during the 1950s and early 1960s conditioned her perception of and response in the late 1960s and early 1970s to the first real international crisis to face Japan since World War II: intensifying balance-of-payments disequilibrium coupled with disintegration of the Bretton Woods system during the late 1960s and early 1970s. This chapter briefly discusses Japan's economic achievements between the end of the war and the late 1960s, with emphasis on the role of the economic bureaucracy, and concludes with a summary of those aspects of the experience particularly important in determining Japan's response to the international monetary crisis.

Economic Recovery Under Occupation and the Early 1950s

Japan's Immediate Postwar Economic Situation. Japan suffered economic chaos and dislocation difficult to imagine during the devastating war that ended with unconditional surrender in August 1945. More than three million lives had been sacrificed in overseas fighting and domestic bombing. The sudden loss of all overseas possessions reduced total Japanese territory by more than

40 percent, while more than six million former military personnel and colonists were forced during the next two years back into the already crowded home islands where one out of five housing units nationwide had been destroyed by fire. Severe food shortages, aggravated by poor harvests in 1945 and 1946, continued for more than two years after the end of the war, with average caloric intake in 1945 estimated at between 1,000 and 1,100 per day, around half the prewar level.

More than ten million individuals were left unemployed after the war. Estimated GNP fell to around 60 percent of prewar levels, and immediate postwar industrial production, strangled by a lack of manufacturing plants, equipment, and other resources, fell to only a fraction of its prewar level. Imports of the food and raw materials essential to maintain Japan's population stopped for a time until the arriving conquerors could arrange resumption of foreign trade under their direct control. As the Allied Army of Occupation began to land in late 1945, Japan lacked the wherewithal to feed, clothe, and shelter a dislocated and dispirited population, let alone to procure the resources and produce the goods required for a postwar recovery.[1]

Uncontrolled inflation twice as severe as that experienced in postwar Italy soon multiplied the economic miseries inflicted upon the Japanese population. By 1948 wholesale prices were more than one hundred times their 1937 level, driven by a combination of underproduction, accumulated wartime savings dumped suddenly into the market, a vigorous black market, and most important, a ballooning money supply caused by war indemnity payments and bank loans to companies shifting from military to nonmilitary production.[2]

Early Occupation Economic Policies. General Douglas MacArthur's initial instructions for conduct of the occupation as defined in the State-War-Navy Coordinating Committee's "Initial Post-surrender Policy for Japan" (SWNCC 150/4) and the more detailed secret Joint Chiefs of Staff memorandum (JCS 1380/15) placed economic policies within the broader context of an ambitious program of political and economic democratization that, it was hoped, would destroy the political, economic, and social foundations of Japanese militarism.[3]

Washington's economic democratization program included deconcentration of economic power through dissolution of the *zai-*

batsu, Japan's enormous prewar financial combines, redistribution of agricultural land ownership from nonfarming landowners to farming tenants, promotion of a powerful Japanese labor movement, and the purge from public employment of business leaders thought to have cooperated with the "militarists" during the war in the hope their younger successors would prove more progressive.[4] Japan also was expected to pay heavy reparations to the nations of Asia that suffered most under her wartime occupation.

True to their initial instructions, the war-weary Allied occupiers showed little interest in Japan's postwar economic relief and reconstruction, or in the near-term dislocations their ambitious program of economic reform might produce. Japan's occupation, in contrast to Germany's, was implemented indirectly, through Japanese political and bureaucratic institutions already in place. The Japanese government itself was assigned responsibility for postwar economic relief.[5] But the danger of mass starvation soon persuaded MacArthur and his advisers to press Washington for emergency shipments of food and medical supplies. These began to arrive in the spring of 1946, but in amounts far smaller than those provided for Europe. Between 1945 and 1949 around $2 billion worth of aid was provided to Japan through the GARIOA (Government and Relief in Occupied Areas) and EROA (Economic Recovery in Occupied Areas) programs.[6]

Japan's Response to Economic Chaos During the Late 1940s. Japan's senior government officials shared the shock and despair that immobilized the nation at the end of the war. In late 1945 they could only guess at the scope of their responsibilities and resources under SCAP[7] control. They lived their private and official lives from day to day, unsure of the extent to which their new military masters intended to punish individual government officials for participation in the war effort and how administrative responsibility would be divided between the forces of occupation and the incumbent Japanese administrators.

Attempting to appear responsive to the occupation's initial demands while at the same time promoting economic recovery, the Japanese government moved quickly to extend large amounts of credit to industry for conversion of war materials facilities into civilian production.[8] Funds also were provided to former Japanese military contractors from the Special Account for Provisional Military Expenses to cover wartime obligations.[9] These payments, combined with other government expenditures such as military separation payments, intensified the inevitable postwar inflation as increasing amounts of money chased too few of the necessities of life around the devastated Japanese islands.

When government efforts to reduce the increasingly severe inflation and to improve production and distribution of badly needed goods proved futile, Japan's key economic ministries with SCAP approval devised and in February 1946 published an ambitious "Emergency Economic Crisis Policy" designed to curb inflation, reform the rationing system, curb the black market, and provide more relief for the unemployed.[10]

Implementation of this new emergency economic policy proved difficult as responsible government ministries and agencies clashed over jurisdiction and priorities. Lack of progress soon led frustrated occupation authorities to encourage formation of a new high-level agency capable of enforcing interministerial coordination and responsible for liaison with SCAP. The resulting Economic Stabilization Board (ESB) was established in August 1946. Chaired by the prime minister, the ESB assumed overall responsibility for economic policy planning and coordination and, theoretically, acted independently of the change-resistant career economic bureaucracy. At the insistence of SCAP the director general, who served as the chief administrative officer, and other key officials were appointed from outside the ranks of the career government bureaucracy, a move guaranteed to sow suspicion and enmity within the ranks of Japan's turf-conscious mandarins.[11]

Later in 1946 a group of economists led by Hiromi Arisawa of Tokyo University proposed a concept that gave the bureaucracy even greater direct control over the national economy, a "priority production system" designed to alleviate production bottlenecks in industries such as coal and steel considered critical to economic recovery. Under this plan the government rather than the market determined the order in which industries designated as critical received supplies of scarce commodities when they became available, and arranged funding for them through the Reconstruction Finance Department of the Bank of Japan, later reorganized as the Reconstruction Finance Bank (RFB).

More conservative SCAP officials were concerned about the long-term impact of the priority production system on the Japanese economy and approved the plan only with reluctance. In an effort to assure more effective SCAP control, they insisted that implementation be managed by the Economic Stabilization Board, an institution with which they enjoyed a better working relationship than with the economic ministries. This considerable expansion of responsibility led in May 1947 to a major ESB reorganization and an increase in personnel from 316 to more than 2,000 staff members. Officials with responsibility for economic planning were transferred to the ESB temporarily from all economic government agencies as part of the staff expansion.[12] Chalmers Johnson describes the considerable influence of the newly organized ESB:

> During 1947 and 1948, when the priority production system was in full operation, the ESB set basic trade policy and drew up a foreign exchange budget; the BOT [Board of Trade of the Ministry of Commerce and Industry] in turn kept the accounts for the fund and supervised the kodan [public corporations], whose fixed capital was supplied by the government and whose working capital was obtained by loans from the BOT's Foreign Trade Fund. The kodan actually purchased goods for export from domestic producers and sold them to the BOT, and they received consignments of SCAP imports from the BOT, which they in turn sold to consumers.[13]

Working with the newly energized BOT, the moderate socialist Katayama Cabinet announced an even more ambitious "Emergency Economic Policy" on June 11, 1947, which once again strengthened direct government control of the economy. Under the new plan the ESB received broad authority over food and commodity distribution, wage and price controls, and measures to expand exports.[14] Production and distribution of essential commodities improved somewhat, but the economy remained in turmoil, suffering from war-related dislocations and an increasingly severe inflation that showed no sign of abating.

The Reverse Course and Its Economic Implications. International and domestic factors combined after two years of occupation to shift Washington's attention from economic democratization to economic recovery, a shift that by the end of 1948 led them to make important changes in SCAP's instructions concerning the occupation's economic role in Japan.[15]

Internationally, Washington's concerns over global stability had shifted from Nazism/Facism to Soviet-led Global Communism. Japan became more attractive as a strategically placed member of the anticommunist alliance under this new bipolar configuration, but one whose long-term reliability and effectiveness would depend greatly upon her political stability and economic vigor.

Conservative critics of SCAP economic policies within the occupation bureaucracy and in Washington for some time had assigned the threat from the left higher priority than the objectives of economic democratization outlined in SCAP's early instructions. They had charged more politically liberal members of the occupation economic team, many of them veterans of Roosevelt's New Deal, with stifling Japan's postwar economic recovery through their excessive economic democratization efforts, and even with promoting a leftward shift in postwar Japan.

This charge naturally found a sympathetic audience within Japan's business establishment and gradually struck a resonant chord among their American counterparts. Conservative critics urged a moderation of economic democratization policies such as trust-busting and development of trade unions and more emphasis on measures to curtail inflation and improve Japan's export competitiveness. The reformers naturally opposed abandonment of their earlier objectives and resisted proposals for a harsh anti-inflation program on the grounds that disadvantaged sectors of Japanese society would suffer most from its implementation.

The 1946 U.S. midterm elections in which the Republican party gained decisive majorities in both houses of Congress guaranteed those conservative critics a more sympathetic hearing in Washington. Although control of the presidency and executive branch remained in Democratic hands until 1952, the 1946 election and resulting tidal change in congressional committee leadership assured the administration's occupation budget proposals more critical attention when they were submitted for congressional approval. As the Cold War intensified in Washington, so did congressional pressure on the executive branch to curb what the conservatives described as the "liberal excesses" of the occupation's "New Dealers." According to Theodore Cohen, a self-described "New Dealer" and SCAP's first Labor Division chief, Washington's changing political winds reached Tokyo soon after the election. Cohen recalled that "reforms and reformers lost prestige and even respectability, while many of the Headquarters brass cozied up to GHQ civilians with big business connections."[16]

Apart from global strategic concerns, budget-conscious Republican congressional leaders began to fear that Japan would remain a financial burden on the United States until able to make her own way in the world economy. During the debate over extending American aid to Japan, critics charged that Japan's enduring inflation would erode the value and effectiveness of Washington's GARIOA and EROA programs.

Establishing a Fixed Exchange Rate for the Yen. It was against this political background that Army Under Secretary William H. Draper, the Pentagon official who supervised both the German and Japanese occupations, dispatched a team of mid-level economic specialists to Japan in June 1948 to recommend a fixed rate of exchange for the Japanese yen, a move considered essential to resumption of a normal pattern of Japanese foreign trade. The interagency group included officials from the Departments of State, Treasury, Army, Commerce, as well as the Federal Reserve, with Ralph A. Young, Associate Director of the Federal Reserve System's Division of Research and Statistics, as chairman of the Mission.

Japan's international economic transactions during the early part of the occupation reflected the confused state of the postwar domestic economy. As specified in the Potsdam Declaration, all of Japan's postwar foreign trade was conducted indirectly through the occupation authorities.

Imports strictly limited to those necessary to "prevent disease and unrest," were purchased largely with U.S. appropriated funds, and were priced in yen in line with the low controlled prices of domestic production. Exports were sold, initially only for dollars, at competitive world prices. Dollar proceeds went into the SCAP foreign trade fund, and the Japanese producers were paid prices in yen based on yen costs. There resulted a series of conversion rates, or implicit multiple exchange rates, which varied greatly from commodity to commodity and even among different sales of the same commodity.[17]

During the immediate postwar period this complex system effectively insulated Japan's production of goods for export and consumption of imports from market discipline and allowed the government to allocate benefits directly according to priorities believed most conducive to realization of the occupation's economic objectives, but at the sacrifice of considerable additional government expenditure. By 1948 Washington was convinced that a fixed rate of exchange was essential if Japan was to develop a truly competitive export sector and reduce inflation-promoting government subsidies.[18]

Draper defined what was to be the Young Mission's charge in a delicately worded letter dated May 14, 1948, that illustrated the sensitivity of Washington's relationship with Douglas MacArthur.[19] Draper instructed Young to study "the practicability of establishing a commercial rate and supplementary measures to accompany the operation of such a rate," or if that should prove premature, to consider "establishment of a new conversion rate for the Japanese yen for military and non-trade international financial transactions." Anticipating SCAP's likely response, Draper also ordered Young "to endeavor to reach an agreed position with the Supreme Commander Allied Powers with respect to the above."[20]

The Young Mission arrived in Japan on May 20, 1948 (after in-depth consultations with concerned agencies in Washington), with less than a month to meet Draper's deadline of June 16, 1948, for submission of its report. Theodore Cohen, by then "kicked upstairs" to serve as special adviser to Economic and Scientific Section (ESS) chief Major General W. F. Marquat, recalls that the ESS staff assumed the Mission had arrived in Japan with their recommendations already determined during interdepartmental consultations in Washington. Cohen says the Mission members spent more of their eighteen-day stay in Tokyo drafting the report than they did examining local economic conditions.[21]

As expected, Young's report of June 12, 1948, recommended establishment of a fixed yen exchange rate as essential for rapid economic recovery and suggested that it should be implemented no later than October 1, 1948, even earlier if possible. The report's specific recommendation was "in the neighborhood of 300 yen per dollar." But it added "that SCAP be authorized to fix a level at the appropriate time within a range of 270 yen to 330 yen per dollar" and that "SCAP should be given authority to make subsequent adjustments in the rate within specified limits, without Washington approval, in accordance with the principles of the International Monetary Fund, as applied to member countries."[22] MacArthur, unaccustomed to such blatant interference from Washington in his affairs, classified the report top secret and flatly rejected its recommendations in a cable to Washington.[23]

SCAP's opposition to the Young Mission's recommendations didn't remove the proposal for early imposition of a unified fixed rate of exchange for the yen from the interdepartmental wrangling in Washington that by December 1948 had produced for President Truman's signature a comprehensive nine-point program of economic rehabilitation designed within a few short years to stop Japan's inflation and to reestablish the competitiveness of Japanese exports in world markets. In addition to normalization of the exchange rate, the nine-point plan required Japan immediately to reduce government expenditure to or below the level of government revenue, eliminate trade subsidies, and suspend Reconstruction Finance Bank financing.

With few special interests left undamaged in the near term by the inevitably severe consequences, it is difficult to imagine any democratic government implementing such an ambitious program of economic reform under normal conditions. Industries considered critical for national economic recovery had become comfortable with direct government subsidies and liberal government-sponsored financing during the past three years. Washington's new program put them under sudden and severe pressure to reduce production costs or face bankruptcy. Export-dependent firms feared the impact of a single fixed exchange rate on their competitiveness in world markets. Importers faced significant increases in the cost of essential materials. Organized labor correctly anticipated massive unemployment as Japan's corporations and government agencies dismissed nonessential employees in the struggle to remain competitive under more stringent conditions. But an Army of Occupation intent upon reform was difficult to refuse.

Even Japan's military occupiers, especially ESS officials responsible for economic policy, considered Washington's new plan draconian and urged modification lest hasty implementation create massive unemployment and even political instability. The combined reluctance of SCAP and the incumbent Japanese government was overcome by the dispatch of Joseph M. Dodge, a respected Detroit banker with recent experience in the German economic recovery effort, to oversee the new program's implementation. Dodge arrived in Tokyo on February 1, 1949, for a three-month visit, assigned officially as special economic adviser to SCAP, but with independent channels of communication to Washington and the clear support of the Truman administration for what soon became known in Japan as the "Dodge Line" of economic reform.

During the three-month stay Dodge and his staff focused most of their attention on revision of the national budget, working closely with the newly appointed Finance Minister Hayato Ikeda and MOF officials to prepare a balanced government budget proposal for Diet approval.[24] By the beginning of April, in spite of intense pressure from other branches of the Japanese government and private special interest groups, Dodge and the MOF had crafted and obtained political approval for a national budget for the following fiscal year (Japan's fiscal year runs from April 1 to March 31) that not only eliminated the deficit, but produced a surplus of one billion dollars. In the process Dodge permanently enhanced the influence of MOF budget officials with his decision to work through them to implement his program of reform.

With the government's budget deficit suddenly under control and inflation beginning to decline, MacArthur on April 23, 1949, announced establishment of the new fixed rate of international exchange for the yen at Y 360 = $1. The new rate was determined through compromise between Washington's economic planners, who had encouraged a higher value on the one hand, and the Japanese business community and SCAP's economic officials on the other, who had lobbied for a much cheaper yen that would make Japanese exports more price competitive in world markets.

The need to improve Japan's position in international trade by establishing a fixed exchange rate for the yen had been recognized for some time. Tatsuro Uchino reports that as early as December 1947 a secret committee of the Economic Stabilization Board under the chairmanship of the noted economist Shigeto Tsuru had proposed replacement of the multiple exchange rate system with a fixed rate, but that the plan was abandoned after ESB personnel changes in the wake of the Katayama Cabinet's resignation.[25] The Young Mission in 1948 had proposed a Y 300 = $1 rate, with discretion for adjustment between Y 270 and Y 330 per dollar. And Theodore Cohen mentions in his memoir that he was asked in late 1948, prior to Joseph Dodge's arrival in Japan, to head a committee within SCAP's Economic Section to determine an appropriate fixed rate of exchange for the yen. His committee settled on Y 330 = $1.[26] Thus the Y 360 = $1 rate finally established by MacArthur in April 1949 was considerably lower than had been anticipated, but it still inspired excited cries of protest from the Japanese business community, especially from those less competitive sectors that had enjoyed the subsidization of their transactions at a much lower rate.

Washington's new program for Japan's economic recovery was implemented by the recently elected conservative Yoshida government under the direction of SCAP and the watchful eye of Joseph Dodge. It quickly achieved the primary objective of ending Japan's destabilizing inflation, but at the cost of a tremendous increase in unemployment and numerous bankruptcies of small and medium-sized firms. Yoshida surely sensed the political danger inherent in support of such a sudden and severe deflationary policy shift. Yet Washington's demands provided Yoshida with the opportunity to channel that inexorable external pressure toward support of his own objectives, steering Japan's economy toward domestic and international market discipline, and suppressing the interventionist economic bureaucracy that earlier in the occupation had attempted unsuccessfully to accelerate the rate of recovery through implementation of their government-managed priority production system.

The Impact of Korean War Special Procurements. The severity of Japan's domestic economic predicament and limited success of industry's attempt to compensate for soft domestic demand with an export drive during a worldwide recession had forced even the conservative Yoshida by April of 1950 to dispatch Finance Minister Hayato Ikeda to Washington for secret negotiations with Joseph Dodge over relaxation of his deflationary program. Ikeda returned to Tokyo empty-handed, and it appeared Japan would be forced to endure the economic and political consequences of Washington's financial clampdown until the end of the occupation.

Just two months after Ikeda's disappointing Washington visit, however, the Korean tinderbox burst into flames with a North Korean strike on June 25, 1950, across the 38th parallel. This attack marked the beginning of hostilities among North and South Korean, Chinese, and American-led United Nations troops that would continue until July 27, 1953. As the only nearby industrialized nation with adequate manufacturing capacity, Japan's underemployed factories and work force benefited enormously from Korea's misfortune between 1950 and 1955, first as suppliers of war material and services for United Nations forces and, after the July 1953 armistice, as suppliers of materials needed for the reconstruction of South Korea.

Former Economic Planning Agency official Tatsuro Uchino estimates that special procurements, broadly defined, during the period pumped between $2.4 and $3.6 billion into the capital-starved Japanese economy and accounted for an amazing 60 to 70 percent of all of Japan's exports.[27] Also significant for Japan's postwar economic development, this unanticipated expansion of demand was strongest in industries such as textiles, steel products, and automotive equipment, the very sectors that would lead Japan's export drive during the 1950s and 1960s. Thus, Tokyo's concern over Mr. Dodge's deflationary policies ended abruptly in late 1950, and by May of 1952 Japan had regained full sovereignty and responsibility for her own destiny with the end of the occupation.

Japan's industrial production recovered to prewar levels within four months of the outbreak of hostilities, and the following fiscal year surpassed its 1934–1936 average by 31.4 percent.[28] Prices and wages also increased sharply in response to the sudden increase in external demand, but the government resisted the temptation to intervene and maintained official price controls only on those products considered most essential.

Rapid Economic Growth During the 1950S and 1960S

Plans for Government Management of Rapid Economic Growth. Less than a year after the outbreak of war, special procurements of military goods and services related to the Korean conflict had peaked and begun to decline. Once again Japan faced the threat of serious recession, this time with the occupation and its direct sponsorship of Japan's economic recovery about to end. Takafusa Nakamura identifies four key strategies devised and implemented by Japan's economic bureaucracy during the late 1940s and early 1950s to cope with the situation through accumulation of capital and allocation of those accumulated funds to favored industries: establishment of the Japan Development Bank; reform of the tax system; coordinated implementation of the foreign exchange allocation system; and government efforts to encourage Japanese companies to import foreign technology.[29] Those policies helped to define the economic role of Japan's postwar government and contributed to the remarkable record of economic growth during the 1950s and 1960s.

Supporters of government-guided economic growth long maintained that Japan's economic recovery had been stymied by the scarcity of capital needed to finance expansion of industrial plant and equipment since Joseph Dodge's anti-inflation-inspired 1949 suppression of the Reconstruction Finance Bank. The basic problem of capital scarcity, as they interpreted it, intensified as Japanese factories scrambled in late 1950 and 1951 to expand production facilities to fill Korean War special procurement contracts.

The Bank of Japan alleviated this chronic capital scarcity for a time by extending credit to Japan's large City Banks sufficient to allow them to loan their best corporate customers amounts far beyond any reasonable assumptions about their ability to repay. City Banks under this precarious "overloan" arrangement reduced their risk by closely supervising how their overborrowed customers used their funds. Bank officials were appointed routinely to membership on the boards of directors of their borrowers, and companies experiencing temporary reversals could expect their main bank to assign a bank official to a supervisory position within the company to oversee the recovery effort.[30]

Chalmers Johnson notes that this highly centralized system of government-sponsored finance gave Japan's economic bureaucracy an effective means of allocating capital to industries judged critical for Japan's economic growth and export expansion since the Bank of Japan took pains to protect its own vulnerable over-loaned position by advising the City Banks to make loans only to companies in industrial sectors especially favored by the Ministry of International Trade and Industry (MITI) for rapid development.[31]

When the overloan strategy proved inadequate to finance the sudden industrial expansion required to meet the demand generated by Korean War special procurements, Japanese economic officials persuaded a reluctant SCAP to approve formation of several government-funded banks designed to allocate capital directly to sectors of the economy slated for government promotion. The bulk of the capital for the government-funded banks was provided from personal savings accumulated within the postal savings system, a convenient passbook savings system for small individual accounts run through post office branches throughout the country that attracted depositors with a favorable rate of tax exempt interest. The most important of those official banks, according to Nakamura and Johnson, was the Japan Development Bank (JDB), which began operation at the end of March 1951. JDB loans provided more than financing at a subsidized rate of interest. Their loans served as a signal to private banks that the company's activities were approved and would be supported by the government, and this greatly facilitated acquisition of additional funding from nongovernment sources.[32]

Tax policy too was modified during the early 1950s to promote accumulation of capital for distribution to critical industries. An ambitious effort to rationalize and democratize Japan's national tax system had been made early in the occupation and later modified under recommendations of the Shoup tax missions during 1949 and 1950. As efficiency and rapid growth replaced democratization as the primary economic objectives of SCAP and the Japanese government, it became clear that the more egalitarian aspects of the postwar tax reform would have to be revised. Kozo Yamamura has concluded that

It can safely be said that the central and prime goal of the tax policy after 1953 was to achieve a high rate of growth, and this goal was pursued by such changes as were necessary to increase saving, that is, to aid rationalization. The results of this policy appeared as a gradually less progressive direct tax burden and an increasingly more regressive indirect tax burden. It appears also clear that this policy was enhanced by giving a preferential tax treatment to the larger firms vis-à-vis the small ones by means of numerous special exemptions.[33]

The Enterprises Rationalization Promotion Law passed in March 1952 also included significant corporate tax incentives for favored sectors of the economy, including promotion of more rapid replacement of manufacturing equipment through accelerated depreciation schedules and government subsidization of the cost of experimental equipment for key industries.[34]

The Foreign Exchange and Foreign Trade Control Law was passed in 1949 soon after the SCAP established a fixed rate of exchange for the yen. This legislation gave Japan's economic bureaucracy the authority to control the extent and nature of Japan's foreign trade. Because Japan was a small, resource-poor nation with a large population, everyone agreed that its chances for economic recovery and improvement of living standards would continue to depend upon their ability to import primary products and semiprocessed goods, to apply those goods to the manufacture of higher labor and technology value-added products, and then to sell its manufactures abroad in quantities sufficient to earn enough foreign exchange to pay for additional raw materials and foodstuffs.

But Japan's economic bureaucracy judged market forces unlikely in the near future to balance Japan's serious trade deficit due to a combination of overall sluggish global trade, a surprise September 1949 devaluation of the British pound that made British goods more competitive in Japan's foreign markets, and the war-scarred condition of the domestic economy. This deficit drained

Japan of the foreign currency necessary to pay for imports required for economic recovery, and made Japan's economic bureaucracy even more desperate to conserve Japan's limited foreign exchange income and to redistribute that earned to those enterprises considered most likely to use it to produce exportable goods.

Rather than allow supply and demand to distribute foreign exchange from exporters who earned it abroad to those who required it to pay for imports, the Foreign Exchange and Foreign Trade Control Law required all exporters immediately upon receipt of foreign currency in payment for their exports to exchange it for yen at the Foreign Exchange Control Board until its abolition in 1952, and thereafter at banks authorized by the government to handle foreign exchange. The government then allocated the foreign currency so collected only to companies wishing to import goods considered necessary for economic recovery under the government's guidelines. Writing during the 1960s about the impact of the law on Japan's foreign trade practices, former senior government official and economist Warren Hunsberger commented:

> In principle nothing may be bought from abroad without permission from the government. Permission has been limited first of all by basic decisions made semi-annually in the foreign exchange budget, which sets limits on the amounts of foreign exchange to be made available for particular uses. Within these limits the Ministry of International Trade and Industry (MITI) exercises wide discretion in issuing licenses.[35]

The final item on Nakamura's list of policies that shaped the economic role of Japan's postwar government was promotion of the acquisition of foreign technology. Technology, like all other imports, had to be paid for in foreign currency. Since the economic bureaucracy controlled access to foreign currency under the Foreign Exchange and Foreign Trade Control Law they were able to control the private sector's technical cooperation agreements with foreign companies. As with other imports, approval was granted for the acquisition of technology only when it was judged likely to promote the government's plans for economic growth and export expansion.[36]

The international environment during the 1950s and 1960s proved favorable for Japanese acquisition of foreign technology. In addition to approving each acquisition agreement, Japan's government participated actively in negotiations with foreign firms, assuring their companies the best possible price and terms. Foreign firms, primarily American, were willing to license their technology on terms favorable to Japan because most of them had little or no interest in exporting their products, and during the 1950s they found it difficult to imagine that Japanese companies would ever reach the point at which they might challenge their American mentors in the United States or in third markets. Those few firms really interested in exporting were well enough informed to be realistic about their chances of ever being allowed to penetrate the Japanese market.

By the end of the Korean conflict Japan's bureaucracy had in place the administrative tools, structural relationships, and political support required to orchestrate remarkable postwar economic growth. Given the importance of the international economy to realization of its objectives, the government granted import licenses for industrial materials more freely to those companies producing goods for sale abroad, provided tax advantages for the export production and sales expenditures of Japanese companies, and assisted in the financing of exports, both long- and short-term. Export insurance and trade promotion abroad, done primarily by the MITI-controlled Japan Export Trade Promotion Agency (JETRO), also contributed to the effort.[37]

All of these measures were far removed from the Bretton Woods spirit of a market-driven flow of goods and capital across national boundaries. But they were tolerated—even encouraged—in the early 1950s by the United States and other countries as essential for Japan's economic survival and reconstruction. With serious trade deficits during the first twelve years after the war, Japan was supported in the effort to improve her foreign exchange earning potential lest she once again require foreign aid and become a burden on the U. S. treasury. Few contemporary observers could have dreamed that within twenty years the situation would be reversed, and Japan's *surpluses* would become an important destabilizing factor within the international system.

Government-Guided Rapid Economic Growth. Japan's "economic miracle" of postwar double-digit growth attracted worldwide attention after the war, attention that ranged from astonishment in the mid-1950s, to admiration in the late 1950s and early 1960s, and to outbursts of open resentment and suspicious reexamination of the means employed to achieve it by the late 1960s. The relationship with the international economy throughout the period was characterized by a series of up-and-down cycles in Japan's balance of payments.[38] Rapid domestic economic growth increased consumption of imports as well as of domestic goods. It also reduced the overall propensity to export, increasing the deficit in the balance of payments, which forced Japan to draw on her foreign currency reserves in order to balance the account.

When foreign currency reserves reached a level considered dangerously low, the government was forced to reduce the rate of growth of the economy with more restrictive fiscal and monetary policy. Tighter money slowed the demand for imports and made exporting once again more attractive for Japanese firms, resulting in an improved balance of payments and an increase in foreign currency reserves. Once reserves had recovered to a level considered safe the government was again free to stimulate economic growth, much to the relief of the business community and Japan's political leadership. This cyclical phenomenon became known as the "balance-of-payments ceiling" on economic growth. Japan's economy thudded up against the balance-of-payments ceiling five times during the 1950s and 1960s, forcing the government to apply the economic brakes in 1954, 1957, 1961, 1964, and 1967.

Temporary slowdowns in the rate of economic growth were no more popular in Japan than in other countries. They reduced business income, increased the chance of bankruptcy, and made workers more apprehensive about their economic futures and therefore less willing to spend. They were equally unpopular with Japan's bureaucrats and politicians who would rather be praised for engineering Japan's postwar economic miracle than blamed for temporarily slowing the rate of growth. As a result of this cyclical balance-of-payments pattern, its importance for Japan's most important postwar national goal of economic growth, and the often-repeated efforts of economic policymakers to explain their growth-inhibiting actions to an anxious public, the level of Japan's foreign currency reserves and balance-of-payments situation received far more public and political attention in Japan than in the United States. Detailed analyses of the problem appeared regularly on the front pages of major newspapers, while similar news was relegated to the financial sections of American economic journals.

Early Foreign Response: Pressure for Trade Liberalization. The architects and engineers of Japan's economic recovery in the postwar catch-up environment were determined to take advantage of every available opportunity to fulfull their mission, including preservation of the occupation-mandated direct and indirect barriers to imports designed to reduce expenditure of precious foreign exchange on nonessential purchases abroad. Such barriers were tolerated by Japan's trading partners for a time as essential to postwar industrial recovery and for lack of foreign interest in Japan as an export market. But by the late 1950s, Japan's economic recovery and penetration of key American markets had inspired pressure from the United States and other Western nations to liberalize her very effective web of trade and investment restrictions.

Japan's commercial success in the American market, concentrated as it was in specific, often politically potent industrial sectors, had inspired the fundamentally free trade Eisenhower administration reluctantly to pressure Tokyo to impose "voluntary" export restraint on several especially sensitive products such as textiles, toys, and tableware, while macroeconomic concern over the relationship with Japan focused more on military aid payments than on trade. Still, as late as April 1959 President Eisenhower was able to tell students at Gettysburg College in Pennsylvania that "More perhaps than any other industrialized nation, Japan must export to live," and added, "For Japan there must be more free world outlets for her products. She does not want to be compelled to become dependent upon the Communist empire."[39] By the end of the second Eisenhower term, however, public and political concern over the U.S. balance of payments had reached the point at which the "gold flow" issue emerged in the 1960 election debate.[40]

Democratic party campaign organizers were well aware of growing public concern over the American position in the world economy in general, and specifically over economic relations with Japan, as they prepared for the 1960 struggle to win back the White House. The Government of Japan's unavoidable decision in June 1960 to cancel their invitation to President Eisenhower in the wake of widespread rioting in Tokyo over renewal of the bilateral security treaty, for example, inflamed anti-Japan feeling throughout the United States. American opinion leaders, including even the president of the Admiral Corporation, took advantage of the situation to propose a boycott of Japanese imports. They had little success, but the publicity their effort inspired provided a clear warning to American political planners of the public's sensitivity.[41]

The Democrats criticized the "do nothing" Republican international economic policies during the campaign and promised if elected to take action to staunch the "gold flow." Once in office the Kennedy administration was faced with the delicate task of fulfilling their campaign promise with an international economic policy that would be perceived by the general public as different from that of the previous administration while not offending the free trade principles of their key supporters. Their approach was to focus government and public attention on foreign impediments to American exports rather than on the problem of imports or of export promotion, and their most important specific initiative in support of that objective was the Trade Expansion Act of 1962.[42]

This legislation granted the president authority to negotiate multilateral tariff reductions, granting cuts in American tariffs for reciprocal reductions abroad. It also established a small international negotiating unit staffed largely by international trade lawyers to pursue those objectives, the office of the Special Trade Representative (STR), which in 1977 would become the United States Trade Representative (USTR).[43] Hereafter the administration's preferred response to all public and congressional complaints about micro- or macrointernational economic issues was to divert attention from protectionist responses by agreeing to increase pressure on American trading partners, including Japan, to open their markets to U.S. goods. This strategy seems to have been based upon the assumption that American exports would automatically increase if unimpeded on the other end. The 1962 Act did provide compensation for American workers displaced by imports, but this politically important program proved ineffective and within a few years was dismissed as "burial insurance" by the increasingly resentful labor movement. Little attention was given to government programs to promote American industries with export potential or to other export promotion measures common in Japan and other major trading nations.

Thus Japan's import barriers took on more political importance in the United States than their economic significance alone would justify. The United States increased pressure on Japan to reduce her barriers, but import protection in any democratic nation is easier to implement than to reduce. Japanese economic officials were reluctant to abandon any advantage during their economic recovery and rapid growth effort, and therefore resisted such pressure with every means available. Flat refusal on selfish national interest grounds was obviously inappropriate given the bilateral configuration of forces. So, resistance took the form of delay rather than refusal.

Basic clashes of national economic interest during the 1950s and 1960s were portrayed by Japan as unfortunate misunderstandings, caused largely by a lack of information abroad about Japan's "true situation." Public relations and lobbying campaigns were undertaken to close the "information gap" with more accurate information which usually included reference to Japan as weak and vulnerable, "four small islands, poor in natural resources," still requiring the protection those tariff and nontariff barriers provided in order to survive. Japan's Foreign Ministry in 1957 sponsored establishment of the United States-Japan Trade Council in Washington, D.C., in part to coordinate such activities. The public relations and lobbying campaigns did little to change basic opinions, but they did buy time and delay Japan's compliance without a major confrontation over economic issues.

Japan began the politically painful task of liberalization in the early 1960s, accepting Article VIII IMF status in 1964, and joining the Organisation for Economic Cooperation and Development (OECD) soon thereafter.[44] The specter of Japan's postwar cyclical relationship with the world economy continued to dominate the thinking of the economic bureaucracy, and progress throughout the 1960s and beyond was slow, made in response only to implied or direct threats of retaliation against Japan's exports by other members of the international economic system. As a result, Japan entered the turbulent latter half of the 1960s with a system that was highly effective when dealing with international deficits, but quite unprepared to cope with the destabilizing international surpluses that she would face in the years to come.

The Legacy of Postwar Recovery and Rapid Economic Growth

Japan's response to the challenges of postwar economic recovery and rapid growth helped to determine its perception of and response to the 1969–1971 international monetary crisis. Four important aspects of that experience were: a greatly strengthened national economic bureaucracy; emphasis on maximization of foreign exchange reserves and maintenance of a fixed rate of exchange for the yen; a weak sense of responsibility for maintenance of the international economic system; and the tendency of the political and bureaucratic leadership to rely more heavily upon external pressure to settle disputes among Japan's powerful domestic groups and their governmental supporters.

A Stronger National Economic Bureaucracy. Japan's prewar "Servants of the Emperor" had enjoyed great influence and prestige, but the national bureaucracy emerged from the occupation even more powerful than its illustrious predecessors, managing to maintain much of its influence and autonomy throughout the high-growth 1950s and 1960s. Officials responsible for foreign trade and international monetary affairs proved especially successful in expanding their domain, due largely to the importance of their work for implementation of the preeminent national objective of economic recovery and rapid growth.

Chalmers Johnson in this regard notes the near doubling in size of the national bureaucracy during the occupation's indirect rule and the weakening of the military and big business, the economic bureaucracy's most vigorous prewar rivals, through SCAP's demilitarization and *zaibatsu* dissolution policies. He also describes postwar politicians and political parties, other potential rivals, as relatively ineffective.[45] Japan's higher civil servants, when compared with politicians, were considered well trained, professional, relatively honest, and dedicated to national rather than regional or particularistic objectives.

The international economic bureaucracy continued to benefit during the 1950s and 1960s from the widespread public perception that their policies and skillful implementation efforts were largely responsible for the rapid improvement in Japan's economic conditions. The Japanese public, their political representatives, and even the business community, thus proved willing to accept a level of government influence over the national economy, especially over international economic affairs, that would have been unimaginable in the United States.

Sanctification of Foreign Exchange Reserves and Fixed Yen Rate. Foreign exchange scarcity has plagued Japan at least since the latter half of the nineteenth century and the onset of modern industrial development. The immediate postwar economic crisis further sensitized the government, business community, and public to the problem since Japan, like other war-damaged nations, was forced to import large quantities of food to survive, as well as most of the machinery, raw materials, and technology required for early postwar economic reconstruction. Foreign currency to pay for those essential imports came either from the sale of Japanese goods and services abroad or from direct and indirect foreign economic aid, a solution not long acceptable either to foreign donors or to Japan. Adequate levels of foreign exchange thus were essential for immediate survival, and in the longer term for greater economic independence.

After the yen's exchange rate was fixed in 1949 and international economic transactions were returned to private hands, an abundance of foreign exchange became associated with good business conditions and foreign exchange scarcity with recession through the mechanism of the "balance-of-payments ceiling" on economic growth. The strong domestic demand that accompanied rapid economic growth increased imports and diverted exports to the domestic market, reducing Japan's foreign currency reserves. At some point the government was forced to reverse this dangerous trend with imposition of a politically unpopular tight money policy until reserves rose again to a safe level. Under those conditions preservation of foreign exchange reserves naturally became a key responsibility of government officials in charge of international monetary affairs.

Change in the parity of the yen, in this case a *de*valuation, was an obvious and politically less odious alternative to domestic economic clampdown as a means of discouraging imports, encouraging exports, and replenishing foreign exchange reserves, especially in light of the strong resistance from the business community that met SCAP's imposition of the Y 360=$1 rate in 1949. Instead, perception of the yen's exchange rate in Japan shifted during this period from the "stable" rate (subject to change in response to "fundamental disequilibrium" as defined under the Bretton Woods system) to a "fixed" rate that served as a benchmark for domestic economic planning and that was considered essential to Japan's economic security.

The government opposed change, even incremental change, in the yen's parity first because they assumed a change once made would make it difficult to resist future international demands for parity changes. Further, they feared that an unpredictable exchange rate would seriously destabilize the domestic economy and place Japan at the mercy of the vagaries of the international market, in the long term threatening Japan's economic autonomy. Japan's economic bureaucracy was hesitant to leave anything as important as the determinant of the yen value of all exports and the yen cost of all imports to the whim of the market, preferring to endure the negative political consequences of temporary government-supervised clampdowns on domestic economic growth to a change in the exchange rate.

Lack of Responsibility for the International Economic System. Throughout the postwar period Japan showed little sense of responsibility for maintenance of the liberal international economic system in spite of the importance of its smooth operation for her national well-being. Even a quarter-century after the end of the war representatives of other nations still considered Japan a largely passive participant in international economic forums whose active involvement was stimulated only in support of her own short-term economic interests. This was most obvious in Japan's response to international pressure for liberalization of restrictions on trade and investment, its flat rejection of IMF reform proposals to increase the flexibility of exchange rates during 1969 and 1970, and the refusal to admit its own shift to surplus-prone balance-of-payments status in the late 1960s. Japan showed little concern over the possibility that the whole international economic system, beginning with the delicately balanced Bretton Woods international monetary arrangements, might tumble down upon its own head as well as those of the other participants.

The national rather than global scope of Japan's primary goals during the 1950s and 1960s—domestic economic recovery and rapid economic growth rather than global stability—accounts in part for this limited international economic agenda. The destructive impact of World War II, the "unconditional" terms of her surrender, and the occupation experience all intensified Japan's prewar sense of isolation and alienation as the sole non-Caucasian member of the Great Powers club and only industrialized nation in Asia of global significance. Postwar Japan remained in many ways a global outsider, forced as a loser to accept most of the responsibility for the war, treading lightly and avoiding international criticism within the diplomatic arena once readmitted, while focusing all energies at home on economic recovery.

Another factor limiting Japan's sense of responsibility and support for the system was Japan's exclusion as an Axis power from the bilateral and multilateral consultations that culminated in the 1944 Bretton Woods Conference and formation of the international system. In contrast to the experience of the United States and the major European nations other than Germany, no cadre of Bretton Woods veterans and staff of specialists emerged in postwar Japan eager to argue for government policies in support of the integrity of *her* global system. Thus, during her economic recovery and rapid economic growth period, Japan became an increasingly important component of the international economic system, but remained an "outsider" with little genuine sense of "ownership" or responsibility for maintenance of the system.

Foreign Pressure as a Substitute for Political Leadership. Japan's top political officials became accustomed to compensating for their difficulty in exercising decisive political leadership through reliance on powerful foreign pressure under the unusual conditions that prevailed during the Allied Occupation. The terms of her "unconditional surrender" had obliged Japan to accept Allied plans for her demilitarization and democratization. So SCAP ruled war-devastated Japan for several years as an undisputed *deus ex machina*, albeit indirectly, through political and bureaucratic governmental institutions retained to promote continuity and efficiency, and to legitimate the occupiers' reform efforts.

The incumbent government, in spite of its official status, was in no position to reject SCAP orders, at least not directly. It did, however, delay or modify less appealing directives through time-honored bureaucratic tactics of requests for clarification and revision—the "prolonged yes"—and the control of information its superior knowledge of the Japanese political, economic, and social environment provided.

Constitutional reform, the crowning achievement of the occupation's democratization program, made Japan's top-level leadership even more dependent upon external pressure when required to implement necessary but politically distasteful measures. This commendable undertaking greatly increased the authority and responsibility of Japan's political institutions and political leadership by shifting sovereignty from the emperor to the people, and ultimate political power from the emperor and his closest advisers to the cabinet and prime minister as agents of the popularly elected parliament. But it proved more difficult to build Japan's political parties into institutions capable of producing political leaders with the popular support and degree of legitimacy required to exercise their expanded responsibilities under the new constitutional arrangements. Weak cabinets were forced under the new system to rely upon their powerful occupying sponsors for backup when faced with politically divisive issues.

SCAP's overpowering presence did allow the occupied government to achieve measures politically impossible under normal circumstances, such as the early efforts to allocate scarce foodstuffs most efficiently, to control the black market, to reallocate farmland ownership from landlords to tenants, to implement the disruptive policies necessary to reduce inflation, and—viewed from the conservative perspective of the Yoshida Cabinet—to reduce the government's budget deficit and the influence of the national planning-oriented economic bureaucrats. Under SCAP's scowling presence the incumbent political and bureaucratic authorities were able to take credit for implementing measures essential to Japan's national well-being while diverting the immediate blame and political retribution inevitably generated onto SCAP and the Allies.[46]

Dependence upon foreign pressure as a substitute for authoritative central political leadership did not end with the 1952 suspension of the occupation. It was particularly evident during the struggle to liberalize restrictions on the inflow of foreign trade and investment.[47] Japan emerged from the occupation as perhaps the most protected from foreign competition of the world's economic powers. But by the late 1950s the increasing global competitiveness of Japan's manufactured exports had intensified international pressure for liberalization of those trade and investment restraints in the name of free trade, fair play, and eventually the stability of the international economic system.

Still, Japan's economic bureaucracy was unwilling to abandon such an important advantage without a struggle. It was supported by that segment of the business community that produced for the domestic market, and it also gained the sympathy of many politicians who feared offending their financial supporters in the business community or the voting public by publicly admitting the foreign demands were reasonable and inevitable. Some of Japan's more internationally minded bureaucrats and businessmen realized the inevitability—even the long-term advantages—of economic liberalization and argued for prompt compliance. But they constituted only a small minority whose voices were heard more clearly abroad than at home.

Flat refusal was still out of the question, given the global configuration of forces and the larger importance of maintaining access to international sources of raw materials and markets for manufactured products, especially the United States. So the government responded with the "prolonged yes" perfected during the occupation, delaying decisive action as long as possible by interpreting basic clashes of national economic interest as unfortunate "misunderstandings" caused largely by a lack of information abroad about Japan's "true situation" in elaborate international public relations and lobbying campaigns.

Japan agreed to liberalize only after foreign pressure increased to the point at which it was obvious to all opposing domestic interests that further resistance would cause unacceptable damage to Japan's essential international relationships. Once again, Japan's top political and bureaucratic leadership was able to implement necessary and inevitable but politically divisive measures while directing the immediate political blame toward the sources of the international pressure.[48]

During the first quarter-century of the postwar period, Japan's econo-political system responded with remarkable effectiveness to the successive challenges of postwar economic reconstruction and the opportunity to achieve unprecedented levels of economic growth. Her own success and changes in the international environment presented a very different challenge by the end of the 1960s when Japan's system was asked to cope with a rapidly deteriorating international monetary system and a fundamental shift from deficit-prone to surplus-prone status in the global economy. Her response to this next challenge, conditioned by a generation of scarcity and domestic preoccupation, proved less satisfactory.

3. From "Surplus-Prone" Status to "Protracted Crisis" State

Japan's international monetary prospects dimmed once again at the beginning of 1968 as the domestic economy boomed and foreign exchange reserves dipped perilously close to crisis levels. But the situation changed dramatically during the next two years, and by the end of 1969 domestic and international observers agreed that Japan's international moneymen thereafter would face international surpluses rather than deficits. There was no agreement, however, on how long this new situation would last. Was it a more permanent change or simply a protracted manifestation of the periodic rises in international monetary fortunes that Japan had experienced throughout the postwar period? Japan's government experts argued publicly that it was only temporary, but American and European observers, and even some analysts in Japan, considered it a more permanent change.

No other advanced industrialized nation felt more dependent than Japan upon an orderly, predictable international monetary system for its economic welfare. But the system established at Bretton Woods in 1944 continued to careen from crisis to crisis, each one making the system's future more uncertain. Turbulent parity changes for the British pound in late 1967, and the French franc and German mark in 1969, had eased immediate pressure for fundamental systemic reform, and an improved U.S. balance of payments during late 1969 and early 1970 delayed the day of reckoning, but basic systemic problems remained.

The early May 1971 West German decision to float the mark once again after months of repeated official assurance to the contrary intensified pressure on Japan, as the world's other major surplus nation, for some response. How long could Japan alone continue to accumulate destabilizing levels of foreign currency reserves earned through huge trade surpluses with the United States and other countries without offering more than the cosmetic measures so far implemented to reduce international—and even domestic—criticism? By May 1971 "something" had to be done.

A Fundamental Shift in Japan's International Economic Status

Four Politically Sensitive International Economic Indicators. Among the many international economic indicators regularly published by Japan's government, four stood out as particularly important to policymakers and private-sector observers during the period of this study: the overall trade balance; the current account balance; foreign exchange reserves; and the bilateral trade balance with the United States.

The previous month's *overall trade balance* was regularly announced to the public on the 15th of each month. It neatly summarizes Japan's overall position in the exchange of manufactures and primary products with the rest of the world. As the simplest, most frequently quoted, and most easily explained international economic statistic available, it has even more political than economic significance. And in Japan, as in other trade-sensitive countries, the trade balance is more directly related to local employment than the other indicators.

The *current account balance* received less public and political attention during the period of the study, but it is economically even more significant since it includes not only trade in goods, but also in "invisibles" such as services, foreign investment income, and private remittances. It is a more comprehensive indicator of a country's business relationship with the rest of the world, but more difficult to present in simple terms to the public. The current account balance was even more important for Japan's international economic bureaucrats since Japan tended to run significant deficits in invisibles that had to be compensated for elsewhere in the account.

The *level* of Japan's official holdings of *foreign exchange*—foreign currencies (mostly U.S. dollars) and a small percentage of gold—was the most significant international economic indicator when considering Japan's participation in the international monetary system. This figure was released by the Ministry of Finance on the last day of each month. Foreign currency reserves have always been watched more closely in Japan than in the United States, and

Table 4
Key Japanese International Economic Indicators by Month, 1969–1971

	Global Trade Balance			*Global Current Account Balance*		
	1969	*1970*	*1971*	*1969*	*1970*	*1971*
Jan.	−45	−42	2	−169	−182	−178
Feb.	227	230	367	113	93	226
March	430	399	702	293	225	511
April	352	312	549	247	186	409
May	237	201	580	123	52	424
June	337	345	648	231	202	504
July	371	375	788	253	213	629
Aug.	334	339	594	217	211	843
Sep.	378	422	597	251	251	690
Oct.	290	398	423	183	269	589
Nov.	281	307	348	168	145	486
Dec.	582	746	870	462	584	1,040

	Foreign Exchange Reserves			*Bilateral Trade Balance with U.S.*		
	1969	*1970*	*1971*	*1969*	*1970*	*1971*
Jan.	2,305	2,564	3,205	−33.65	−96.55	−50.99
Feb.	2,449	2,546	3,538	45.61	−1.65	−13.18
March	2,575	2,773	4,285	150.92	−10.74	164.47
April	2,453	2,828	4,481	114.95	26.03	158.27
May	2,441	2,775	5,545	81.36	47.25	181.95
June	2,385	2,638	6,238	88.17	−4.14	302.11
July	2,305	2,384	6,567	121.38	103.33	343.52
Aug.	2,313	2,395	11,069	102.88	70.13	435.93
Sep.	2,466	2,423	11,939	95.47	105.09	255.65
Oct.	2,472	2,542	12,653	54,62	12.43	233.82
Nov.	2,654	2,761	13,384	20.92	49.73	221.60
Dec.	2,614	3,188	13,783	93.69	163.61	404.24

Source: OECD, *Statistics of Foreign Trade*, Series A, 1971.
Note: Units U.S. $1 million

repeatedly during the postwar period low reserves were used by government officials to help justify unpopular deflationary policies.

During 1971 the level of foreign currency reserves received even more public attention as a source of international criticism. Other nations saw Japan's rapid accumulation of foreign exchange as a destabilizing element within the Bretton Woods system, and as the months went by this figure was presented frequently by public

Japanese observers, much to the dismay of international monetary officialdom, as evidence that official "stand fast" policy on the yen's parity would have to be changed.

The fourth international statistic, the *bilateral trade balance* with the United States, was of less economic importance. In a properly functioning international trading system, bilateral surpluses and deficits naturally occur and are accepted as long as each country tends to maintain an overall balance with all of its trading partners taken together. But Japan's large and growing trade surplus with the United States was of great *political* importance because of the importance of the bilateral economic and defense relationship.

The End of International Deficits. The domestic economic upswing that began early in 1966 had by 1967 created an international deficit problem for Japan's economic policymakers. Domestic economic factors combined with an overall slump in world imports to end the increase in Japan's world market share, while demand for imported goods at home continued to increase. For the first time in many years foreign currency reserves fell for several months below the psychologically important $2 billion level, and after a rebound in the fourth quarter they dropped below that mark again for the first six months of 1968.

The Ministry of Finance responded to the tightening international situation with the traditional remedies used to combat cyclical balance-of-payments problems throughout the postwar period. In September 1967 the Bank of Japan raised the official discount rate from 5.48 percent to 5.84 percent, and the rise in the discount rate signaled a simultaneous and more important clampdown on commercial bank lending through "window guidance." When the balance of payments continued to deteriorate the discount rate was raised again in January 1968. By March reports had begun to circulate in Japan suggesting that Japan was about to request standby credits of $400 million from the IMF to cope with her deficit situation, and by April rumors were sweeping Tokyo and European capitals of plans for a *de*valuation of the yen in order to improve the export competitiveness of Japan's exports and to limit imports.[1]

Devaluation rumors had spread during previous deficit periods, but in early 1968 their credibility was strengthened by the turbulent international monetary situation and the recent devaluation of the British pound. An official responsible for international monetary policy at the time confirmed in an interview several years later that some government consideration actually had been given to the idea of approaching the IMF to discuss a devaluation, but Finance Minister Mikio Mizuta and other MOF officials as well as the Bank of Japan released strongly worded statements of their intention to maintain the Y 360 = $1 parity in spite of the dangerously low level of Japan's foreign currency reserves.[2] They expressed confidence in their ability to handle the deficit problem through traditional means.

Their confidence proved well-founded. June 1968 was the last month to date during which Japan's foreign exchange reserves dropped below $2 billion with an improvement in the trade account and an end to the growing deficit in the services account. By August the outlook was bright enough to allow the official discount rate to be lowered once again to 5.48 percent. This, together with a loosening of the Bank of Japan's "window guidance" for private banks, increased the availability of credit for Japan's businesses and further increased the tempo of domestic economic growth.[3] External and internal factors combined to bring the balance-of-payments deficit crisis back under control by the end of the year, and for the first time in the postwar period balance was achieved without seriously dampening domestic economic growth. The boom that had begun in 1966 continued on to set new records for a sustained period of economic growth.

The upward trend continued throughout 1969 with foreign currency reserves accumulating to $3 billion during the first quarter, and by the end of the calendar year they stood at close to $3.5 billion. Nontrade factors, such as investment by foreigners in Japanese securities, had helped to boost the total, but the primary contributor was the expanding trade account surplus. By the end of 1969 Japan's exports exceeded imports by $3.7 billion, a figure 46 percent larger than the 1968 year-end surplus, and a startling 300 percent over 1967's performance.

Rapid balance-of-payments recoveries had been recorded in the past. But the 1968–1969 situation was unique in that the recovery occurred while the domestic economy continued to boom. Japan's GNP growth in 1969, at 13.5 percent, was only slightly lower than the 13.8 percent recorded in 1968. And there was no indication that the longest postwar boom was about to end.

The OECD's 1969 Assessment of Japan's New Status. This fundamental change in Japan's relationship with the international economy attracted the attention, and eventually concern, of her major trading partners. Each year the Economic and Development Review Committee of the OECD meets to discuss the domestic and international outlook for each member nation and to prepare a report of its findings. The final texts of these annual OECD country surveys are the result of considerable discussion, negotiation, and compromise among the OECD secretariat, the representatives of all the other member countries at the meeting, and the representatives of the country under review. Since they received at the time widespread media attention in the nation under consideration, and were referenced during subsequent discussions of international economic policy coordination, the annual OECD surveys had considerable political as well as economic significance during the late 1960s and early 1970s. Each country does its best to avoid specific criticism and to assure a favorable assessment of the domestic and international economic policies of its current government.

The Japan review was held in Paris on June 26, 1969, and two months later the OECD published its annual "Japan Survey." The introduction stated:

> The radical change of Japan's external position sets a promising new frame for future developments, but will also pose new problems. Relieved for the foreseeable future from the necessity to protect the country's low level of reserves and to submit the economy every two or three years to a "recession" or cooling off period, the problem of maintaining cost and price stability over time and of avoiding the building up of excess capacity may require greater attention than hitherto. In the likely absence of important balance of payments constraints, the enforcement of quick policy adjustments may become more difficult and the reaction of business slower. Moreover, with the attainment of a more adequate level of external reserves, Japan is, for the first time in her history, experiencing the problems of surplus countries trying to avoid undue strains on international liquidity.[4]

Considering its institutional origins, this was quite a frank assessment of Japan's international monetary position. The report clearly demonstrated that the important members of the world trading system had concluded by mid-1969 that Japan had moved from deficit-prone to surplus-prone status, and hoped for domestic and international economic policy adjustments in Tokyo to cope with the new situation. The report specifically mentioned the need for more rapid trade and investment liberalization:

The Japanese authorities are seeking progressively to fulfill their commitments for the adoption of more liberal policies concerning imports, current invisible transactions and capital exports. Since, if present trends continue, a large surplus on Japan's balance of payments may remain even though fast growth in the economy is maintained, further progress in liberalizing current external transactions and capital exports is highly desirable from the international point of view. . . . The present strong domestic expansion should make it easier for the Japanese authorities to overcome the social problems that have to be taken into account when accelerating the movement towards the removal of the remaining restrictions on imports.[5]

The initial public response of Japan's economic bureaucrats to their newly achieved international monetary status was cautious, as might be expected after decades of struggle against balance-of-payments ceiling restraint on domestic economic growth. At the beginning of 1969 Finance Minister Takeo Fukuda told journalists that external reserves of nearly $3 billion were by no means excessive when compared with the holdings of other large countries and the volume of Japan's foreign trade, and suggested that the level should even increase.[6] He and other officials repeated this assessment time and again throughout the year as reserves continued to climb, stressing the need for Japan to remain prepared to cope with future declines in her export competitiveness and surges of imports that once again might dictate domestic deflationary measures.

But MOF officials were well aware of the significance of the change. Taizo Hayashi, in 1969 the director of the Research Division of the Finance Minister's Secretariat, in a 1977 series of articles revealed that in addition to their regularly published projections, MOF economists each quarter prepared what they called a "*shojiki besu*" (candid basis) projection of domestic and international economic trends for the next six quarters. These projections were kept secret and used only for internal MOF policy discussions. Hayashi wrote that according to MOF's 1969 *shojiki besu* estimates, it was obvious that Japan's balance-of-payments situation had hit bottom around 1961 or 1962 and that thereafter it would continue, with periodic ups-and-downs, to register a surplus.[7] In other words, the MOF economists privately agreed with the main contention of the 1969 OECD report.

Japan's Initial Response to the New Surplus Situation

The international monetary system, already destabilized by concern over the future of the British pound, the West German mark, the French franc, and most important, the U.S. dollar, hardly needed another "problematic" currency. As Japan's growing reserves also clouded the future of the yen, international criticism of Japan became more frequent and more intense. In spite of their cautious public pronouncements, Japan's international economic officials began to implement measures designed to cope with the increasingly embarrassing surpluses and, more important, to appease their international critics.

The Yen Shift. The most effective measure, in terms of its immediate (although short-term) impact on Japan's foreign currency holdings, was the government effort to encourage Japan's exporters and importers to shift from international to domestic sources of credit. Nearly all of Japan's postwar foreign trade transactions had been denominated in U.S. dollars. The MOF had opposed yen financing of foreign trade during the 1950s and most of the 1960s, even when domestic interest rates were lower than foreign rates, because it made their control of international aspects of the economy more difficult and because it reduced, at least temporarily, the level of Japan's foreign currency reserves.[8]

Japan's interest rates during 1969 were somewhat lower than those abroad, making government policy compatible with natural market forces as the government began to encourage Japanese companies to switch their borrowing from foreign sources to Japanese sources. In early April the Ministry of Finance instructed Japan's foreign exchange banks to release some of their short-term foreign currency funds, and to provide their customers with yen financing for international transactions.[9] Later in the month Governor Makoto Usami of the Bank of Japan announced that the Bank was considering a revision of the export bill re-discount rate to further encourage the shift of the yen.[10]

The yen shift program was received enthusiastically by the business community, and by June other industrial sectors with large international sales and purchases joined the steel and petroleum industries in requesting even more yen financing. At the end of June the Bank of Japan announced that foreign exchange banks would be allowed to expand the yen shift an additional $400 million.[11]

An increase in Japanese interest rates during the latter half of 1969 made domestic yen financing less attractive for Japan's foreign traders and reduced the shift to yen financing. This prompted the Bank of Japan to participate more directly in the effort by announcing on September 22 that it would supply yen funds to foreign exchange banks through its buying operations and the extension of short-term loans. The same day the Ministry of Finance announced that dollars would be made available to the banks on a deferred-payment basis with which they could repay some of their Eurodollar loans as well.[12]

The exact amount by which the government's yen shift program reduced Japan's foreign currency reserves during 1969 is difficult to measure, but the total increase for the year was considerably less than what normally would have been expected from the large trade surplus. Of course, this effort had no impact at all on the growing international competitiveness of Japan's exports or on the Japanese economy's receptivity to imported goods, and made Japan no less surplus-prone in the longrun than it was before.

Trade and Investment Liberalization. The increase in international economic competitiveness, and the resulting shift from deficit-prone to surplus-prone status, brought more insistent demands from Japan's trading partners for rapid liberalization of the restrictions that remained on trade and investment. During the "dollar shortage" days of the early 1950s those restrictions had been tolerated abroad, even encouraged in some cases, as necessary for Japan's economic reconstruction. But conditions had changed radically by the late 1950s, and under considerable international pressure Japan made a commitment in 1960 to begin the politically painful process of liberalization.

Sufficient progress had been made by 1964 to enable Japan to become a full member of the three most important international economic organizations: the IMF (with Article VIII rather than Article XIV status), the GATT (General Agreement on Tariffs and Trade), and the OECD. A four-stage capital liberalization program was announced in 1965, with the first step implemented on schedule in 1967 and the second in February 1969.[13] However, by 1969 countries suffering bilateral deficits with Japan, such as the United States, found her remaining trade and investment barriers all the more irksome and demanded more progress on their removal as part of the effort to correct the international imbalance.

Those demands were received sympathetically by Japan's economic policymakers, especially those responsible for international monetary affairs. In a pattern that would be repeated over and over during the next few years, officials returning from international economic conferences in 1969, at which they had been scolded by the representatives of other countries for Japan's combination of surpluses and domestic economic protection, announced upon arriving in Tokyo that trade and capital liberalization was urgently needed. The Bank of Japan's Governor Usami, for example, brought that message back from the regular Basle meeting of the Bank for International Settlements on May 18, 1969. In an airport press conference he insisted that more rapid liberalization was necessary if Japan was to avoid foreign pressures for a revaluation of the yen.[14]

Increasing international monetary instability later in the year heightened Japan's sensitivity to the international resentment caused by her remaining restrictions. Yusuke Kashiwagi, director general of the International Monetary Bureau of the Ministry of Finance and Japan's most influential monetary affairs expert, told an interviewer on September 28, 1969, that more rapid liberalization was required in order for Japan to remain a proud member of international society, and that the current domestic prosperity provided the ideal political timing for its implementation.[15]

As the pressures increased, even the organized business community joined the chorus. An October 13, 1969, meeting of the chairman and vice chairmen of Keidanren (The Federation of Economic Organizations) strongly endorsed rapid trade and capital liberalization, and promised to hold more meetings of their liberalization-related committees to promote the process.[16] By 1969 it seemed that all of Japan—in principle—supported more rapid liberalization. And soon after the annual IMF and World Bank meetings, during which Japan's delegation came under particularly heavy fire from the United States and other countries, the government announced a stepped-up schedule for import liberalization covering 55 items to be liberalized by the end of 1971.[17]

Significant progress was made during 1969, but it came nowhere near the level of proposals suggested at airport press conferences by returnees from international economic meetings, nor anywhere near the level required to make a real impact on world opinion. In spite of the efforts of international monetary policymakers worried about the impact of a failure to liberalize more quickly on the fixed parity of the yen, the process dragged on throughout the period of the study—even into the 1980s—and remained a point of vulnerability in Japan's international economic relations.[18]

Foreign Aid. Japan's embarrassing surplus situation during the late 1960s also provided an opportunity to expand foreign aid programs.[19] During the 1950s, and even in the first half of the 1960s, economic recovery had not yet reached a level at which much foreign aid activity was expected from Japan. Most that was given took the form of reparation payments to those countries with claims from World War II. With membership in the OECD, Japan had made an international commitment to increase foreign aid, accepting the OECD's target of 0.70 percent of GNP for official development assistance (ODA), that aid which could be categorized as direct government grants, official loans with liberal repayment terms, and official contributions to international organizations. Even after joining the OECD, Japan's representatives often cited the chronic shortage of foreign currency as a restraint on the amount of aid they could give. The buildup of international surpluses during 1968 and 1969 stimulated more calls from abroad for significant improvements in the quantity and quality of Japan's aid efforts.

By 1969 Japan's international economic policymakers had a good opportunity to respond to foreign pressure to expand their foreign aid program while at the same time helping to reduce the buildup of foreign currency reserves, since disbursement of dollars would reduce the current account surplus and reduce net excess demand for yen in the exchange market. Some progress was made. For example, Finance Minister Fukuda, during an Asian tour in April 1969, expressed his government's intention to increase aid to Southeast Asia. After attending the annual meeting of the Asian Development Bank in Singapore, he announced in Sidney, Australia, that Japan planned to double aid to Asian countries within five years.[20]

Overall aid statistics for the decade reflected some effort to implement the commitment. During the first half of the 1960s, Japan's ODA had increased by only about 2.5 percent per annum. But the figure rose to 16.2 percent during the years between 1966 and 1971. The effort began from a rather low level, however, and the progress made was hardly adequate to dampen international criticism of Japan's foreign aid program, let alone to reduce significantly the troublesome foreign exchange reserves. In 1969 Japan's ODA represented only 0.26 percent of GNP (compared with the OECD's 0.70 percent target) and she remained vulnerable to criticism that foreign aid was essentially engineered to facilitate Japan's trade with less developed countries.[21]

Miscellaneous Measures. In addition to the yen shift, liberalization, and expansion of the aid effort, a few less significant attempts were made to cope with international disapproval of Japan's surplus situation during 1969. In March, for example, the limit on the amount of foreign currency that Japanese tourists and businessmen traveling abroad could take out of the country was increased by 40 percent. MOF officials also announced plans to begin negotiations with the IMF for an increase in Japan's quota from its relatively low level of $725 million. Toward the end of the year plans were made to repay Japan's World Bank loans before they came due, and arrangements were made for the purchase of medium-term World Bank bonds. The government's "Supreme Export Council," headed by the prime minister, was even renamed the "Supreme Trade Council," and a subcommittee was established within the organization to encourage the import of foreign goods.

The one measure Japan refused to consider was any change in the parity of the yen, or even reform of the international monetary system that would increase overall rate flexibility. After details of the efforts by IMF executive directors and their staff to introduce more flexibility into exchange rates became public in mid-1969, Governor Usami of the Bank of Japan stated categorically during a press conference that Japan's economy was based upon the assumption of exchange rates fixed as they were, and that even though reform to provide more flexibility was a growing possibility, Japan would be opposed to any such change.[22]

Just prior to his departure for Washington to attend the annual IMF meeting, Finance Minister Fukuda confirmed earlier off-the-record hints from MOF officials that he intended to oppose the reform proposals, stressing the need to maintain a system of solidly fixed parities.[23] Japan did agree after some initial hesitation to participate in the continuing IMF staff-level reform deliberations.

But Fukuda, just one day after West Germany's surprise announcement of the decision to float the mark, told the IMF in his main address that Japan was absolutely opposed to any systemic reform that might lead to a change in the parity of the yen.[24]

Japan Applies Economic Restraints for the First Time for Domestic Reasons

First quarter declines in the rate of growth of industrial production and increases in inventory levels stimulated speculation in 1969 that Japan's longest economic boom in history was about to end. Business spokesmen began to call for a loosening of the tight money policy, and expressions of sympathy for their point of view echoed in the corridors of the Ministry of International Trade and Industry. Economists in the Ministry of Finance, Bank of Japan, and Economic Planning Agency remained skeptical, however, and insisted that any lowering of the official discount rate or relaxation of administrative guidance to banks concerning the level of their lending was inappropriate since other economic indicators suggested that the economy was likely to continue on its upward course. These officials were particularly concerned about the rise in the wholesale and consumer price indexes, and by June their concern was reflected in the authoritative monthly report of the overall economy published by the EPA.

Japan had been more willing to accept moderate inflation as a cost of rapid growth than the other postwar economic superstar West Germany. But the possibility of upper single-digit inflation could not be ignored. In 1968 the December wholesale price index was only 0.2 percent higher than it had been in January. But by the end of the first quarter of 1969 wholesale prices were increasing by 0.3 percent per month, well over the rate of inflation for the whole previous year. By midyear it was certain the economy was overheating and that without corrective policy of some sort inflation would soon be out of hand.

Japan's economic policymakers began to consider economic restraint measures to cope with the new situation. In the past such measures had only been applied as a result of alarming declines in Japan's international monetary position, when foreign currency reserves had reached a dangerously low point and there was some question of her ability to generate sufficient foreign earnings to pay for needed imports. Economic restraint measures were never popular with Japan's business community and public, but the "external threat" of running out of money to pay for imports provided indisputable support for temporary sacrifice, greatly facilitating implementation.

The mid-1969 situation was quite different. Japan's external economic accounts were well in the black; the surpluses themselves were even becoming a source of foreign discontent. This deprived economic officials of their accustomed "external threat" argument during the extended ritual preceding the change in the official discount rate.[25] Not only had tight money policies not been used in the past to cope with anything but international deficits, opponents further argued that Japan's inflation was being imported from abroad in the form of higher-priced imported goods, and that Japan's business community should not have to sacrifice for the economic transgressions of the United States and other countries. Japan's international monetary authorities also feared that a shift to domestic restraint would make domestic markets less attractive and encourage Japan's manufacturers to put more emphasis on exports, thereby increasing the trade account surplus and boosting foreign currency reserves. Nonetheless, with the distinct possibility of double-digit inflation by the end of the year, a large increase in the official discount rate—from 5.84 percent to 6.25 percent—was finally decided upon by the Ministry of Finance and Bank of Japan and announced on August 30, 1969. Reserve requirements for the large banks were raised at the same time.

For the first time in the postwar period restraint policies were used to cope with domestic rather than international economic problems. The international reaction was predictable. Given the sensitivity of the international monetary situation at the time, and the domestic and international predictions that Japan's surpluses were likely to continue for the foreseeable future, this move increased foreign pressure on Japan to consider other measures to cope with their new economic situation.

Fixed Exchange Rate Defense Measures During 1970 and Early 1971. Pressure eased somewhat on Japan's politically sensitive international economic indexes during the first three quarters of 1970 after substantial increases during 1969. But surpluses returned with renewed vigor during the final quarter of 1970 and continued throughout 1971. A sharp downturn in Japan's domestic economy exacerbated the situation, encouraging exports and reducing demand for imported raw materials. Repeated demands from the business community, combined with fear that declining interest rates abroad would attract foreign capital to Japan, persuaded the government to reduce the official discount rate a quarter point to 5.75 percent effective January 19, 1971. But the Ministry of Finance and Bank of Japan rejected demands for further reductions, even in the face of British and German cuts at the end of March, because of a sharp increase in consumer prices.[26] The resulting disparity in U.S. and Japanese interest rates tended to reverse the effect of the government's "yen shift" policy, and the swing back to dollar financing of foreign trade further increased Japan's foreign currency holdings during 1971.

The overall trade balance for the first quarter of 1971 alone, $1.1 billion, was nearly double that for all of 1970, and a surge in U.S.-bound exports created a bilateral trade surplus with the United States of approximately $80 million, compared with a $123 million *deficit* in the first three months of 1970. When the final trade figures for fiscal year 1970 (April 1, 1970, to March 31, 1971) were announced at the beginning of May, they showed Japan running the largest surplus in that account of any country in the world.[27] Japan's foreign currency reserves jumped another $1 billion in just over two months, topping $5 billion by early March. This nice round figure of $5 billion seemed to stick in the minds of government policymakers and public observers, intensifying public speculation about the possibility of Japan being forced to consider a parity change for the yen as the only way to control the situation.

Official Public Denials of Plans to Up-Value the Yen. After March 1971 the relentless pressure of international surpluses forced MOF and Bank of Japan officials and their political masters to issue increasingly frequent public denials of any intention to change the parity of the yen and to devise alternative policies to cope with the growing imbalance. These public denial exercises were taken very seriously by Japan's international moneymen, who feared the discussion of revaluation that followed every public announcement of all four critical international economic indexes would encourage domestic and international holders of dollars to convert them to yen in anticipation of a quick profit equal to the margin of revaluation. Japan maintained strict and effective government control over foreign exchange transactions, but even they could not stop all speculative purchases of yen.

Speculative purchases of yen tended to drive up the price, a trend the government had to counter with official market intervention managed by the Bank of Japan, offering to purchase dollars with yen to stabilize the parity within the tight margins around the official Y 360 = $1 rate defined under the Bretton Woods system. The intervention purchases, of course, increased Japan's official U.S. dollar holdings. Higher foreign currency reserves, in turn, when announced at the end of the month, increased public speculation about the possibility of a revaluation, resulting in more purchases of yen and even bigger official foreign currency holdings.

By March 1971 even Cabinet members were making frequent public denials of plans to revalue the yen, or even of foreign pressure to consider a revaluation. Finance Minister Fukuda and Foreign Minister Kiichi Miyazawa, for example, were grilled during Upper House Budget Committee hearings by JSP (Japan Socialist party) member Yoshihachiro Kimura about the possibility of a revaluation. Fukuda admitted that Japan's foreign currency reserves were rising rapidly and that reductions in American interest rates were likely to drive short-term capital out of the United States in search of higher yields. But he denied that there was any real foreign pressure for a yen revaluation since all influential European and American government and business leaders agreed there was no need for a parity change.[28]

During a regularly scheduled press conference a few days later Bank of Japan Governor Tadashi Sasaki told reporters that he knew of no real foreign pressure for a revaluation, and that Japan's government would firmly resist such pressure in the unlikely event it ever should occur. Sasaki flatly rejected revaluation as an appropriate policy with which to deal with the situation, saying that a change in the yen's parity would have widespread adverse impact on the Japanese economy as a whole, much of which would be unpredictable.[29]

Sasaki's first major public denial on March 10 of any plans for a revaluation had little impact on the Japanese communications media's speculation that a revaluation plot was brewing in the bowels of government, and he was questioned on March 25 at the Foreign Correspondent's Club in Tokyo about government plans for the yen. He repeated his strong denial in much the same terms that he had used two weeks before, adding for the foreign press the significant point that Japan's current high level of foreign reserves was, in part, the result of overprotection of the real value of the yen by import restrictions. He agreed that Japan's reserves were higher than in the past, but added that the accumulated funds could be used to develop foreign sources of raw materials and to provide foreign aid to needy countries without revaluing the yen simply to get rid of the money. He also repeated his opinion that a parity change would adversely affect Japan's domestic economy.[30]

By the end of March the public position of Japan's government officials responsible for international monetary affairs was established and did not change substantially, until announcement of the controlled float in late August:

1. Surpluses in the four critical statistical indexes were accumulating at an undesirable speed and were impossible to ignore, but the hypersurplus situation was only temporary and not evidence of "fundamental disequilibrium."
2. In spite of growing press speculation there was no real official—or significant private sector—foreign pressure on Japan to consider a parity change.
3. Even if the government wished, it would be impossible to calculate the appropriate level of parity adjustment because the yen's "true value" was still disguised by trade and investment restrictions that would first have to be removed to see how the economy performed at the old rate in a truly free market climate.
4. A parity change was sure to have a devastating effect on Japan's overall economy, especially during the current business slump.
5. It still was possible to formulate and implement nonrevaluation countermeasures with which to deal with the growing surpluses.

During interviews several years after the event all of the key international monetary officials confirmed that their public statements at the time accurately reflected the real climate of opinion within the Ministry of Finance and Bank of Japan. Only Taizo Hayashi, then in charge of the Research Division of the Finance Minister's Secretariat, had a significantly different opinion. Although more concerned about the upward trend in the international economic indexes than they would admit in public, government officials were even more concerned about the immediate impact of public discussion of the issue on the market. Confidence in their position and fear that intraministerial discussions might leak to a jittery public combined within the MOF even to prevent formulation of a secret contingency plan to deal with any possible international ultimatum demanding a parity change (of the sort issued from Washington on August 15). Concerned officials instead directed all their energies toward quieting public speculation through skillful argument and minor liberalization efforts.

Modest Trade and Investment Liberalization Efforts. As pressure from the economic indexes and public skepticism intensified during early 1971, trade and investment liberalization became even more attractive for Japan's international monetary policymakers. Official rejections of a parity change solution to the imbalance problem often included mention of the government's commitment to trade liberalization. The most dramatic specific example of that effort came in late March when it was announced that effective April 1, 1971, tariffs on nearly 2,000 imported items would be reduced nine months prior to the date they were to be cut under the Kennedy Round schedule. At the same time the Export Contribution Corporation was also abolished, bringing to an end the preferential tax treatment Japanese companies had long received in proportion to the percentage of their total production devoted to exports.[31] The anticipated effect of these efforts was modest when compared with the seriousness of the surplus problem, but Japan's representatives in the United States gave the initiative widespread publicity as proof of their commitment to make Japan a more attractive export market for foreign countries.[32]

By mid-April rumors were circulating in Tokyo about government plans for Japan to play a leading role in the next round of GATT tariff reductions. Sources close to Prime Minister Sato and Finance Minister Fukuda reported that the two had met on the evening of April 12 to discuss proposing a "Japan Round" of tariff reductions that would begin in 1973 modeled on the "Kennedy Round" initiated by the United States in the early 1960s.[33] This report was later officially confirmed and representatives of the Ministry of Finance, MITI, and the Ministry of Foreign Affairs began to discuss how the idea should be presented at the GATT meeting scheduled for the end of April in Geneva.[34] This proposal eventually led to the Tokyo Round of GATT negotiations later in the decade.

Tighter Exchange Controls. The government also tightened its foreign exchange controls in order to limit speculative, short-term inflows of foreign investment and to restrict speculative currency transactions by Japanese trading companies and exporting manufacturers. These complex measures are described by Wilbur Monroe, a Treasury Department official assigned to the U.S. embassy in Tokyo, as "ad hoc for the most part; measures were taken to deal with situations as they evolved and if there was any design at all it would appear that the government's primary intention was to block inflows of short-term capital by foreigners. Only slightly less exuberant efforts were devoted to controlling leads and lags in commercial transactions."[35]

By the end of April 1971 the Finance Ministry was hinting to the press that concern over Japanese corporate speculation in foreign exchange and its effect on Japan's international balances was forcing consideration of an overall revision of the law that set the standard for international trade settlements *(Hyojun Kessei Hoho)*.[36] Like so much of the legal framework for international economic transactions, this law was formulated in the early postwar period when Japan's economy suffered from a shortage of foreign exchange, and as a result was biased toward the expansion, rather than reduction, of foreign currency reserves. Government sources cited foreign exchange bank estimates that international traders could increase Japan's foreign exchange holdings by as much as two to three billion dollars through such activity, all justified under liberal interpretation of the existing law.

Tighter foreign exchange controls undoubtedly slowed the inflow of foreign capital into Japan. But they also complicated legitimate transactions, and their very announcement demonstrated the growing seriousness of the situation and increased the speculative attractiveness of the Japanese yen. As the months passed their effectiveness tended to decline and their negative "announcement" effect to increase.

The Skeptical Public Response

The confidence of Japan's international monetary officials in their ability to avoid a change in the yen's parity was not shared by Japan's press or business community. These two sectors evidenced increasing skepticism in the government's ability to resist the international pressures they took such pains to deny during early 1971, and eventually even in the wisdom of the government's "stand fast" policy itself. That is not to say that either the business community or the press hoped for or encouraged a yen revaluation during early 1971. They did not. Persuaded by the periodic warnings of government officials that revaluation would have a disastrous effect on the economy—warnings made as much to convince the world they had no intention of revaluing as to impart accurate information—nearly every public observer anticipated serious economic repercussions from what was widely regarded as the inevitable result of Japan's endless accumulation of surpluses.

Japan's Communications Media. The yen revaluation story was big news in 1971. Vats of ink, tons of newsprint, thousands of hours of high-powered newsmen's time, and millions of yen of expense account money were expended in its pursuit. First, a revaluation would be an event of great economic importance should it occur. There was room to argue over the actual effect it would have on the economy, but once done it would fundamentally change the relationship of Japan's economy with the rest of the world.

Second, Japan's economic journalists realized that the nature of the yen parity issue would force the government to make the announcement as a surprise to avoid uncontrollable pre-announcement financial speculation. Government officials would have to lie about their intentions if asked in order to keep the surprise. Journalists do not like to be surprised—especially by other journalists—and this element heightened the tension between government officials and the journalists who covered them. They would have to stay alert to avoid being "scooped" by the competition.

Third, in spite of the fact that Japan's journalists tend to form close relationships with individual politicians and bureaucrats, they take their "public watchdog" and "public tutor" roles very seriously. In principle, Japan's journalists maintain a more adversarial relationship with their government than do their American counterparts. So it was no surprise to find journalists from the print and electronic media highly suspicious of the public statements of the international monetary officials in 1971. They are always suspicious, and usually critical.

All of this is appropriate, even predictable. But constant speculative reporting throughout the year, intensifying after the end of the first quarter, did complicate the government's handling of the yen issue. After March 1971 hardly a day went by that the subject was not mentioned on the front page of every major newspaper. Senior economic policymakers always were asked at least one question about their intentions for the yen at their public weekly news conferences; they were squeezed in private for background or off-the-record comments that might provide more information. Important foreign visitors to Japan were asked for their opinions. And Japan's international correspondents in New York and Washington even sought out those who didn't visit Japan to ask their opinion of the likelihood and advisability of a yen revaluation—if they hadn't given the matter any thought before being asked, they would in response to the question. On days when no responsible government official could be found to deny plans to change the parity, stories were written about the likely effect such a change would have on Japan, or about public and elite opinion polls on the likelihood and advisability of such a move.

Whether or not a unilateral revaluation prior to the August "Nixon shock" would have been a good thing for Japan, the drawn-out anticipation of the event generated uncertainty about Japan's future that made recovery from the economic slump more difficult in 1971. Businessmen do not like to expand their activities in times of uncertainty. It also stimulated foreign and domestic speculation in the foreign exchange, attracting even more unwanted foreign exchange. And, perhaps most important, the long period of press speculation made Japan's international monetary officials even more cautious as they considered the issue. Official discussion—even secret discussion—was kept to a minimum within the Ministry of Finance for fear of disastrous leaks of information. The more the media pressure intensified in 1971 the less willing the policymakers were to discuss the subject, even among themselves. This hesitancy helped to keep decision making confined to a very small group at the top of the bureaucratic system.

The Japanese Business Community. By March 1971 moves within the Japanese business community heavily involved in international trade indicated a suspicion of the government's intentions, or at least of its ability, to resist what seemed to the businessmen to be almost insuperable pressure for a revaluation. Two such industries were shipping—builders and owners—and the large trading companies. Various industrial sectors heavily dependent upon export markets had already begun to protect themselves from the serious losses that would result from a sudden exchange rate change by trying to denominate contracts for the delivery of goods or services in yen rather than dollars. In the event of an up-valuation, companies committed to the delivery of significant amounts of their product abroad in prices denominated in dollars would suffer losses proportionate to the percentage of the upvaluation. With yen-denominated contracts their foreign customers would be required to absorb the loss.

The Japanese shipbuilding and shipping industries were particularly sensitive to the problem. Since 1970, due to the long lead times their contracts required, shipbuilders had been careful to negotiate yen-based contracts for future delivery. But the industry still claimed to hold over five billion dollars worth, including interest, of dollar-denominated contracts for future delivery and to fear any change in the yen's parity.[37] During a meeting of shipping company magnates on March 24, agreement was reached to try to expand their revaluation defense measures by thereafter denominating their shipping rates for North American routes in yen rather than in dollars. However, the companies feared strong opposition from their international customers.[38]

Although the most vociferous and best organized, Japan's shipbuilders and shipowners were not the only concerned businessmen who took action to avoid sudden losses should the yen be revalued. On March 13 Matsuyuki Wakasugi, head of the Boeki Shosha-kai (Association of General Trading Companies), a group of presidents of 15 of Japan's major trading companies, had visited Yoshihiro Inayama, president of Japan Steel, to ask his company to share foreign exchange loss risk with them. It was reported that the steel company was only the group's first stop. The trading companies hoped to spread exchange risk among their suppliers throughout the Japanese business community. Wakasugi and his group argued that in the event of revaluation the trading companies would bear an unfair proportion of the resulting loss since their purchases were denominated in yen and their sales contracts were denominated in dollars. They added that the steel companies actually would benefit from a revaluation since the prices they had to pay for their imported raw materials would be reduced if the yen's international value were to increase. Inayama was reported to have received their suggestion quite coolly, with the comment that nothing could be done for the time being and that any action on the part of the steel companies to share exchange loss burdens would have to await assessment of the trading companies actual losses.[39]

During the early months of 1971 other trade-dependent industrial sectors announced "revaluation defense" measures in order to assure their business associates that they would not be caught flatfooted by a surprise announcement. Each "revaluation defense" announcement was given prominent coverage by the Japanese press as further evidence of the likelihood of a revaluation. Through March members of the business community most likely to be affected by a parity change focused their efforts on specific revaluation defense measures rather than on the question of whether or not the government should make such a move. The Shipbuilders Association was the only exception. Its members vigorously lobbied the government through public statements and office visits for maintenance of the fixed rate. But even at this early stage they took care to add that the government should share their losses through direct compensation or tax relief if it eventually did decide to revalue the yen.

The business community may have focused their lobbying efforts during early 1971 on avoiding loss from being fenced in by dollar-denominated contracts for future delivery rather than on any effort to influence the government's parity policy because they believed the government was already doing all it could to prevent a revaluation of the yen. During later interviews, moreover, several senior businessmen said they thought it inappropriate for private-sector representatives to "interfere" in the area of international monetary policy, and that even if they had wished to comment they were sure their efforts would have been sharply rejected by MOF officials.

The leaders of Japan's business community dutifully avoided making significant public references to the government's international monetary policy throughout the first quarter of 1971 in compliance with the wishes of the international monetary officials. But they too were becoming more concerned with the growing pressure at home and the more frequent reports coming from their international branches of American and European frustration with Japan's official passive posture. By early April senior business spokesmen began to express their concerns directly and indirectly in public statements that received widespread media attention.

For example, in a speech given to a large group of Japanese bankers in Tokyo on April 9, Kogoro Uemura, chairman of Keidanren, specifically stated that Japan's government must intensify efforts to liberalize restrictions on international trade and investment in order to avoid giving foreigners the impression that Japan preferred a revaluation of the yen to a serious liberalization effort.[40] For some time official Keidanren policy had included encouragement of more rapid liberalization, but Uemura's early April speech was the first time it had been linked explicitly in public to Japan's international monetary problems.

Less than one week later Chairman Kikawada of Keizai Doyukai sent even more intense shock waves through government and business circles during his opening address to the Keizai Doyukai General Meeting. On February 18 he and other business leaders had received identical letters from William Blackie, chairman of Caterpillar Tractor, a large American construction equipment manufacturer, that asked the Japanese business community to press their government for a yen revaluation to help relieve the competitive pressure on American business created by Japanese exports. Seiichi Yamashita, Keizai Doyukai's executive director, later recalled that the letter was taken very seriously by Mr. Kikawada and the Doyukai staff as a signal from the United States that Japan was in for serious trouble in the near future. In mid-April, without going so far as to call for a parity change, Kikawada decided to state in his opening address to the General Meeting that it was his personal opinion that the question of whether or not a revaluation should be considered as one policy alternative should be given more serious consideration by the government, especially from the standpoint of cooperation with Japan's important international economic partners. The suggestion had to be made as Kikawada's personal opinion rather than the opinion of the whole organization because many of the other members of the organization strongly opposed the idea.[41]

The government's response was immediate and sharp. Morning newspapers carried front-page news of Kikawada's "bombshell" together with strong negative reaction from unnamed senior MOF and Bank of Japan officials. They repeated the official line that the imbalance was only temporary, that the pressure could be handled through liberalization, that exchange rate policy was the sole responsibility of government officials directly involved, as well as a stern warning that it was inappropriate for nongovernment individuals to make such public statements.[42] Yamashita added that immediately after his statement became public Kikawada received an angry telephone call from Finance Minister Fukuda, as well as many other hostile personal calls from MOF officials. One such senior official vividly recalled the incident five years later and said that Kikawada was accused privately by some MOF officials of advocating examination of a revaluation simply for selfish business reasons since his own industry (he was chairman of Tokyo Power and Electric) would be bound to profit from a change in the parity of the yen because it would reduce the cost of importing power-generating fuel.[43]

MOF and Bank of Japan officials continued, and even intensified, their heavy-handed efforts to retain control of public discussion of international monetary affairs in the face of evidence that by April Japan's business leaders had begun to lose confidence in their ability to formulate a credible alternative to cope with the worsening situation. As the weeks went by, business elites began to discuss the problem openly and to call upon Japan's international moneymen for a more credible plan of action.

In the midst of this increasing public criticism, senior government officials assured a jittery Japanese public in early May that the unexpected West German decision once again to float the mark, and the shock waves that decision created within the international monetary system, would have no impact upon Japan. Even Prime Minister Sato was asked to join in the public assurances due to the gravity of the situation. MOF officials drafted immediate explanations of the difference between Japan's position and the West German predicament, stressing Japan's maintenance of effective exchange controls with which they would be able to head off speculative attacks on the yen should the tide of international dollars head next for Japan.[44] In spite of these explanations, Japan's foreign currency reserves had jumped another $1 billion in just the two short months before the West German float was announced.

The deutsche mark crisis helped to finalize Japan's decision to ease interest rates for the second time in 1971, beating back the more conservative policymakers' fears of inflationary repercussions similar to those experienced in the United States. On May 7 the Bank of Japan announced that the official discount rate would be lowered by a quarter point beginning the following day. In contrast to previous announcements, this statement emphasized that the reduction was being made to cooperate in the cause of international monetary stability, and that hereafter the government would have to consider more rapid stimulation of Japanese domestic economic demand as part of the effort to stabilize the international situation.[45]

By the end of May the West German float, increasing public pressure from American congressional and business leaders, and public hints from senior Nixon administration officials that the yen was seriously undervalued had stimulated public concern in Japan to the point that Keidanren, Keizai Doyukai, and the Zenkoku Ginko Kyokai (National Banking Association), Japan's most influential banking organization, all were openly demanding that the government reexamine its international monetary position and either consider adjustment of the yen's relationship with the international monetary system (Keizai Doyukai's position) or at least formulate and implement a more effective system of liberalization countermeasures to help reduce growing resentment toward Japan among her important international economic partners.[46] The government could no longer hope to silence public comment on the yen issue with a raised official eyebrow, or even with blatant arm-twisting. Japan's international moneymen realized they not only were under severe international pressure, but even more important, that their aloof, "stand fast" posture had cost them the confidence of the most important elements of Japan's business community leadership. Their public denials of plans for a yen policy change, even when made by the prime minister himself, were taken by the Japanese press in the same spirit as the annual announcement of the return of the swallows to Capistrano: worthy of note, but not unexpected. Something more dramatic was required than to maintain their standpat position.

4. The "Eight-Point Program to Avoid Yen Revaluation"

By the beginning of June 1971 domestic and foreign pressure had reached a level at which Japan's international monetary officials had to announce some dramatic plan to demonstrate that they were in control or risk losing the confidence of the Japanese business community, the public, and even their own political superiors. The West German float in May had calmed international money markets, but only temporarily. Japan's foreign currency reserves had increased over $1 billion in May alone, the largest monthly increase in that important indicator to date. And even though U.S. government officials were careful not to make direct reference to the yen's parity after the celebrated Trezise statement of late May, official and unofficial American criticism of Japan's overall foreign economic policies became increasingly shrill with each passing day. Congressman Henry Reuss even introduced a "Sense of the Congress" resolution on June 3, 1971, calling for the suspension of the convertibility of the U.S. dollar into gold and a float as the only means for the United States to cope with the situation.[1]

Closer to home, and even more important, Japan's business community—even the traditionally cautious, team-playing bankers—was becoming increasingly restless and concerned.[2] After a June 2nd meeting of vice chairmen of the Japan Foreign Trade Council (Nihon Boeki-kai), it was announced that the group had agreed upon a position paper to be submitted to the government calling for more rapid trade and investment liberalization, more foreign aid, and a loosening of foreign exchange controls. All of these suggestions had been made in the past. But this announcement from Japan's most influential business group reflected declining confidence in the government's ability to cope with the situation by including a request that a program be established through which

Japanese companies could be compensated for losses resulting from changes in the yen's exchange rate should the government eventually be forced to revalue.[3] Even Keidanren had refrained from discussing this possibility in the past.

Japan's political leaders were poorly informed about the details of international economic policy, and lacking personal staffs of professional economists they had to depend for their information and advice upon the very government bureaucrats whose activities they were supposed to supervise. But by late May and early June the Liberal Democratic party was well aware of the issue and especially anxious to avoid criticism of their leadership as preparations began for the Upper House elections scheduled for June 27. Party leaders hoped to see something done before the election that would deprive their political opposition of the opportunity to charge the government with inability to handle the widely publicized international monetary issue and bilateral relations with the United States.[4] This political unease increased pressure on Japan's bureaucracy for some dramatic response prior to the late June election.

The "Eight-Point Program to Avoid Yen Revaluation" was announced on June 4. Reflecting in its very title Japan's resolve to avoid change in the yen's parity at all cost, it included a number of nonexchange rate measures to cope with foreign criticism of Japan's economic policies. From the time of its announcement to the August 15 "Nixon shock"—and even after—Japan's economic officials focused much of their energies on the promotion of this plan as an alternative to revaluation.

The effort failed. The eight-point plan had been hastily formulated by the Ministry of Finance with a minimum of preliminary interministerial consultation, so it surprised no one when efforts at implementation met stiff resistance from the government agencies and industrial sectors most directly affected. The plan failed to impress observers at home and abroad. Government officials and business representatives met repeatedly throughout June and July to hammer out agreement on implementation, but with little success as the four critical international economic indicators continued to climb. With a new wave of unrest in international money markets in early August, it was only a matter of time before the dollar-dominated Bretton Woods system would collapse.

The Eight-Point Program: "Top-Down" Decisionmaking in Japan

Toward the end of May rumors began to circulate among government office workers in Kasumigaseki about plans for a comprehensive set of measures to deal with Japan's international monetary predicament. Newspaper articles too, obviously the product of purposeful leaks and background briefings by senior government officials, described the government's growing concern over foreign criticism of Japan's past international economic policies within the current tense world situation. The articles suggested that Japan's representatives would have to present a comprehensive and meaningful program to liberalize official restrictions on foreign economic activity to the annual meeting of the IMF scheduled for late September in Washington. Front-page stories on June 2 speculated that the whole program would be approved at a special meeting of the Economic Cabinet on June 4. That same day an interministerial directors-general meeting was held at which MOF officials explained the outline and purpose of the program to the senior officials who would be responsible for its implementation.[5]

The "economic cabinet" met in emergency session as anticipated on Friday afternoon, June 4, with Finance Minister Fukuda, Foreign Minister Aiichi, MITI Minister Miyazawa, Agriculture Minister Kuraishi, Economic Planning Agency Director General Sato, and Chief Cabinet Secretary Hori in attendance. Fukuda presented the new eight-point program to the group for final cabinet-level approval and immediately thereafter provided the waiting press corps with an official version of the plan they had heard so much about off the record during the past few weeks.

The eight points were:

1. *More rapid implementation of import liberalization measures*
    - Decide by the end of September on items among the 40 remaining restricted imported products to be liberalized by the end of the calendar, or fiscal, year
    - Increase import quotas on items that cannot be liberalized
2. *Rapid implementation of preferential tariffs for imports from less developed countries*
    - To be implemented by August 1, 1971

3. *Acceleration of the tariff-reduction timetable*

   - Unilateral tariff reductions for items of importance to the livelihood of the Japanese public
   - Efforts to promote a new round of international tariff reductions

4. *Promotion of the liberalization of restrictions on international investment*

   - Reduce the number of industries in which foreign investment is not permitted and increase the number of industries that are completely liberalized
   - Liberalize all investment by Japanese abroad in principle, investigate the lending of foreign currency for that purpose by the Export-Import Bank and other institutions, and increase bank loans for foreign investment

5. *Removal of nontariff barriers to trade*

   - Review the automobile import quota system
   - Review automatic import-approval procedures and other nontariff barriers

6. *Expansion of foreign aid*

   - Make both quantitative and qualitative improvements in the whole program

7. *Orderly exports*

   - Work to ensure the "orderly" expansion of Japan's exports
   - Consider the suspension or abolition of the export promotion tax system
   - Reexamine Bank of Japan preferential financing for exports
   - Consider shifting the emphasis of Export-Import Bank financing from export financing to import and investment financing
   - Investigate measures to promote the stockpiling of important raw materials

8. *More flexible management of fiscal and monetary policy*

   - Consider measures to stimulate the economy and to promote social capital expenditure[6]

Fukuda then went directly to the prime minister's office to report the results of the meeting to Sato who approved both the specifics and spirit of the plan. Sato then held his own press conference to express support and ask each government ministry and the business community to cooperate in implementing the specific measures decided upon by the cabinet.

Given the political and bureaucratic climate, the eight-point program was an ambitious undertaking. And although Japan in response to foreign pressure continued to propose implementation of several of the points well into the next decade, the program did include responses to virtually every point of criticism Japan had received from abroad—every point, that is, but a change in the parity of the yen.

Important government decisions normally are made no more quickly in Japan than they are in other industrialized democracies. In fact, the Japanese process may be more tortuous because of the great importance placed upon the responsibility of Japanese policy initiators to make all reasonable efforts to obtain the input and agreement of everyone involved before a final decision is reached. While this greater emphasis on consultation and consensus usually slows the decision-making process, it reduces the time and friction required to implement decisions that have been properly coordinated. But it also justifies resistance by subordinates to ready-made policies handed down from on high without adequate consultation.

The formation and announcement of the eight-point program to avoid yen revaluation did not follow the preferred "consensus" pattern. The specific measures were drawn up by a small group of MOF officials under the leadership of vice minister for international monetary affairs, Yusuke Kashiwagi, with a minimum of interministerial consultation.[7] Takeo Fukuda, as a former MOF official, already concerned about the economic implications of the situation, and as a senior LDP politician increasingly sensitive to the political implications of continuing to support a "stand fast" policy, was convinced of the need for such drastic action. He, in turn, persuaded his fellow LDP cabinet members, including the prime minister, to endorse the proposal as the official government position. Once the plan was finalized it was announced to the public and to the other economic bureaucracies as the only hope for Japan to cope with the international monetary situation short of a disastrous change in the parity of the yen. The MOF plan naturally included many items that were under the jurisdictions of other ministries.

This "top-down" formulation of the eight-point program resulted first from the assumption that only international monetary specialists had the experience and technical knowledge required to deal with international monetary affairs. Japan's international monetary professionals were used to working alone, protected from the customary bureaucratic give-and-take and public pressure. The general public and business community were beginning by April to question the judgment of the professionals. But their concern still was expressed in general terms rather than as demands for implementation of specific alternative policies.

A second factor was the growing sense of crisis throughout Japan concerning the yen problem. Everyone agreed that something dramatic should be done, and done quickly, to quiet domestic and international criticism of Japan's position and to counter the continuing rise in the four critical international economic indicators. If every government and business organization affected were to be consulted in good consensus policy formulation style, the final decision would be unacceptably postponed.

A third factor was less specific, but no less important: the personal style and reputation of Yusuke Kashiwagi, the undisputed leader of Japan's international monetary professionals. Born in 1917 in Dairen, China, Kashiwagi spent much of his childhood abroad as the son of an international banking family. His colleagues even joked that Kashiwagi spoke better English than Japanese. Upon graduation from the Law Faculty of Tokyo University, he entered the Finance Ministry in 1941 and served in the Budget Bureau and other key sections of the Ministry up through the mid-1950s. Since then he spent the remainder of his career in the highly specialized field of international finance. During those years Kashiwagi was said to have been involved in every major Japanese international monetary event. He had good personal relationships with all of the important European and American international monetary specialists, who found him easier to deal with than most of his colleagues because of his command of English and his personal style. Kashiwagi by the early 1970s was Japan's international monetary expert's expert.

Equally important, his expertise was recognized and appreciated by other MOF officials, the business community, the press, and senior members of the Liberal Democratic party. An official who worked closely with Kashiwagi for many years noted during a personal interview that the more senior post of vice minister for international monetary affairs was even specially created in the late 1960s to keep Kashiwagi in a position to handle Japan's international finances after his term as director general of the International Monetary Bureau expired in 1968.[8] His indispensability was demonstrated once again in June 1971 when he was asked to remain at the MOF as Special Adviser to the Finance Minister rather than retire as was customary after a colleague who entered the ministry the same year assumed the top administrative post of vice minister for administrative affairs. Few things are more difficult in the Japanese bureaucracy than expansion of the number of top-level personnel positions, especially when done to avoid the retirement of a favored official. For Kashiwagi the impossible was accomplished with relative ease—a tribute to his abilities.

In addition, according to the universal evaluation of officials who worked with him, Kashiwagi had at least as much confidence in his own abilities as others had in him. His personal style reflected that self-confidence. The frequently heard comment that Kashiwagi's English was better than his Japanese was not always made as an expression of personal affection. Some observers added that during his long experience abroad he had developed a management style they thought more appropriate to the European or American systems, that he was more inclined to make decisions on his own than to consult his colleagues in good Japanese fashion, and that he was more effective when dealing with foreigners than with other members of the Japanese bureaucracy.

These three factors—the traditional isolation of international monetary policy from outside interference, the late May 1971 sense of crisis, and the personal style and reputation of Japan's most influential international monetary official—combined to produce the sudden announcement of Japan's final response to her international monetary predicament. Its rapid formulation and announcement were a credit to its supporters. But difficulties experienced during implementation, and even its effect upon domestic and international opinion, were to prove a major disappointment.

Efforts to Implement the Eight-Point Program

The eight-point program was presented in early June not as the first of a series of planned responses, or even as a stopgap measure with which to ride out temporary international monetary market turbulence. Rather, it was designed and presented as Japan's *final effort* to cope with the problem. Since there already was absolute opposition among the monetary professionals to any consideration of a parity change—opposition so strong that no contingency planning was done to prepare for an action such as that taken by the United States on August 15—the eight-point program was all that was left. So the top political leadership and international monetary specialists immediately began the Herculean task of persuading the rest of the bureaucracy and Japan's international business community to accept the need for the program and to cooperate in its rapid implementation.

Finance Minister Fukuda, the cabinet minister most responsible for the fate of the program, followed up his splashy public announcement of the measures in early June with another widely publicized meeting with Prime Minister Sato on June 15. The meeting was given top billing in the communications media, indicating that press officers in the MOF and the prime minister's office were making every effort to impress the public with Sato's and Fukuda's commitment to the program.[9] They reviewed implementation efforts to date and urged more bureaucratic and business cooperation in implementation during the press conference that followed their meeting.

Three days later another emergency meeting of the "economic cabinet" was held to review progress and to assess initial foreign reaction.[10] Members approved formation of a special task force within the Finance Ministry to prepare Japan's proposal for a new round of international tariff-reduction negotiations in time for the annual GATT meeting in the fall as promised in point three of the plan.[11] The tone of the public statements of the economic cabinet members following the meeting was optimistic, but it was obvious they felt compelled to increase political pressure against bureaucratic resistance to achieve more rapid compliance with the program.

The need to continue top-level political pressure to achieve rapid implementation of the eight-point program was even mentioned prominently as a factor in the selection of the new members of Sato's third cabinet when he announced its formation on July 5, 1971, soon after the Upper House elections. Sato shifted Takeo Fukuda from Finance to Foreign Affairs where he could play an international coordinating role and named Mikio Mizuta to succeed Fukuda as Finance Minister. Mizuta, known for his liberal economic views, was expected to be more sympathetic to the economic stimulation measures in point eight of the program than the inflation-shy former MOF bureaucrat Fukuda.[12] Kakuei Tanaka, a vigorous, outspoken politician and Fukuda's most formidable opponent in the race to succeed Sato as prime minister, was given the difficult MITI portfolio, where he was expected to wring compliance with the trade and investment aspects of the program out of the recalcitrant bureaucracy and business community. And Munenori Akagi, a senior LDP member with high credibility within Japan's powerful agriculture organizations, was given the Ministry of Agriculture.[13]

After more than a month of frustrating delay since announcement of the program, these new cabinet members plunged into the implementation effort. Mizuta told the press soon after his appointment that even though implementation of the whole program was likely to prove difficult because of conflicting opinions about the timing and specific measures, he fully supported the effort and would do all he could to make it succeed. When pressed with questions about whether or not the program actually would solve Japan's problems with the yen, he replied that rapid implementation of the whole program had come to be considered an international promise by Japan, and on that grounds alone it should be supported and implemented. He also insisted that domestic economic stimulation would have a positive impact on Japan's international statistics.[14]

The new MITI minister, Kakuei Tanaka, also proved an active salesman for the MOF's program. He put his bureaucratic subordinates and the business community on notice that he placed high priority on rapid implementation and that he would tolerate no foot-dragging. On July 6 he publicly suggested that the solution to the implementation problem might be the passage of legislation in Japan similar to the 1962 U.S. Trade Expansion Act under which the president was given more flexibility in the implementation of foreign economic policy. He went into some detail during the interview, an indication that staff work had been done beforehand on the proposal. He said in part:

> Of course, these are problems that cannot be dealt with by MITI alone. The Finance Ministry, the Foreign Ministry, Agriculture Ministry and other Ministries all have to work together. I am thinking about the establishment of what would be called an "international economic adjustment law" which would be like the 1962 Trade Expansion Act which gave the President of the United States authority over the enactment of international economic policy. For example, it would make it possible for the rapid and flexible decision and implementation of matters such as tariff rate reductions at the cabinet level rather than

having to send each one through the Diet. If we implement all of these policies I am absolutely convinced that we can avoid a revaluation of the yen.[15]

After the Upper House election at the end of June, speculation over the timing of the prime minister's retirement and over his likely successor increased. Takeo Fukuda and Kakuei Tanaka were the two front-runners, with Fukuda in the lead. Since the eight-point program had been initiated by the Finance Ministry under Fukuda's leadership, and since its public reception at home and abroad during June had been less than enthusiastic, it would not have been surprising to find Tanaka lukewarm in his endorsement of the plan. He might well have tried to expand financial support for his candidacy from sectors of the business or agricultural communities that opposed or gave only half-hearted support to certain specific aspects of the plan. He might also have been tempted to withhold wholehearted cooperation out of concern the initiative would fail and an understandable desire to avoid association with such a serious policy failure.

But even Tanaka proved an active public supporter of the program throughout July and August of 1971. Perhaps to appear like a prime minister, (or maybe just for lack of an acceptable alternative), he joined Fukuda in agreeing to give the effort full political support, citing the hostility Japan's negotiators would face at the IMF annual meeting in late September if nothing were done. He told the press after a meeting of the economic cabinet on July 9: "If we continue along like this our foreign exchange reserves will amount to $10 billion by the middle of September when we have the U.S.-Japan Joint Trade and Economic Meeting and the annual General Meeting of the IMF, and there is a strong likelihood that we will be put in a difficult international position through greatly increased pressure for a revaluation of the yen."[16]

Several of the most politically sensitive liberalization measures fell under the jurisdiction of the Ministry of Agriculture. Agriculture was far from internationally minded and was expected from the beginning to pose the most serious implementation problems. The new minister, Munenori Akagi, was an assertive individual accustomed to speaking his mind in private and in public. Although he agreed to support the eight-point program since it was considered by then to be Japan's last hope for avoiding yen revaluation, he made clear his sympathy for the agricultural sector and the sacrifice it required of those in it. During an interview on July

19 he responded to the suggestion that Japanese agriculture might simply wither away as a result of further exposure to international competition by saying:

> Agriculture cannot collapse! When agriculture collapses all of Japan will collapse too and become a colony! I believe that Japan is in good shape precisely because of the spirit of agriculture, of the Japanese race with a thousand years of tradition, and the position that Japanese agriculture maintains within society. It's quite likely that Japan's high rate of growth has been made possible by our level of agricultural self-sufficiency.[17]

Akagi added that since the prime minister had decided to move ahead with the eight-point program of liberalization it would have to be supported. But, as befitted a man with his agricultural sympathies, he also suggested that the government should give thought to a supplementary plan to increase the buying power of agricultural families disadvantaged by the results of the liberalization.

These public suggestions were no comfort to the Finance Ministry, which already had begun to feel pressure from manufacturers for similar compensation. Five years later former MOF officials who participated in the early implementation struggle and the subsequent bilateral trade and investment negotiations with the United States remembered Akagi as the most reluctant (some even went so far as to say "stubborn") of the political leaders when it came to reaching agreement on liberalization measures. The question of government compensation was to plague the MOF throughout the year. The Ministry's international monetary men were anxious to press their liberalization plan on the rest of the economic bureaucracy as the solution to the problem they were charged with solving, but the Ministry's budget men were most reluctant to agree to open the public purse to pay compensation as the price of interministerial and private-sector cooperation in the implementation effort.

Other senior LDP members not included in the third Sato Cabinet joined the political sector's early effort to solve the international monetary predicament through nonparity change measures during the June-August period. One example of their contribution was formation of a temporary LDP committee to oversee the deteriorating relationship with the United States—the Ad Hoc Special Committee on Relations with the United States (Rinji Tai-Bei Kankei Tokubetsu Iinkai), chaired by Naokichi Kitazawa. Along with textile trade, Okinawa reversion, and Japan's stake in the U.S.-China relationship, this committee examined the bilateral implications of the yen problem.

The committee held its first meeting on July 26, 1971. After being reminded by the director general of the Foreign Ministry's North American Bureau, Bunroku Yoshino, of the importance of rapid implementation of the eight-point program for U.S. Senate approval of the Okinawa Reversion Agreement, members of the committee decided to dispatch a special delegation to the United States during mid-August to meet with their American counterparts. Zentaro Kosaka, former foreign minister and chairman of the LDP's Policy Affairs Research Council, was suggested to head the delegation, and plans for the visit were made public on July 26 by Chief Cabinet Secretary Hori.[18] The announcement, however, proved premature and the proposed parliamentary visit was never made. The LDP on July 30 was forced to announce cancellation of their plans after consultation with the U.S. side revealed that most American politicians and senior officials would be on vacation in mid-August. Kosaka decided to postpone the trip to the United States and went instead to the Soviet Union to talk about fishing rights.[19]

As seen in these examples, the international monetary specialists' eight-point program to resist international pressure to change the parity of the yen enjoyed strong support from the political sector during June and July 1971, and even as late as the announcement of President Nixon's plans for the international monetary system on August 15. At least, it enjoyed the support of LDP members senior enough to fear public blame for mismanaging relations with the United States should it fail. As pressure increased for agreement on the more specific items of liberalization, representatives of industrial and agricultural interests appealed to rank-and-file LDP parliamentarians for protection. The bureaucracy feared possible withdrawal of LDP support for their effort and growing political demands for government compensation in response to those pleas.[20]

The forceful and highly visible commitment of Japan's top political leadership was not sufficient, however, to ensure rapid implementation of the eight-point program. Each specific item of the Finance Ministry's proposal had to be sold to the particular ministry responsible, and the government-wide effort had to be coordinated and monitored. At the suggestion of the MOF, a task force composed of the directors general of the Minister's Secretariat from each economic ministry was established soon after announcement of the program to accomplish that task. It was hoped that, given their normal intraministerial coordinating roles and their immediate personal access to the minister himself, they would be more effective and responsive to this political effort than would their bureaucratic colleagues more removed from the political concerns of the ministry. Included were the ministries of Finance, International Trade and Industry, Agriculture, Transportation, Foreign Affairs, and the Economic Planning Agency.

Yusuke Kashiwagi, by then retired from the vice ministership for international monetary affairs and appointed special adviser to the finance minister, addressed the task force's first meeting in June. He reiterated the opposition of the MOF and of Japan's top political leadership to any change in the parity of the yen and presented the eight-point program as the only policy alternative left to Japan to cope with her international predicament. Kashiwagi told the group that the program had been discussed at the recent OECD meetings in Paris with European and American representatives who were skeptical of the bureaucracy's ability to implement the plan in time to have much impact on the situation. A more favorable international reaction required evidence of the successful implementation of the plan as early as possible. The members of the task force agreed to press the relevant sections of their respective ministries to obtain agreement on all phases of the plan, and to meet at regular intervals to review the progress of their efforts.

The second meeting of this task force was held on June 25 to review progress made through the month. To soothe the territorial sensitivities of the other ministries, the MOF did not call them as usual to the spacious, if austere, conference facilities on the third floor of their own Kasumigaseki headquarters, but rented a room in the Hotel Okura just across the street from the American Embassy. MOF representatives listed the steps their ministry had taken toward realization of the project and urged the other ministries to intensify their efforts, judged lackluster at best to date.[21] Perhaps because of the modest record of accomplishment this meeting was given very little publicity.

The tone of the task force's third meeting, held a month later on July 20, was somewhat more optimistic. After nearly two months of struggle, in the midst of a rapidly deteriorating international environment, the Finance Ministry was able to report progress on the liberalization of outgoing foreign investment and some optimism about a modest expansion of import quotas. Even the MITI and Agriculture representatives were reported by anonymous sources to be more forward-looking on the items under their jurisdiction than they were a month before.[22]

Some Progress. Although the overall implementation effort during June, July, and August must be described as a failure, the Government of Japan had more success in some areas than in others. The eighth point, stimulation of the domestic economy, proved easy to implement. Even prior to the plan's official announcement, Finance Minister Fukuda told the press on June 3 he had instructed the ministry to begin preparations for implementation of the "flexibility clause" of the current fiscal year's budget. The flexibility clause was first written into the budget in 1971. It allowed an increase of up to 50 percent in the current year's deficit if more government expenditure was judged necessary to handle unforeseen changes in Japan's economic environment. In his announcement Fukuda stressed the dampening effect on exports and expansionary effect on imports that such stimulative measures were expected to have as a major reason for proposing the move.[23] Fukuda and his advisers also hoped that early demonstration of the government's willingness to stimulate the economy would help overcome the business community's resistance to some of the less palatable items in the rest of the program since trade and investment liberalization is always easier during economic upswings than during periods of slow growth when the business community is less optimistic about the future.

Announcement of the program on June 3 was positively received in Japan, but by the middle of the month the release of gloomy domestic economic statistics began to generate new concern over the 1971 business slump. On June 11 the Economic Planning Agency made its scheduled announcement of the growth rate for the last fiscal year (April 1, 1970 to March 31, 1971). At 9.9 percent it was the first time Japan had failed to achieve double-digit growth in the past five years.[24] This disappointing news was followed later in the month by the release of industrial production statistics for May. They were even more gloomy, showing the largest monthly decline in growth in that important indicator since 1953.[25]

The outlook had not improved by July, and the peak business

organizations began to pressure the government for stimulative action. During a meeting with the prime minister on July 15 during which he urged the adoption of measures to protect small business from the effects of the liberalization program, Chairman Shigeo Nagano of the Japan Chamber of Commerce urged Sato to consider another reduction in the official discount rate in order to bring Japan out of its slump.[26] Keizai Doyukai proposed the same measures during the regular meeting of its senior members on July 21 with Vice Minister Iichiro Hatoyama and several MOF bureau directors, and also suggested that the government work up a more effective plan to increase spending on public works projects such as roads and sewers.[27] Keidanren came out a few days later with a more comprehensive proposal after a meeting held to discuss promotion of the eight-point program. While agreeing in principle to support the whole program since it had already been presented to the world as an international promise, this organization concluded that the only really effective part of the package was economic stimulation. Keidanren recommended that long and short-term interest rates be lowered, that public debt be expanded by one trillion yen ($2.78 billion), and that a large-scale supplementary government budget be implemented within the current fiscal year.[28]

It was not long before the business community's high-level pleas bore fruit. On July 27, Finance Minister Mizuta announced a comprehensive economic stimulus package that was intended to cope with the sagging business environment while improving Japan's international economic position. The official discount rate was lowered for the third time since the beginning of the year by another quarter point and significant additional funding was committed for development of social infrastructure.[29] While the government expected the economic effect of its stimulation package to have some positive influence on the four critical international economic indexes, it had even higher expectations for the influence the package would have on the willingness of key elements of the business community to support more actively the remainder of the eight-point program. The stimulative measures taken were hardly extreme, but they did represent partial accomplishment of at least one point of the anti-revaluation program.[30]

MITI's position in the implementation effort proved most difficult of all ministries concerned. Its officials were pressured from one side by MOF and LDP leadership to gain the business community's acceptance of the proposed liberalization, and from the other side by the affected industrial sectors to resist. Also, some of MITI's more internationally minded officials were sympathetic to the plan, which created internal as well as external cross-pressures for the ministry as the weeks went by. MITI's close relationship with Japanese industry was an important reason for its success in the postwar development of the economy. Relations of mutual trust and confidence had developed over the years with the business community that enabled ministry officials to influence the course of economic events more effectively than their legal mandate alone would have allowed. MITI officials were therefore hesitant to order changes in the system without adequate prior consultation with the private sector lest that mutual trust and confidence be damaged and make ministry's job more difficult in the future.

The Ministry of Agriculture too had a close relationship with Japan's farmers and central agricultural organizations. But the Agriculture Ministry's situation was somewhat more comfortable since international interests there were less important than in MITI. Japan's agricultural exports were negligible. What few Ministry internationalists there were concerned themselves more with imports than with maintaining an international environment receptive to Japan's exports. The Agriculture Ministry's attitude—especially under Akagi—toward the Finance Ministry's plan was simply decided: resist to the extent politically possible all efforts to sacrifice the well-being of Japan's farmers through agricultural liberalization for the sake of the manufacturing sector.

MITI got off to a good start in mid-June with the formation of a "Yen Problem Project team."[31] This team was charged with reviewing all policy changes under MITI jurisdiction required in the eight-point program and coordinating their implementation. On June 19 the Ministry announced that investigations were under way of the stockpiling of raw materials mentioned in point seven, focusing on nonferrous metals and oil.[32] Initial MITI estimates indicated Japan's foreign currency reserves could be reduced by about 90 billion yen ($250 million) during the next fiscal year through the program. Of course, stockpiling was only a short-term cosmetic measure since it would reduce the current account surplus in the year it was implemented but would increase it in subsequent years when the purchases normally would have been made.

Stockpiling was one of the least controversial parts of the antirevaluation plan, perhaps accounting, in part, for its early announcement. Later in the month the yen project team tackled the subject of export restraints. This was a politically more difficult area, but also in a sense more attractive from the bureaucratic perspective since its implementation would both expand bureaucratic employment and enhance MITI's regulatory powers over important industrial sectors. In the initial announcement five items were singled out for their political sensitivity in foreign markets: color television sets, automobiles, small desk calculators, steel, and cosmetics.[33] It was proposed that the restrictions would be implemented under existing provisions of the Export-Import Exchange Law (Yushutsu-Nyu Torihiko-ho) and would not require new legislation. But the actual implementation of the program would still take some time since it would require formation of export cartels and careful investigation of export prices.[34] Although the late June MITI announcement did not lead immediately to official export restraints, the early selection and public announcement of the five targeted products was clear evidence of progress.

MITI also initiated widely publicized negotiations with the Japanese computer industry on investment liberalization in mid-July. This was an area of particular concern for U.S. government and industry circles. MITI Minister Tanaka met with Toshiwo Doko, chairman of the industry's main trade group, the Japan Electronic Industry Development Association (Nihon Denshi Kogyo Shinko Kyokai) on July 13 to press for agreement.[35] The effort ended in failure, and both the government and industry took pains to defend their positions in the press. After another week of effort MITI presented the industry with the Ministry's "final" position and by the end of July hopes were high for liberalization of the rules restricting foreign investment in Japan's computer industry by the end of the year.[36]

In late July the Ministry took up the second section of point four of the MOF program with announcement of a proposal to reduce foreign currency reserves through the establishment of an "Industrial Development Cooperation Public Corporation" (Sangyo Kaihatsu Kyoryoku Kosha) that would invest in big projects in foreign countries. The plan was to focus on electric power or water projects with 50 percent of the total investment coming from Japan and the rest from local sources. This proposal was expected to reduce Japan's foreign currency accumulation by as much as $1 billion per year.[37] A few days later MITI presented the Finance Ministry with a proposal for directly loaning foreign exchange reserves to Japanese companies involved in the development of natural resources and energy supplies through the foreign exchange banks.[38] Although these two measures would have no effect on Japan's trade or current account balances, they would help to recycle rapidly accumulating foreign currency reserves.

MITI officials proved willing to cooperate with the MOF-initiated eight-point program to avoid change in the parity of the yen when the measures proposed were unlikely to affect the long-term international economic competitiveness of Japanese industry and were likely to expand MITI's budget and influence within the private sector. Agriculture, on the other hand, demonstrated a less flexible attitude right from the beginning. Encouraged by its own highly competitive and politically influential agricultural sector, the U.S. government placed great importance on the rapid liberalization of Japanese quotas that restricted U.S. exports of farm products such as beef, grapefruit, oranges, and other citrus products to Japan during bilateral economic discussions. The Japanese press made something more than there actually was of the fact that President Nixon himself came from California, a large citrus-producing state.

But during the critical June, July, and August period the only specific accomplishment was liberalization of the quota on grapefruit. A battle between Japan's mandarin orange *(mikan)* growers and the government in late April had delayed an earlier liberalization program, and the subject resurfaced with announcement of the eight-point program. The LDP leadership, mindful of the forthcoming Upper House election on June 27 and the need for agriculture's support, decided to postpone specific discussions until the end of June. Two days after the election, on June 29, some liberalization of grapefruit restrictions was announced, effective the following day.[39] Mandarin orange growers were predictably outraged. Agriculture had lost one round, and the fallout from that loss strengthened its resolve to resist further measures later in the year.

Those specific measures of the anti-revaluation program that required only bureaucratic agreement to implement were difficult enough for Japan's beleaguered government. Those that required approval of the cabinet and Diet were even more difficult. Changes in tariff levels and the liberalization of restrictions on foreign investment proposed under points three and four were in the latter category. The government's recommendations for tariff changes had first to be submitted to the Tariff Advisory Commission (Kanzei-ritsu Shingikai), the advisory body of government officials, nongovernment experts, and representatives of the private interests involved. The council's recommendation was presented to the finance minister who then ordered legislation to be drafted and submitted to the Diet for approval. Foreign investment liberalization proposals similarly were given first to the Foreign Investment Council, which made recommendations to the finance minister who then presented them for final approval to the cabinet. The whole process was, by design, very open to public scrutiny and vulnerable to efforts by the private sector to block progress.

On June 28 the Planning Committee of the Tariff Council met at the Ministry of Finance to discuss tariff reductions proposed under the eight-point program. They set mid-August as the date by which the council should decide which specific items should be reduced by the end of the current fiscal year (March 31, 1972). Soybeans, automobiles, kerosene, black tea, and beer were among twelve items proposed for immediate consideration. The committee hoped to reach agreement in mid-August and report their conclusions to the full Tariff Council in time to have the package ready for presentation to the next diet session later in the year.[40]

The Foreign Investment Council was even more successful in carrying out its part of the program. Although increased direct foreign investment in Japan would not reduce pressure for yen revaluation—indeed, quite the opposite since it would increase demand for yen—liberalization would help to reduce overall foreign criticism of Japan's economic policies. During a meeting of the full council on July 29, members ratified the MOF liberalization proposal in its entirety.[41] The proposal was then presented to the finance minister, who was to seek cabinet approval on August 3, allowing implementation on the following day. All but seven industries were opened to 50 percent automatic approval of foreign ownership, and 151 industries were added to the 100 percent liberalized list. The only disappointment was the exclusion of computers, the most important industry on the list. Negotiations between the industry and MITI had broken down and consideration of further liberalization of that critical industry was deferred until August 1974.

Obstacles in the Path of Rapid Implementation. The effort to implement the eight-point program was judged a failure even by its primary author and strongest supporter, Yusuke Kashiwagi.[42] In spite of intense pressure from the Ministry of Finance and the

Liberal Democratic party the government's last-ditch effort to maintain the fixed parity of the yen resulted in only a few significant changes in Japan's foreign economic practices. Several factors contributed to that failure.

First and most important was the unusual manner in which the program was presented to the government and private sector. As described above, the plan was hastily assembled within the Finance Ministry and presented to the political leadership for approval without the customary detailed interministerial and government-private-sector discussions that proceed such action in Japan. This was in spite of the fact that most of the specific measures required the consideration and agreement of two or more government agencies.

For example, approval of both MITI and the Bank of Japan was required to abolish the export-preference financing system proposed under point seven. By mid-June government officials were expressing public skepticism about reaching interagency agreement within the month, and the most optimistic estimates for actual implementation were early October.[43] Bank of Japan Governor Sasaki was questioned about this on June 16 during a regular weekly press conference. He replied that the Bank and other responsible organizations were doing their best to accelerate the process but that he understood the program would adversely affect medium and small business, and that a system to compensate these companies for their losses would have to be worked out before final agreement could be reached.[44] This statement was made with full knowledge that the Ministry of Finance was most reluctant to provide the funding required to implement point seven, or any other point of the program.

In Japan's system, as in our own, top-level political support is not always sufficient to assure immediate implementation of a program, especially a complex program. Japan's politicians lack personal professional staffs to which they can turn for the specific information with which to counter bureaucratic resistance to their wishes, even when they do want to move quickly (which is seldom). In many cases, they have to rely for advice upon the very bureaucrats who are resisting their efforts. Further, while the tradition of filling all top-level bureaucratic positions (with the exception of the ministership and one or two parliamentary vice ministerships) with career officials who have worked their way up through the system has as one important advantage the improvement of policy continuity, it has the short-term disadvantage of making politically initiated changes in policy far more difficult to devise and implement. (Political appointees within the American bureaucracy are said to spend much of the first half of their tenure reinventing the wheel, and much of the latter half looking for their next job, but they at least are more sensitive to demands for change proposed by top political leadership.) Bureaucratic inertia has become a highly refined Japanese art form. Its most debilitating effects are avoided, when time permits, by elaborate predecision consultation and negotiation. This consultation was insufficient for the eight-point program and doomed its implementation.

The official bureaucracy was not the only source of resistance. Japan's business community helped to delay implementation. All the major organizations expressed their support during June, July, and August to the principle of rapid implementation of the eight-point program in order to decrease pressure for a revaluation of the yen. But they were less reliable when it came to support for specific points of the program. Throughout the period, Keidanren continued to cluck reassuringly in favor of the idea, but was not motivated to twist powerful corporate arms to achieve rapid compliance with specific measures because there was considerable doubt among the professional staff and active directors about the value of the program even if implemented.[45]

The Japan Chamber of Commerce as well officially endorsed the program. Yet by mid-July their support was contingent upon the government's implementing a compensation package for small businesses adversely affected by the resulting liberalization, a measure the government was on record as opposing.[46] Keizai Doyukai too officially supported the program but at the same time continued its public calls, begun in May, for a reexamination of the fixed parity system as an alternative. Perhaps the most remarkable example of business community noncooperation was the Japan Foreign Trade Council's (Nihon Boeki-kai) opposition to abolition of the export promotion tax system mentioned in point seven. The Japan Foreign Trade Council, given the nature of its business, should have been especially sensitive and receptive to any measure that might improve Japan's position in the international economy and preserve her market position abroad. It also was free of the domestic-international tension that stymied other business organizations. But on June 19 the council publicly announced plans to forward an urgent protest against the proposed abolition of the export promotion tax system to the MOF, MITI, Ministry of Foreign Affairs, Bank of Japan, and Economic Planning Agency out of fear that loss of that advantage in the long term would result in a decline in overall trade.[47]

Another factor inhibiting rapid implementation of the eight-point program during and after June that was mentioned by former finance minister Mikio Mizuta, finance vice minister Iichiro Hatoyama, and vice minister for international monetary affairs, Takashi Hosomi, was the domestic economic slump that continued on into 1971.[48] Government economists had been predicting the end of the slump since the first quarter of the year, but conditions were still gloomy in July. Finance Minister Mizuta was forced to admit to a meeting of the Lower House Finance Committee on July 23 that growth during the current fiscal year might not even reach 8 percent—a shocking prospect for a nation accustomed to more than a decade of double-digit economic growth.[49] The slump provided business interests and sympathetic government officials with a good argument against rapid implementation of those points of the program that would reduce the export competitiveness of Japanese industry and increase import competition in their home market.

The Upper House elections, both before and after the June 27 balloting, also slowed implementation of the anti-revaluation program. As these were scheduled to be held just three weeks after the program's announcement, the Liberal Democratic party was reluctant to press too hard for any measures that might offend their business and agricultural constituency. The previously mentioned problem with grapefruit was only one of many. Although the Upper House has only limited power in Japan's political system, the forthcoming election was considered important as an indicator of support for Prime Minister Sato, then in the seventh year of his premiership. The LDP approached the election on Sunday the 27th confident of a comfortable victory, but Monday morning headlines told a different story. The LDP not only failed to gain seats, but the Socialists did much better than expected, with much of their unanticipated support coming from agricultural areas, traditional LDP strongholds.[50] Socialist success in rural areas resulted from the opposition of rice farmers to what they perceived as a weakening of the government's price support policies for rice. But the election's outcome made the agricultural liberalization issue, a critical part of the overall anti-revaluation program, more sensitive for the LDP. The ruling party's poor showing also reduced public confidence in the Sato regime and intensified speculation about the timing of his retirement, which furthermore made it more difficult for Sato and his cabinet to exercise forceful leadership on the implementation issue.

In addition, many of the senior personnel changes in Japan's national bureaucracy are made during the month of June, and in 1971 those changes included many of the bureaus and divisions most responsible for implementing the eight-point program. It naturally took some time for newly appointed officials to settle into their jobs and to establish the working relationships with subordinates colleagues required to pursue their assignments. This too tended to delay program implementation. The finance minister announced appointment of Budget Bureau director general Iichiro Hatoyama (son of former Prime Minister Ichiro Hatoyama) to the top career post of administrative vice minister on June 10th, together with a general reshuffling of bureau directorships. Although inexperienced in international monetary affairs, Hatoyama was known as an excellent coordinator during his years in the Ministry. It was hoped those coordination skills would facilitate the implementation effort.

With the retirement of Yusuke Kashiwagi as vice minister for international monetary affairs and his appointment as special adviser to the finance minister, Takashi Hosomi, a tax system specialist with a wide range of associations and friendships within the MOF, other ministries, and the business community, was named his successor. Hosomi too had little international experience at the time of his appointment. But his domestic experience was considered more important in June 1971 since the immediate task was to persuade the other ministries and the business community to implement the eight-point program to avoid a change in the parity, rather than to propose changes in international monetary policy. Both Hatoyama and Hosomi were expected to rely upon Kashiwagi for advice on the technical aspects of the international system.

A final factor that impeded the implementation of the eight-point program was the public skepticism with which it was received. The combination of continuing increases in Japan's four critical international economic indicators, reports of continuing instability in the international monetary system, and increasingly intense foreign criticism of Japan for maintaining an undervalued currency seemed too much for the eight-point program to counter, even if implemented in its entirety, and private-sector observers from the very beginning doubted the government's ability to implement most of the program.[51] Why endure the painful process of liberalization if the program was unlikely to save the fixed rate?

Since the government was absolutely opposed even to consideration of a parity change as part of Japan's response to the international economic predicament, there was no reason to commission opinion polls on the subject. And during subsequent interviews none of the key policy participants recollected ever seeing any. But the Japan Economic Research Center, an affiliate of *Nihon Keizai Shimbun,* did commission such a poll on June 30. The results, published the following day, provide an interesting glimpse of elite opinion on the yen issue during this critical period.

Asked their opinions about yen revaluation were 222 political, academic, business, labor, and consumer group leaders. Of those questioned, 72 percent were opposed to any change in the parity, and 52 percent thought the yen was not undervalued at the current rate. But 76 percent of all respondents thought the yen rate would be changed by 1972.[52] The poll must have simultaneously comforted and distressed Japan's international monetary officials. The bad news was that after nearly one month of intensive sales effort seven in ten of Japan's opinion leaders considered the eight-point program to avoid revaluation as likely to fail. Still, the MOF could take some comfort in the knowledge that Japan's opinion leaders would not be shocked into panic should a parity change eventually have to be made.

Through June, July, and August the MOF continued to discourage public suggestions of the need for a parity change, but with diminishing success. Already in June the newspapers and weekly business magazines were full of advertisements for books about *en kiriage* (yen revaluation), written by economists, businessmen, and economic journalists of greater and lesser reputation, that presented analysis of the international monetary situation and predicted the time and amount of the eventual revaluation. Bookstores established special *en kiriage* sections, and many of these hastily prepared volumes became almost as popular on evening commuter trains as the more traditional pulpy *manga,* (thick comic books that not infrequently have explicit sexual themes). In addition to the popular literature about *en kiriage,* more credible reports were released after the beginning of June that tended to reinforce public doubt. For example, in mid-June the prestigious research division of the Long-Term Credit Bank of Japan issued a report entitled "World Inflation and Japan's Price Problem," which concluded that Japan would be unable to deal with the problem of imported inflation through any way other than revaluation of the yen.[53]

The most damaging study of this sort, from the point of view of the "stand fast" international monetary officials, was yet to come. On July 10 a group of 36 Japanese economists, headed by Ryutaro Komiya, a respected University of Tokyo professor who maintained good relations with MITI, published a report that concluded Japan's international imbalance problem would not be corrected by the government's eight-point program, and therefore Japan should move unilaterally to change the parity of the yen. The specific method of exchange rate adjustment they suggested was a modified version of the "crawling peg." Under their modified crawling peg system, the yen's parity would be allowed to change once every three to five months by one percent or less. This would limit the annual allowable change in the exchange rate to between 2.4 percent and 4 percent. Komiya's group predicted that it would take approximately three years for Japan to return to equilibrium under this method of adjustment. Made up of well-known economists from Japan's major universities (from whom many in the government had learned their international economics), the international monetary officials found it difficult to criticize the findings of the Komiya group either as ill-informed or as special pleading in support of one special economic interest or another. The opinions of this group could not be ignored, and the front-page treatment of their findings demonstrated their public clout.[54]

The MOF tried to rebut their argument with an official statement on the very same day. Japan, in the opinion of the Ministry, was not in basic imbalance and needed no change in the exchange rate. As for the specifics of the proposal, the Ministry reminded the authors that the floating peg system had yet to be tried even by other countries, and therefore more investigation of that method of adjustment was required before it could be considered for Japan. They also warned that once Japan's exchange rate had been changed, it would be far easier to change it again (the so-called "Pandora's box" thesis, which would be heard more frequently as the weeks went by). Government spokesmen repeated official policy that all efforts should be turned toward the implementation of the eight-point program, especially those efforts to stimulate the domestic economy, in the expectation that as domestic economic activity picked up exports would be reduced and imports increased.[55]

By the end of July it was clear that the eight-point program had failed to achieve two of its most important objectives—to suppress public anxiety over Japan's international monetary predicament and to raise public confidence in the ability of the experts to control the situation. It also had little impact on the four politically critical international economic indexes.

Foreign Reaction to the Eight-Point Program

The eight-point program was designed to accomplish more than restoration of domestic confidence in the ability of Japan's international monetary professionals to handle the yen problem. The MOF also hoped that the June 3 announcement (June 2 in the United States) would dampen foreign criticism of economic Japan, convince the governments and private sectors of the United States and other large trading nations that Japan was ready and able to do something about her lopsided foreign trade statistics (without a yen revaluation), and reduce the likelihood that other countries would propose their own remedies, such as changes in the Bretton Woods system or more protective trade policies. But the plan was as much a failure abroad as it was at home.

Throughout 1971 Japan's international monetary officials were much more concerned about the reaction of the United States than about Europe's. The policy participants spoke later of the issue in almost exclusively bilateral terms.[56] West Germany and other European countries also were important within the international monetary system, but for Japan their primary significance was the impact their policies might have on the United States. The United States was, after all, Japan's largest and most open overseas market, her closest international ally, and the keeper of the commitment to maintain the convertibility of the dollar into gold—the cornerstone of the Bretton Woods system.

Early response from the Nixon administration to Japan's anti-revaluation program was far from encouraging. Economic Planning Agency Director General Sato on June 7 presented the plan in some detail at the Paris ministerial meeting of the OECD, asking for the "understanding" of the American delegation, headed by Secretary of State William Rogers, together with that of the European representatives. But after the meeting Deputy Under Secretary of State Samuels bluntly told a press conference, "The Japanese government's eight-point liberalization program is insufficient," adding that tariff and non-tariff barriers as high as Japan's were unacceptable for a country with such a large surplus.[57] Commerce Secretary Maurice Stans and other top administration officials continued to criticize Japan's efforts later in the month during testimony at June 24 hearings of the Foreign Economic Policy Subcommittee of the Joint Economic Committee, chaired at the time by Congressman Hale Boggs.[58] President Nixon himself even joined the chorus with tough anti-Japan comments in a speech given in Kansas City, Missouri, early in July.[59] The administration was impressed with neither the substance of Japan's program nor with the record of implementation during June and July.

But the strongest blow from the Nixon administration came from a quarter unrelated directly to economic policy. Japanese newspapers on the evening of July 16 carried huge headlines announcing President Nixon's decision to visit Peking before May of the following year.[60] The administration's sudden move was dubbed in Japan as the first "Nixon shock." However, official Japanese reaction to the announcement was positive, emphasizing the hope that the move would help to stabilize the security of East Asia. But the positive impact was overwhelmed by adverse reaction to the administration's decision not to inform the Sato government until only a few minutes before its public announcement. This was judged a deliberate American snub of Sato and a demonstration of the low priority the Nixon administration assigned relations with Japan. The China shock undermined the credibility of the Sato Cabinet in handling relations with the United States and increased Japan's sense of international vulnerability—both factors also adversely affecting the ability of the government to rapidly implement its liberalization program.

During June, July, and August the response of Washington's executive branch to Japan's liberalization efforts was a model of restraint when compared with that of the American Congress. Congressman Henry Reuss of the Joint Economic Committee, an important voice in congressional economic policy debate, followed up his June 3 call for a float of the dollar with a June 17 announcement of an investigation of the problems of the international monetary system, including the position of Japan.[61] Much was made of Japan's closed market and protectionist foreign economic policies.

Wilbur Mills, chairman of the House Ways and Means Committee, recently embroiled in the bilateral textile trade crisis, called in a speech on June 17 for tougher American insistence on her rights under GATT against trading partners like Japan who continued to trade unfairly.[62] By the end of July Mills went even further, proposing in a speech to the Washington Press Club that the administration consider an across-the-board surcharge on imports and rebates on exports as a means of coping with the unfair trading practices of American trading partners like Japan.[63]

By 1971 Japan's government had become aware of the increasing congressional influence on U.S. economic policy. The embassy in Washington was instructed to intensify efforts to communicate with Capitol Hill, and not to rely solely upon official statements or traditional contacts in the Department of State and other executive agencies for its assessments of Washington's intentions. By June and July career officials of the embassy's economic and political sections were meeting more frequently with senators, congressmen, and key staff members. These contacts confirmed the growing congressional frustration with economic Japan and the skepticism with which the government's liberalization efforts were received.[64]

The American business community provided no encouragement to Japanese supporters of the eight-point program. After the program's announcement the Japanese press still reported frequent public demands by senior American businessmen for more drastic corrective Japanese action, including a revaluation of the yen, and private and public pressure from the U.S. business community on the Nixon administration for retaliatory trade measures. Since 1969 the administration had been pressed by American industries faced with import competition for government action to reduce the flow of foreign goods into their markets. Producers of steel, color televisions, automobiles, footwear, and a host of other industries developed effective lobbying and public relations techniques to support their pleas. But not all U.S. industry agreed with their position. Multinational firms dependent upon the international economy and fearful of foreign retaliation against their own interests—more often an investment than an export position—quietly urged the administration to resist pressures for reversal of the free-trade principles that had guided U.S. foreign economic policy throughout the postwar period.

With the hope of encouraging the U.S. business community to develop a consensus position on their foreign economic policy recommendations (thereby avoiding having to make the hard decisions itself), the administration earlier in the year suggested formation of a high-level U.S. business advisory group on economic relations with Japan. Under Secretary of State U. Alexis Johnson contacted John Caldwell, then executive secretary of the American delegation to the U.S.-Japan Businessmen's Conference, with the suggestion and asked him to find an appropriate chairman and committee members.[65] Caldwell then persuaded Pan American chairman Najeeb Halaby, a relatively neutral party in the Washington "free trade-protectionism" debate, to accept the chairmanship. Approximately 50 influential American businessmen were chosen as members, and the Advisory Council on U.S.-Japan Economic Relations was founded.[66]

Formation of the U.S. advisory group triggered Japanese efforts to create a counterpart. Yoshizane Iwasa, chairman of Fuji Bank, a director of Keidanren, and an organizer of bilateral businessmen's meetings in 1961, sought the agreement of Keidanren Vice Chairman Horikoshi to separate the secretariat of the new organization from the international division of Keidanren that handled the arrangements for the annual U.S.-Japan Businessmen's Conference. Horikoshi agreed, a move Keidanren later regretted since coordination of the two group's activities became somewhat difficult as the years went by.[67] It was hoped on both sides of the Pacific that the new organization would be more effective at translating business concerns into concrete political action. The first meeting of the new bilateral business advisory groups was held in New York on June 14, 1971. The Japanese delegation, headed by Iwasa, had expected some hostility, but their reception was even more acrimonious than anticipated. Their explanation of the new eight-point program met with angry complaints about Japan's growing trade surplus with the United States, unfair trade practices, and "Japan Incorporated."[68]

The New York meeting was followed by the eleventh annual U.S.-Japan Businessmen's Conference, held in Washington June 16–18. The tone of discussion at the Washington meetings was similar to that of the New York performance. A joint communique was issued on June 18 in which the U.S. side called for more rapid Japanese trade and investment liberalization. The Japanese side insisted upon the inclusion of the statement that "before Japan can make any decision on whether to revalue the yen, its barriers to trade and exchange transactions must first be dismantled."[69] Iwasa and Kogoro Uemura, chairman of Keidanren and head of the Japanese delegation to the Washington meetings, held a joint press conference in Tokyo just after their return from the United States in which they described the tough American reaction. But they concluded that U.S. businessmen were more interested in trade and investment liberalization than in a change in the parity of the yen.[70] Whether or not their assessment was accurate, it pleased MOF supporters of the eight-point program who expected the foreign pressure to aid them in their effort to reach agreement on liberalization.

The major international economic organizations—the IMF, OECD, and GATT—also were problematic for Japan during this period. No public proposals were made, but staff discussions continued within the IMF of the growing international monetary instability and an appropriate response. It was expected that new proposals for parity adjustment reform would be presented at the September annual meeting, a change Japan still opposed, considering it the beginning of an era of more flexible exchange rates which would weaken Japan's economy.[71] Public discussion in the American and Japanese press of the likely outcome of this debate weakened the position of those trying to implement the eight-point program in Tokyo.

The OECD released its annual assessment of the Japanese economy in July. Published on the 23 and widely reported in Japan, the report avoided any direct reference to a Japanese "basic imbalance" or to the advisability of a yen revaluation, a considerable victory for the Japanese participants in the negotiations that preceded publication.[72] After describing the eight points of the program, the report went on to conclude:

> Any judgment on the likely impact on the balance of payments of the points just outlined will have to be postponed until the exact timing, the full details and the precise ways of implementation will be announced for each set of measures. The government has, in any case stated its firm intention to translate the various programmes into concrete action. Both the measures of liberalisation already taken and the more recent set of decisions, notably on trade account, can be expected to have some medium-run effects on the Japanese balance of payments. But in the current year it seems difficult that such measures could impinge significantly on the strength of the current account.[73]

GATT released its own pessimistic report in July entitled "Japanese Economic Growth and Trade Between 1955 and 1970." It too was skeptical of Japan's liberalization measures and their likely impact on the international statistics. The report concluded that Japan had a large-scale structural surplus resulting from the success of Japanese development policies over the past 15 years, increases in productivity, and her ability to reduce dependence on imports while improving her ability to exploit foreign markets.[74]

International criticism of Japan's trade and investment barriers, while resented, was also welcomed by Japan's international monetary officials as additional support for their increasingly lonely effort to implement an alternative to a change in the yen's parity as a solution to their foreign economic predicament. Internationalists in Japan were accustomed to using—even encouraging—such external "support" to strengthen their efforts vis-à-vis more powerful domestic interests. But as time went by the foreign comments on Japan's economic situation more frequently included the conclusion that the eight-point program, even if implemented, would fail to affect the statistics, and the only solution to the problem was a change in the yen's parity—making foreign criticism less desirable as leverage.

Prior to the December 1971 realignment of the world's exchange rates the parity of each nation's currency was considered the exclusive business of that nation. Official public comments about other nations' parities were not made in polite company. Since the flap created by Treasury Secretary John Connally's congressional testimony in May and Assistant Secretary of State Trezise's statement in Tokyo about the undervalued yen, the Nixon administration took pains to avoid any official mention of the need for a parity change. For example, Treasury Under Secretary Paul Volcker, the senior U.S. official most directly responsible for this policy issue, responding to a specific question about the yen's parity from Senator Charles Percy during a June 24 hearing of the Joint Economic Committee Subcommittee, agreed that revaluation would have to wait until there was more progress on trade and investment liberalization in order to see just how much of a change was required.[75]

Further, prior to the August 15 surprise Nixon announcement, no official proposal for a change in the parity of the yen was made to Japan by U.S. officials even in private. Recalling the events of 1971 several years later, former MOF vice minister Hatoyama repeated several times during personal interviews that he simply could not understand why the U.S. government did not make a secret request for a yen revaluation prior to the August 15 shock treatment. He recalled that Yoshizane Iwasa, in contrast to his public statements, had told him and other MOF officials upon his return from the June bilateral businessmen's meetings that the U.S. business community supported a revaluation. But the Ministry all through June, July, and early August continued to assume that if the Nixon administration finally did decide a parity change was necessary, a senior administration official would ask for one in secret.[76] This point was confirmed by other senior Japanese policy participants during their interviews.

Japan Prepares for September Monetary Meetings

By the beginning of August 1971 the Finance Ministry's international monetary officials may well have been the only people in Japan who still believed they could resist foreign pressure for a change in the parity of the yen. One journalist jokingly wrote: "It has already come to the point that when people meet, 'What do you think of the outlook for a yen revaluation?' has replaced usual forms of greeting."[77] Yet the MOF and most political leaders continued to devote their efforts to implementing the eight-point program.

The preferential tariff system for developing countries mentioned in point two finally was agreed upon and implemented on August 1 with MOF acceptance of the business community's proposal that smaller firms be monitored for adverse impact by the Medium-Small Industry Modernization Council (Chu-sho Kigyo Kindai-ka Sokushin Shingikai).[78] Some progress within the MOF was made on the more difficult abolition of the export promotion tax system, but Keidanren continued to demand adjustment of the corporate tax structure in compensation.[79] Finance Minister Mizuta also announced on August 11 that legislation was being prepared for presentation in the next session of the Diet that would expand Japan's foreign aid (point six) and limit its export promotion character.[80]

The rest of the package, however, was in trouble. MOF and MITI were at odds over the proposal to lend foreign exchange abroad to reduce Japan's holdings (point four). MITI had publicly announced a proposal, but the MOF was concerned about the government's financial responsibility should funded projects lose money. MITI Minister Tanaka grumbled that the MOF should present its own plan if they disapproved of MITI's since the commitment had already been made to implement the system in the MOF's own eight-point program.[81] The outlook for agricultural liberalization was even less promising. Instead of the usual ministry-private-sector pattern of negotiations that characterized industrial liberalization talks, officials in the Ministry of Agriculture were meeting in August with the Agriculture Committee of the LDP to try to select the seven items promised for liberalization by the end of the year. On August 10 Chief Cabinet Secretary Hori felt obliged to denounce the liberalization program as excessively harsh and incompatible with Japan's program of agricultural self-sufficiency.[82] As the days went by there was little reason to believe that Japan's delegation would have much progress to report on agricultural liberalization when they visited Washington in September.

The Economic Planning Agency did its best to brighten the picture with the release of its monthly economic report for July. The first optimistic report in the series since the fall of 1970, it concluded the recession had finally reached bottom and that the economy would steadily improve during the remainder of the year.[83] But editorial comment following its release speculated that the report's conclusions were more political than economic, that it was designed as ammunition for use by the Japanese delegation during the September international monetary talks in Washington. Even cabinet member Kakuei Tanaka disputed the EPA's conclusions in a press conference after the August 3 cabinet meeting and called for more direct government stimulation of the economy.[84]

The four critical international economic indexes continued to climb while implementation battles raged at home during the first two weeks of August. Foreign currency reserves passed the $8 billion mark in spite of the MOF's and Bank of Japan's efforts to reduce speculative purchases of yen; the international monetary system entered its most unstable and unpredictable state since the May 1971 crisis. In Europe the French took measures to reduce the speculative inflow of U.S. dollars and to improve their gold holdings at the expense of the United States during the first week of August.[85] The West Germans continued to allow the mark to float, and other European countries were experiencing problems with the U.S. dollar as global confidence in the American ability to maintain the link with gold continued to erode.

On August 12, a Thursday, the U.S. Federal Reserve Board was forced to increase its currency swap arrangements with two European countries: Switzerland and Belgium. The swap arrangement with the Swiss was expanded from $600 million to $1 billion, and the Belgian agreement was increased from $500 million to $600 million.[86] These swaps increased the American official line of international credit and were intended to discourage the sale of dollars and the purchase of European currencies such as the German mark and Swiss or French franc in anticipation of a quick profit when they were revalued. They provided little relief, however, and as long as the world's exchange markets remained open during the second week in August the U.S. dollar continued to take a severe beating.

On Monday morning, August 16, Japanese government and business workers rode Tokyo's impressive public transportation system to their offices reading newspapers that carried on their front pages reports of the Sunday, August 15, ceremonies commemorating the 26 anniversary of the Japanese surrender at the end of World War II. After a particularly hot and sticky weekend, those unable to take a few days of vacation during Tokyo's most unpleasant season prepared to return to their telephones and conference tables to continue hammering out the specifics of a program of liberalization that was proving increasingly difficult to implement. The evening editions that awaited their return home carried reports of events that were to permanently change Japan's relationship with the international economic system, and the quality of their relationship with the United States.

5. The "Nixon Shock" and the Decision to Float the Yen

Two of the most remarkable weeks in Japan's international monetary history began on Monday, August 16, with news the Nixon administration finally had decided to do something about the international role of the dollar. Japan alone among all of the major American trading partners allowed foreign currency transactions to continue for eleven trading days while deciding and implementing an initial response to the U.S. action. In less than two weeks the government purchased more than $3.7 billion—dollars inevitably worth considerably less once the dust had settled—increasing Japan's foreign reserves by an incredible 42 percent at an eventual cost to the Japanese taxpayer of over $600 million. Although small by today's standards, the scale of Japan's market intervention was enormous in 1971. After twelve days of frantic internal debate, Finance Minister Mizuta finally announced late Friday, August 27, the end of more than 22 years of support for the fixed Y 360 = $1 rate and the move to a controlled float.

The Nixon Announcement and Japan's Immediate Reaction

Because of the thirteen-hour time difference between Washington and Tokyo, Monday, August 16, began in Japan with a continuation of the tense and wary atmosphere described in the last chapter. Japan's monetary authorities, like their counterparts in other countries, try to time the announcement of any decision likely to affect either the stock market or foreign currency exchange for the end of the week, after markets are closed, to avoid panic buying and selling. Traders then are able to consider the impact of the announced decision for a day or two, so that sales and purchases may begin the following Monday morning with cooler heads. This Monday was no different from previous Mondays since the beginning of the uneasiness over the yen parity earlier in the year. Large flows of U.S. dollars into Europe the previous week had failed to trigger any Friday night or Saturday announcement from the Japanese monetary authorities. And they had received no particularly disturbing news from Washington or from other international centers over the weekend. Many senior government officials, while still concerned about the situation, managed to take a few days off from Tokyo's heat and humidity, sufficiently confident that the "protracted crisis" would continue. Their subordinates, with a skeleton crew of top-level supervisors, began another week of effort to achieve agreement on the implementation of the eight-point liberalization program, hoping to have something ready for presentation a month later in Washington. The stock market opened normally and foreign currency transactions began with as much of a "business-as-usual" attitude as the protracted crisis environment had allowed since May.

But at Camp David, the presidential retreat near Washington, meetings had been held over the weekend that soon would end Japan's state of "protracted crisis" and initiate a period of "intense crisis." Economic affairs continued to trouble the Nixon administration at home and abroad. With little more than a year left before the 1972 election, the president was being urged by his economic advisers to reconsider the policy of gradualism followed for the first three years and to take more dramatic measures to cope with stagflation at home and the declining credibility of economic America abroad. For some time, chairman of the Federal Reserve Board Arthur Burns and other moderate economists of the Republican persuasion, had been proposing a limited wage-and-price freeze as the only solution to the twin threats of inflation and unemployment. Their arguments, distasteful as they were to the conservative president, were supported by the announcement earlier in August of the steel industry's agreement to labor's demand for a 30 percent increase in wages over the next three years.

On the international side, discussions had continued throughout the year within the Washington policy community about the eventual need for unilateral American action to resolve foreign economic problems caused by the overvalued dollar. Just after the disturbance caused by the refloating of the German mark in early May, Lyle Widman, an experienced member of the Research Department of Treasury's International Affairs Division, had written a "Confidential: Eyes Only" memorandum for Under Secretary Paul Volcker that suggested taking advantage of the unsettled situation to achieve:

1. A significant revaluation of the currencies of major European countries and Japan as a result of floating rates or other actions.
2. A fairer sharing of the balance of payments and budgetary costs of the military burden.
3. An improvement in the trade policies of the European countries and Japan.
4. A sharing of foreign aid, which takes into account U.S. defense burdens.
5. Monetary improvements, including greater flexibility and phasing out of gold and avoidance of excessive use of controls.[1]

Widman went on in his memorandum to suggest that at the appropriate time:

The U.S. should be prepared to indicate, and if necessary, use the following measures as negotiating leverage:

1. suspension of gold convertibility;
2. imposition of trade restrictions;
3. diplomatic and financial intervention to frustrate foreign activities which interfere with the attainment of our objectives; and
4. reduction of the U.S. military presence in Europe and Japan.[2]

Widman's proposal (edited by Paul Volcker) and others such as that of William Dale, U.S. Executive Director to the IMF, had attracted the attention of Treasury Secretary Connally. Ten years later during an April 1981 interview with the NHK television network that aired in Japan later in May, Connally recalled discussing the deteriorating international situation with President Nixon throughout the summer. By August 1971 he and Nixon were prepared to suspend the convertibility of the dollar into gold when the right time arrived.[3]

The "right time" came with reports reaching Washington late in the week of August 9 that British monetary authorities were planning to request a $3 billion gold purchase from the United States in response to the unsettled situation that week in Europe. Replying to a question from the NHK interviewer about the immediate reason for convening the Camp David meeting, Connally said:

The Camp David meeting was convened by President Nixon on very short notice. I had just come home from the weekend, that weekend, I got a call when I landed in San Antonio, from Paul Volker [sic] who was the Under-Secretary of Treasury for monetary affairs, who told me that great trouble had erupted in the international monetary markets and that he thought there was a crisis and I should come back to Washington. So immediately I returned to Washington and called and asked for an appointment with President Nixon before I even left Texas. When I got there I went straight to the White House and told him that I thought we were going to have a possible crisis on Monday when the money markets opened and that we needed to make some decisions over the weekend. So he immediately called the Camp David meeting which set up the August 15 or 16 announcement. . . . The immediate crisis was that we thought on Monday that we probably would be called on by at least one company [sic] in the world to exchange gold for dollars in the amount of approximately 3 billion dollars.[4]

President Nixon and Connally were joined on the evening of Friday the 13th at Camp David by Arthur Burns, Budget Director George Shultz, Council of Economic Advisers (CEA) Chairman Paul McCracken, CEA member Herbert Stein, Peter G. Peterson (head of the newly established office on International Economic Affairs), Treasury Under Secretary Paul Volcker, and Nixon's speechwriter, William Safire.[5] After a preliminary meeting on Friday it was decided the following day that President Nixon would announce a "New Economic Policy" in a speech to be televised live on Sunday night at 9:00 P.M. Washington time.

A few minutes before 10:00 A.M. Monday morning (just before the telecast Sunday night in Washington), Prime Minister Sato received an unusual direct call from Secretary of State Rogers. Since the prime minister's English was only a little better than the secretary's Japanese, there was some immediate confusion as assistants scurried about to find a reliable interpreter. Once that problem was solved, Rogers told Sato the president was about to make an important economic policy address that would affect the interests of Japan, and suggested that he and his advisers listen to the short-wave Voice of America broadcast. The style of prenotification was reminiscent of that just a month before when Nixon had announced his plan to visit China. The short-wave, static-punctuated speech and follow-up explanatory calls from Volcker and Burns to their MOF and Bank of Japan counterparts shook the Japanese government to its very foundation. Within an hour it was clear to Sato and those who heard the speech and explanations that Japan's international monetary situation had fundamentally changed.

In his Sunday night speech, Nixon announced a comprehensive program to deal with the domestic problems of unemployment and inflation, and the international problems of decreasing American foreign economic competitiveness and declining international trust in the dollar. On the domestic side he announced a ninety-day freeze on all wages and prices to be administered by a new Cost of Living Council, a $4.7 billion cut in federal spending (including a reduction in government personnel and a postponement of scheduled federal pay increases), individual and corporate tax cuts, and the postponement of plans for revenue sharing and welfare reform.

The international measures, described as efforts to protect the American dollar from "international speculation," were temporary suspension of the American commitment under the Bretton Woods system to convert upon demand the dollar into gold at the rate of $35 an ounce and an imposition of a 10 percent surcharge on dutiable items imported into the United States. Exchange rates were mentioned several times. Speaking of the decision to impose the surcharge, the president said, "It is an action to make certain that American products will not be at a disadvantage because of unfair exchange rates." And, he added, "The time has come for exchange rates to be set straight, and for the major nations to compete as equals. There is no longer any reason for the United States to compete with one hand tied behind her back." He assured the American public that the actions decided upon did not constitute a devaluation of the dollar, and that the New Economic Policy would not raise prices for those Americans who purchased products made in the United States.

American action of some sort to deal with the weakening dollar was by no means unanticipated. But the timing and the content of the Nixon announcement caught Japan by surprise. The communications media and private observers had been speculating for some time that Japan would be forced eventually to revalue the yen through an American policy initiative, probably some time in 1972, and certainly not before the annual IMF meeting scheduled for the end of September. None of the seers had predicted that the anticipated American action would combine a suspension of the dollar's convertibility *and* a surcharge on imports. This combination affected the interests both of international monetary authorities and foreign exchange banks on the one hand, and those of manufacturers and trading companies dependent upon exports on the other. Of all the major American trading partners, Japan would be the most seriously hurt since it had such a large stake in the U.S. market, and because more than 90 percent of Japanese goods sold in the United States were dutiable items that would be subject to the surcharge.[6]

News of the Nixon announcement spread through Tokyo as soon as the speech ended, with special radio and television bulletins and calls from Japanese corporate representatives stationed in the United States. By noon Japan's business community was in the midst of a genuine panic. American and European foreign exchange and stock markets were closed at the time of the announcement. Tokyo was not so fortunate. There was a sudden rush to sell the stocks of export-dependent companies, with sellers willing to take heavy losses. The foreign exchange market was in even worse turmoil. By midday dollar sales were reported to be over $400 million, nearly all of which had to be absorbed by government intervention purchases. Japan's journalists, long anticipating a dramatic international monetary development, dropped their assignments and rushed to government and business contacts hoping for some comment with which to flesh out stories for the Monday afternoon editions. Everyone scrambled for more specific information about the American move and objectives and its likely effect upon Japan's international monetary policy.

The Ministry of Finance in Kasumigaseki attracted the most attention. Journalists assigned to the MOF Club at the time recounted their Monday morning and afternoon frustrations with amusement several years later. Those junior officials available for discussion and off-the-record briefings had no idea of what was going on, and could only confidentially confirm the general severity of the situation. Those few top-level people involved in substantial policy-making discussions were so busy meeting that even the close personal relationships the journalists had carefully cultivated over the years for just such instances were useless in trying to obtain newsworthy interviews for the afternoon edition of the papers. The senior officials simply did not come out of their meeting rooms, even to eat. One enterprising veteran economic reporter remembered stationing himself in the men's room on the red-carpeted third floor of the Ministry, the one nearest the top-level offices, in the hope of exploiting the vulnerability of one or more senior officials to the call of nature. His lonely vigil ended some hours later in failure.

Television and radio news of the Nixon announcement brought all of Japan's vacationing international moneymen back to their MOF offices. Throughout the rest of the morning and early afternoon every effort was made to collect the information necessary to decide what Japan should do in response. This was not easy since by noon, Tokyo time, it was already 11:00 P.M. Sunday night in Washington. The few people still there who were available for comment when reached by telephone were as surprised by the move as their Japanese callers had been. The MOF did not even have a definitive version of the text of Nixon's speech until late Monday afternoon. Takehiro Sagami, who played a critical staff role as director of the Research and Planning Division of the Minister's Secretariat, recalled phoning the American embassy Monday morning for a copy of the speech text, and was surprised to learn that even the embassy had not yet received an official draft from Washington. Until late afternoon MOF officials worked with a summary taken from the Dow Jones wire.[7] MOF officials assigned to the Japanese embassy in Washington were able to give Tokyo the details of Secretary Connally's press briefing just after the president spoke, but Connally's comments were general and intended for a public rather than a technical audience, as was reflected in the U.S. press on Monday, and of little help.[8] Most of the Ministry's counterparts in European capitals were themselves on vacation, enjoying a long holiday on Monday, August 16, thus reducing the value of that channel of information. The need for secrecy further reduced possible sources of information and advice from the Japanese private sector on Monday, and remained so throughout the crisis, since officials feared that even requests for advice would further stimulate speculative dollar selling.

By late afternoon the Ministry finally obtained the complete text of Nixon's speech. Through this, and notes taken during the earlier calls from Burns and Volcker, MOF officials knew that the United States was determined to reverse the decline in its international economic statistics, that the suspension of the dollar's convertibility into gold was the beginning of a major effort to realign parities, and that U.S. officials were serious enough to impose an import surcharge of dubious international legality to achieve their objectives. They also knew that the Tokyo stock and foreign exchange markets were severely destabilized by the news, that government intervention purchases had reached $600 million by the close of business the first day, and that all of Japan—not to mention the rest of the world—was anxiously awaiting Tokyo's response.

There was much more they didn't know. Just how much of a balance-of-payments turnaround would the United States consider sufficient? What level of yen up-valuation did they want? Was Washington planning a multilateral currency settlement or a series of bilateral arrangements? Would the dollar be devalued as part of the final settlement? Under what conditions would the import surcharge be lifted, and when? And, most immediate, how did the Europeans plan to react to the Nixon administration's initiative?

The MOF could have closed the foreign exchange market at any time during the day. This option was suggested and supported by Administrative Vice Minister Iichiro Hatoyama, newly appointed to the most senior career position in the Ministry. His argument, perhaps reflecting his Budget Bureau background, was that the government could not afford to continue to spend public money to purchase huge quantities of U.S. dollars in order to maintain the fixed exchange rate when they were sure to be worth less after the currency realignment. Hatoyama, however, was the first to admit that he had only a rudimentary knowledge of international monetary affairs, and therefore deferred to the contrary opinions of Kashiwagi and other specialists who opposed his suggestion. The specialists argued that Japan should not be the first country to suspend trading, that they should wait to see how the Europeans would react on Tuesday morning, European time. Once the exchange was closed, Japan would be forced to make some change in the yen's parity when it was reopened—a move the specialists still strongly opposed.[9]

After nearly eight hours of nerve-racking individual consultation, information gathering, and observation of the foreign exchange market, a meeting was convened about 6:00 P.M. That included Hatoyama, Kashiwagi, Hosomi, Takeuchi (chief of the Minister's Secretariat), Koichiro Inamura (director-general of the International Monetary Bureau), Taizo Hayashi (Inamura's deputy), and Sagami. Four possible options were considered:

1. Immediate revaluation of the yen vis-à-vis the dollar to a new fixed rate
2. Suspension of the commitment to maintain the parity of the yen

within the 0.75 percent plus-or-minus band around the Y 360 = $1, or a "free float"
3. A "controlled float" under which the parity would be allowed to increase gradually but at a rate strictly controlled through government intervention in the market
4. Continued maintenance of the fixed Y 360 = $1 rate

The first option, a simple unilateral revaluation, had been the response most frequently discussed in the communications media during 1971, perhaps because of its simplicity. It had no support at the Monday night MOF meeting, however, since it would have been impossible to determine just how much change was required. An initial change too small to satisfy the United States would have to be changed again, at great embarrassment to the government and inconvenience to the international business community. If the initial change was larger than actually needed it would adversely affect the competitiveness of Japan's economy abroad. The second "free float" option was rejected because it was thought the market had been too destabilized by the "Nixon shock" to respond responsibly. There would be no telling how high the rate would go when trading began in such a volatile environment. The third option, a controlled float, was supported at the meeting by Hatoyama, who had been arguing throughout the day that the exchange should be closed and support for the old rate ended. Other participants agreed with Kashiwagi's strong determination to keep the exchange open and to continue support at the fixed parity until more information could be obtained about American intentions and the European reaction.

In spite of Hatoyama's lack of international monetary expertise, as the highest ranking career official in the Ministry his opinion could not be ignored. After approximately thirty minutes of intense debate it became clear that Hatoyama would not change his position and that agreement among the top career officials on a unified position to present to Finance Minister Mizuta could not be reached. Therefore, the meeting was moved into the minister's office at about 6:30 P.M. to present both opinions to Mizuta for his personal decision.

After hearing arguments by Kashiwagi for holding open the exchange and maintaining the fixed rate, and Hatoyama's for temporarily closing the exchange and reopening it after announcing a controlled float, possibly after an initial small revaluation, Mizuta reminded Hatoyama that he had train reservations to leave that evening to give a speech to the Osaka business community the following day. Mizuta gave Hatoyama "permission to leave," and asked that he not blame him for the final decision. Hatoyama left the meeting fully expecting that Mizuta would decide to close the exchange temporarily and move to a float. Before leaving for Osaka he even gave his deputy authorization to use his seal in his absence to sign the order.[10] Hatoyama was to be disappointed. Mizuta was persuaded to allow the exchange to open as usual on Tuesday and to continue support for the fixed Y 360 = $1 rate by the confidence the international monetary specialists expressed in their ability to handle the situation without floating the yen, by his fear that a change in the yen's parity would have a severely deflationary impact on the already depressed Japanese economy, and by reluctance to have Japan take any such fundamental action before knowing what the European nations were going to do. Looking back on the August 1971 events five years later nearly to the day, Mizuta said that he regretted his decision that Monday night and wished that he had followed Hatoyama's advice rather than sending him to Osaka.[11]

Late Monday night Mizuta issued an official statement to the expectant Japanese press corps, the first since news of the Nixon initiative reached Japan, assuring the public that the government would continue to support the current parity of the yen and to press for more rapid implementation of the eight-point program. Mizuta said that Japan's strict foreign exchange controls would enable the government to prevent unacceptable speculative purchases of yen with U.S. dollars once the market reopened.[12] Bank of Tokyo Governor Sasaki echoed Mizuta's statement during his own press conference at the same time, and Toshio Kimura, head of the Economic Planning Agency and Acting Foreign Minister (Fukuda was in the hospital recovering from a gall bladder operation), told the press that the government planned to pursue the same policies that it had during the past few months, at least until the late September IMF meetings. He predicted that the United States would propose specific reforms of the Bretton Woods system at the meeting and that Japan would play an active role in the preparatory meeting.[13]

With the Monday night decision to wait and see what the rest of the world would do about the "Nixon shock" and to allow the market to open the next day with continued government support for the fixed rate, the Japanese government lost its best opportunity to agree upon and implement a more responsible policy response, such as an immediate move to a controlled float, that would have prevented the accumulation of more billions of unwanted U.S. dollars and perhaps would have hastened return to a new fixed parity, a tortured process that in the event ultimately required four months of bitter multilateral wrangling.

The Decision to Float

On Tuesday morning, August 17, after the regular Cabinet session, a special meeting of the members of the "economic cabinet" was held, with Governor Sasaki of the Bank of Japan, the top three officials of the LDP, Kashiwagi, and Hosomi of the MOF in attendance. Due to the seriousness of the discussion, Prime Minister Sato himself chaired the meeting. Mizuta's decision to accept the "stand fast" advice of his international advisers was presented and accepted. It was also decided that Kashiwagi should leave on a quick fact-finding trip to Europe and the United States the following day.[14] Just after the meeting Mizuta told a press conference there would be no change in Japan's yen policy: the exchange was to remain open, the yen's fixed parity would be supported, and work would continue, with renewed vigor, on the implementation of the eight-point program to avoid a yen revaluation. He also suggested the possibility of a large-scale supplementary budget during the current fiscal year to cope with the recessionary impact the Nixon announcement would have on the Japanese economy.[15] Later in the day, in an attempt to bolster the credibility of Mizuta's statement among the increasingly skeptical press corps, MOF officials expanded on his comments, detailing some of the public works projects that would be considered.

This public posture was maintained by the Ministry throughout the week, and even during the following week, until the controlled float was announced on August 27. Any sign of doubt or hesitation on the part of the senior officials directly responsible for the yen policy would have been big news indeed, and would have triggered an immediate and uncontrollable flow of U.S. dollars into the Tokyo market. The only breach in the Ministry's public discipline came on Tuesday when Hatoyama was reported in Osaka to have suggested during his speech to the business community that the exchange might be closed if demand for yen continued to be strong.[16]

This was flatly denied by Hosomi the following day in a special news conference.[17]

As decided the previous day, Kashiwagi left for Europe on Wednesday night, choosing first to go to Paris. France was chosen as the first stop on his fact-finding tour because the French position seemed to be more in line with the position of Japan's international moneymen.[18] Before leaving, he asked for and received the agreement of Hosomi and Hatoyama that the exchange would not be closed or any other major change made in the position announced after the Tuesday cabinet meeting prior to his return to Tokyo on Sunday.

But the domestic and international environment refused to stand still for the Japanese authorities as they worked feverishly to gather information with which to guide their slow-moving policy-making process. As the days went by during the first week after Nixon's surprise announcement, international and domestic pressures continued to build for a change in Japan's announced "stand fast" position. Most immediate was the news that the Europeans had decided not to open their markets on Tuesday morning after the three-day holiday. This information naturally fueled speculation on Tuesday that Tokyo would follow suit since the MOF had said in its earlier public statements that it would closely watch the European reaction to the American initiative. A meeting of the finance ministers of the European Economic Community (EEC) was scheduled for the August 19 in Brussels, during which the West Germans were expected to press for a reopening of the exchanges with a joint float. If realized, this move was expected to intensify pressure on Japan to join the float.[19] As it turned out, on August 19 the French opposed the German position, and pressed for Community-wide adoption of their two-tiered exchange rate proposal (official transactions at the old fixed rate, and others at a market-determined rate). The European meeting ended in disagreement, with each country planning to reopen its own exchange under rules it judged most appropriate. The only thing the Europeans could agree on was that the Japanese were not being helpful, and some officials openly charged Japan with intensifying the European crisis by refusing to take any cooperative action.[20] This tough talk from Europe discouraged those Japanese government and private observers who had hoped Japan might join with the Europeans in a united front against Washington.

The Americans did their best to increase pressure on Japan for some immediate action after the Sunday night speech. Treasury Under Secretary Volcker was dispatched to London on Monday, the 16th, to explain the U.S. initiative to the Europeans. A meeting was scheduled for 4:00 P.M. in London (local time; midnight on Monday in Tokyo), which allowed no time to send a senior Japanese representative. Monetary officials from Britain, Germany, France, and Italy were joined by two relatively junior MOF representatives assigned to the Japanese embassy in London, who could only participate as observers. The Japanese were justifiably disappointed not to have been included in the critical briefing. Volcker told the group that he came not to negotiate, but to explain that the United States was seeking a major improvement in the balance-of-payments situation, and that the surcharge would not be lifted until actions to achieve that goal had been taken by other countries.[21]

The administration's intentions gradually became clearer after a period of initial confusion in Washington. Treasury Secretary Connally held a news conference on Monday during which he answered questions about the intent of the Nixon initiative. Although he again was careful to deny U.S. plans to "devalue" the dollar, he said he believed the major American trading partners understood the problem and that he intended to achieve more appropriate exchange rates.[22] President Nixon himself, in a speech to the annual Knights of Columbus dinner in New York the following night, called for American support for his international economic policy initiative, and said he hoped to make the terms of America's international trade fairer.[23] And in Washington on Monday and Tuesday, analysts close to the administration, and government officials themselves on an off-the-record basis, were quoted as saying that the main objective of Nixon's international economic initiative was an adjustment of exchange rates, especially for the Japanese yen, that would improve the competitiveness of American goods abroad. A figure of 20 to 25 percent was often hypothetically floated.[24] So, by Wednesday it was clear to everyone in Japan that the United States intended to force Japan to make a parity change as one of the most important goals of the international side of the New Economic Policy.

Japan's ambassador in Washington, Nobuhiko Ushiba, visited the Treasury Department for a meeting with Connally on Wednesday, the 18th, to hear firsthand his explanation of the administration's objectives. After the meeting Ushiba denied during his Japanese press briefings that the subject of the parity of the yen was even discussed.[25] But five years later he recollected that there had been strong U.S. pressure just after the announcement for an immediate and large revaluation. Prior to the meeting there had been some speculation within Japanese government circles that the administration's real objective was a 10 percent revaluation, equal to the 10 percent surcharge that had been put on dutiable imports. But Ushiba recalled that the U.S. side was not willing even to consider such a small amount at that time.[26]

American public reaction to Nixon's New Economic Policy also intensified U.S. pressure on Japan. Although Senator William Proxmire and others expressed early reservations about the advisability of the import surcharge, the overall response immediately after the announcement was very favorable.[27] The *New York Times,* long critical of the administration's economic policies, ran an editorial the following day that praised Nixon's move as a bold initiative![28] The American business community was even more enthusiastic. Observers in Tokyo realized from the beginning that it was unlikely the American public or their elected representatives would discourage any part of the administration's initiative.

Dollar sales on the Tokyo exchange also pressured the Japanese international monetary authorities to reconsider their "stand fast" policy. In spite of tight exchange controls, $600 million had been absorbed by the government by the end of trading on Monday, and this was followed by a $700 million record on Tuesday. The MOF and Bank of Japan privately and publicly asked foreign exchange banks to exercise all possible restraint and to observe the regulations against speculative transactions.[29] On Wednesday the MOF announced the beginning of an official investigation of the banks for transactions that violated the rules. This action reduced Wednesday's volume to only $280 million, since the banks feared public government accusations that they were trying to profit from the national crisis. The lull in trading was short-lived, however, as $600 million had to be absorbed on Thursday, even as the official investigation began.[30] Japan's tight control over foreign exchange transactions failed to live up to the expectations of the international monetary officials.

The Japanese government from the beginning of the crisis received little support from the public sector for their effort to maintain the fixed yen rate. The business community until the "Nixon shock" had been almost unanimous in opposition to any change in the yen's parity, and during the first few days they continued to issue cautious public statements.[31] But the import surcharge, combined with the suspension of convertibility, greatly increased businessmen's concern over their export position. Up-valuation of the yen would reduce price competitiveness of Japan's goods abroad, but it also would reduce the price Japan's manufacturers had to pay for the imports they needed to make their goods. The surcharge, in contrast, would only reduce the price competitiveness of Japanese goods in the American market with no compensating decline in import prices. On Wednesday, Chairman Nagano of the Japan Chamber of Commerce publicly stated that if Japan was forced to choose between a revaluation of the yen and the 10 percent surcharge, a revaluation would be the preferable course of action.[32] Keidanren's chairman Uemura added his voice to the call for a change in policy the following day saying that a parity change seemed inevitable and that the government should quickly begin to work out appropriate compensatory measures.[33]

Takashi Hosomi later recalled that members of the Japanese business community were even more forceful in their private conversations with MOF officials during the first few days, and that the Ministry's specialists were shaken by the sudden shift of *zaikai* opinion. The businessmen mistakenly believed that the government could negotiate with the Americans on a bilateral basis for an immediate 7 or 8 percent revaluation in return for removal of the surcharge. They doubted the government's claim that the Nixon administration was making much more severe demands in private and was unwilling to consider removal of the surcharge.[34] MOF officials were even pressured during this early period by other government agencies, such as the Foreign Ministry and MITI, to try to work out a bilateral deal through which Japan would agree to a small immediate yen revaluation in exchange for suspension of the surcharge. But by midweek the MOF was certain that Washington would reject any offer of a revaluation so insufficient as that being considered by the Japanese business community and the other economic ministries.[35]

Thursday morning Japan's international monetary officials, already shaken by the domestic and international response to their early reaction to the "Nixon shock," were faced with an unusually critical editorial in Japan's major economic newspaper, *Nihon Keizai Shimbun*. Newspaper editorial and news analysis comment during the past few days had been less than complimentary. But the

Thursday morning piece directly questioned the wisdom of the government's policy of keeping the exchange open and maintaining the old rate. The editorial noted that Japan was the only major nation in the world to keep its exchange open, and that as a result the government had to buy enormous amounts of depreciating dollars, an action likely to have a detrimental effect on the Japanese economy long after the international monetary issue was settled. The editorial accepted the Ministry's explanation that Japan's international monetary situation would never again be the same once the exchange was closed. But it interpreted this as evidence of the government's failure to make a decision rather than as an appropriate policy response. The editorial charged that the government's failure to establish a solid position had caused the Japanese public to lose confidence in its ability to handle the problem. Without mentioning Special Adviser Kashiwagi by name, or his trip to France, the editorial accurately predicted that any attempt to strike a deal with the French on the grounds of mutual Japanese-French interests was bound to fail since France's economic relationship with the United States was far different from that of Japan's. The piece concluded that it was not in Japan's national interest to keep buying U.S. dollars and that the government would be held accountable later on for its actions.[36] The Thursday editorial gave a serious jolt to the remaining supporters of the "stand fast" position within the MOF, but it closely paralleled the concerns of Hatoyama, Hosomi, and other officials who were coming to the conclusion that some hard decisions about the parity had to be made, and the sooner the better.

By midweek, even cabinet-level support within the LDP for the MOF position was openly weakening. Toshio Kimura, director general of the Economic Planning Agency and Acting Foreign Minister, gave an exclusive interview on the subject to *Nihon Keizai Shimbun* economic editor Tsuruta that made the front page of the Thursday morning paper. Kimura clearly stated that under present international monetary circumstances Japan could not afford to take a passive posture, and he indirectly criticized those in the government who were opposed to taking a more flexible stand on the parity issue. Kimura said that he feared Japan's isolation if the members of the European Economic Community should agree to a float at their meeting scheduled for Thursday (Brussels time), and suggested that Japan's officials should devise a more appropriate position beforehand: "Up until now, the idea of strongly supporting the old position has been prevalent within the government. But I think the time for that has passed." Kimura also criticized the government's failure to predict the U.S. August 15 action, and although he did say the government should continue to support the eight-point program, he again indirectly criticized MOF officials by suggesting that their opposition to a shift toward floating exchange rates or wider bands of allowable fluctuation derived in part from their fear of the difficulties they would encounter in implementation: "In the end there probably will be resistance to being forced to revalue, but we must focus on the larger problem of rapidly stabilizing the international monetary system which is now unstable. . . . We can no longer afford to chart Japan's future course in a casual fashion, sticking to long-held political and economic ideas, in the face of the important changes occurring in both the political and economic international arena. It is time for Japan to move positively and directly, giving due consideration to our national resources."[37]

None of the other cabinet members or senior LDP officials were as openly critical of the Finance Ministry's "stand fast" position as Kimura during the first week of the crisis. But after Tuesday neither did any of the senior political leaders make statements of strong support for maintaining the old fixed parity as the primary objective of Japan's international monetary policy. Senior LDP members also criticized the Nixon administration's simultaneous demands for liberalization and exchange rate adjustment, hinting that the eight-point liberalization program should be reevaluated in response to changed circumstances.[38] With foreign and domestic opposition to the continued maintenance of the parity growing and support for the MOF's alternative program of liberalization nearly evaporated, an alternative had to be considered.

With Kashiwagi's departure for Paris late Wednesday night, Administrative Vice Minister Hatoyama and Vice Minister for International Monetary Affairs Hosomi became Finance Minister Mizuta's two most senior advisers on the issues of the yen's parity and the foreign exchange market. Hatoyama maintained his belief throughout the week that the market should be closed immediately and the yen's parity allowed to rise, as he had insisted during the Monday night meeting in the minister's office. Each day he urged Hosomi, Mizuta, and Kashiwagi (before he left for Europe) to take that action.[39] Hosomi was more cautious during the early part of the week. Having only limited knowledge of what he then considered the highly complex problems of international finance, he thought it best to accept the advice of Kashiwagi and his specialist subordinates in the MOF, who continued to believe that maintaining the fixed parity of the yen was the most important objective of Japan's international monetary policy, and to believe that Japan still had a chance to survive the current attack on that goal. Under the pressures described above, however, his confidence in the internationalists began to weaken.

Late Thursday night, the 19th (Thursday morning Washington time), Hosomi received a telephone call from Hideo Suzuki, Japan's senior IMF representative in Washington.[40] Suzuki, who had joined the Ministry of Finance in 1940, making him one year senior to Kashiwagi and Hatoyama, had spent much of his career in the international policy arena and was a senior member in good standing of the international monetary policy community. He briefed Hosomi on the increasingly tense mood in Washington and growing frustration with Japan's refusal to consider a change in the parity of the yen. Suzuki said there was no possibility the MOF would be able to maintain the fixed rate in light of the impact of the Nixon announcement on the international monetary system, and that the Ministry was only compounding Japan's problems by delaying their response. Suzuki urged Hosomi to close the exchange and to reopen with a floating yen as quickly as possible, in spite of Kashiwagi's opposition. He further argued that the change should be made even though the U.S. side was unwilling to agree beforehand to remove the import surcharge in response since he was convinced through conversations with American officials that they had no intention of maintaining the surcharge once multilateral agreement on new exchange rates had been achieved.

This advice from a senior international monetary specialist finally persuaded Hosomi to oppose the Ministry's stand-patters. The next day, Friday the 20th, Hosomi reported his conversation with Suzuki to Hatoyama and they agreed that the yen had to be floated whether or not Kashiwagi approved after his return from Europe and the United States. They informed senior officials of the MOF International Monetary Bureau of their decision that same day. Hosomi and Hatoyama also agreed to honor their commitment not to make any change before Kashiwagi returned to Tokyo.

Finance Minister Mizuta himself still could have overruled this administrative decision, but by Friday of the first week Mizuta himself was resigned to the inevitability of the parity change. That morning he summoned Takehiro Sagami, director of the Research and Planning Section of the Minister's Secretariat, to his office to discuss the report on the Finance Ministry's activities he was scheduled to deliver to the emperor the following week. As written, the report reflected the government's determination to maintain the yen's parity. Mizuta told Sagami he now realized that a parity change was inevitable and that the report should reflect that change. He further told Sagami to begin preparations for the parity change, with emphasis on the measures required to counter its negative impact on the domestic economy.[41] Since Prime Minister Sato earlier in the week had given Mizuta full authority to take any action he considered appropriate to handle the problem, all the officials with responsibility for the parity issue were agreed on the need for a change by Friday, August 20.[42]

Implementation of the Float Decision

After several days of intense discussions in Paris and Washington, Yusuke Kashiwagi returned to Tokyo at 7:40 P.M. Monday, August 23. He was met at Haneda Airport by an army of reporters anxious to be the first to hear any comments he might have that would give a clue to the government's plans for the yen. Finance Minister Mizuta had stated at the time of Kashiwagi's departure that no action would be taken until he returned. By the following Monday night Tokyo was awash with rumors that the other shoe was about to drop. The most common speculative scenario was that a secret bilateral deal had been arranged between Kashiwagi and Volcker during their lengthy talks in Washington through which the United States would lift the surcharge in return for a 10 percent revaluation of the yen. Kashiwagi disappointed the waiting reporters, brushing by without a word. He and Takashi Hosomi, who had been waiting at the airport for him to arrive, immediately went to their official black limousine to be driven to the Ministry of Finance. On the way to Kasumigaseki, Hosomi told Kashiwagi of the Ministry's decision to close the exchange and to float the yen. According to Hosomi's recollection of the conversation, Kashiwagi was still opposed to the plan even after his conversations in Paris and Washington.[43]

Finance Minister Mizuta was waiting in his office for Kashiwagi's report on the international scene and his opinion on the exchange market and parity. After meeting with the minister for over one hour Kashiwagi, understandably tired and irritable after his long trip, met with reporters in the MOF press room at 10:00 P.M. for an unusually tense and confrontational one-hour briefing during which he did his best to quiet speculation that any fundamental change in policy was about to be announced. He was quoted as saying: "This trip was only to gather information from various countries. No negotiations were involved at all. Even so, when I read the Japanese press I get the strong impression that the only thing we can do is to revalue the yen. Things are more quiet in Europe and the United States than they are here."[44]

Kashiwagi made two additional important points during his press briefing. First, in spite of growing public pressure from the business community and the communications media, a quick-fix bilateral arrangement with the United States, or some dramatic unilateral action that would solve the whole problem, was out of the question. The U.S. authorities, and even the Europeans, seemed in no hurry to reach a final agreement, and therefore there was no need for Japan to make any sudden change in policy. The second point was that the international objectives of Nixon's New Economic Policy were broader than just a realignment of exchange rates. The United States was pressing Japan for a "package deal" that would also include trade and investment liberalization, more foreign aid, and defense "burden sharing." It was unrealistic to assume that the United States would remove the surcharge on Japanese exports and stop pressuring Japan in return for an immediate small revaluation.[45]

Kashiwagi's warning of the multiple objectives of the Nixon administration was confirmed by Ambassador Ushiba, who had returned to Tokyo Sunday night from Washington for consultations. After briefing Foreign Minister Fukuda (still recuperating from his operation) and the Policy Affairs Research Council of the LDP on Monday the 23rd, Ushiba told the press that Japan would have to continue the liberalization effort in spite of Nixon's sudden action in light of the 30 percent increase in exports to the United States over the previous year. He also said that an early bilateral agreement that would include immediate suspension of the surcharge was most unlikely.[46] Ushiba repeated his assessment of Washington's ultimate objectives when he and Kashiwagi briefed the "economic cabinet" on Tuesday morning, the 24th, just after the regular cabinet meeting. This meeting was billed as "The Preliminary Meeting of the Participants in the U.S.-Japan Trade and

Economic Talks," scheduled for mid-September in Washington, to reduce public speculation that it had been convened to approve a decision about the yen.

Listening to the reports of their bureaucratic experts, Japan's senior political leaders realized that they faced a situation even more distasteful than they had feared the previous week. Since the early June announcement of the eight-point program, MOF and top political leaders had urged agreement on trade and investment liberalization with the argument that it had to be done to avoid a change in the parity of the yen. Now they realized that the United States was demanding both liberalization *and* a parity change, and that with the import surcharge in effect it would be difficult to resist either demand. Domestic opposition to the MOF liberalization plan, especially from agriculture, had been strong even prior to the mid-August shock. That opposition had intensified considerably during the past week. The major farm organizations had come out flatly opposed to any more sacrifices by agriculture in light of the inevitability of a revaluation, and even cabinet members such as MITI Minister Tanaka and Agriculture Minister Akagi were publicly arguing that the MOF liberalization program should be reassessed after Nixon's high-handed announcement.[47]

Increases in foreign aid and defense burden sharing, the third and fourth elements of the U.S. package, would be politically difficult to realize, but nowhere near as difficult as any meaningful trade liberalization after a change in the yen's parity. Still smarting from the domestic repercussions of the July 15 "China shock," plagued by the emotion-charged textile dispute, and concerned over final U.S. Senate ratification of the Okinawa Reversion Agreement, the Sato Cabinet found little comfort in Japan's most important bilateral relationship during the latter half of August 1971.

After the Tuesday meeting of the "economic cabinet," Finance Minister Mizuta told the press corps there would be no change in the government's position on the yen, and that the issue would have to be settled through multilateral negotiations rather than through bilateral arrangements with the United States.[48] He also said the MOF was prepared to take stimulative measures necessary to counter the deflationary impact of the situation. Kashiwagi pressed the multilateral theme during an interview the following day, arguing that even West Germany had not made a bilateral agreement with Washington, and that France was demanding a devaluation of the dollar as part of the final settlement. He added that the parity adjustment was now a political problem that would require a political, rather than bureaucratic, decision, and that the level of revaluation eventually agreed upon in multilateral negotiations would be dependent in part upon Japan's progress in trade liberalization and increases in foreign aid and defense expenditures.[49]

Japan's international monetary officials had assumed prior to the "Nixon shock" that any change in the fixed exchange rate would create panic within the Japanese business community. Up until the announcement of the suspension of the dollar's convertibility into gold and the imposition of the 10 percent surcharge, no business spokesmen had proposed revaluation as the most logical solution to Japan's international economic predicament, and some, like shipping and automobile industry representatives, had actively opposed it. In May, Chairman Kikawada of Keizai Doyukai mentioned the subject in a highly publicized speech. But even he only suggested that parity adjustment be considered, along with other measures, as a possible option. Kikawada was strongly criticized by other businessmen, as well as by MOF officials, for even that.

The combination of the impact of the suspension of the dollar's convertibility on the international monetary system and the imposition of the surcharge quickly changed the business community's attitudes toward a parity adjustment. While they still preferred maintaining the fixed rate, it took them only a few days to realize that change was inevitable after the "Nixon shock," and their attention turned toward the eventual impact of the New Economic Policy on Japan's economy. The import surcharge was considered a more serious threat to the immediate interests of members of the business community than a parity change of the level they anticipated just after the Nixon announcement. Part of the reason for this sudden change of heart was their underestimation of the level of revaluation being demanded by the United States. But equally important was their desire to have the unsettled international economic environment returned to normal as quickly as possible since uncertainty was making international business almost impossible to conduct. The forward exchange market had collapsed; both suppliers and customers were hesitant to sign contracts for delivery of goods the price of which depended upon some future political decision about exchange rates.

The business community's public and private proposals focused on three main points during the second week of the intense crisis:

1. Quick government action to appease the Nixon administration on the exchange rate and hopefully to end the imposition of the surcharge
2. A concrete economic stimulus package from the Ministry of Finance and MITI to counter the widely anticipated deflationary impact of the international monetary realignment and import surcharge
3. The Finance Ministry's agreement to compensate corporations and industrial sectors for losses suffered from currency realignment

Business community spokesmen gave the revaluation issue itself little attention during this period, other than to recommend as small a change as possible. Nippon Steel president Yoshihiro Inayama, an influential Keidanren member destined to become chairman in ten years, even went so far as to suggest during an August 23 speech to the Tokyo Foreign Correspondents' Club that in spite of its short-term recessionary impact, a revaluation of the yen might be a good thing for Japan in the longrun.[50]

By the end of the first week of the crisis this change of attitude in the business community deprived opponents of the yen float in the MOF and Bank of Japan of an important source of support for their position. Japan's business community obviously was ready to accept the decision to float. Indeed, they had begun to demand an end to the "stand fast" policy by the beginning of the second week. The only remaining domestic impediment to an immediate announcement of the decision to float was the large dollar holdings of Japan's foreign exchange banks.

This subject, even five years after the event, proved during interviews with the major policy participants to be the most sensitive of any aspect of the government's handling of the yen issue. Few interviewees were willing even to discuss it except in the most general terms, and none for attribution. Their reluctance is understandable. Throughout the period between President Nixon's television speech and Mizuta's August 27 announcement of the decision to move to a controlled float, the government was hammered constantly by criticism from the press, opposition party leaders, and private-sector experts for its willingness to accumulate huge amounts of U.S. dollars that were certain to depreciate in value in the near future. Many of the critics charged that in spite of the long-term unsettling impact on the Japanese economy these funds were bound to have, the government was allowing foreign exchange banks and international traders to shift the burden of their losses to the Japanese taxpayers. Some critics went further, suggesting even darker motives on the part of the policymakers, citing their close personal relationships with private bankers and traders, and the frequency with which MOF and Bank of Japan senior officials retired from their government posts to take up managerial positions in the very institutions they had been regulating, charges that less cynical critics of the government's action labeled groundless and unfair. This criticism remained fresh in the minds of the interviewees and made it difficult to obtain information sufficient to assess the motives of the key policymakers at the time of the crisis.

Several former officials did confirm during interviews that key officials both in the Bank of Japan and the Ministry of Finance were strongly opposed to a change in the parity of the yen immediately after the Nixon announcement and throughout the twelve-day "intense crisis" period because of the huge losses it would create for the foreign exchange banks—but that their position was unrelated to any expectation of immediate or future personal gain. Rather, they believed these key officials felt a sense of moral obligation to the banks since the MOF and Bank of Japan had required foreign exchange banks to maintain large U.S. dollar holdings over the years (holdings which had increased greatly during the international monetary instability in 1971) with the promise that the government would never agree to a change in the parity of the yen. The banks had cooperated with the government in good faith, and it was unfair, they argued, to expect them to suffer such serious losses as a result of their cooperation.

Further, just as MITI and the Ministry of Agriculture found it easier to carry out their official responsibilities within a relationship of mutual trust with that sector of the economy with which they worked most closely, MOF and Bank of Japan officials were reluctant to take action that might jeopardize their relationship with the banking community and make future enforcement of administrative guidance more difficult.

Therefore, from the day of the decision to float the yen until the August 27 announcement of the float, concerned officials argued behind closed MOF and Bank of Japan doors that foreign exchange banks should be allowed to sell down at least part of their U.S.

dollar holdings at the expense of the public treasury before the change. Opponents argued that the Ministry would be criticized severely if such an effort ever became public, and that it would be impossible to allow only the foreign exchange banks to sell off their holdings without providing speculators at home and abroad with a heaven-sent opportunity to profit at the expense of the Japanese treasury at the same time. This debate also contributed to the delay in implementing the decision to float.

During the early part of the second week after the Nixon announcement the MOF was quite successful in its effort to reduce speculative dollar sales on the open Tokyo exchange through both its tough public warnings to foreign exchange banks to follow exchange regulations and its publicly announced investigation of the banks' activities. The Ministry further strengthened its position with the announcement on Friday, August 20, that under active consideration was a revision of the Foreign Exchange and Foreign Trade Control Law that would shorten the allowed period of a "lead" (the time between which foreign currency could be purchased and the actual purchase of the goods for which it had been obtained).[51]

At the beginning of business on Monday, the 23rd, Japan's foreign currency reserves were reported to be $11.5 billion, an increase of $2.7 billion, or 30 percent, in one week. On Monday, Tuesday, and Wednesday, due to the government's insistence that the banks strictly comply with foreign exchange regulations, the yen's parity even *rose* from the lower limit of the .0075 percent allowable band of fluctuation under the fixed rate system (Y 357.3 = $1) as banks bought back dollars to correct their oversold positions. This phenomenon ended abruptly on Thursday morning, and dollar sales for the day rose again to $540 million.[52] The sudden shift fueled public speculation that the monetary authorities had reversed their tough line vis-à-vis the banks and were allowing them one last chance to sell off dollars prior to a parity change announcement. Trading the following day provided additional circumstantial evidence to support that thesis. On Friday alone a total of $1.2 billion was sold on the Tokyo exchange, of which the Bank of Japan was reported to have purchased $1.19 billion. Traders found it impossible to keep up with demand, and for the first time in history transactions were allowed to continue for a short period after the closing bell.[53] The $1.2 billion purchased on Friday made Japan the second largest holder of foreign currency reserves in the world, with $12.5 billion, larger than the $12.2 billion estimated at the time for the United States.

According to one anonymous official who was involved in the planning, the MOF had agreed with the Bank of Japan in midweek that the exchange would remain open throughout the remainder of the week, including the normal Saturday schedule, under more relaxed observation of the foreign banks' transactions. Then the decision to float would be announced after the close of business on Saturday. After the frantic trading on Friday, however, it was decided not to open on Saturday and to move the announcement up to Friday night. Finance Minister Mizuta informed Prime Minister Sato of the decision early Friday evening and received his approval.

At 8:00 P.M. on Friday, the 27th, 200 journalists jammed into the MOF press room to get the story for which they had been waiting nearly two weeks. Finance Minister Mizuta opened the press conference with the following statement:

> In light of the current international monetary situation, we have decided that while continuing to support the current parity of the yen, as of August 28 we will tentatively suspend restrictions previously imposed on the level of fluctuation allowed for transactions in the foreign exchange market. Since joining the IMF in August of 1952 Japan has continuously maintained the plus-or-minus one-percent band of fluctuation of its currency stipulated in the IMF Agreement. However, the international monetary system has recently become extremely fluid, and transactions for a majority of the currencies of the major European countries are occurring at rates that exceed the allowable level of fluctuation stipulated by the IMF Agreement.

Recently, reflecting the efforts of the Japanese people over the past 20–odd years, the yen has rapidly strengthened. And under the current unstable international monetary situation, the IMF-stipulated band of allowable fluctuation itself has come to prevent the smooth execution of export, import, and other international transactions. I believe that through this action we will both accelerate the move toward new agreement on the international monetary system, in cooperation with other countries, and also try to re-establish the stability of our foreign exchange transactions as quickly as possible. To compensate for the decline in exports and slackening domestic demand that will accompany this action and the U.S. imposition of the import surcharge, we will work to further stimulate domestic demand, improve the Japanese people's standard of living, and improve our social infra-structure. To accomplish this we plan to implement a supplementary government investment and loan program in addition to the implementation of a public bond policy and proposal of a supplementary budget during the next session of the Diet. We will devise positive policies both for the financial and tax systems.[54]

After reading his prepared statement Mizuta told the crowd of journalists that it finally had been decided that Japan could not be the only country holding out with a fixed exchange rate and open market after the Nixon announcement. And he added the critical detail that the government would not tolerate an "unruly" market during the float. In other words, Japan intended to implement a controlled float rather than a free float, or, a "dirty" rather than "clean" float, as it was later characterized by American critics. He also emphasized the importance of the economic stimulative measures planned, but avoided promising government compensation to industries suffering losses as a result of the parity change. With this announcement the twelve-day "intense crisis" ended at last. In spite of attempts to present the decision to Japan's public as part of an international effort to achieve a new balance, Japan had been forced by U.S. pressure to abandon its primary international monetary policy objective: maintenance of the fixed exchange rate.

Japan's inevitable response was delayed far longer than necessary because of: the failure of Japan's international monetary specialists to prepare a contingency plan to deal with a sudden action such as that taken by Washington on August 15; the needlessly belligerent public posture of U.S. officials toward Japan just after that announcement; Japan's misreading of the international situation by her international monetary specialists; and the difficulty in reaching agreement among bureaucratic actors intent upon protecting the private-sector interests with which they were associated. This delay reduced the credibility of Japan's international moneymen with the Japanese public and with the American and European officials with whom they would soon begin to negotiate for a new fixed-rate arrangement.

6. Hopes Dashed for an Early Settlement

The August 27 announcement of the yen float was a politically and psychologically important milestone on the long journey toward realignment of the yen's parity with changing international reality. The government admitted publicly that it had been forced to reconsider its 22–year policy of maintaining the occupation-established Y 360=$1 rate as the cornerstone of Japan's foreign economic relations. This first step, bitterly opposed by hard-liner international moneymen, was the most difficult to take and paved the way for the unexpectedly large parity change eventually required. It signaled to domestic and international observers that Japan's policy formulation process had moved off dead center at last and that Japan's political and bureaucratic leadership were beginning to respond to the crisis precipitated by Nixon's August 15 announcement. No longer could they be accused of total policy immobility.

During public statements immediately after the announcement Finance Minister Mizuta and other senior officials insisted the float was only a temporary measure taken to cope with the immediate international situation. They expected international events to develop in a way that would allow them to return to a new fixed rate in the near future. The officials made no public predictions about the timing of the return to a fixed rate, but during interviews several years later they recalled that at the end of August MOF and Bank of Japan officials thought it likely a solution would be achieved through one or two multilateral meetings, and none of them expected the process to drag on until the end of the year. Perhaps to emphasize that point, Mizuta stressed that, technically speaking, the official parity of the yen hadn't really been changed. Japan had only agreed to relax temporarily the traditional .0075 percent band of rate fluctuation.

Anticipating domestic criticism for knuckling under in the face of U.S. pressure (*tsuizui seisaku,* "following in the wake of another craft," was the phrase then favored by opposition politicians), especially after the embarrassment of the July 15 "China shock" and the ongoing battle over textile exports to the United States, Mizuta and other government spokesmen insisted that the decision to float the yen was made "in the spirit of international cooperation," rather than in response to unilateral pressure from the United States. Bank of Japan Governor Sasaki stressed this theme in his press conference: "After re-opening, nearly all of the European markets went to wider bands of fluctuation. So, it became difficult for only Japan to maintain a fixed rate under such conditions. We can think of it in terms of falling into step internationally."[1]

Most important, from the very beginning the government made clear its intention to control the level of the float and to avoid any sudden change in the exchange rate. This would be done with continued intervention in the market and strict enforcement of foreign exchange controls. In theory, the government could maintain the rate at any level it chose, as long as it was willing to continue to absorb U.S. dollars accumulated through intervention purchases and to withstand domestic business complaints about the inconvenience caused by the tighter exchange controls. So, it could have been—and soon was to be—argued that the August 27 move had little economic significance in spite of the political importance as the first step in the policy-making process.

The Immediate Post-Float Agenda

The float decision was an important step in the right direction, but it alone was insufficient to provide Japan's international moneymen with the peace of mind required to resume their interrupted summer vacations. From the announcement of the float four major tasks occupied most of their time. First, the experts had to determine exactly what the American side wanted from Japan, or more accurately, what they were willing to settle for. What mix of trade and investment liberalization, foreign aid increase, expanded defense burden-sharing, and yen parity change was required before Washington would agree to return to a new fixed rate for the yen and removal of the import surcharge? And, how would Treasury Secretary Connally eventually respond to European demands for a devaluation of the dollar as part of the final settlement? The Japanese authorities assumed that the early, vague American demands were an inflated preliminary negotiating position rather than a starting point for actual negotiation. They were to be surprised by the lack of flexibility in the U.S. position as the weeks and months went by.

A second important task after the float announcement was the management of domestic public reaction to the handling of the yen issue. Most immediately, the MOF feared a negative reaction from the uninformed public against its decision finally to float the yen, especially after having reinforced previous statements of continued support for the fixed rate over the past year with dire predictions of a negative impact such a move would have on Japan's economy. A negative reaction to the government's "surrender" among the uninformed public could be manipulated to the political advantage of opposition parliamentarians during Diet debate.

Monetary authorities also feared more sophisticated public criticism for waiting so long to float the yen, and in the process purchasing such a large amount of U.S. dollars. Already during the weekend just after the float rumors began to circulate in Tokyo of prior government notification of foreign exchange banks that allowed them to unload their depreciating dollars at the expense of the public treasury. Japan's journalists smelled blood and the opposition was calling for Diet hearings during which they could exploit the issue.

The international moneymen also had to counter public demands, mostly from the business community, for some quick unilateral action that would appease the Americans and bring an end to the import surcharge and exchange rate uncertainty. Most often those demands took the form of a call for a small unilateral revaluation of the yen (less than 10 percent). Although the government specialists themselves underestimated the "bottom line" of the U.S. demands at this early stage, even they were sure that such a small gesture would be insufficient to obtain removal of the surcharge and end the inflow of U.S. dollars without heavy enforcement of exchange controls. The public proposals of the Japanese business community for a unilateral revaluation helped to weaken the position of Japan's negotiators during talks with their American and European counterparts. They could no longer claim at the bargaining table that the Japanese public was unwilling to accept a change in the parity of the yen.

A third task for the MOF and Bank of Japan officials was the difficult technical problem of how to manage the foreign exchange market under the new controlled float until a new fixed parity could be agreed upon. Each day the MOF would have to decide—and obtain Finance Minister Mizuta's political agreement—just how far to allow the float to rise, balancing market demand for the yen against intervention purchases of U.S. dollars, dollars that further bloated Japan's foreign currency reserves. On the one hand, too rapid a rise could induce panic buying, destabilize the market, and possibly overshoot the ultimately acceptable level of revaluation. On the other hand, too slow a rise could swamp the treasury with unwanted dollars and increase foreign criticism of Japan's "dirty" float. The experts had no postwar experience with such a system to serve as a guide and justification for their daily decisions.

The fourth task was the effort to persuade the other ministries and private interests that Japan should still implement the eight-point liberalization program. They knew the United States planned to demand liberalization as part of the package settlement, and suspected that the eventual level of the revaluation demanded would be affected by progress in that area. Mizuta had confirmed government support for the eight-point program during his press conference after the float announcement. But if progress was difficult to achieve prior to the "Nixon shock," it would be even more difficult to achieve afterward. The Finance Ministry's most persuasive argument in favor of implementation—avoidance of a parity change—had been lost; the other government ministries and the public resented the high-handed manner of the Nixon initiative and the failure of the U.S. side to respond to the float decision with some quid pro quo. Why, representatives of sectors scheduled for liberalization asked, should they sacrifice for a cause already lost? But the international moneymen still pressed the liberalization issue in the hope of achieving some trade-off on the level of the final parity adjustment and in response to U.S. liberalization demands that intensified as the weeks and months went by.

On August 28 Japan's policymakers began a long and delicate balancing act, pressed on one side by international forces and on the other by domestic interests, as they struggled to achieve their new goal of resettling the yen as quickly as possible at a new fixed parity as close as possible to the old.

International Reaction to the Float

In spite of all the public statements at the time of the float assuring the Japanese public that the government was responding to multilateral pressures rather than unilateral American demands, Yusuke Kashiwagi and other senior participants confirmed later during personal interviews that the yen crisis was for them from beginning to end more a bilateral U.S.-Japan issue than a multilateral issue.[2] Nonetheless, the Europeans could not be ignored. Even if Japan was most interested in final agreement with Washington on the new parity for the yen, and even after they learned that no Euro-Japanese coalition vis-à-vis the Americans would be possible, they still had to keep close track of European developments because of their impact on American decision makers and on the future of Japanese economic relations with Europe.

The Europeans. Even prior to Nixon's August 15 announcement there had been public suggestions from European capitals that Japan either unilaterally revalue the yen or move to a float. After Nixon's initiative French and German officials continued to criticize Japan for intensifying the American protectionist mood with her "stand fast" international monetary policy and lack of progress on liberalization. All the major European countries also feared that Japanese exports would become even more competitive in their markets if Europe agreed to substantial parity changes and Japan was allowed to escape with only a modest up-valuation. This problem of the final spread between the yen and the European currencies troubled the Europeans right up to the Smithsonian settlement in December.

The European situation was complicated by a difference of opinion between the French and West Germans over how the European Economic Community should respond to the Nixon initiative. West Germany continued to support a joint Community float, but France insisted on implementing its two-tiered system and demanded from the beginning that the United States agree to a devaluation of the dollar vis-à-vis gold as the basis for the final settlement. Representatives of the finance ministries and central banks of the European Six met on September 2 in Brussels to try to achieve a more unified position, but no progress was reported. They could only agree that Washington should suspend the import surcharge and that the United States should take action of its own to correct its deficit position.[3]

By September 10 some progress had been made toward unifying the European position during a meeting of the EEC's Executive Committee at which it was agreed that the EEC would formally propose that the United States devalue the dollar.[4] The finance ministers of the European Six met again on September 13, just prior to the Group of Ten's meeting in London, in another attempt to unify their positions. But that meeting too failed to resolve the Franco-German split, and the EEC went into the London meeting officially agreed only that the dollar should be devalued and the surcharge suspended, two points previously agreed upon.[5] This lack of European unity helped to prolong the final settlement and left Japan without a comfortable "consensus" international position with which they might align themselves.

The Americans. The immediate reaction from Washington to the announcement of the float was quite predictable. Treasury officials welcomed the move as the first step toward achieving a realistic rate adjustment.[6] But there was no indication that the United States was ready even to consider suspension of the surcharge or any other quid pro quo in response to the Japanese move. Rather, U.S. government spokesmen cautiously stated that they would have to wait to see just how far Japan was willing to allow the yen to float upward and how much progress could be made toward implementation of the June liberalization program before they could respond. During a Sunday morning August 29 television interview Commerce Secretary Stans said that the United States had no definite target rate in mind for the yen but a larger parity adjustment was required for Japan than for any of the European currencies.[7] Although the lack of a positive U.S. response to the float was predictable, given the unyielding posture of Connally and his colleagues since the August 15 announcement, this tough attitude increased the sensitivity of the Japanese government's position and made it more difficult for it to justify its decision to float to the Japanese public.

Assistant Secretary of State for Economic Affairs Philip Trezise arrived in Tokyo on Sunday afternoon, August 29, to discuss the bilateral cabinet-level meetings scheduled for September 15 and 16 and to help clarify the New Economic Policy as it related to Japan. During talks the following day at the Foreign Ministry with directors general of the various economic ministries, he disappointed his Japanese hosts by drawing a sharp distinction between the import surcharge and the parity issue. In addition to rejecting the argument that the surcharge violated the GATT, he reported that the United States had no intention of making an exception from the surcharge for Japan because of the recently announced yen float, and insisted that Japan had to make more progress on the implementation of the eight-point liberalization program to achieve a final settlement.[8] In spite of Trezise's explanation, Japan formally petitioned the U.S. government the following day through the embassy in Washington to suspend the surcharge, citing the float gesture and criticism of the surcharge at a recent GATT council meeting. Washington was unsympathetic.[9]

Throughout the period between the August 15 announcement and the mid-September bilateral meetings, Treasury Secretary Connally and other administration officials continued to take a tough, aggressive stand on the international aspects of their new economic program. They argued that the current U.S. misfortune was the result of past American permissiveness and generosity in dealing with Japan and Europe, and that it was now time for the beneficiaries of past American generosity to conceive and implement measures to help turn the U.S. international balance around.

But for all its aggressiveness, the administration was vague when it came to specific demands. It simply insisted that the dollar's convertibility would remain suspended and that the surcharge would be maintained until the Europeans and Japanese proposed countermeasures adequate to correct the U.S. imbalance. The sudden August 15 announcement had been intended to create an international economic crisis, and administration officials were betting that the other major trading nations felt sufficiently dependent on an orderly world trading system to make significant concessions.

In this spirit Connally and his advisers were intentionally vague about how long the surcharge would be maintained and the specific measures required to achieve its removal. Deputy Under Secretary of State Samuels told a GATT meeting convened on August 30 to discuss the subject that the United States had no idea how long it would last, and he was quoted in the American and Japanese press as suggesting it might be as long as two years.[10] Connally confirmed Samuels' position a week later during testimony before the House Ways and Means Committee, rejecting the idea that the surcharge might lead to a trade war and assuring the committee members that the purpose of the move was to achieve the removal of tariff and nontariff barriers to U.S. exports in other countries.[11] And President Nixon told the American press the following week that the surcharge could remain in effect for some time since the United States was trying to achieve a long-term, rather than a temporary, solution to international economic problems. He went on vaguely to link removal to agreement on a new system of more appropriate parities, defense burden-sharing, and trade liberalization.[12]

One subject the administration was not vague about during September was its absolute opposition to any change in the official price of gold. An increase in the gold price would amount to a devaluation, a measure demanded with special vigor by the French as part of the final settlement. Treasury Under Secretary Volcker expressed firm opposition to the proposal during a press conference on September 4, and that position was reaffirmed by Connally later in the week.[13] Connally's refusal even to consider a change in the dollar price of gold at this early stage was especially disappointing to Japanese and European observers since it meant that a final multilateral settlement would be far more difficult to achieve and indicated that the United States felt little pressure for an early settlement.

Domestic Response to the Float

Throughout the yen crisis an important reason cited for not even considering an adjustment of the parity was the adverse public reaction such a move would generate. But after two weeks of intense crisis, waiting for some reaction from the international monetary policymakers, the rest of Japan received the August 27 float announcement with relative calm. Rather, it was the hard-core international moneymen of the MOF and the Bank of Japan who were most disappointed. For them the decision to float was not a tactical maneuver in a larger battle. It was unconditional surrender.

Over the weekend and early the following week the heads of all the large business organizations released moderately supportive statements expressing their agreement that such a dramatic step had to be taken to cope with the international crisis. Also, commentators and editorialists in the communications media did not attack Minister Mizuta and his bureaucratic subordinates, much to their relief, for the decision to "surrender." Indeed there seemed to be a general sense of public relief over the government's decision finally to respond to the international situation.

The Political Reaction. The opposition parties, of course, could not ignore an opportunity to criticize the government's handling of such a highly visible issue. They were quick to issue statements of protest after Mizuta's announcement of the float. Torao Takazawa, secretary general of the Japan Socialist party's executive committee, labeled the float a "de facto revaluation," and said the government would have to accept responsibility for the untold damage its failure to avoid revaluation would cause since it had insisted that Japan remain under the umbrella of the U.S. dollar.[14]

Komeito's policy committee chairman, Yoshiaki Masaki, agreed that the float was only the first step toward a revaluation and criticized the government for abandoning its promise to maintain the parity. Masaki also added that the government should be prepared to implement economic measures to counter the blow it would deal the economy.[15] Democratic Socialist Party Secretary-General Ryosaku Sasaki also opposed the float decision but did not deny the need for an international adjustment of currencies. He argued that devaluation of the U.S. dollar was the only solution to the problem and criticized the government for floating without first obtaining American agreement to remove the surcharge on Japan's exports to the United States.[16] Japan Communist party spokesman, Susumu Kondo, chairman of the party's economic policy committee, was also critical during his Friday night statement of the government's handling of the yen issue. He mentioned a problem that would trouble the government during the next few weeks even more than the float decision itself: the maintenance of an open exchange market between August 16 and August 27, and the resulting government purchase of over $3 billion worth of additional foreign currency.[17]

Soon after the Nixon announcement Japan's opposition parties began calling for Upper and Lower House Diet hearings at which Finance Minister Mizuta and other senior officials would have to appear to answer questions about their handling of the yen issue. Considering the delicacy of the subject and the government's internal confusion, Mizuta had been reluctant to appear. Opposition members, and even disgruntled LDP members, often used such hearings as a forum in which to embarrass the government and to gain public sympathy for their point of view. Seemingly endless press conferences and interviews were difficult enough for the government to handle, but at least officials being grilled by the press could refuse to answer the more sensitive questions. Diet hearings were a different situation altogether. Senior LDP members and ministry officials were old hands at parrying sharp questions with vague, noncommittal answers when they chose not to divulge information judged harmful to the national interest—or to their own reputations—if made public. But the answers they did give had to be accurate. It was, and still is, a very serious offense for a government official to make an inaccurate statement in the Diet. And the government would look foolish—perhaps even guilty—if they simply refused to answer questions posed by the committee members.

Just prior to the announcement of the float Mizuta agreed to appear before the Upper and Lower House Finance Committees. Hearings were scheduled for Wednesday and Thursday of the following week, September 1 and 2. Socialist, Komeito, and Democratic Socialist party representatives met on Monday night to discuss the line of questioning they would pursue to make the most of the opportunity. After the meeting participants informed the Japanese press they intended to demand that the government obtain American agreement to remove the surcharge, and that all three parties were still opposed to a revaluation of the yen.[18]

The hearings began as scheduled in the Lower House Finance Committee on Wednesday September 1 at 10:00 A.M., with Finance Minister Mizuta, MITI Minister Tanaka, Economic Planning Agency Director General Kimura, and Bank of Japan Governor Sasaki in attendance. As expected, opposition members strongly criticized the government's decision, calling it the first step toward an unnecessary and unwanted revaluation. Mizuta countered by saying that rather than a move toward revaluation, the float should be considered the first step toward revision of the whole international monetary system, repeating the "multilateral pressure" arguments he and other officials had made at the time of the announcement.[19]

LDP Member Katsushi Fujii brought up the eight-point liberalization program, suggesting the Cabinet should reconsider plans for its implementation since circumstances had changed so dramatically on August 16. The responses of Mizuta and Tanaka to his question were significantly different. Mizuta insisted that the liberalization program must be continued since Japan was already internationally committed to carry it out. But Tanaka openly repeated his reservations about the advisability of pursuing the program and suggested the government should reconsider the subject before final implementation.[20]

Both LDP and opposition members sharply questioned the assembled economic cabinet members and Governor Sasaki about the decision to keep the foreign exchange market open after the

"Nixon shock." During the Upper House Finance Committee hearings the following day, LDP member Tokutaro Higaki even suggested the MOF and Bank of Japan might have done so in order to protect certain private interests, implying the foreign exchange banks. Mizuta hotly denied the suggested impropriety, saying the government had no such plan and that MOF specialists estimated that between 70 and 80 percent of the transactions made during that period were purchases by the banks for their customers. He repeated the argument made during the previous day's hearings that the exchange was left open mainly because such a large percentage of Japan's trade was denominated in dollars and the government feared the turmoil caused by closing the exchange would have a worse effect on the economy than the purchase of additional U.S. currency.[21] Mizuta and Sasaki did their best to put public concern over the decision to hold the exchange open to rest during the hearings. But the subject was to come up again with renewed strength.

Under heavy pressure during the Thursday hearings to justify his recent decisions, Mizuta for the first time suggested that a yen revaluation might be a good thing for Japan: "The current international monetary instability is not necessarily all bad since if—hypothetically speaking—the yen were to be revalued, we would have a good chance to improve the structure of our economy."[22] The two days of hearings finally closed without further serious damage to the reputations of Japan's government officials. But many questions about its actions remained to be asked and answered.

Managing the Float. Japan's more inflexible international moneymen may have felt "defeated" by the announcement to float on August 27. But as time went by their surrender proved less than unconditional. The government stood by its commitment to avoid a rapid increase in the parity through a combination of intervention purchases in the market and more strict enforcement of existing foreign exchange controls. Immediately after the float the foreign exchange banks were warned against transactions with even a slight speculative tinge and told that the MOF and Bank of Japan would be the final judges of whether or not they were speculative after the transactions had been made.

During interviews five years later the two senior MOF officials most responsible for the management of the float, Administrative

Vice Minister Iichiro Hatoyama and Vice Minister for International Monetary Affairs Takashi Hosomi, recalled that there was strong political pressure from the very beginning to keep the parity increase as small as possible.[23] Hosomi said that he was given a ceiling every three or four days by Minister Mizuta that the yen rate was not supposed to exceed. He was informed each day by the Finance Ministry's International Monetary Bureau just how much intervention (purchase of dollars) was required to maintain the rate within that ceiling. When the level of intervention required became unreasonable due to market pressure on the yen, Hosomi had to go to Mizuta and recommend that he authorize a higher ceiling. He recalled that Mizuta often became upset with such requests, and at one point when an increase was absolutely necessary Hosomi had to ask Vice Minister Hatoyama to intervene with Mizuta in order to obtain his agreement.

Hatoyama, Hosomi, and other MOF officials said that MITI Minister Tanaka, whose economic advice Mizuta highly valued, was a strong source of pressure on Mizuta to keep the exchange rate increase as small as possible, especially during the early phase of the float. Hosomi himself received calls from other senior LDP members, who asked him to do what he could to reduce the increase, often citing the adverse effect the change was expected to have on small and medium-sized export-dependent industries in their electoral districts. During the early part of September it would have been difficult for government and business figures to imagine the level of yen revaluation they eventually would be required to accept to achieve agreement on a new parity.

On the last day of August, a Tuesday, unhappy with the performance of the market the first few days of the float during which the yen had risen by the end of trading on Monday to Y 341.77 = $1—a 5.6 percent increase—the MOF announced new restraints on trading that would strengthen Japan's already draconian foreign currency exchange controls. Export "leads" (the purchase of foreign exchange to pay for transactions yet to be consummated) were prohibited in principle, and other measures were taken to better control international short-term capital flows.[24] The effect was immediate. The yen dropped to Y 338.9 = $1 the day of the announcement.

Throughout the rest of the week the exchange remained quiet. Even on the first day of the month, normally a heavy transaction day, activity was quite light. Foreign currency market participants were not sure just how the government planned to handle this revolutionary change in their market system and therefore were cautious in making sales or purchases. Officials of the MOF and Bank of Japan were anxious to avoid any panic or destabilizing waves of dollar selling, and did their best to keep the foreign exchange banks and currency traders in line, exercising their duties with more than usual zeal. They were under pressure from their political superiors to maintain the level of the float within limited boundaries, and they had to do so with a minimum of dollar purchases in order to avoid international criticism of a "dirty" float.

On Sunday, September 5, an emergency meeting of MOF senior international monetary officials was held to assess the exchange's first week of performance under the float. Although transactions had been relatively moderate and the MOF had been able to maintain the increase in the yens's value within 6 percent of the old rate through the tough enforcement of existing regulations, officials decided at the meeting to issue a Ministerial Ordinance *(Shorei)* the following day under the authority of the Foreign Exchange and Foreign Trade Control Law that would further limit transactions. This new ordinance specifically tightened controls on short-term transactions, such as Eurodollar sales. It was publicly justified as necessary because the Ministry was having difficulty with acceptance of its administrative guidance by the Tokyo branches of foreign banks in Japan. The ordinance was approved by Minister Mizuta on the 6th and implemented immediately.[25]

Although the new Ministerial Ordinance did not restrain foreign exchange transactions any more than the previous informal administrative guidance, it did have the force of law and violators could be prosecuted. This more serious attitude further dampened exchange transactions on the Tokyo market during the next couple of weeks and by Saturday, September 18, the yen rate was up only 6.3 percent, to Y 337.25 = $1.[26]

This relatively moderate increase in the yen's parity was not achieved without cost. It was obvious to observers in Japan and abroad that under a free float there would have been far more purchases of yen than was allowed under the controlled float, driving the rate considerably higher than the 6 percent accepted by the MOF. Cynical foreign observers began to consider the float little more than a public relations ploy, and Japan's foreign exchange banks and large international traders began to grumble about the difficulty the tight controls necessitated by the float caused them in export and import negotiations.

Yen Recession Countermeasures. For more than a year MOF officials had been trying to strengthen the credibility of their denials that yen revaluation was under consideration by emphasizing the disastrous effect it would have on the Japanese economy. After the August 27 float the international moneymen were forced to harvest the crop they had sown during the past year. The memory of their predictions, based more upon guess and persuasive value than statistical calculation, intensified the post-float fears of the business community and political leaders that the parity change would be severely recessionary, and strengthened their resolve to persuade the government to offer compensation.

Highly conscious of the domestic public response to its action, the government moved quickly after the float to announce plans for a comprehensive economic stimulation program. The outline of the plan was first announced by Mizuta together with the float on August 27. It included a supplementary budget during the current fiscal year of Y 500 billion (about $139 million at the old rate), to be spent on the development of sewer systems, housing, and roads. Mizuta even responded favorably to questions during the press conference about the deferral of corporate taxes to help compensate companies for exchange-related losses, and other measures to aid export-dependent small firms.[27] Plans were soon announced for increased government spending during the next fiscal year, beginning April 1, 1972. Early the following week the Economic Planning Agency released preliminary calculations suggesting that the budget would have to be increased by 20 percent in order to compensate for the deflationary impact of the yen rate change.[28]

MITI became an even more vocal supporter of "yen-recession countermeasures" than the MOF for two main reasons. First, due to the nature of its government responsibilities, MITI had closer relationships with Japan's manufacturers and international traders than did the MOF. Just as the MOF and Bank of Japan tried to protect the interests of the foreign exchange banks, hoping to avoid losses for them as a result of the parity change decision, MITI went to bat for its manufacturing and trading "clients." Second, all of the compensatory proposals, one way or another, would require expenditure of government funds, most of which would go through

MITI bureaucratic channels. The Ministry of Finance, which housed the powerful Budget Bureau, eventually would have to balance proposed expenditures against anticipated revenues. Compensatory proposals examined within the MOF were tempered by current and former (like Hatoyama) Budget Bureau officials. MITI had no such restraint. Officials who hoped to rise to positions of responsibility within MITI pursued budget negotiations throughout their careers as an exacting bureaucratic life science. Making events even more exciting, the yen crisis came just at the time when interministerial negotiations over the shape and size of the supplementary budget had reached a critical phase.[29]

The floating of "trial balloons" in the communications media is an important part of the annual interministerial struggle over the apportionment of Japan's national government budget.[30] A ministry official, usually anonymous, describes for a sympathetic reporter his ministry's plans in the hope of receiving favorable press coverage and public support (or the appearance of public support) that will help to overcome the nay-saying propensity of Budget Bureau officials. Each year many such "trial balloons" are decorated to best demonstrate to the press and public that the ministry's proposed project is appropriate to cope with whatever national or international problem happens to be receiving widespread public attention at that time. High-growth economic policy, quality-of-life improvement, antipollution, energy conservation, international public relations, and a host of other topics have served as the annual magic phrase over the years. "Yen-recession countermeasures" was the most popular theme during late 1971.

Just after the float announcement MITI released its own calculations of the impact of the "Nixon shock" on Japan's economy, estimating that an eventual revaluation of 10 percent would reduce Japan's exports during the next fiscal year by about $3 billion. Adding the projected loss of $2.4 billion in exports estimated for imposition of the surcharge, MITI predicted that Japanese exports would drop a total of about $5.4 billion, a loss that would severely affect the domestic economy and require large-scale (MITI-directed) compensation. The day following the float MITI announced plans for a special financing program to avoid bankruptcies in industries most affected, especially small and medium-sized firms.[31]

By September 16, MITI's plan had progressed to the point of submission for Cabinet approval. It included a program to facilitate foreign exchange transactions for small and medium-sized exporters. The strong MOF control of exchange transactions had nearly dried up the market for those businesses, and the new proposal would reinstate permission for the Bank of Japan to buy export bills and allow for the expansion of foreign currency deposits in foreign exchange banks. A new small business finance corporation was also included.[32]

A cynical observer of the public discussion in Japan during the post-"Nixon shock" period might be inclined to question the sincerity of the government's stated concern for small business and lack of attention to the large business sector. The public reputation of big business in Japan may be more positive than that of its counterpart in the United States, but not by much. As a result, it is as rare in Japan as in the United States when the government presents a business aid program to the public as support for *big* business. When questioned later during interviews about the real objectives of the government's business aid package, however, Kenjiro Taguchi, then director of the Foreign Exchange Division of MITI's Trade Bureau (the division from which the foreign exchange transactions countermeasures program originated), replied that during the yen crisis MITI was genuinely more concerned about small business.

According to Taguchi, MITI was besieged just after the Nixon announcement with complaints from representatives of small manufacturers, especially textile and sundry goods, for some relief. Their most immediate concern was lack of a forward foreign exchange market which prevented them from making export contracts. Although small in economic terms, their political power was feared by Taguchi and his MITI colleagues since many textile and sundry goods manufacturers maintained close relationships with influential LDP members. MITI took seriously the threats of these small businessmen to seek political rather than bureaucratic relief, and were concerned their efforts would stimulate more political "interference" in the government process at the very time the bureaucracy needed all the flexibility it could muster to cope with a fast-moving, unpredictable situation.[33]

Business Response. The early public response of Japan's business leaders to the float announcement was moderately supportive. Even though they were not pleased to see Japan forced to change the yen parity, and expected the move to complicate their international transactions and to reduce the competitiveness of their products in foreign markets, Keidanren, the Japan Chamber of Commerce, and Keizai Doyukai all released statements of "understanding" over the first weekend.[34]

Shipowners and shipbuilders associations were important exceptions. They had vigorously opposed the move from the beginning. The two associations held a joint meeting early Saturday morning, the 28th, at which they decided to demand government compensation for their inevitable exchange rate-related losses. They predicted a Y 2 trillion ($2.8 billion at the old rate) loss and presented their case to the Transportation Minister the same day.[35] According to the recollections of the international moneymen, the shipping interests were the most effectively organized and most vocal (troublesome, from their point of view) of any of the business groups. They skillfully presented their case through the communications media and political contacts, and were openly critical of the government's handling of the issue. However, their concern focused almost entirely on the issue of compensation for losses created by a change in the exchange rate rather than on the rate change itself. Their complaints about the float were intended to strengthen their compensation request rather than to influence the final decision on the new parity.

The former government officials' recollections were confirmed during a personal interview with Kazuichi Murai, a senior staff member of the Association of Japanese Shipbuilders, who had worked closely with Chairman Taguchi on political affairs at the time of the yen crisis. Murai said that his association had been expecting a parity change for some time prior to the announcement, and that in contrast to other business organizations, they prepared for the change with careful calculations of the losses they expected. They also printed pamphlets that explained their position for distribution to government officials and the communications media.[36] For the Ministry of Finance the compensation issue was a long-term problem. But during the first phase of the float the international monetary officials worried more about the effect of the industry's criticism on the public's perception of their handling of the parity issue itself.

The shipping interests soon were joined in their compensation demands by organizations representing other manufacturing sectors. The Japan Machinery Manufacturers (Nihon Kikai Kogyo Rengokai) and Japan Electrical Equipment Manufacturers (Nihon Denki Kyokai) and the shipbuilders presented Prime Minister Sato

—and the press—with a compensation petition at the end of August that followed the shipping interests' line of argument. And in early September such diverse groups as the Canned Goods Association (Kanzume Kyokai), Japan Scientific Equipment Manufacturers Export Association (Nihon Kagaku Koyohin Yushutsu Kumiai), the Japan Chemical Importers Association (Nihon Kagakuhin Yunyu Kyokai), and the Japan Industrial Machinery Association (Nihon Sangyo Kiko Kyokai) joined the chorus.[37]

All of these organizations were institutional members of Keidanren, and on Monday, September 6, Keidanren held a vice chairmen's meeting to discuss the exchange loss compensation question. After this meeting, Keidanren added its powerful voice to the call for compensation. However, the peak association was more cautious than its member organizations, pointing out that since there were few foreign examples of direct government compensation the use of the tax system might be a more appropriate method of accomplishing the purpose.[38] A second meeting on the compensation issue was held at Keidanren the following Thursday, September 16, chaired by Vice Chairman Horikoshi, that confirmed Keidanren's position that compensation should come through the tax system, and possibly through the extension of payment periods for export financing or reductions in interest on such financing rather than direct government compensation payments. Representatives from shipbuilders, industrial machinery makers, electrical equipment manufacturers, and sectors as diverse as automobiles, ocean freight, nonferrous metals, steel, trading companies, and synthetic fabrics participated. One difficulty encountered was that the shipping industry was the only group with credible estimates of the losses they were likely to suffer. This complicated presentation of a comprehensive Keidanren position to the government.[39]

The government was cautious in its reaction to the compensation demands, fearing that it might be forced in the heat of immediate concern over the float to make commitments it later would regret. Earlier in the month there had been rumors that the MOF had decided on a compensation plan for business based upon the tax system and changes in business accounting principles through which foreign exchange losses could be declared as tax deductions over a longer period of time.[40] Minister Mizuta's conciliatory tone during the August 27 press conference when announcing the float helped to fuel the speculation. MITI officials too were reported sympathetic to the plan in spite of the fact that it would do little to expand their share of the national budget. But as of mid-September no specific decisions had been announced sufficient to satisfy business demands.

Japan's business community also began during September to complain about strict enforcement of exchange market controls, an issue that would become an even bigger source of concern for the international monetary policymakers. The MOF and Bank of Japan were forced to tighten exchange controls under the controlled float in order to dampen the appreciation of the yen without buying an unacceptable volume of U.S. dollars through intervention purchases. Their efforts soon began to complicate even legitimate transactions and to frustrate Japan's international traders. This concern, combined with fear of the effect of the continued assessment of the U.S. import surcharge, led by mid-September to public proposals from the business community that the government consider a unilateral revaluation of the yen to a new fixed parity as a more acceptable alternative to the heavily controlled float.

After a September 7 meeting of the National Banking Association (Zenkoku Ginko Kyokai), Chairman Goro Koyama held a press conference during which he said it now appeared that a settlement of the problem would take longer than originally expected, and that some "policy breakthrough" was necessary in order to normalize foreign exchange markets, hinting at the need for a small unilateral revaluation. Koyama expressed concern over the stifling effect of the Finance Ministry's increasingly strict foreign exchange controls placed on foreign exchange banks.[41]

On Saturday, September 11, Keidanren finally formally asked the MOF to consider a relaxation of Japan's foreign exchange controls because of the dampening effect they were having on exports. The MOF quickly responded that it had no intention of relaxing its restrictions and that it planned to aid the small and medium-sized industrial sector through policies other than the exchange rate. Although the article did not directly quote any Keidanren official, it went on to report that certain influential businessmen would prefer a shift in government policy from the current float to a small unilateral revaluation to a new fixed rate that Japan could hold until the final international exchange rate adjustment took place.[42]

By Tuesday the following week, September 14, there was a front-page article entitled "Gap in Domestic Support for Long-Term Currency Strategy" in the *Nihon Keizai Shimbun*. The article reported increasing business resentment over the strict foreign exchange controls and even suggested there was pressure from within MITI for a change in this policy in order to get export sales talks moving again.[43]

Soon thereafter, business leaders ended their anonymous prodding and began openly to ask the government to change its exchange rate policy. Keizai Doyukai was the first organization openly to support the position. At an emergency leadership meeting on September 13 they decided to issue a public statement that urged the government to move more quickly toward an international settlement, and went on to propose an immediate unilateral yen revaluation. The statement was quite critical of the government's handling of the problem and lack of policy.[44] Doyukai's announcement was quickly followed by similar statements from the Association of Trading Companies (Boeki Shosha-kai),[45] the Industrial Problems Research Committee (Sangyo Mondai Kenkyukai), made up of about 24 of Japan's most influential business leaders,[46] and the Central Committee of the National Small-Medium-sized Business Association (Zenkoku Chusho Kigyo Dantai Chuokai), chaired by Shoji Oyama.[47]

MOF officials later recalled private suggestions from the business community that the government implement a unilateral revaluation of less than 10 percent, and said they had greatly underestimated the magnitude of the American demands on Japan and misunderstood the technical difficulties of such a move. Even when MOF officials attempted to explain the problem, their business audience assumed that the Ministry's reluctance to revalue unilaterally was simply a continuation in modified form of their earlier standpat policy. These public calls for a revaluation complicated the task of Japan's international moneymen during the early phase of the float as they prepared for the mid-September meetings abroad.

The Mid-September International Monetary Meetings

During the week after the announcement of the float, Japan's international monetary policymakers continued preparation for a series of international cabinet-level meetings, the first since the announcement of the Nixon administration's New Economic Policy. The first to be set—the eighth annual U.S.-Japan cabinet-level economic discussions—were scheduled for Washington on September 9 and 10. Finance Minister Mizuta, Foreign Minister Fukuda, MITI Minister Tanaka, Agriculture Minister Akagi, and the rest of the "economic cabinet" were to participate. While in Washington Mizuta also planned to confer privately with Pierre-Paul Schweitzer, executive director of the International Monetary Fund.

After Washington the Japanese delegation was scheduled to fly to Canada for similar bilateral economic discussions with their Canadian counterparts. The Canadian meetings had more significance than usual in 1971 since Canadian Finance Minister Edgar Benson currently chaired the Group of Ten. The Japanese authorities held some hope that the Canadians and Japanese might find some points of interest in common vis-à-vis the United States. The final meetings in the international series were scheduled for London on September 15–16. This was to be the first Group of Ten Ministerial-level gathering since the "Nixon shock." Treasury Secretary Connally was expected to explain the U.S. position on resolution of the international monetary crisis directly to his counterparts.

During preparation for their trip to Washington, MOF officials were most concerned about the American position on the parity of the yen and what it would take to get Secretary Connally and the rest of the administration to agree to a new fixed parity system. But the international moneymen still felt compelled to press the politically distasteful subject of trade liberalization at home in the hope of making some progress before the U.S.-Japan meetings. Information received from the embassy in Washington confirmed Assistant Secretary of State Trezise's explanation that the American initiative would place great importance on trade and investment liberalization as part of the final "package settlement."

The June 3 "Eight-Point Program to Avoid Yen Revaluation" was still official government policy, and the Sato Cabinet continued to insist at home and abroad that Japan looked forward to its implementation in the not-too-distant future, even though the initial end-of-August deadline had come and gone with no progress on the significant points. In early September, with an eventual revaluation obvious to all observers and resistance to further efforts growing stronger each day, the only leverage the MOF had to press its case was the vague argument that some progress before the Washington meetings might help to reduce the level of yen revaluation demanded by the United States and hasten the final settlement.

After cabinet-level meetings at which preparations for the international conferences were discussed, all the ministers told the press they agreed "in principle" to the need to implement the liberalization program. Even MITI Minister Tanaka and Agriculture Minister Akagi made supportive public statements. But when it came to specific items, such as beef and citrus imports or increased investment opportunities for foreigners in Japan's computer industry, their agreement evaporated. Tanaka and MITI Vice Minister Morozumi were openly making statements about the unfairness of the U.S. position and the need to reexamine the package in light of the surcharge and failure of the United States to respond to Japan's float gesture.[48] Akagi had never pretended to be sympathetic to agricultural liberalization, even before the "Nixon shock."

The LDP Agriculture Committee held a special meeting on September 2 during which members restated the party's opposition to any relaxation of beef or citrus quotas, but they did leave the door open for movement on less important items at the personal discretion of Minister Akagi.[49] Just prior to the group's departure for the United States, Akagi met with his bureaucratic subordinates and instructed them to begin preparations for administrative countermeasures should he be pressed in Washington for some concessions. After the meeting he told the Japanese press that there was some possibility of progress on sugar, mixed fodder, beans, peanuts, tomato products, ham, and bacon.[50] None of those products was likely to create much excitement in Washington.

Preliminary Multilateral Meetings in Paris. Koichi Inamura, director general of the MOF International Monetary Bureau, was dispatched to Paris at the beginning of September to participate in the Group of Ten's deputies' meeting on the 3rd. He stopped in Bonn the day before to confer with West German officials, the first Japan-German consultations at that level since the "Nixon shock." After the meetings he told the Japanese press corps that Germany and Japan were able to agree that the United States should suspend the surcharge immediately, but there was no mention of agreement on the issue of dollar devaluation, the timing of the settlement, or appropriate levels of adjustment for exchange rates.[51] The only points Japan and West Germany had in common were large foreign currency reserves and surpluses with the United States.

The deputies' meeting in Paris the following day, chaired by Rinaldo Ossola of the Bank of Italy, was no more encouraging for Inamura and his colleagues back in Tokyo. It too ended with only the most general agreement that the international system was suffering an imbalance that required parity adjustment to correct. The American representatives were no more specific about their objectives, and the Europeans no more willing to compromise than they had been since the "Nixon shock." In a preview of the position Mizuta would present in public and in private while in Washington, Inamura at that meeting denied the contentions of the other participants that Japan was in "basic imbalance" with the United States and the rest of the world, even though Japanese foreign currency reserves had much more than doubled during the past few months and the outlook for export performance remained strong.[52]

The Paris meetings were a disappointment for Japan. There was little to be done but wait to see what position the United States would take at the upcoming cabinet-level meetings in Washington and London, and how the Europeans would respond. A final meeting of the cabinet was held in Tokyo on Friday, September 3, just prior to the ministers' departure, with Prime Minister Sato in attendance. The press was told that the Japanese delegation planned to demand an immediate suspension of the surcharge, and that Mizuta would refuse any U.S. proposal for a unilateral revaluation of the yen, insisting instead on a multilateral settlement.

Again, "in principle" agreement on the implementation of the eight-point program of liberalization was announced, but it was clear to all observers that the principle did not extend to any specific politically sensitive items.[53] The international monetary specialists failed to achieve interministerial cooperation in pursuit of their new international monetary goal: the smallest possible upward adjustment of the yen's parity. In light of the intense drubbing the delegation expected from Secretary Connally in Washington, they agreed to meet one final time in San Francisco to see if that city's more international environment would soften the attitudes of Tanaka, Akagi, and their bureaucratic subordinates. On this discouraging note Foreign Minister Fukuda, Finance Minister Mizuta, MITI Minister Tanaka, Agriculture Minister Akagi, Transportation Minister Niwa, and EPA Director General Kimura left Haneda Airport at 5:00 P.M. Monday, the 6th, for the United States.

Discouraging Bilateral Consultations in Washington. Upon their arrival in San Francisco on September 6, members of the group assured the expectant Japanese press corps that their position still remained firm. Nothing would be done about the yen without significant change in the U.S. position, and there was no plan to agree to any of the politically sensitive American liberalization demands. In short, no progress was reported in spite of the more "international" San Francisco environment. The only real news was the unfortunate leak to the press from the Japanese side of the advance text of the speech Secretary of State Rogers planned to make in Washington, which included a request for an early large-scale revaluation.[54] From San Francisco the group flew to Williamsburg, Virginia, for a final day of rest at the Williamsburg Inn.

Japan's cabinet members and their assistants arrived in Washington the following day at 6:00 P.M. in three helicopters to be greeted by an actual red-carpet welcome from their American hosts. The choppers landed on the grass near the Washington monument where Secretary of State Rogers, Treasury Secretary Connally, and Commerce Secretary Stans were waiting. Rogers graciously greeted Fukuda in a few phrases of polite Japanese, and Fukuda replied in English. After short ceremonial speeches, the group was driven to the Shoreham Hotel escorted by a fleet of motorcycles with red lights flashing.[55]

Official meetings began at 9:45 on Thursday morning, September 9, in the large State Department conference room. Secretary Rogers opened with the speech that had already been leaked to the Japanese press, including the demand for a large revaluation. Fukuda, as expected, responded with a statement about the importance of the bilateral relationship to the United States and to Japan, and strongly urged the American side to consider immediate removal of the surcharge.[56]

In contrast to Japan's behavior, the Americans did their best to keep details of the meetings as private as possible. The State Department even pressed a number of its in-house Japanese-language specialists into service as interpreters, avoiding the usual outside contract interpreters readily available in Washington, to reduce the possibility of leaks. Many of the Japan specialists recruited for the interpreting job were unfamiliar with the complex economic terms used during the conference and the more obscure product names that arose during discussions of liberalization. Agriculture Minister Akagi further complicated the situation with a thick provincial accent difficult at times even for his Japanese associates to understand. At one point as he referred to dairy products and grapefruit, the translation of his remarks referenced flowers and trees. After a few confusing moments one member of the Japanese delegation pointed out the translation error to Akagi in Japanese, suggesting that he stop talking about that subject, and the matter was dropped.[57] The somewhat comical translation problem symbolized the atmosphere of the whole first day of the conference. By the end of the day agreement seemed no closer than the tone set in the two opening speeches.

The following day, Friday the 10th, was devoted to one-on-one talks between the Japanese ministers and their American counterparts in the hope that some progress might be made in a more intimate setting, with Rogers urging increased defense expenditures on Fukuda and Commerce Secretary Stans and Agriculture Secretary Hardin pressing Tanaka and Akagi for more progress on liberalization.

Mizuta met Connally in his office at the Department of Treasury. According to detailed notes taken during the meeting by a participant from the Japanese delegation, Connally insisted on three main points:

1. A large change in the parity of the yen
2. The importance of the textile issue to the Nixon administration (an issue Mizuta suggested that Connally discuss with MITI Minister Tanaka)
3. More meaningful Japanese efforts to reduce tariff and nontariff barriers to U.S. exports to Japan

Connally told Mizuta and his assistants that reduction of tariff and nontariff barriers to U.S. exports to Japan was of even more immediate importance to the United States than the yen's exchange rate. He restated the administration's public position that their basic objective was a large turnaround in the American international accounts and that the United States was prepared to wait until Japan and the Europeans presented proposals to achieve that objective before considering any change in its current trade and monetary posture.

Mizuta's response was polite but firm. He replied that Japan was ready to assist the United States during its time of need out of gratitude for American help in the past. But he insisted that he and Japan's international monetary specialists did not believe Japan was in a "basic imbalance" situation that required a large parity change. He admitted that the current year's international surplus was large, but added that he expected it would soon be corrected through the combined impact of the government's domestic economic stimulation measures, the import surcharge, and the yen float, and that it would likely fall back into deficit within two or three years without any change in the exchange rate. Mizuta was particularly concerned by Connally's comment that the liberalization issue took priority over parity adjustment for the administration, knowing full well that this could delay the final yen settlement.[58]

The long-awaited Washington meetings ended with little agreement at 5:00 P.M. on Friday the 10th (6:00 A.M. the 11th, Japan time). The obligatory joint communique reaffirmed the mutual trust and friendship between the two countries, but it reported no progress on any of the important issues concerning the yen. It included a statement by the Japanese side encouraging the United States to lift the surcharge as quickly as possible, especially in light of the yen float, and the U.S. side assured Japan that the surcharge was only a temporary global measure not aimed exclusively at them.[59]

Both sides left the conference so frustrated with the theatrical and nonproductive aspects of the cabinet-level meetings during a period of such international tension that it was suggested the following year's session be downgraded to the subcabinet level, and that "specialists" be detailed to work on the liberalization problems.[60] One Japanese participant reported that the Japanese ministers—and he assumed their American counterparts as well—found it particularly tedious to sit during the first day through the reading of speeches that had already been circulated to the participants, many of which were unrelated to their specific interests. CEA Chairman McCracken's hour-long dissertation on the state of the American economy was said to be particularly frustrating for the Japanese side, especially since EPA Director General Kimura was able to respond with only a five- or ten-minute presentation of Japan's situation.[61]

During their briefing for the Japanese press on Friday night, the ministers did their best to present the results of the meetings in a positive light, saying the discussions had been "atypical" (referring to the heated exchanges between Tanaka and Stans), and that the United States now better understood Japan's position. But in private they were far less optimistic about an early solution to the exchange rate problem than when they arrived. The discussions persuaded them that the U.S. side was in no hurry to reach an agreement and that the liberalization issue would have to be addressed as part of the final settlement. Casual mention of U.S. expectations for an eventual yen revaluation of between 25 and 35 percent had been made by Connally during one of the dinner meetings, and he gave the impression that the United States would drop down from that incredible level only in return for dramatic liberalization concessions. The Japanese delegation left Tokyo expecting a difficult time, but the reception they received in Washington considerably exceeded their expectations.

Just before leaving Washington, Finance Minister Mizuta went to IMF headquarters on Saturday the 11th at 10:00 A.M. for a confidential meeting with Executive Director Schweitzer. The meeting was held in the office of Hideo Suzuki, Japan's representative at the IMF, in order to avoid publicity. After the tough treatment they had received during the bilateral meetings, Mizuta and his aides were able to take some comfort in Schweitzer's insistence that the most logical solution to the current crisis was U.S. agreement to an immediate 10 percent devaluation of the dollar and modest up-valuation of the Japanese yen, German mark, and other currencies, that the surcharge should be suspended immediately, and that U.S. demands for a huge turnaround in the balance of payments were "fantastic." But that was the extent of the good news.

Schweitzer too seemed unconvinced by Mizuta's argument that Japan was not in a "basic imbalance" situation that required a substantial parity change, and that the current surplus eventually would be corrected by countermeasures already in place. Even more discouraging, Schweitzer said he did not believe that Connally and the administration were in any hurry to settle the matter, and suggested that an early removal of the import surcharge was unlikely. Like Japan, the IMF hoped for an early settlement of the problem and considered its prolongation very dangerous. But realistically, little progress could be expected in the near future. In fact, no settlement was likely even at the annual IMF meetings scheduled for the end of the month.[62]

Talks with the Canadians. The Japanese cabinet-level delegation arrived in Toronto on Sunday the 12th for bilateral economic talks similar to those just concluded with the United States. Some minor points of discontent concerning penetration of Canada's market by Japan's manufactured exports were expected, but Canada too was suffering from the effects of the import surcharge. Mizuta, Fukuda, and the rest of the delegation hoped their conversations would produce sufficient bilateral agreement to dampen the growing impression in the domestic press that Japan was standing alone against the rest of the world. The visit also presented Mizuta with an opportunity to explain his position to Finance Minister Benson, then chairman of the Group of Ten and responsible for the agenda of the London meetings scheduled for later in the week.

Mizuta made no progress on his agenda during a preliminary meeting with Benson on Sunday night. He could only tell the Japanese press that night that Canada agreed the surcharge was unfair and that it should be suspended immediately.[63] The Canadian side, however, showed no inclination to ally itself with Japan's position and stressed its economic dependence on the United States. The Canadians even politely reminded Mizuta that their dollar had been floating against the U.S. dollar for some time, and that the United States had imposed the surcharge in the first place to get other countries—especially Japan—to agree to changes in their parities.[64] To make matters worse, during the bilateral economic discussions the following day the Canadians were more critical of Japan than had been expected, suggesting the government exercise more "prudence" in its export policy vis-à-vis Canada and expressing concern over the lack of progress in liberalization of the Japanese domestic market.[65] Canada, it was clear by the end of the bilateral discussions, would be no source of support for Japan during the upcoming multilateral talks.

The First Postshock Group of Ten Meeting. The Japanese delegation divided into two groups at the end of the Toronto meetings, with Mizuta and his international monetary assistants leaving for London and the rest of the group returning to Tokyo. Just after his arrival at Lancaster House, site of the Group of Ten conference, a somewhat discouraged Mizuta warned the Japanese press not to expect anything significant from the upcoming meetings. Citing recent comments in Washington by Secretary Connally that the United States had no specific proposal to present to the group, and warning that he (Mizuta) expected the international monetary confusion to continue for some time, the Finance Minister said he planned to use the meetings as an opportunity to explain Japan's position in more detail, especially the critical point that Japan's current balance-of-payments surplus was the result of the domestic recession and U.S. inflation, not the exchange rate, and that the

Japanese economy was really more fragile than it appeared to be when viewed from abroad.[66]

That afternoon Mizuta met British Finance Minister Anthony Barber for preliminary discussions. After asking about the results of the Washington talks, Barber said he did not believe the United States would be willing to end the surcharge until other major countries—like Japan—agreed to a large revaluation. Mizuta replied with the same position that he had presented to Connally, Schweitzer, and Benson a few days earlier and added that Japan was surprised by the extent of international "misunderstanding" of Japan's balance-of-payments situation. Rather than a "basic imbalance" that required a large parity change, the 1971 surplus resulted from temporary factors. Barber then asked if Japan would agree to a parity change if the United States devalued the dollar as part of an international settlement. Mizuta agreed that would be an easier position to accept.[67]

Discussion went much as expected on September 15 and 16 during the first ministerial-level meetings of the Group of Ten since the "Nixon shock." As they had agreed on the 13th, the finance ministers of the European Six, with the support of Japan, urged Secretary Connally to suspend the surcharge immediately and to agree to devalue the U.S. dollar as part of the final settlement. And, as he had promised the Japanese press corps, Mizuta told the group Japan was willing to cooperate in an international settlement plan, but that he could not agree to a unilateral revaluation of the yen.

IMF Executive Director Schweitzer, who had been invited to attend the meeting, appealed for an early settlement of the exchange rate problem, citing the danger of continued international monetary instability for the whole Bretton Woods system. In particular, he called on the United States to reconsider its anti-devaluation position. "So far, there has been no contribution from the United States, and he considered it unlikely that a solution could be found to the realignment problem if one major country refused to accept its share of adjustment."[68]

Treasury Secretary Connally was unmoved by the arguments of the other participants. He refused to consider a dollar devaluation, saying that it was unnecessary since all the other major countries were either floating or had revalued their currencies. He went on to insist that final settlement of the problem required measures by the other countries that would result in a $13 billion improvement in the U.S. balance of payments during the next year, including substantial parity adjustments, trade and investment liberalization, and greater military burden sharing.[69]

The communique issued by the ministers on Thursday afternoon stated their agreement that the current situation required a large-scale reform of the international monetary system, including parity adjustment, and that the ministers' technical representatives should meet again before the annual meeting scheduled for September 26 to prepare a plan of action.[70] This was in spite of the conclusion of those same international monetary specialists at their last meeting in Paris on September 3 that the situation could be settled only through political agreement among the ministers themselves.

Reassessment

From President Nixon's announcement of the New Economic Policy until the mid-September international meetings, Japan's international monetary policymakers continued to maintain the hope they would be able to ride out the crisis that the suspension of the U.S. dollar's convertibility and imposition of the import surcharge had created with only a modest realignment of the yen's parity and a few politically painful concessions on trade and investment liberalization. Pursuing their careers in a postwar economic system organized and operated with the accumulation of foreign currency reserves as one of its primary objectives, and still genuinely skeptical in 1971 about the long-term basic strength of their economy's international competitiveness, they considered any policy measure that would permanently weaken that competitiveness a threat to Japan's national interests. As a result, they took U.S. pressure for a significant change in the parity of the yen as an unfair, unreasonable, and unnecessary demand that they, as public servants, were duty-bound to resist. The Nixon administration's blunt presentation of those demands helped to justify and intensify their natural defensive inclination. Why, they wondered, should Japan be punished for overcoming through hard work, skillful management and sacrifice—at least for the present—its tendency to run balance-of-payments deficits?

In spite of the symbolically important float announcement, Japan's international monetary position in early September remained much the same as that already pursued throughout the year—stand firm, buy time, gather information, and wait to see what the rest of the world would do. But by the end of the mid-September round of international meetings, Japan's key international moneymen, and Finance Minister Mizuta himself, had begun to realize they had miscalculated their position. While they still thought a large-scale change in the yen's parity would be against Japan's long-term economic interests, their personal exposure to the opinions of Japan held by policymakers in the United States and Europe convinced them that some significant sacrifice in that area had to be made to maintain Japan's existing economic relationships with her major trading partners. It seemed possible that other nations, even the United States, might abandon their postwar commitment to an open international trading system. The Nixon administration seemed to enjoy strong public approval of its tough international initiative. Even the blatantly protectionist import surcharge was supported by 72 percent of the American public according to an early September 1971 Harris public opinion poll.[71]

During discussions between meetings in Washington, Toronto, and London, Hosomi and his accompanying support staff decided to advise Finance Minister Mizuta that a final solution to the parity problem would require more time than originally expected and that the eventual revaluation of the yen would be larger than they had anticipated. By the end of the London conference even Yusuke Kashiwagi endorsed this more pessimistic reading of the situation. The group decided that if a large-scale change was inevitable, they should move more positively in that direction and try to avoid the public impression that they were being forced to go along.

Taking advantage of the fresh memory of the international reaction against Japan at the various meetings and their exclusive access to the minister while he was away from Tokyo, Hosomi and Toyo Gyohten drafted a speech for Mizuta to deliver to the Japanese press immediately upon his return to Tokyo. Mizuta, realizing the significance of the move, accepted their working draft and made extensive changes in the wording and tone himself.[72] On Saturday morning, September 18, he read the statement to the welcoming press corps assembled at Haneda Airport's Tokyu Hotel. It warned that settlement would take longer than originally expected, and included a dramatic appeal to the Japanese public to remain patient and persevere while the government conducted the difficult negotiations required to settle the international monetary problem. The statement also rejected recent calls from the business community for an immediate, small-scale revaluation of the yen as an alternative to the tightly controlled foreign exchange market, and—most significant—suggested that an eventual revaluation to an appropriate level (unspecified), as part of a multilateral settlement, would not be against the long-term interests of the Japanese economy.[73]

7. The Waiting Game

Fourteen days of direct exposure to the intemperate European and North American climate of negotiations within which Japan's international moneymen had indirectly struggled these past months seemed to inspire a note of sincerity in Finance Minister Mizuta's appeal for patience and perseverance as he addressed a waiting crowd of economic journalists upon his return to Tokyo September 18. Consultations with Secretary Connally, other Nixon administration officials, and their equally obdurate European counterparts had convinced Mizuta and his bureaucratic subordinates that settlement of outstanding international economic issues would take longer than expected, and require even more of a sacrifice by Japan.

Mizuta and the key MOF international moneymen knew they would be expected to maintain even longer their difficult and politically dangerous efforts to manage the upward float of the yen's parity with a minimum of economic and political disruption—a job Mizuta himself found particularly distasteful—while working to persuade their counterparts in other ministries, influential members of the LDP vulnerable to special-interest constituent pressure, and the business community to support the eight-point program of international trade and investment liberalization the Ministry had proposed back in June.

These international moneymen, with parliamentarian Mikio Mizuta as their titular leader and primary interface with the Japanese political scene, also would be expected to continue to monitor the moves of their American and European counterparts as they all struggled to reach agreement adequate to warrant the convocation of a final negotiating session at which the arrangements required to set the international monetary world to rights would be decided. From time to time they would participate directly in those delicate interim negotiations, mostly as gatherers of more accurate information, sometimes as representatives of a nation anxious to appear sufficiently cooperative to avoid domestically embarrassing overt foreign criticism, yet careful not to agree to any concessions until they were absolutely necessary and justifiable as such back home.

The nerve-racking confrontations with Tokyo's carnivorous economic press corps was to continue for another few months, but the lavish attention and publicity was admittedly exciting while it lasted. At home, status-conscious neighbors were impressed by the black, flag-decked media limousine awaiting the late-night return of even upper-medium level monetary officials, and wives enjoyed complaining about the rude and demanding nature of "yo-mawari" (night-rounds) journalists at a stage far earlier in their husband's careers than they had anticipated.

But every government player knew that one mistake—one unintended leak—could lead to uncontrollable speculative transactions on the foreign exchange market, even to the end of a long and exemplary bureaucratic career. In spite of the danger, the press could not be ignored. Apart from the often-cited principle of the public's "Right to Know," supported in practice by the communications media's "Desire to Sell," those sharp-eyed journalists helped in large measure to determine how the "public" would feel about the government's handling of this critical issue, and more important, how other powerful players would *believe* the public felt. Reliable journalists had to be fed just enough accurate information to generate articles that would help prepare the Japanese public and business community to accept as reasonable the demands the international moneymen would be required to agree to as the price for a reordered and stable international monetary system. But Japan's news market proved to be even more treacherous and unpredictable than the foreign currency market.

The Nixon administration, preparing for a reelection battle complicated by continuing problems with inflation, high unemployment, and an unpopular war, could hardly afford to approve a settlement that might be judged by the American public as less than total victory. Nonetheless, the United States—the player with the least to lose in the event of failure—still defined the "rules of the game." During late September and October time remained on Secretary Connally's side, but as the weeks and months passed even Connally would begin to feel powerful domestic pressure to settle the issue.

Japan's negotiators, however, were under much more immediate pressure. Their public and elite understood Japan's dependence on the international economic system; they felt vulnerable and insecure even in the best of times. Sharp conflict with their most important ally, the United States, combined with the most serious international monetary crisis in the postwar period, had greatly heightened that sense of insecurity. All of Japan looked forward to a resolution of the matter and expected the politically troubled Sato Cabinet to achieve that objective as quickly as possible. Exposed to criticism from home and abroad, Finance Minister Mizuta and his bureaucratic subordinates continued their delicate domestic-international balancing act, managing the floating yen, foreign exchange controls, a recessionary economy, and public opinion at home, while at the same time trying to convince the American and European players that they were doing their best to cooperate in the effort to reach a final international settlement.

The major European countries continued to squabble among themselves, and with the Americans, over the nature of the final settlement, dollar devaluation, cross-rates among their currencies, and the level of responsibility each should assume for reducing the U.S. trade deficit. They agreed only that Japan's sacrifice should be much greater than that of any European country, and that any final settlement must include a devaluation of the U.S. dollar as well as up-valuations of the other currencies.

Multilateral ministerial and expert-level meetings were held one after another, interspersed with criss-crossing bilateral consultations during which the participants exchanged information, opinions, and threats of varying intensity. Japan participated in her familiar passive-defensive fashion: gathering information, assessing the intentions of the other actors, and trying to avoid public criticism that might embarrass the government at home, while waiting for the Americans and Europeans to achieve agreement sufficient to warrant the convocation of a final multilateral conference at which the new fixed rates would be established that would include the smallest possible change in the yen's parity.

The whole process was complicated by the American "package settlement" approach that included vigorous demands for trade and investment liberalization as well as a large yen revaluation. While understandable from the American point of view (one could argue that Japan's representatives had even encouraged this approach in the first place by proposing to ease the imbalance problem with their eight-point liberalization program), this particular wrinkle complicated and delayed Japan's decision-making process by increasing the number of government and private actors and interests involved.

By early November all participants—even the Americans—were tiring of the game. For Connally there was more political advantage in achieving a settlement than in continuing to talk tough to foreigners while prolonging international economic uncertainty. And the European and Japanese international moneymen were beginning to conclude that their respective publics and business communities had reached the level of tolerance necessary for the concessions required for multilateral settlement, so that it was safe to try for a "final" agreement by the end of the year.

Japan Settles In for a Long Wait

The Government: Objectives and Action. As Japan's international moneymen faced the mid-September prospect of a few more months of combat duty before a "final" settlement would return things more or less to normal, their three most pressing concerns were control of the yen float, promotion of the eight-point trade and investment liberalization program, and the formulation and implementation of government programs to mitigate the negative impact of yen revaluation in anticipation of strong public and business expectations.

Control of the Prolonged Float. The most immediate problem was the parity of the yen. After four months of trying to manage the float Japan's international moneymen would develop a greater appreciation for the utility of the market mechanism. When the decision was made in mid-August to institute a "controlled" float, none of the senior players imagined they would be required to perform this delicate balancing act until the end of the year. By September foreign governments and business interests were joined by Japan's politicians, the business community (even the Finance Ministry's normal allies, the banks), and the communications media in a chorus of criticism over the government's management of the float. Some of the complaints were justified.

The controlled float was instituted in August to restrain, or at least delay, foreign demands for yen revaluation by allowing market forces to gradually press the yen's parity up from its original Y 360=$1 level on the one hand, while on the other allowing the government to restrain the market-determined speed of ascent through a combination of intervention dollar purchases and strict application of controls on foreign exchange transactions.

Any miscalculation that resulted in too rapid a rate of increase ran the risk of igniting complaints to sympathetic politicians from manufacturers (many of them small and medium-sized firms) of price-sensitive export items about the government's insensitivity to their plight, and also of further heightening public fears of the dire economic consequences of revaluation. Excessive government market-dampening efforts ran the risk of setting off international protests of "dirty" floating, further swelling the government's holdings of dollars purchased in intervention, and provoking complaints from Japan's foreign exchange banks and trading companies that over-zealous application of foreign exchange transactions was drying up the market, making it impossible to conduct business abroad.

By the end of mid-September's international meetings, Japan's international moneymen realized they would have to improve their control of the float and revise the exercise of exchange transaction controls in a way that would allow just enough transactions to satisfy the business community, but not so many that the Bank of Japan had to accumulate an unacceptable amount of U.S. dollars. And all of this had to be done while the exchange rate was maintained at an acceptable level. This was in addition to participating in a series of ongoing international meetings to hammer out solutions to a number of basically bilateral economic problems.

American government and business leaders soon became frustrated with Japan's unwillingness to let the yen rise under the float to what they considered an appropriate level. Donald Kendall, chairman of the American corporate giant, Pepsico, and chairman of the Emergency Committee for American Trade (ECAT), a big-business group organized in the late 1960s to promote a more internationalist American international economic policy, arrived in Japan on the evening of September 25. Known as a friend and economic adviser of President Nixon, he had no difficulty arranging appointments with Tokyo's financial "movers-and-shakers," including even a private meeting with Prime Minister Sato for the 29th.

Just after his arrival Kendall held a press conference during which he strongly criticized the government's management of the yen float. He said that he and other members of the American business community did not believe the float as currently managed adequately reflected actual conditions in the Tokyo exchange market.[1] Kendall hinted that the float was, in practice, more effective as a public relations tool than as a source of economic adjustment.

Kendall's comments were taken seriously by government officials and the communications media. In addition to his personal relationship with President Nixon, Kendall's organization, ECAT, was considered in Tokyo circles to be fundamentally internationalist and antiprotectionist, one of the few policy-relevant Washington institutions that might be expected to nudge the Nixon administration toward a more cooperative foreign economic policy. Therefore his warning could not be dismissed as the mere rumblings of a neoisolationist.

Treasury Secretary Connally soon made the same point during the Washington IMF meetings in September. In a major speech at the annual meeting, Connally linked the administration's willingness to suspend the surcharge to the willingness of other countries to allow their currencies to float freely, rather than heavily controlling the amount of parity change.[2] Connally again raised the "dirty float" charge at a meeting with the Business Council on October 15, saying that even by mid-October the yen hadn't been allowed to rise anywhere near the level it would reach if allowed to rise freely.[3]

Influential individuals and organizations in Japan took the opposite view, complaining the rate of increase was too rapid and likely to cause serious long-term economic damage. Their complaints were noted and amplified by MITI Minister Tanaka who on October 8 commented at a hearing of the Upper House Commerce Committee that in his personal opinion any revaluation of over 10 percent would be a severe shock for Japanese industry, adding that he didn't believe the final figure would be over ten percent. Although he admitted a stronger yen would reduce the price Japan had to pay for imported raw materials, Tanaka said he thought small and medium-sized business would eventually require some sort of compensatory government economic policy.[4]

Each day the specialists had to determine the amount of upward float required and implement it through sensitive dollar-buying operations coordinated through foreign exchange banks by the Bank of Japan. Finance Minister Mizuta recalled during interviews several years later the considerable pressure he received from LDP colleagues to slow the rise of the yen and his own frustration with his bureaucratic subordinates' inability to maintain a slower and more politically comfortable rate of increase.[5]

Although the government was able to control the day-to-day yen rate with a high degree of accuracy once a new level was agreed upon (just as they had been able to maintain it within 0.075 percent of the old fixed rate of Y 360 = $1), the determination of appropriate medium- and long-term rate objectives during the float were far from exact scientific economic calculations, according to the recollection of a senior MOF official directly involved in the effort. Research Division staffers of the Minister's Secretariat went through reams of paper supporting one position or another, but the actual decisions were based more on the pressures of the moment than on long-term econometric calculation.

The government's research efforts were supplemented by several top-secret discussions with private-sector academic, and even banking community, foreign exchange experts—many of them MOF "Old Boys"—to seek advice on how to handle the float. But none of the experts consulted were able to give the government particularly useful ideas on how to deal more effectively with this unprecedented situation that faced the MOF in late September and October.[6] The international moneymen were on their own, responsible for the most critical economic job in Japan, yet doomed to face criticism no matter which direction they turned.

Japan's communications media was yet another factor in the government's efforts to manage the float of the yen. Since the outbreak of the crisis MOF and Bank of Japan officials had been extremely cautious in their comments to the press, much to the disappointment of MOF press club members who were used to better treatment by their news sources. After the float, however, key officials were forced to pay more attention to the impact of yen-related press reports as they mapped their control strategy. To help balance what sometimes became for the government the costly impact of press speculation on the future of the yen, off-the-record interviews were given to "responsible" journalists in which hints were dropped about plans for the foreign exchange market. More often than not such "leaks" were designed to convince currency traders that the government was prepared to defend the current rate through large-scale intervention should it be attacked, making quick speculative profits at the expense of the public treasury impossible.

For example, the front-page lead story in *Nihon Keizai Shimbun* on October 12, 1971, reported that the government and Bank of Japan had decided not to allow the yen to float upward beyond the 325 yen to one dollar mark.[7] This was just after a Monday of exchange transactions that had pressed the yen over the IMF-calculated 9 percent up-valuation level. The "reliable government source" added that the yen had reached its "actual value" in the opinion of the government monetary authorities, and they were prepared to intervene strongly to maintain it. The "reliable government source," of course, hoped to discourage potentially speculative purchases of yen, reducing the need for government intervention purchases through "jawboning." Such "leaks" became more frequent as the weeks and months of the controlled float went by. Their effectiveness as a market-controlling tool naturally declined in proportion to the frequency of their use.

Throughout late September and into October the yen continued its gradual rise while Japan's foreign currency reserves piled up, the latter reaching $13.3 billion by the end of September. By mid-October the official exchange rate had risen the equivalent of a 9 percent revaluation when calculated by the IMF method, and all expectations were that it would go even higher. The government learned that although it was able to reduce the speed of rate change through its jawboning, intervention purchases, draconian application of foreign exchange transactions rules, and press manipulation, the resources of the government were insufficient to staunch the flow of the market once it headed firmly in one direction.

Trade and Investment Liberalization. Japan's international moneymen continued throughout September to press their more domestically oriented government colleagues and the business community to act quickly on the trade and investment liberalization package the MOF had proposed in early June as an alternative to yen revaluation. Unpopular from the beginning, and characterized by its reluctant institutional targets as a scheme concocted by the international monetary sector to solve its own exchange rate problem through politically and economically difficult changes in other sectors of government and business (and all without adequate prior consultation), the liberalization package received an even less sympathetic hearing after the Y 360=$1 rate the original plan was designed to protect crumbled more than a month before. Nonetheless, at its regular Tuesday meeting on September 28 the Cabinet with considerable public fanfare endorsed a proposal to liberalize trade restrictions on 25 items at the beginning of October, a move described as bringing Japan's liberalization effort in line with that of West Germany.[8]

Many official statements after regular cabinet meetings during September and October included mention of top-level discussions among members of the "economic cabinet" of the need for more progress on liberalization. These reports were often either purposely vague in detail, or attributed to unnamed sources. For example, following the October 15 cabinet meeting (the same day Ambassador David Kennedy and MITI Minister Tanaka signed the bilateral textile agreement), the Japanese press reported cabinet discussion of a "post textile" strategy for relations with the United States that focused on the remaining bilateral liberalization problems. In case either intended audience—the domestic bureaucratic and private-sector targets of the liberalization efforts, or the governments and business communities of Japan's foreign trading partners—missed the point, the briefing officer emphasized that the government hoped its positive attitude toward liberalization would reduce the level of yen revaluation demanded by the United States.[9]

Not all of the liberalization commotion was empty international public relations. In the semifrantic atmosphere of late September and October, some real progress was made. For example, the Planning Subcommittee of the Tariff Advisory Commission (Kikakubukai, Kanzei-ritsu Shingikai) met at the Finance Ministry on October 19 to discuss Japan's tax situation for the upcoming year. The committee agreed that in spite of the shock of the August 16 U.S. action vis-à-vis the yen, Japan should still work toward tariff cuts in order to reduce domestic price levels, increase imports, and dampen protectionist sentiment in foreign countries. At the end of the meeting the members released a public statement detailing their agreement and announcing plans to consider further tariff reductions on refrigerators, whiskey, and soy beans, all items highlighted in the June eight-point liberalization program.[10]

But throughout the late September-October period Japan's international moneymen had far greater success selling their countrymen the appreciating yen through market intervention than they did selling the concept of swapping trade and investment liberalization for vague American commitments to a smaller level of revaluation. American trade officials continued to demand meaningful liberalization as part of the final "package" settlement in which they would remove the surcharge and repeg exchange rates. Japanese agriculture, Japanese business, and the bureaucrats who administered the current system of restraints were not about to agree to anything "significant" under such fluid conditions.

Special Revaluation Countermeasures. In anticipation of private-sector demands for help to survive what most observers still expected to be a serious domestic economic crisis, the Sato Cabinet and all sectors of the economic bureaucracy spent much of September and October developing special government programs to help soften the impact revaluation was expected to have on business. In addition, much of their remaining time was devoted to encouraging the Japanese press to publicize the fruits of these efforts.

One month into the float the actual economic impact of the parity change was still highly overrated, as indicated by the EPA's early October revision of the official current fiscal year growth rate projection from 10.1 percent to 5.5 percent.[11] Realizing now that a substantial up-valuation of the yen was inevitable, the government instructed the Economic Advisory Council (Keizai Shingikai), then headed by Keizai Doyukai chairman Kikawada, to begin work on a replacement for its existing 1970–1971 national economic plan that would take the yen's parity change into consideration. When this move was announced the government emphasized its intention to include expensive government-spending projects (such as increases in social welfare spending, which would stimulate the overall economy), and also proposed changes in Japan's overall industrial structure.[12]

A MITI official involved in planning the policy and implementation of that ministry's late 1971 yen revaluation countermeasures stated during an interview several years later that MITI and the rest of the government was especially concerned just after the float about the disruptive political potential of small and medium-sized companies. They feared that small businessmen might follow agriculture's example and appeal directly to sympathetic LDP members for economic relief if not satisfied with the answers given them by the bureaucracy. Such appeals to higher political authorities—unfiltered by the bureaucracy—would generate noisy parliamentary demands for unrealistic direct or indirect government compensation on behalf of the politicians' constituents or financial supporters that would be difficult or impossible to deliver, yet equally difficult to refuse, thus seriously complicating the policy process at a critical juncture.[13]

This concern combined with others to force interministerial cooperation in mid-September on the formulation of an extraordinary set of economic countermeasures designed to ease the impact of yen revaluation on medium and small-sized companies. The program was approved by a special cabinet meeting on September 23. A fund of Y 150 billion (nearly $500 million) was established through which small and medium-sized companies suffering excessive inventories, declining production, or industrial adjustment problems related to the change in the parity of the yen could obtain loans of between five and ten million yen ($15,000 and $30,000).

The countermeasures also improved the terms under which small and medium-sized corporations could obtain credit insurance, and established a fund from which foreign currency was deposited in exchange banks that was equal to the bank's total holdings of export bills from medium and small-sized corporations. In addition, the period during which losses could be declared for tax purposes was extended from one to three years, and funds were earmarked for industrial association projects designed to promote adjustment from one industry to another. Considering the complexity of this undertaking and the inevitable bureaucratic wrangling required to reach agreement on its final form, it is remarkable that the plan saw the light of day less than one month after the decision was announced to float the yen. During mid-October, the Cabinet also quickly approved a fiscal year 1971 supplementary budget of Y 244.68 billion (about $732 million) designed to help the economy ride out the revaluation storm.[14]

Japan's Business Community. Finance Minister Mizuta's dramatic mid-September warning upon his return from Europe that final settlement would require both more time and more concessions from Japan only increased the business community's frustration with the uncertainty of its international monetary position as the days of crisis lengthened to weeks, and weeks became months. Once careful to avoid direct criticism, or even to mention the existence of problems in the past, by late September business spokesmen were openly discussing the yen and related issues, and giving the government the benefit of their advice, whether it was wanted or not.

During this waiting period between mid-September and early November, Japan's business leaders focused their expressions of concern on three main issues: the yen rate and how agreement on a new fixed system should be achieved; the need to agree in advance on more government-spending programs to help counteract the depressing effect of yen revaluation on the overall economy; and the question of direct or indirect government compensation of foreign currency–related business losses. Most serious for the international moneymen, business spokesmen were even publicly stating that a unilateral revaluation of the yen would be preferable to the continued imposition of the American import surcharge and the inconvenience created by the measures necessary to manage the float.

Business Speaks Out on the Yen. The "territorial" sensitivity of Japan's career government international moneymen is, and was, at least as well developed as that of their foreign counterparts. They justified claims of exclusivity with explanations of the sensitivity of the issues involved, the vulnerability of foreign exchange markets to external manipulation, the technical complexity of international monetary affairs, and the possibility that even peripherally involved "outsiders" might end up accused of trying to manipulate the market to their personal advantage.

Accustomed to a pattern of government policy formulation and implementation in all other areas that put the emphasis on consulting with representatives of any business interests likely to be affected by contemplated changes, this "territoriality" of the international moneymen had long been a source of irritation for Japan's business community, especially the internationally sophisticated banking and trading circles.

In the past, fear of MOF retaliation had effectively stilled most direct business criticism. That which did appear—unnamed sources in articles by "unreliable" journalists who wrote for the sensation-prone weekly magazines—was usually confined to ad hominem complaints about the "internationalist" affectations and/or arrogance of individual officials. Even "unreliable" journalists didn't criticize the professional performance of Japan's international moneymen prior to the 1971 crisis. The system continued to work through thick and thin; the yen remained pegged at Y 360=$1, a reassuring point of reference in a turbulent world trading system. A little bureaucratic snootiness was a small price to pay for such a sense of security.

Accusations of personal rudeness or foreign affectation might sting for a moment, but they posed little threat to the bureaucracy's continued absolute control over international monetary affairs. Only a loss of public confidence in the bureaucrats' ability to handle the situation on their own could threaten that control. And this threat could only come from the business community. In contrast to the political opposition, labor unions, consumer groups, or any other potentially hostile parties, the business community—especially the banks and international trading companies—combined a relatively high level of expertise on the subject with easy access to Japan's national communications media. If the internationally sophisticated bankers and trading company executives began to complain that the government was mishandling the yen issue, they would be heard.

MOF and Bank of Japan officials grappling with the international monetary crisis were well aware of this potential threat to their control of the issue, and therefore keenly interested in the opinions and public statements of Japan's business community. Bluntly put, they knew the business community had to be "kept in line" or the government ran the risk of public and political intervention in its handling of the yen issue, which might seriously restrain their options and make final settlement much more difficult to achieve.

During the earlier stages of the crisis, before the Nixon administration decided to force a settlement with the August 15 surprise announcement, there was little cause for concern. The long- and short-term international monetary objectives of the government and the business community were the same: contain the international pressures resulting from the sudden growth of balance-of-payments surpluses and the unseemly accumulation of foreign currency reserves through a combination of maximum efforts to portray Japan in multilateral and bilateral international forums as concerned, sympathetic, and ready to cooperate; make minimum trade and investment liberalization concessions when absolutely necessary, avoiding altogether any which might damage Japan's long-term foreign exchange earning ability; and wait for the inevitable macroeconomic changes to correct the temporary imbalance situation. This fortunate congruence of mutual interests crumbled with the suspension of the dollar's convertibility and imposition of the 10 percent surcharge. Members of Japan's business community became impatient watching the government play its "stand fast" waiting game, while their position in international markets rapidly evaporated. Their frustration was reported in the press with increasing frequency throughout September.

After weeks of public complaints by knowledgeable and responsible businessmen, Chairman Shigeo Nagano even included pointed reference to the lingering international monetary crisis in his opening address on September 12 to the 34th Annual General Meeting of the Japan Chamber of Commerce. Nagano said it was his hope the government soon would exercise "strong leadership" to resolve outstanding problems quickly in order to spare Japan's small and medium-sized businesses the negative consequences of the continued float of the yen. With Prime Minister Sato and several other cabinet members in attendance, Nagano and his Chamber of Commerce constituency could be sure this expression of frustration with government's apparent lack of progress on this important issue went straight to the top.[15]

Keidanren, with a superior professional staff and more political clout than the Japan Chamber of Commerce, loomed as an even greater potential problem for the government in mid-September. A special committee of concerned Keidanren members, mostly bankers, had already been established to investigate the yen problem and to propose a general policy statement that would prove acceptable to the whole Keidanren board. Yoshizane Iwasa, then chairman of Fuji Bank, was chosen to lead the group. He recalled during a later interview that many of his committee members were sympathetic to the proposal put forward earlier in the year by Professor Ryutaro Komiya of Tokyo University for a modified "crawling peg" currency realignment.[16] After the events of mid-August this "crawling peg" proposal was hardly a radical position. Still, recalled Iwasa, representatives of "industrial" interests within Keidanren remained opposed even to this concession, let alone to a significant level of revaluation, making it impossible for Keidanren to issue a coherent policy statement supported by the whole organization and greatly weakening its role in the policy debate.[17] In mid-October Iwasa accepted an invitation to present his personal opinions about current U.S.-Japan economic relations, including the yen issue, to a seminar arranged by the Japan Productivity Center. He repeated the *keizai-kai* theme that Japan should return as quickly as possible to fixed exchange rates and suggested that when this occurred Japan would have to accept a revaluation of the yen of about 10 percent with an increase in the allowable bands of fluctuation from 2 to 3 percent.[18]

Frustrated with the apparent lack of progress in the negotiations, a few Japanese business leaders intensified pressure on the government by suggesting that business should establish its own "diplomatic" channels of communication with the United States and Europe to facilitate an earlier solution to the international monetary crisis. The September 20, 1971, Tokyo financial press carried an article on "Businessmen's Diplomacy," reporting that Keizai Doyukai chairman Kikawada and Yoshizane Iwasa intended to discuss the yen problem with their American counterparts during mid-October visits to the United States while attending various annual regional bilateral business conferences. Keidanren chairman Uemura too would join in, with planned visits to several European capitals in mid-October.[19]

Given the sensitivity of the situation in which Japan's international moneymen found themselves toward the end of October, they were appalled by the thought of what this diversification of communication channels the business initiative represented. It was one thing to send cooperative business executives abroad to explain Japan's "actual situation" to foreign audiences, and it was quite another to have them trotting the globe spouting their own opinions about sensitive issues. The businessmen involved not only had excellent access to Japan's communications media, they also met on a regular basis with Japan's senior political leaders. It now was likely that their interpretations of international monetary reality in foreign countries for Japan's communications media and political leadership would differ from the official line, thereby eroding the tight control Japan's international moneymen had maintained for so long over the vital flow of information.

This newfound public assertiveness of the business community naturally bruised the feelings of some government people accustomed to greater public deference. During off-the-record interviews five years later they recalled a sense of "betrayal" at the time. Up to the August 16 "Nixon shock," business had been absolutely opposed to any change in the parity of the yen. Then, almost overnight, it had begun to criticize the government's lack of flexibility in its management of the difficult international negotiations. The business community's public scoldings were particularly irksome, one victim remembered, because the most vocal critics obviously underestimated the level of up-valuation required to satisfy the international pressures faced by the yen.

A 10 percent up-valuation, a figure often heard during the mid-September-October period, even if offered, would have come nowhere near to moving Connally toward agreement on a final settlement or even removal of the import surcharge. It would instead, government officials believed, have weakened Japan's negotiating strength right at the end of the game where it really counted—especially if the gesture were made as a "unilateral revaluation." The government officials also feared some businessmen might be manipulated by the Americans into taking public positions that would, in the end, work against their own long-term interests.

In spite of the government's denials that any "unilateral revaluation" plan was under consideration, such rumors continued to spring up in Tokyo, especially after every publicly reported official contact with the United States, thus making the international moneymen's lives more difficult by destabilizing the foreign exchange market. Senior government officials continued to deny the possibility time and time again, in statements such as that given by Finance Minister Mizuta before the Upper House Budget Committee on October 5, just after returning from the IMF's annual meeting in Washington. Mizuta said that bilateral conversations were continuing between Japan and the United States and West Germany. But, he insisted, such bilateral contacts were necessary in order to pave the way for an international agreement. They in no way signaled a change in Japan's basic policy of changing the parity of the yen only within the framework of an international settlement.[20]

Business Demands More Help to Counter a Yen Recession. Although basic disagreements within the business community continued throughout the period over issues such as the amount the government should be willing to compromise on the parity up-valuation, and whether or not industries with long-term export contracts, such as shipbuilding, should be compensated directly by the government for their inevitable losses, everyone seemed agreed that the parity change would greatly slow domestic economic growth, and that its dampening impact should be countered by more government spending during the next fiscal year. Beyond that, the business community was less specific, even vague.

The size and diversity of Keidanren's business membership accounts for its considerable political influence. Yet its very size and diversity also often complicates the group's decision-making process, making it difficult for the organization as a whole to take public positions on any but the most general issues of economic policy. Even relatively simple problems can require busy senior business executives to sit through meeting after lengthy meeting, to explore possible compromise positions, only to produce after many hours a purposely vague statement of general principles, the chief virtue of which is that it offends no member of the group, but which also because of its vagueness has little chance of influencing the policy-making process either for or against business.

The yen revaluation issue cut back and forth across important corporate interests within Keidanren. It was, to be sure, vitally important to every member. Everyone was concerned about it. Yet any specific settlement scenario had different implications for different companies and sectors of business. The interests of Japan's bankers were not necessarily those of her manufacturers; exporters differed with importers; heavy industrial interests with long-term contracts saw things differently from representatives of lighter industry with their more rapid turnover periods.

All Keidanren members could agree on the need for a healthy Japanese economy in which to pursue their interests, and an international economic environment as open as possible to Japanese commercial and financial penetration. They all agreed that government officials should "do something" to help undo the inevitable damage caused by "their" revaluation. The trick was to reach agreement on the specifics. Toward this end, Vice Chairman Horikoshi was asked to form a "Roundtable on Parity Adjustment Countermeasures" (Heika Chosei Taisaku ni Kan-suru Kondankai) to discuss the impact of the yen float on business negotiations and the question of compensation. Horikoshi's group included fifteen representatives of many of the industries most sensitive to revaluation, including the shipping, automobile, and the heavy and electrical machinery sectors.

After a meeting on October 4 at Keidanren's headquarters building, the group announced basic agreement on the need for a rapid settlement of the yen problem, and on the need to increase government funding for the export-bill-buying program designed to facilitate exchange transactions. The group also agreed to support the government's opposition to direct compensation for yen revaluation-related losses suffered by business, concluding it would be more appropriate to pay any compensation required indirectly through the tax system. Finally, in place of more specific recommendations, the Horikoshi group urged the government to devise an overall program through which to deal together with the problems of economic stimulation and compensation.[21]

The yen compensation issue also appeared on the agenda of the Commercial Law Subcommittee of Keidanren's Legal System Advisory Council. This group, headed by Professor Takeo Suzuki of Tokyo University, held a meeting on October 6 to explore the possibility of a revision of the commercial law which would allow exchange loss-impacted companies to spread out the declaration of those losses for income tax purposes over a number of years, thereby increasing the total deduction. The subcommittee also considered proposals for the formation of a special fund to compensate business losses during periods of fluctuating exchange rates.[22]

On Monday of the following week the Japan Chamber of Commerce announced basic agreement with Keidanren's earlier suggestion that the national tax system should be revised to allow indirect compensation to corporations suffering foreign exchange loss during the float, especially an extension of the length of time losses could be declared,[23] and the following Tuesday the Nihon Boeki-kai (Japan Foreign Trade Council) published its petition to the government for the formation of an exchange loss compensation similar to that recently proposed by Keidanren, noting they had been suggesting the implementation of such a system since 1968.[24]

In sum, by September members of Japan's business community had become badly shaken by the difficulties they were experiencing with foreign exchange transactions caused by management of the float. They were rapidly losing confidence in the international moneymen's ability to handle the critical situation on their own with no business feedback; they felt justified in demanding government compensation for business losses attributable to foreign exchange problems, and reached the point that they were willing to press their complaints and demands for compensation in public.

But to the international moneymen this public bickering seemed very much like playing with matches near gasoline. Finance Minister Mizuta himself led the effort to reestablish congruence of opinion between the government and Japan's business community on international monetary affairs. Soon after his return from London he announced plans to breakfast with the leaders of both Keidanren and Keizai Doyukai to ask for their "cooperation" on the international monetary issue, especially on the suggestion that Japan move to a unilateral revaluation rather than continue the float.[25] The same day he took his message to the bankers at a meeting of the Association of Financial Organizations [Kinyu Dantai Kyogikai]: exchange rate adjustment would take time; a unilateral revaluation of the yen was neither wise nor contemplated; and the MOF was doing all that was possible to formulate long-term policies with which to cope with the inevitable dislocations.[26]

By late October the business community's leadership understood that a unilateral revaluation wouldn't accomplish Japan's long-term objectives and that they must wait for a multilateral political settlement. Much to the relief of the MOF and Bank of Japan, this quieted for the time being overt business criticism of their actions. Still, business's skepticism of the government's abilities continued to be expressed in other ways. For example, in light of the textile restraint situation and the drawn-out process toward a revaluation of the yen, the Keidanren staff began to study the feasibility of improving the government's institutional framework for coordinating economic policy. They planned to study the American system of presidential assistants, especially the Council on International Economic Policy recently established by President Nixon.

On October 26 Keidanren announced plans to call a meeting of the other major Japanese business organizations in a "Joint Conference of Economic Organizations to Promote Administrative Reform" [Gyosei Kaikaku Suishin Keizai Dantai Godo Kaigi]. Although no substantial progress was made on bureaucratic reform in the end, they were able to politely express their dissatisfaction with the Japanese government's handling of the yen issue by public disclosure of their plans.

Looking back on the confused first few months after Japan's plunge from an exchange rate fixed at Y 360 = $1 for over 20 years to a floating rate, the record shows that both government and business estimates of the negative economic consequences were far worse than actual performance. The 1971 yen crisis in the long-term was a far more important political than economic shock, and by October the government's statistical releases had begun to indicate this more moderate impact. One of the earliest statistical indicators of foreign trade performance is MITI's monthly announcement of export approval figures for the previous month. On October 12 MITI reported that export approvals for September 1971 were up 19.7 percent over the previous year. Although like increases for previous months of 1971 had all been larger than 20 percent, this announcement indicated that Japan's exports were nowhere nearly as severely stymied during the first full month under the float as expected.[27]

This optimistic trend was confirmed a few days later by the Finance Ministry's release of its preliminary estimates of actual balance-of-payments transactions—as opposed to MITI's previously mentioned approval figure—during September. According to the MOF, Japan's exports during September were nearly 6 percent lower than those during September 1970, a disappointment to be sure, but not the avalanching decline that both government and business had feared. The MOF was careful in its release to attribute the decline to the U.S. import surcharge and the American West Coast dock strike rather than to problems with the yen float.[28]

More official reassurance of economic life after the yen shock was released by MITI the following Monday, this time the results of a September survey of the 14 largest trading companies. According to MITI, the immediate effect of the yen shock was a severe blow to their ongoing export contract negotiations, but by September the companies estimated they were back to between 50 and 70 percent of normal.[29] These and other similar public announcements made it clear that by October the government was doing what it could to reduce public panic over the negative impact of the yen float, and by the end of the month the panic that struck Japan's business community had given way to a more rational appraisal of the situation, even with the inconveniences of the managed float to contend with.

Domestic Political Opposition. LDP antimainstream faction leaders and the policy strategists of the major opposition parties recognized the international monetary crisis as an appropriate instrument with which to attack the Sato Cabinet during its waning years. By September 1971 Eisaku Sato had served continuously as prime minister for nearly seven years, longer than any of his predecessors, whose average tenure in office (excepting those who held office less than a year) was just over three years. Tokyo was full of speculation about "post-Sato" Japanese national politics, particularly about who would emerge victorious from the LDP factional bloodletting that would decide Sato's successor.

MOF "Old Boy" Takeo Fukuda, then Foreign Minister, was the odds makers' favorite by late 1971. He had served in all of the LDP and government positions usually expected of a serious prime ministerial candidate. Particularly well known for his expertise in economic policy, he had served as Finance Minister until May 1971. Fukuda looked and acted like a traditional Japanese prime minister. It was clear that he expected to succeed Sato when the change was made.

Although Fukuda seemed to have the edge over other candidates, the race was far from decided in late 1971. Kakuei Tanaka, who sat next to Fukuda in the Cabinet as Minister of International Trade and Industry, was another strong contender. Tanaka, a "party politician" rather than a former career bureaucrat and graduate of the elite Law Faculty of Tokyo University, had a political style quite different from that of the more traditional Fukuda. A plainspoken "wheeler-dealer" who certainly was expected to play an important behind-the-scenes role in determining the outcome of the race, Tanaka was so unlike past prime ministers in background and political style that his prospects had to be given rather long odds.

Underdog Tanaka, however, made it clear that he intended to make a serious run to succeed Sato once he decided to step down. And as the months of 1971 went by, the skill with which he manipulated his personal relationships in and out of government and his highly visible cabinet position to that end had impressed even the skeptics. Tanaka knew that as a cabinet member, out-and-out opposition to Sato or his policies—or even to chief opponent and fellow cabinet member Fukuda—was beyond the pale of acceptable political behavior. Such action would expose him to charges of political opportunism and selfishness, and label him as being more concerned about becoming prime minister than about the party—all essential attributes for a prime ministerial candidate, but attributes that winning candidates succeeded in disguising one way or another.

So, in contrast to antimainstream LDP faction leaders unfettered by cabinet positions, throughout the crisis Tanaka avoided overt criticism of the Sato Cabinet and MOF officials' handling of the yen issue and instead focused his efforts on being perceived within the party as being as much a team player as one could expect a prime ministerial candidate to be, and on being perceived by the general public and business community as an innovative MITI minister devoting full time to the protection of their economic interests in the face of world economic crisis.

Masayoshi Ohira took advantage of his exclusion from the current cabinet to make a direct attack on the Sato Cabinet's handling of the yen issue. Speaking to the youth group organized by his *koenkai* (personal political support group) in Hakone on September 28, 1971, Ohira criticized the length of time it was taking the international moneymen and the current cabinet to reach agreement on this critical issue.[30] He hammered away at the need for Japan to return immediately to a fixed exchange rate, implying by his criticism that such a move was possible under existing conditions. He even suggested publicly that Japan should consider a unilateral revaluation of the yen if that was the only method of reestablishing the fixed rate system. Of course, suggestions for such action by an influential member of the ruling party only intensified the sense of pressure on the policy core of Japan's international monetary bureaucrats, who feared the reaction of their international negotiating partners upon hearing that news item.

Takeo Miki, another antimainstream LDP faction leader who always seemed more comfortable at the edges of power playing the "barely inside outsider" role, and who had spent most of his long parliamentary career preaching the need for party reform, took up the international monetary issue during a September 30 speech to a research group affiliated with his faction. In a statement even more hostile than Ohira's, Miki called for Prime Minister Sato's resignation. Although the yen issue was not the only thing about Mr. Sato's stewardship troubling Mr. Miki in late September, he suggested in his widely published remarks that for Japan to overcome its international difficulties—including international monetary difficulties—domestic problems first had to be solved through a change in political leadership. In case anyone missed the point, Mr. Miki informed the group that he was available to succeed Sato as prime minister should Sato decide to accept Miki's political advice and step down.[31]

It was not surprising that Ohira, Miki, and other LDP antimainstream leaders took political advantage of the Sato Cabinet's international monetary predicament. But their actions placed even more psychological pressure on the overburdened international monetary bureaucrats, who feared such public statements would be picked up by their American and European counterparts and used to weaken Japan's position during the upcoming negotiations. While the Americans and Europeans battled over the configuration of the final settlement, the professionals were doing their best to "hold the line" with as little change in the status quo as possible, while at the same time projecting the international image of a cooperative economic partner. Such charges might well be used by foreigners dissatisfied with Japan's liberalization progress or the level of yen parity increase allowed under the float as evidence that even the Japanese agreed among themselves that Japan should be doing more to reach a settlement.

For the Japan Socialist party (JSP), Komeito (KMT), Democratic Socialist party (DSP), and Japan Communist party (JCP), yen revaluation lacked the raw emotional appeal of nuclear disarmament, but it did concern Japan's relations with the United States. It seemed almost tailor-made as an issue with which to press the opposition parties' long-espoused contention that successive postwar LDP cabinets had been "in error" in pursuing high-growth economic policies at all costs, and that there were hidden costs to be paid for Japan's excessive reliance on the United States.

Each opposition party set up an ad hoc yen problem committee, such as the JSP's Yen Problem Committee (En Mondai Kenkyukai), established in September under the Policy Advisory Council (Seisaku Shingikai), and the DSP's Special Committee on International Monetary Policy [Kokusai Tsuka Taisaku Tokubetsu Iinkai].[32] These committees met as often as possible, coordinating information and analysis on this poorly understood subject, and calling leading economic experts and government officials to testify at public and closed hearings. The committees were always striving to take maximum advantage of the issue's high visibility to gain publicity for their contention that Japan found herself in the current crisis because of both the LDP's excessive reliance on the relationship with the United States in the past, and its failure to adopt opposition-supported welfare-state economic policies.

The JSP's Yen Problem Committee was the most active of these ad hoc investigative opposition groups. But, like the rest of the opposition parties' activities, these groups had little or no influence on the actual formulation and implementation of government policy. Designed to appeal more to individuals already committed to a particular opposition party's overall position than the average citizen, it is unlikely their efforts even swayed heretofore uncommitted public opinion—the one avenue of actual policy influence open to them—either one way or the other. Their activities were reported by the print journalists assigned to the opposition party press clubs, but the stories usually appeared in the midst of other economic or political news with little emphasis, almost as if their opinions and actions were too predictable to warrant extensive coverage.

According to one JSP member who played an important role in the party's consideration of the yen problem, party members realized the importance of the issue but its specifics were only vaguely understood by most of the participants. There was little discussion of the actual economic implications of a parity change during party committee and subcommittee meetings. Conventional "opposition" wisdom was that a parity change would weaken Japanese labor's position in the international market and therefore that revaluation should be resisted.[33] In other words, the opposition agreed with the position of the LDP and business community—if for slightly different reasons. This congruence of ultimate objectives made it more difficult for the JSP and the rest of the opposition parties to exploit the yen issue more effectively.

Charges of Government-Big Bank Collusion. In early October, at the very time the confidence of the public and the business community in the abilities of the international moneymen was at its lowest level in memory, the opposition did unearth one issue that had potential political impact. They questioned the credibility—indeed, the personal honesty—of the international monetary officials of the Bank of Japan and Ministry of Finance, suggesting they had manipulated the yen crisis at the expense of the public treasury and to the benefit of Japan's big banks—banks where many of these same officials could expect to get comfortable jobs after retirement.

Meetings of the Upper and Lower House Budget Committees traditionally serve as stages for public display of the give-and-take between the LDP and the opposition, and even between the mainstream and antimainstream factions of the ruling party. Often televised and routinely covered by communications media reporters, these question-and-answer sessions of the two committees often provide as interesting political theater as is normally available in Nagata-cho (Tokyo's "Capitol Hill").

The Thursday, September 30, offering proved more interesting than most. Socialist party member Shizuo Wada unexpectedly charged during an impassioned statement to the Upper House Budget Committee that an unnamed Bank of Japan official had notified "certain interests" of the government's decision to float the yen just prior to the public announcement. This advance notice, Wada charged, gave those "interests" time to sell off huge portions of their dollar holdings—dollars that would lose value vis-à-vis the yen after the float—in the foreign exchange market while the government was still obligated to absorb them through intervention purchases under the fixed rate system.[34]

Deputy Director General of the Finance Ministry's International Monetary Bureau, Taizo Hayashi, detailed to attend the hearing that day to respond to any questions concerning international monetary affairs, replied to Wada's charge by admitting that four foreign exchange banks and five trading companies alone had been responsible for sales of around $2.6 billion after the dollar shock. Hayashi even admitted that it was quite possible some of the exchange transactions made were to cover fictitious international contracts, in violation of foreign exchange regulations, to allow the companies to purchase yen with what looked like an inevitably depreciating U.S. dollar. When pressed, Hayashi refused to give the names of the banks and trading companies.

Wada was not satisfied with Hayashi's response. He continued his attack by charging that Bank of Japan international monetary official Shiro Inoue had made a personal visit to the Dai-Ichi Bank the day before the float was announced to inform Senior Vice President Muramoto of plans for the float, and to suggest the bank sell down their huge stock of dollars while it still could at the old, more beneficial rate. Wada said he had obtained information that indicated that the Dai-Ichi, Sumitomo, Tokyo, and Tokai banks were the four largest sellers of dollars in the market just prior to the float announcement, and that their sales could have been made only on the basis of prior information. Wada demanded that the Budget Committee call Inoue of the Bank of Japan and Muramoto of Dai-Ichi Bank as witnesses before the committee to answer his charges. LDP committee members would not agree to Wada's demand that the committee call Muramoto, a private citizen, as a witness. But they did agree that Inoue would be called to testify on the 5th of October, as soon as he returned from the annual meeting of the IMF, then in progress in Washington.

The Ministry of Finance knew that somehow Wada had obtained specific information about the government's activities during that sensitive period because of the accuracy of his statement concerning the banks' transactions. The MOF finally released the information Wada had demanded on October 30. It detailed the foreign exchange transactions of the banks (including those mentioned in

Wada's statement), and trading companies between August 16 and August 27, as requested. Approximately $3.9 billion had been traded during that period alone, over five times the market volume during the Deutsche mark crisis in May, the largest disturbance in the foreign exchange market prior to August. The data released also indicated that most of those purchases made in advance of actual transactions ("leads"), in violation of foreign exchange regulations and laws, did not have contracts to back them up, indicating their speculative nature.[35] Upon hearing the news of Wada's Budget Committee bombshell, Dai-Ichi Bank's Muramoto issued an immediate and flat denial. Muramoto said that his responsibility for foreign exchange at the bank brought him in frequent contact with Mr. Inoue, but he denied any meeting on August 26 as Wada had charged. He offered to so testify before the committee should they request his presence.[36]

Preoccupied with the discussions in Washington during the IMF and World Bank annual meetings, Inoue waited until his return to Tokyo on November 3 to respond publicly to Wada's charge. That afternoon he was questioned about the incident during a press conference arranged for the Japanese delegation at Haneda Airport. In contrast to Mr. Muramoto's recollection, Inoue remembered his personal visit to Muramoto on August 26, the day before the float announcement. But in contrast to Wada's charge, he said he visited the bank to warn against excessive sales of dollars during that sensitive period. Inoue added that he had contacted several other banks on the afternoon of the 26th and the morning of the 27th, both by telephone and personal visits to the banks. When asked why he took the unusual step of a personal visit to the banks, Inoue said that he did so to impress them with the importance of holding down dollar sales that might later be considered speculative by the government.[37]

Inoue was able to face directly Wada's accusation that he had leaked information prior to the yen float on the following Tuesday during an appearance before a morning session of the Upper House Budget Committee. Wada, seeming to have obtained additional information over the weekend, began by accusing Inoue of contacting seven foreign exchange banks on the 26th and 27th to inform them of the government's decision to announce a float of the yen on Friday evening, August 27. Inoue responded that he had, in fact, personally visited the Tokyo, Fuji, Mitsubishi, Sumitomo, Sanwa, Dai-Ichi, and Mitsui banks on the 27th. But he repeated his contention that the visits were to warn the banks against speculative sales of dollars for yen rather than to give any advance warning of the float decision. He reminded the committee that Japan's foreign exchange market had been relatively quiet on the 23rd, 24th and 25th of August. But on the 26th a large amount of dollars were sold, and it was this sudden increase in dollar transactions, he said, that prompted his somewhat unusual action.[38]

Inoue further argued during the Upper House Budget Committee hearing that it would have been impossible for him to have given the banks prior notice of the float because he himself didn't know the decision to move to a float had been made. He said he knew there was strong support for a float within the MOF and Bank of Japan but he had not been informed of its timing. Later in the hearing, Finance Minister Mizuta confirmed Inoue's statement, saying that he kept the timing of the announcement to himself until the very last moment, hoping to avoid any such leaks of information and the financial confusion that would result. Mizuta told the committee he did not believe Inoue knew when the float was to be made.[39]

Mr. Inoue's spirited self-defense, and the supporting testimony by Finance Minister Mizuta and others, helped to contain this potentially explosive issue within manageable boundaries at a time when Japan's international moneymen could ill afford further weakening of their authority through what could have become a serious scandal. Yet, five years after the event, several policy observers and participants—all most reluctant to discuss the subject—hinted during off-the-record interviews that Japan's government officials had decided to notify the foreign exchange banks of the government's decision to float in advance to allow them to sell down their large holdings of dollars—dollars that had been accumulated earlier in the year, in part, at government insistence and with a guarantee that the parity of the yen would never be changed. When pressed, they justified the decision on the grounds that the disastrous financial impact on Japan's banking community would have been unfairly distributed if the government had simply floated the yen without such prior notification. Those banks that in the past had been the most cooperative with the government by agreeing to absorb large quantities of dollars when requested (and assured by the requesting officials that the parity would never be allowed to change) would have suffered the heaviest losses. The interviewees also suggested that the public treasury was better able to absorb the loss than were the banks, and that the immediate financial losses to the government created less overall damage in Japan than would have occurred should the major exchange banks have been required to shoulder the losses themselves. Bank failures were a possibility, and surely the working relationship between Japan's major banks and the government—a factor they considered important in effective economic policy implementation—would have been seriously damaged.

The International Scene: Europe and the United States Square Off

More International Meetings. During this anxious period of mid-September to early November, Japan's international moneymen prepared for and participated in two sets of important international meetings. The first focused on the long-anticipated annual meeting of the International Monetary Fund and the World Bank held in Washington between September 27 and October 1. The second, the previously decided-upon meetings of subcabinet "working-level" officials, was scheduled for Paris in mid-October, between the 18th and the 20th. Japan's strategy remained the same: appear concerned, cooperative, and willing to compromise; gather information on the timing of a final decision; and avoid mistakes. As usual, Japan's representatives seemed more concerned about how they would be required to respond to the decisions agreed upon by other participants than they were in trying to affect outcomes.

The 1971 IMF and World Bank Annual Meetings. With fundamental differences of opinion still dividing the Nixon administration's negotiators and their European counterparts, no one expected the 1971 international monetary crisis to be resolved at the IMF annual meeting. The various conferences in Washington—formal and informal, multilateral and bilateral—were expected to provide the key actors with yet another opportunity to measure the impact of their own behavior on that of their international counterparts in preparation for another, hopefully more successful, round of discussions.

On the evening of September 23, Finance Minister Mizuta and his entourage left Tokyo for Washington prepared to propose to the assembled representatives a two-part systemic reform that would shift "key currency" responsibility from the U.S. dollar to the SDR

(Special Drawing Rights), thus allowing more flexibility in the fluctuation of exchange rates. These were solid, safe proposals, neither new nor radical, unlikely to surprise the assembled European dignitaries or their American hosts. More significant, Mizuta publicly announced he was authorized to agree to a change in the parity of the yen if such change could be made in the context of an overall international agreement.[40] This aspect of Japan's position at least had some relevance for the eventual solution to the crisis situation, and indicated Japan's flexibility and willingness to cooperate to achieve an eventual solution to the problem.

Taking advantage of the annual IMF and World Bank meetings in Washington, the Group of Ten finance ministers' representatives were scheduled to meet on September 25 from 3:30 P.M. (4:30 A.M. the 26th, Japan time), in preparation for a meeting of the ministers themselves the following day. According to Yusuke Kashiwagi, the key Japanese participant, some progress was made in Washington. In contrast to the last meeting of the group earlier in the month, during which they couldn't even agree on a list of topics for discussion, all participants at the Group of Ten's meeting in Washington agreed on the need for solutions to the following four questions:

1. The amount and method of parity adjustment, with "method" referring to whether or not the parity adjustment would include a dollar devaluation, and if included, the form it should take
2. Whether or not the final settlement should include wider margins of allowable rate fluctuation
3. Specific requirements for the removal of the American 10 percent surcharge on dutiable imports
4. Whether or not trade and investment liberalization issues and levels of defense spending should be included in the overall discussions[41]

After more than a month of direct and indirect discussion, the world's ten most important finance ministers by the beginning of the 1971 annual meetings had only decided what it was that they should discuss. But, given the difficulty of the issue, even this was judged great progress. The *New York Times* even suggested Connally and the rest of the administration might have become more flexible on what was shaping up to be the key issue: dollar devaluation.[42] During a meeting with the Japanese press following the meetings, Minister Mizuta expressed modest optimism. After noting the situation was considerably better than that which he had faced earlier in London, Mizuta said many difficult "technical problems" still remained that would have to be resolved at the working-level meetings scheduled for mid-October before any final multilateral agreement could be achieved by the ministers themselves.[43]

The most important international monetary discussions were concluded in Washington at the end of the Group of Ten's ministers' meeting on Sunday night the 26th, and most of what remained was ceremony. The following Tuesday, September 28, the IMF opened its annual meeting. In his opening address, Executive Director Schweitzer told the assembled delegates that abolition of the 10 percent American surcharge was the most important business before the group, and reminded the American representatives that agreement to devalue the dollar would help solve the problem.[44]

Finance Minister Mizuta spoke on the following day and urged rapid return to fixed exchange rates. He also proposed, as planned, that the role of the SDR be expanded while that of the U.S. dollar be limited, and he expressed Japan's willingness to adjust the yen's parity as long as such adjustment occurred within the context of a multilateral exchange rate settlement.[45] Having completed his part in the program, Mizuta left Washington on Wednesday afternoon, the 29th, for a one-night stopover in Los Angeles and the long return flight to Tokyo, without even hearing the speeches of Connally and the other delegates to the annual meeting.

That efforts to solve the most serious international monetary crisis in the postwar period were being staffed and conducted within the organizational framework of the Group of Ten's finance ministers' meetings rather than that of the IMF itself did not go unnoticed at the Fund's Washington headquarters. Earlier in the month, fearing further weakening of the Fund's role in international monetary affairs, Pieter Lieftinck, executive director (Netherlands), suggested that the IMF Executive Board should prepare its own suggestions for dealing with the situation in the form of a resolution the board would present at the upcoming annual meeting.

The board's initiative was delayed, however, by disagreement over the specific role it should play and the wording of a resolution. Nevertheless, lack of progress in other areas increased pressure on the Board to produce something that would help to defend the IMF's position within the debate. Working with a preliminary draft prepared by Edwin Dale, executive director (United States), the executive directors met during the annual meetings—an unusual event—to draft a resolution to be presented to the IMF Governors on Friday, October 1, the last day of the meetings.

The resolution called upon all IMF members to collaborate with the Fund and with each other to bring about a reversal of the tendency to maintain and extend restrictive trade and exchange practices, and to establish as promptly as possible a satisfactory structure of exchange rates, to be maintained within appropriate margins for their currencies.[46]

Mizuta's critical comments about the role of the United States in international monetary affairs were mild when compared to those of the Europeans. The French were particularly hostile, insisting that the United States agree to participate in any scheme for exchange rate readjustment with devaluation of the U.S. dollar.[47] Secretary Connally replied to his critics in a September 30 address to the group. In response to the French demand that dollar devaluation (a change in the official U.S. dollar price of gold) be part of the final settlement, Connally insisted that arguments over the price of gold were meaningless since the United States hoped for a reduction in the monetary role of gold as part of the settlement. As for suspension of the 10 percent surcharge on imports, Connally agreed to consider its abolition as soon as other countries were willing to allow their currencies to "float freely."[48]

The long-awaited 1971 annual meeting of the IMF ended with little more than an endorsement of a nonbinding resolution to return as soon as possible to fixed exchange rates and promote a more open international trading system.[49]

Mizuta returned to Tokyo on Friday evening, October 1. He seized the opportunity provided by the public's heightened interest over Japan's participation in a major international conference to argue against domestic and foreign criticism of the government's handling of the controlled float. A unilateral revaluation of the yen without prior multilateral agreement on exchange rates, Mizuta insisted, would prove meaningless. And in anticipation of domestic demands that the government suspend the float as suggested by Connally in order to win suspension of the U.S. import surcharge, Mizuta insisted that under current circumstances no country in the world could expect to maintain a truly free floating exchange rate. Again Mizuta stressed the point he had made at the end of the Group of Ten's ministers' meeting that "technical" problems remained for the specialists to work out before any final agreement could be reached at his level.[50]

Even after the late September annual IMF meetings, the Group of Ten's political actors hoped their international monetary specialist subordinates could bring the diverse national positions of Europe, Japan, and the United States closer to agreement through solution of what Mizuta and his counterparts described as "technical" problems. To the extent the compromises required could be thrashed out among the specialist deputies, the political risk the ministers ran during the final settlement was reduced.

The Mid-October Technical Meetings. The last major technical staff-level efforts were made to resolve the international monetary crisis in mid-October during the OECD's Working Party Three meeting in Paris on October 18 and the Group of Ten's representatives' meeting the following two days. Japan's delegation, led by Vice Minister Hosomi and Special Adviser Kashiwagi, hoped to counter the growing European and American anti-Japan rhetoric by announcing their intention to propose a "Japan Round" of tariff reduction negotiations at the next annual meeting of GATT (The General Agreement on Tariffs and Trade) in November. This proposal had been strongly encouraged by GATT Executive Director Long during a recent visit to Tokyo.[51] Long also assured the senior officials with whom he met in Tokyo that the European members of his organization intended to demand that the United States remove the import surcharge on the grounds that it was a clear violation of GATT.

The OECD's Working Party Three began to discuss the international monetary situation at 10:30 A.M. on the 18th, with emphasis on the sensitive issue of cross-rate adjustment. With most of its trade denominated in U.S. dollars, Japan was concerned primarily with the parity of the yen vis-à-vis that single currency. The European situation was far more complex. They had to worry about sudden changes in competitiveness among themselves—and with the Japanese. The OECD group's meeting continued over to the following day. The discussions were described later as "very difficult," meaning the U.S. representatives were still in no mood to compromise on what the Europeans loudly characterized as their unreasonable demands. Under Secretary Paul Volcker still insisted that he and Secretary Connally intended to hold out for assurance of a $13 billion turnaround in the American trade balance before they would consider removing the surcharge or any final agreement on exchange rates.[52]

After the Group of Ten's representatives' meeting the following day, Chairman Rinaldo Ossola (vice governor of the Bank of Italy) announced that he and his colleagues had advanced to the point at which they could discuss the *overall* amount of up-valuation required to achieve various levels of improvement in the U.S. balance of payments. But, Ossola said, it proved impossible for this "technical" group to discuss the level of change required for any specific currency since that was a "political" and not a "technical" question.[53] Ossola also confirmed information leaked earlier by Japan's delegation that the next Group of Ten's ministerial meeting (i.e., the people required to make the "political" decision) was expected in mid-November.

Vice Minister Hosomi echoed Ossola's pessimism during his post-meeting press briefings in Paris and after his return to Tokyo: "The negotiations have moved away from the administrative level and now depend upon the political decisions of the leadership of the various countries. I have the impression that the outlook for a solution within this year is about forty percent."[54] Special Adviser Kashiwagi, writing after the event, agreed. Surveying the process of reaching an agreement between August 15 and December 18, he identified the mid-October Paris meetings as the point at which the specialists finally realized that no "technical" fix was possible, and from which the negotiations moved to the more purely "political" realm. But persuading their political superiors to accept that conclusion was another matter.[55]

Recognition—at least among the specialist "technicians"—of the impossibility of a "technical" fix meant that the contending countries were at least better positioned by mid-October to reach final settlement than before. Hopes for a solution by the end of the year grew brighter. But this realization also brought with it more direct involvement of the political principals, which meant future negotiations were likely to be less controlled and less predictable than those in the past. Since August 15 Secretary Connally and the Nixon administration had been calling for a "comprehensive" settlement to the American balance-of-payments problem—trade-investment liberalization and more defense "burden-sharing" as well as parity adjustments. The expansion of the "political" component of the negotiations after mid-October made discussion of the "comprehensive" solution more likely.

The Europeans. Japan's international moneymen kept close track of their European counterparts throughout the period. At the beginning of the intense crisis there had been some hope in Tokyo that Japan might join an informal alliance, either with Canada or with one or more of the European countries, to more effectively resist Connally's unreasonable demands. Those hopes had evaporated by the end of the bilateral talks in mid-September. Japan's representatives discovered that mutual frustration with Connally's excesses was an inadequate base upon which to build such an "alliance." Even if the Europeans were willing—a very big "if" in late 1971—Japan's greater economic, diplomatic, and military dependence upon the United States, when compared with that on Europe, meant opportunities for an international coalition with European partners were severely limited on the Japanese side.

Another possibility, with the potential for real change in the way the game was played, was the achievement of agreement among some or all of the European countries on their points of difference that would be adequate to permit joint action vis-à-vis the United States. This too proved difficult. But Japan kept close track of developments in Europe as the EEC countries struggled to accommodate their differences. Japan joined Europe in rejecting Connally's demand for a $13 billion balance-of-payments turnaround. And Japan was also inclined to support the European demand that the United States agree to devalue the dollar as part of any move to change parities.[56]

The United States Bides Her Time. Nixon Administration Objectives and Actions. During the latter half of September and the month of October, Treasury Secretary John Connally remained in firm control of American international economic policy. If the international bankers and monetary professionals found him inexperienced and unpredictable, Connally's "take-charge" attitude, self-confidence, and willingness to talk tough to foreigners seemed to appeal to President Nixon. Complaints from abroad did little to shake Connally's firm control of the international monetary aspects of U.S. economic policy.

Connally continued to play the international economic game as he defined it for the world on the night of August 15 during his explanation of President Nixon's celebrated speech:

1. Render the international economic status quo unacceptable to other national players through suspension of the convertibility of the dollar and imposition of the 10 percent surcharge
2. Define only a broad, ultimate objective—a $13 billion turnaround

in the U.S. balance of payments—as the price to return things to normal by agreement on a system of new fixed parities and abolition of the surcharge
3. Refuse to discuss specific compromise measures which affect the turnaround in the U.S. balance of payments, hoping to heighten international tensions, confuse the opposition, and win higher levels of concession than otherwise possible

This negotiating strategy was criticized as unnecessarily tough and risky at the time, but viewed from Connally's side of the table it made sense. After the August 15 surprise announcement, the United States held only two bargaining chips of interest to the Europeans: suspension of the 10 percent surcharge and agreement to reset the parities of the world's currencies at "reasonable" levels. In contrast, the administration could identify several causes for the rapid deterioration in the U.S. balance of payments during the last few years, each representing a bargaining chip of interest to the Americans held by the Europeans and/or the Japanese. An improvement in any single one or even two causes of the U.S. deficit would have had little effect. A "chip-for-chip" approach for the United States risked the danger of running out of "chips" before significant progress had been made toward her primary objective.

The Europeans—especially the French—had long resented the privileged position the U.S. dollar enjoyed as the world's "key currency." They demanded the United States join, even if only symbolically, in the final adjustment process through a devaluation of the dollar when other currencies were up-valued. Connally and the rest of the administration from the beginning flatly refused even to consider any dollar devaluation proposal. Pointing to the need for congressional approval of a change in the official price of gold, Connally said a devaluation was politically impossible. In addition to the domestic political dimension, he said the administration itself opposed the idea since that would strengthen the role of gold in the international monetary system, in opposition to their wish to reduce gold's international monetary role.

Secretary Connally stood firmly opposed to any dollar devaluation scheme throughout September and October, convincing most observers that he and the administration were serious in their opposition. On September 24, after nearly two hours of sharp questioning by the Senate Finance Committee, he announced that there was no change in the administration's opposition to a change in the price of gold.[57] He repeated this position during a press conference after the Group of Ten's ministers' meeting in Washington on September 25, and added that it was his hope to reduce, rather than expand, the monetary role of gold.[58]

By September the dollar devaluation issue had become a key issue in the multilateral and bilateral search for a final settlement. The political situation in Europe had reached the point at which a settlement that did not include at least token dollar devaluation would be most difficult. So, with the other participants more anxious than the United States to regain international monetary stability, the question became what was required by the U.S. side in order to make them soften their opposition to considering a devaluation. Secretary Connally found one more bargaining chip on his side of the table.

The administration throughout September and October also maintained its firm opposition to removal of the import surcharge. Revocation, they insisted, would be considered only after the United States could be sure of a long-term solution to the balance-of-payments problem. The surcharge, even more than the suspension of the convertibility of the dollar into gold, stimulated charges at home and abroad of "protectionism," a criticism to which Republicans have some historical sensitivity. By October Connally and other administration officials were responding to these charges of "protectionism" by linking removal of the surcharge to improvement in the unfair trading practices of foreign countries. The surcharge, they argued, was not itself a protectionist measure. It was a tool employed temporarily in the fight against protectionism. President Nixon added his weight during a nationally televised speech on October 7 in which he distinguished between "free trade" and "fair trade." The United States, Nixon insisted, was not protectionist, and still believed in "free trade" that was at the same time "fair trade."[59]

During a press conference the following day Secretary Connally responded indirectly to a question about removal of the surcharge by saying the administration expected the elimination of many foreign barriers to U.S. exports in the near future.[60] Although still not specific about the type or level of liberalization the Administration required, he clearly linked such liberalization to the suspension of the surcharge. He also avoided speculating on the timing of the surcharge's suspension.

The first mention Connally made of any time limit for the surcharge was during an ABC television interview on October 17.[61] When asked how long the surcharge would remain in place, he hinted it could be removed within two or three months. But, then again, it might take as long as three or four months. This mention of a specific period of time was big news in Japan. A few days later he seemed to revert to his more rigid position, telling the American Bankers Association's annual meeting in San Francisco that the surcharge would be maintained until the United States was again in a position to defend its balance of payments.[62] And, in case anyone got the idea that the administration had tied surcharge removal considerations to trade and investment liberalization progress alone (excluding parity changes), during a speech on October 16 to the Business Council in Hot Springs, Virginia, Connally hinted the United States was considering suspension of the surcharge for West Germany alone because the Germans were allowing the mark to float more freely than were other surplus countries.

Domestic Opposition to Connally's Hard Line Grows. By far the least dependent of the industrialized, market-economy countries on the international monetary system, the United States occupied the most comfortable seat in the house while playing its waiting game. But by September, Connally's hard-line strategy was making even some domestic American interests nervous about the future of the world's trading system and even about the possibility of direct or indirect damage to American economic interests. Presidential candidate George McGovern told an audience of Japanese businessmen at Keidanren in Tokyo on September 17 that he believed the Nixon administration should agree to devalue the dollar.[63] McGovern's statement could be dismissed as politically motivated, if distasteful, addressed as it was to a group of foreign businessmen. But by late September the early public enthusiasm with which President Nixon's New Economic Policy was greeted had subsided, and previously whispered criticism of Secretary Connally's implementation tactics was becoming an audible chorus.

Congressman Henry Reuss, chairman of the International Subcommittee of the Joint Economic Committee began to question the wisdom of Connally's ham-fisted approach to international economic diplomacy.[64] During a September 19 public appearance before the JEC, Reuss asked Connally when he planned to abolish the surcharge. Connally replied with his stock answer that the surcharge would be removed only after a "comprehensive" settlement of the U.S. balance-of-payments problem had been achieved.[65] Dissatisfied with Connally's approach, fearing it was responsible for unnecessary confusion at home and abroad, Reuss soon wrote a letter to Connally advising him to make more specific the administration's requirements for the removal of the surcharge.[66]

Congressman Reuss also publicly criticized the administration's refusal to consider a dollar devaluation as part of the final solution. Reuss said he had come to believe a small increase in the dollar price of gold would be appropriate if it led to an earlier multilateral settlement of the foreign currency issue.[67] He added that House Speaker Carl Albert and Ways and Means Committee chairman Wilbur Mills agreed with his position. Having heard Secretary Connally tell the world since mid-August that the administration would not consider dollar devaluation as part of the final settlement largely because of congressional opposition, Reuss' statement created great excitement in Tokyo. Reuss confirmed his change of opinion in an interview with a Japanese journalist published on September 29, adding that he believed a revaluation of the yen of between 15 and 20 percent would be appropriate.[68]

As with McGovern, Reuss' opposition—and even that of Congressmen Albert and Mills—could be dismissed by the administration as political opportunism. All three were powerful Congressional figures, to be sure. And Congressman Reuss was universally respected as one of the few members of either House who really understood international economic policy. But all three were Democrats who could be expected to have little good to say about any incumbent Republican administration's economic policies. The situation became more serious for the administration on September 30—just in the midst of the annual meeting of the International Monetary Fund—when Republican Senator Jacob Javits announced his support for Reuss' position on dollar devaluation.[69]

Throughout October this erosion of domestic support for Connally's hard-line opposition to dollar devaluation created colorful headlines abroad. On October 13 IMF official Edward M. Bernstein, one of the world's most respected international monetary authorities and an architect of the Bretton Woods system, suggested publicly that the dollar should be devalued by 12 to 15 percent, and that he believed both the U.S. Congress and the Department of Treasury were ready to move in that direction.[70] Even David Rockefeller, chairman of the board of Chase Manhattan Bank—hardly considered a "Republican Basher"—added his support for a change in the value of gold in an October 20 speech to the British National Committee of the International Chamber of Commerce in London.[71] First National City Bank chairman Walter Wriston followed Rockefeller's lead in a few days.[72] By late October it was more difficult, if not impossible, for Secretary Connally to justify his opposition to dollar devaluation on domestic political grounds. He was being publicly attacked by both political foes and supporters of the Nixon administration.

From the time of its announcement on August 15, the import surcharge had generated even more opposition than the devaluation issue. Considered likely to be a violation of international law, the surcharge was attacked by the indignant major trading countries of Europe and Japan directly and indirectly through their agents in the United States. American free trade interest groups and individuals were quick to join the foreign protesters. George Ball, Robert Roosa, John Tobin, Arthur Okun, and Richard Cooper, well-known economic authorities who had served in previous Democratic administrations, all were on record by mid-September as opposed to the surcharge.[73] Some of the critics acknowledged the effectiveness of the surcharge as a short-term threat to press foreign governments toward needed exchange rate adjustment. But its prolonged imposition, they argued, would have serious consequences for the United States as well as for foreign countries.

C. Fred Bergsten, a young economist who had recently launched a successful career in the Washington policy community with a noisy resignation from Henry Kissinger's National Security Council, suggested, for example, that continuation of the surcharge was serious enough to risk damage to our security relationships around the world, and to negatively affect overall U.S. foreign policy interests.[74] On October 8 Wilbur Mills told the U.S. Chamber of Commerce in New York that maintenance of the surcharge was likely to invite foreign retaliation, and a little over a week later Congressman Reuss pointed to the preparations for retaliation being made by France and Denmark as evidence of the harm it could cause, adding that he saw no evidence that it was actually helping to improve the American balance-of-payments problem.[75]

Secretary Connally retained control of American international economic policy as the search for agreement sufficient to warrant convocation of a final multilateral conference to reestablish a stable international monetary system dragged on from September to October. But with each passing day the international and domestic effectiveness of his "hard-line" policy declined, reducing his options and pressing even Connally toward the final settlement.

Connally's Tokyo Visit

Soon after the frustrating mid-October multilateral meetings in Paris, Secretary Connally decided the time had come to visit Japan for more detailed bilateral discussions of the international monetary crisis. Public disclosure of the visit came first from White House spokesman Ronald Zeigler on October 18.[76] Anticipation of their opportunity to confront Connally once again stimulated Japan's bureaucratic and political policymakers to reach some agreement among themselves on the issues most likely to emerge during the talks, including the yen's parity, defense burden-sharing, and the trade problems that still remained between Japan and the United States after the recent agreement on textiles.

Japanese government officials considered the Connally visit an important step toward final settlement of the yen problem. Tales of his use of loud, blustery negotiating tactics made the rounds at diplomatic receptions throughout the world, and had been reported in gruesome detail by the Japanese press. So, by the end of October all of Japan was braced to receive what came to be called the "Connally Typhoon." The international moneymen and their political superiors fully expected Connally to blow into Tokyo with a number of unreasonable and unfulfillable demands, which he would present in a loud voice to the government and the press, and then blow back out again, leaving them to clean up the mess.

The significance attributed to the Connally visit by the U.S. side was evidenced by President Nixon's comments to former Prime Minister Kishi during his October 22 visit to Washington.[77] After the meeting Kishi told the press that Nixon had nothing specific to say about the yen revaluation issue, but that he did say that he expected a final resolution of all the outstanding U.S.-Japan problems during Connally's visit to Japan. This naturally heightened Japan's expectations for the visit. Press reports of Kishi's October 30 conversation with Prime Minister Sato upon his return to Tokyo emphasized the importance President Nixon placed on the Connally visit.[78]

Paul McCracken, chairman of the president's Council of Economic Advisers, arrived in Tokyo on November 5 at the invitation of Yoshizane Iwasa's U.S.-Japan Businessmen's Conference. McCracken, cast in the role of Connally "advance man," was closely observed by the government, business community, and press for clues to what Connally really expected to accomplish after he arrived on the 9th. Speaking to a group assembled by Mr. Iwasa's organization that afternoon, McCracken insisted the United States was unable to solve its balance-of-payments problem alone, and that other countries would have to cooperate with exchange rate adjustment. He refused to speculate on the eventual amount of that adjustment, saying the decision would be more political than economic.[79]

After meeting with the business community sponsors of his visit, McCracken was entertained by Japanese government officials over the weekend. On Saturday morning he met with Prime Minister Sato, MITI Minister Tanaka, and Toshio Kimura of the EPA, and with Finance Minister Mizuta in the afternoon.[80] After McCracken's one-hour meeting with Minister Mizuta, MOF officials told the press corps that McCracken had encouraged Japan to be prepared to make firm decisions once Connally arrived, and that Mizuta had asked McCracken to relay their concern over the sluggish state of the Japanese economy and the impact of that concern on their ability to compromise on the yen.[81]

The "Texas Typhoon" himself arrived as scheduled late Tuesday night, the 9th, by government jet at Haneda Airport to begin a five-day visit. Connally was met by Finance Minister and Mrs. Mizuta and a large official welcoming party that accompanied him from the airport to his suite at the Hotel Okura. Just that day a supplementary budget had been passed by the Diet, and Connally, after being greeted by Minister Mizuta, congratulated him upon that legislative accomplishment.[82] Connally's thoughtful gesture and his surprisingly polite demeanor convinced his hosts that the Americans had made careful preparations for the visit and that the visit could well turn out to be more than a casual stopover at the end of his Asian tour. Connally told Mizuta at the airport that he had come to Tokyo to exchange opinions, not to negotiate a settlement. He hoped to close the perception gap between Japan and the United States on international monetary problems.

The following day, after a briefing by Ambassador Armin Meyer and the U.S. Embassy staff, the discussion meetings began at the Hotel Okura at 9:45 A.M. Mizuta was accompanied by Yusuke Kashiwagi, Takashi Hosomi, and Koichi Inamura of the International

Monetary Bureau of the MOF. The interpretation was done by Toyoo Gyohten, Hosomi's office director. After the morning discussions, Mr. and Mrs. Mizuta hosted a midday reception for Connally to which various high-ranking Japanese government officials were invited.

The Japanese newspapers reported in their afternoon editions that during a brief discussion Mizuta had encouraged Connally to work toward an early international monetary settlement and not to hold out for unreasonable demands, to which Connally had responded that the inability of the Europeans to reach agreement among themselves might well delay the next scheduled Group of Ten meeting.[83] The press was not told, and therefore did not report, that Connally told his Japanese hosts he hoped to obtain their secret agreement to a substantial level of yen up-valuation, which he could then use behind the scenes to persuade the Europeans to fall into line. He strongly, but politely, urged Mizuta to agree to a parity change of more than 20 percent, while at the same time pressing the case for beef and citrus liberalization. Mizuta and his colleagues listened politely to Connally's arguments and did their best to explain the domestic political and economic difficulty such agreement would cause for them. But they did not agree to Connally's proposal at the first morning meeting on the 10th, or subsequently during his Tokyo visit.[84]

By the end of the first day's meetings, Connally's hosts realized the program was far different than they had expected. Connally hadn't come to Japan to play the "Texas bull-in-a-china-shop" role for which he had become so famous. Further, he demonstrated sensitivity to Japan's problem of interministerial coordination during visits with political and bureaucratic decision makers outside the international monetary policy loop. He met with Foreign Minister Fukuda between 6:00 and 8:00 P.M. on Wednesday evening, the 10th, to discuss foreign aid, the world economy, and Southeast Asia after his 3:00 P.M. meeting with Mizuta at the Finance Ministry.[85] The following day meetings with EPA Director General Kimura, Agriculture Secretary Akagi, and MITI Minister Tanaka were scheduled at each individual minister's office, rather than at some central point, a gesture of cooperation that won Connally considerable good will in Japan at little cost to himself.

Connally encouraged EPA Director General Kimura and others to reduce the level of their intervention in the foreign exchange market to allow the yen to rise more rapidly.[86] In addition to the monetary issue Connally emphasized trade problems, especially agricultural liberalization, with the other ministers, asking Akagi to consider the liberalization of oranges and beef.[87] It was reported after the Thursday meetings that Connally had proposed to MITI Minister Tanaka a bilateral cabinet-level meeting in Honolulu or Anchorage toward the end of the year to finalize agreement on a few liberalization problems.

The Thursday schedule concluded with a two-hour meeting starting at 6:00 P.M. with Prime Minister Sato. Connally and Sato met alone with only one interpreter. Even Ambassador Meyer was not asked to attend.[88] Press reports of the substance of the discussions were sketchy, but rumors spread after the meeting that Connally had received Sato's agreement in principle on a bilateral cabinet meeting to be held in Honolulu sometime in December, and that Finance Minister Mizuta was fully empowered by Sato to make the final judgment about the yen revaluation.[89]

Although he denied knowledge of the specific details of the Sato-Connally discussions on the 11th of November, Kashiwagi later commented that Prime Minister Sato personally held a far more flexible attitude toward up-valuation of the yen than did other members of the government. Kashiwagi remembered Sato as being more concerned about the tone of the overall bilateral relationship, and therefore willing to approve change in the parity required to reach an international settlement.[90] Connally's visit to Japan—so different from what the Japanese had expected—concluded with an unscheduled evening visit with Sato at his official residence on Friday evening. Again, they met alone with only one interpreter.[91]

Secretary Connally's early November visit to Tokyo was an unexpected success. Although no final agreement on the parity of the yen was reached—an impossible expectation due to the multilateral nature of the issue—the Texan Treasury Secretary did a remarkable job of diffusing the anticipatory animosity that had built up during the month prior to his visit in expectation of his unreasonable behavior and demands. He helped to make the American negotiating position on the international monetary issue more legitimate in the eyes of the Japanese policy-making establishment. He earned some valuable political goodwill in Japan by avoiding the political grandstanding that had been expected in an effort to strengthen his own political position in the United States.

On the afternoon of November 11, Connally held a news conference at the American Cultural Center that attracted over 200 correspondents. He told the assembled crowd he still opposed a dollar devaluation, and that he had not asked for any specific level of increase in the parity of the yen. When asked if the international monetary crisis would be solved by the end of the year, he replied that he wouldn't be surprised if it happened, but he also wouldn't be surprised if it took longer.[92]

From the perspective of Japan's international moneymen, the most disappointing part of the visit was Connally's reaction to their contention that the Japanese economic recession made it impossible to make a large-scale revaluation of the yen. He warned Mizuta that reluctance to up-value the yen because of Japan's domestic recession was perhaps not as effective a defense as he might expect, since growth rates that seemed recessionary to Japan actually were attractive levels of economic performance for most European countries.

Secretary Connally left Tokyo with much more than he brought. In spite of his refusal to be more specific about the timing of the suspension of the surcharge, or even about what was demanded to obtain its suspension, and in spite of his continued refusal even to consider devaluation of the dollar, Connally was a far more popular figure in Japan after his visit. He left his negotiating counterparts in the MOF and the LDP in a better position to compromise with American demands than they had been before he arrived—perhaps his primary objective.

8. Japan and the United States Face the Inevitability of Meaningful Change

Predictability is an essential ingredient of smooth interpersonal relations in any society. But it seems more important in Japan than elsewhere. And it seems even more important for Japan when dealing with foreigners. The "Tough Texan" public image Secretary John Connally chose to show the world during the latter half of 1971 as he struggled to adjust the dollar's international value to postwar economic reality disturbed and confused Japan's policy-makers and implementers. Japan's international monetary officials, more comfortable with the patterns of exaggerated politeness usually adopted by both sides during Japan's international exchanges, were shocked by reports they received of Connally's blunt —almost reckless—statements, and of his disregard for customary international monetary diplomatic behavior. They weren't as much offended as puzzled. They weren't sure just what made Mr. Connally tick.[1] This complicated the process of achieving domestic consensus on Japan's response to the U.S. initiative.

During his early November visit to Tokyo, Secretary Connally convinced Japan's negotiators that they were dealing with a rational, reasonable individual, who was at least willing—if not anxious—to settle the world's international economic problems. Connally confirmed his demand that Japan contribute to a huge turnaround in the U.S. balance of payments through significant upvaluation of the yen (as much as 24 percent), liberalization of laws and regulations restricting international trade and investment, and increased defense spending. And he still refused to consider his hosts' suggestion that he accept European demands for a devaluation of the U.S. dollar to hasten progress toward a final settlement. But in spite of all this, Minister Mizuta and his bureaucratic subordinates emerged from the Tokyo meetings with Connally more optimistic about the prospects for an international monetary settlement within the calendar year than they were before the visit. Now it was time to get down to business.

Japan After Connally's Visit

Government Preparations. For Japan's government, getting down to business meant the time had come to prepare for the final act of the yen drama, shifting from the "stand fast" posture required while Japan waited for the bickering between the Americans and Europeans to quieten sufficiently to allow meaningful multilateral negotiations.

Secretary Connally convinced his hosts in Tokyo that he was a reasonable and responsible negotiator. But he also convinced them of his determination to wring greater-than-expected concessions from Japan and Europe during the final round of negotiations. With "final" settlement likely by the end of the year, the international moneymen had at the most seven weeks in which to prepare the business community, the communications media, the political sector and the public to accept without panic—or without faulting the government—the level of revaluation to which Japan would be forced to agree as the price of readmission to a fixed-rate international monetary system. Judging from Connally's comments, they also would have to continue to press trade and investment liberalization on their reluctant colleagues. Also, the delicate subject of the business community's demands for government programs to compensate for the foreign exchange-related losses they expected to suffer had to be addressed as well. All in all, life in Kasumigaseki was likely to get worse before it got better.

Government officials in charge of Japan's economic policy have demonstrated remarkable skill at taking credit for those of their actions that have proved popular, and at avoiding blame for those that have proved unpopular. They have gone to considerable effort to promote the high reputation they enjoy at home, and even abroad, aware that public perception of their abilities can either help or hinder their efforts to influence Japan's economy. In spite of this, each time Japan has faced an international balance-of-payments crisis in the postwar period, the government has responded with an unpopular and tighter domestic economic policy rather than with a change in the fixed parity of the yen, which, at least earlier in the postwar period, would have created less public resentment.

Public complaints about the severity of the economic belt-tightening measures were countered with bleaker pictures of the dangerous alternative: tampering with Japan's position in the international fixed exchange rate system. Once the first change in the yen's parity was made, it was argued, future changes would become more acceptable, introducing the factor of costly instability into Japan's economic relationship with the world, and even running the risk of weakening her ability to earn foreign exchange adequate to pay for the imports required to sustain Japan's postwar standard of living. The danger of any change in the yen's fixed Y 360=$1 exchange rate was stressed (in hindsight, even exaggerated) by economic government officials eager to justify their unpopular belt-tightening measures to a reluctant Japanese business community and public. The success of such past propaganda efforts would come back to haunt them during the 1971 crisis as they struggled to calm public fears over the effects of yen revaluation once it became inevitable they would be forced to comply with U.S. demands.

By November the government's public position on the likely impact of a change in the yen's parity had come full circle. Efforts were made to persuade the business community and public that the negative impact of the revaluation would be nowhere as severe as previously thought. Government officials themselves pointed out the benefits an up-valuation would bring, notably a reduction in the cost of Japan's imports. They no longer scolded business spokesmen for mentioning the once taboo phrase "yen revaluation" in public, and they were in fact encouraged by signs of its growing acceptance. When asked during personal interviews several years later what they considered the best example of misinterpretation or distortion of fact by the Japanese communications media during the yen crisis, former officials often complained that the Japanese press tended to exaggerate the adverse impact of yen revaluation on the economy, conveniently forgetting the source of the journalists' bias.

This sudden reversal of official attitude after the August float was inspired, first of all, by the international moneymen's realization that they were going to be forced to accept an up-valuation of the yen whether they liked it or not, and their desire to avoid public criticism for failing to avoid such a move as promised. A second source of encouragement was official concern over intensified business-lobbying efforts in favor of government compensation for revaluation-related losses. Public fear of the revaluation's adverse economic impact tended to generate sympathy for the lobbyists' arguments; alleviation of that fear weakened their influence. Although the bureaucrats and their political superiors could ill afford to appear insensitive to the plight of business—especially small business—adversely impacted by the yen crisis, they were well aware of the danger of being trapped in the heat of battle into long-term commitments to provide huge sums from the public treasury to bail out every sector of the business community involved in international trade. The substantial contribution already provided indirectly to the foreign exchange banks just before the float was enough of a drain on government resources.

By November the government was able to support its new official argument with statistical evidence. Three months after the destruction of the old Y 360 = $1 fixed rate, the international economic figures were showing some evidence of the parity change, but nowhere near what had been expected. Although this evidence of the yen float's limited impact was sure to stimulate charges of "dirty float" abroad, government spokesmen were able to reassure the business community and public that they were bringing the crisis under control by emphasizing these facts during regular public announcements.

For example, on November 15 the MOF released its usual preliminary estimates of the previous month's balance-of-payments figures, indicating a surplus at the end of October in the overall balance of only $140 million. This figure was down more than $100 million from the previous month, but still in surplus and far better than expected.[2] The following day the MOF released the preliminary estimate of October's exports to the United States. In spite of the float and the 10 percent surcharge, at $654 million it was a surprising 28.5 percent greater than sales in the United States during October of the previous year.[3] The impact of all this on Japan's international "bottom line" was confirmed by the regular announcement on the last day of the month of the official foreign exchange reserves estimate. During November reserves had increased by $738 million, to $14.8 billion.[4]

A report released by a business group in late November confirmed the same trend. According to data collected by the Association of General Trading Companies [Boeki Shosha-kai], the nation's 14 largest trading companies reported surprising increases in export contracts during October, up 16.4 percent over the same

Table 5
Year-on-Year Monthly Comparison of Key Japanese Trade Balances, 1970–1971

	Global Exports		*Global Trade Balance*	
	1970	*1971*	*1970*	*1971*
Jan.	1,093	1,258	−42	2
Feb.	1,366	1,654	230	367
March	1,672	2,148	399	702
April	1,533	1,899	312	549
May	1,496	1,919	201	580
June	1,640	2,048	345	648
July	1,717	2,168	375	788
Aug.	1,599	2,078	339	594
Sep.	1,738	2,109	422	597
Oct.	1,779	2,119	398	423
Nov.	1,563	2,069	307	348
Dec.	2,168	2,616	746	870

	Exports to U.S.		*Bilateral Balance with U.S.*	
	1970	*1971*	*1970*	*1971*
Jan.	309	391	−97	−51
Feb.	431	472	−165	−13
March	487	664	−11	164
April	454	605	26	158
May	480	652	47	182
June	510	709	−4	302
July	568	722	103	344
Aug.	528	733	70	436
Sep.	591	567	105	256
Oct.	518	662	12	234
Nov.	489	662	50	222
Dec.	663	793	164	404

Source: OECD, *Statistics of Foreign Trade*, Series A, 1971.
Note: Unit U.S. $1 million

month the previous year. The same 14 firms reported their import contracts during October down some 26.3 percent, due in part to the domestic economic slump.[5] The Council of Trading Companies' report was even more encouraging for those at home concerned about Japan's post-revaluation ability to maintain a trade surplus since it was based upon reports of contracts made during October for future delivery, rather than on transactions made during the month that might have been contracted for prior to the events of August.

Throughout the final phase of the 1971 yen crisis Japan's economic officials continued, with considerable public fanfare, to work on government policies designed to counter the anticipated negative impact of the parity change on Japan's economy. The banking community was one important focus of their concern. In spite of the support they received between the August 15 Nixon announcement and the decision to float the yen, spokesmen for banking interests had been complaining loudly about the impact on their business of government efforts required to control the yen float.

In late November the MOF began to publicize plans to relax some of the controls on international bank transactions imposed to help control the float. Specifically, the MOF reported that it was considering a suspension of the ceiling placed on the total amount of Japanese banks' foreign loans and borrowing implemented in September to help reduce speculative foreign exchange transactions. The banks argued that the restrictions were forcing their foreign branches to lose business to the local banks with which they competed.[6] With a resolution of the crisis now likely by the end of the year, the government had little to lose even if conditions on the foreign exchange market took a turn that made relaxation inadvisable, since the controls would become unnecessary once the yen's parity was repegged at a fixed rate.

Government spending during the following fiscal year (April 1, 1972 to March 31, 1973) was expected to have considerable impact on the Japanese economy's response to the yen crisis, making the annual budget discussions in late November a subject of even more than usual interest. In response to current and anticipated pressure from the business community the LDP announced after budget discussions during a meeting of the party's Roundtable Conference [Somu Kondankai] at the beginning of December that "the recovery of the economy is the most important objective of next year's budget, with emphasis on social welfare."[7]

For both international and domestic reasons, in late 1971 social welfare spending was an attractive option for government efforts to counter the impact of the yen. First, social welfare spending programs ran no risk of stimulating international complaints since they contributed only indirectly to Japan's international economic competitiveness. Second, the impact of such programs would be felt quickly by the business community since contracts for construction projects that fell under the "social welfare" category could be let immediately. These included sewers, roads, civic centers, and other undertakings of the sort dear to the hearts of elected officials.

Policy Affairs Research Council Chairman Kosaka announced soon after the LDP's Roundtable Conference on December 2 that his council would begin budget deliberations on the 9th of the month, and he made it clear the LDP would do what it could to press Japan's tight-fisted MOF budget officials to make special allowances for the unusual situation created by the yen revaluation crisis. Finance Minister Mizuta confirmed those intentions a few days later with public announcement of his proposal to increase next fiscal year's budget by a whopping 18.4 percent, adding that he would even consider a supplementary budget in the middle of the year should it prove necessary.[8]

Business Community Adjustment. By mid-November Japan's business community had begun to adapt to the new international monetary environment. Few welcomed the changes forced on Japan by President Nixon's New Economic Policy. But after more than three months of uncertainty, including less than satisfactory experience with the government-controlled float of the yen, spokesmen for the various international trading companies and export-dependent manufacturers were once again "cautiously optimistic" about the future. When possible, contracting parties were agreeing to split exchange risk rather than delay consummation of business deals. By November the major trading companies had reached informal agreement to use the tentative exchange rate of Y 320 = $1 in those instances where agreement to split exchange risk proved difficult.[9]

Everyone looked forward to the stability that repegging of the yen would bring, and speculation about the level at which it ultimately would be set was a popular topic of discussion in Japan's business circles. In early November *Nihon Keizai Shimbun* reported the rumor that during Secretary Connally's visit to Tokyo Japan had proposed a 12.5 percent up-valuation if the United States would agree to remove the surcharge. During interviews five years later, the Japanese officials involved denied making the proposal, but the report had significant impact on the public perception of the eventual level of the yen's up-valuation in Japan. In early November most nongovernment estimates of the eventual up-valuation were around 12 to 13 percent, and the Nihon Keizai Shimbun story was even reported the following day by the *New York Times*.[10]

The announcement that the previously delayed Group of Ten's ministers' meeting would be held in Rome at the end of November further excited exchange market speculation against the dollar and in favor of the yen, as well as less costly public speculation about the eventual level of the new rate. By late November, just before Minister Mizuta and his subordinates were ready to leave for the Rome Conference,[11] conventional wisdom had moved the level up from around 12.5 percent[12] to about 15 percent. According to recollections of the key policy participants, the government was comfortable with this level of public expectation since it was fairly close to their own estimates at the time.

No responsible business spokesman was pleased with the prospect of a revaluation, and to that limited extent there was a negative business consensus on the parity issue. But by late November Japanese business opinions differed when it came to recommendations for government action. The business organizations in which export-dependent manufacturers were influential—Keidanren, the Japan Chamber of Commerce, Keizai Doyukai—since late August had urged the government to seek an early end to the "controlled float," even if it meant an interim unilateral revaluation of the yen against the dollar. Prolonged uncertainty was more of a problem for them than a higher exchange rate (within reason) as long as it was a fixed rate. In spite of three months of vehement government opposition to this interim unilateral revaluation proposal, as late as November 18 Japan Chamber of Commerce vice chairman Togawa told a press conference that the organization's chairman and vice-chairmen's meeting had just agreed to urge the government to commence bilateral negotiations with the United States as quickly as possible to arrange an interim fixed yen rate vis-à-vis the dollar since a multilateral settlement was taking so long to achieve.[13]

The banking community, or at least the majority of those banks that were members of the National Association of Banking Organizations [Zenkoku Ginko Kyokai Rengo-kai] urged the government to proceed at a prudent pace, and publicly warned Finance Minister Mizuta and the MOF bureaucracy not to be rushed at international meetings into agreeing to a level of parity adjustment that would later prove disastrous for Japan. After the regular meeting of the National Association of Banking Organizations's Board of

Directors on December 7, Chairman Goro Koyama (chairman of Mitsui Bank) discussed his organization's position with the press. Koyama insisted, as he had since mid-August, that the government should hold out for as small a revaluation as possible, even if it took a little more time. When asked about the impact of the then most frequently heard guess of a final Y 315 = $1 rate, Koyama suggested that such a steep increase would adversely affect the overall Japanese economy, and he urged the government to consider economic countermeasures appropriate to deal with the situation.

Koyama's publicly stated reluctance to see the yen's exchange rate rise as high as Y 315 = $1 was of more than routine significance for the international moneymen, first because as chairman of the National Association of Banking Organizations he spoke officially for most of the Japanese banking community. In addition, Koyama was one of the businessmen who earlier in the year had been reprimanded by officials of the MOF for hinting in public—and taking an even stronger position in private—that the ministry should at least study the possibility of revaluation of the yen as a means of dealing with the ballooning balance-of-payments surplus.[14] Koyama's statements increased pressure on Japan's government negotiators to resist to the extent possible Connally's efforts to push them into agreeing on a higher level of revaluation since the remarks demonstrated that even business community spokesmen known to take a "liberal" view of the revaluation issue were reluctant to see the yen up-valued as much as 14 percent.

One subject upon which there was little disagreement in the business community in mid-November was the importance of countering the anticipated deflationary impact of the yen revaluation with a beefed-up government budget during the next fiscal year. The possibility that government overspending could exacerbate a destabilizing round of inflation, such as Japan was about to experience, was hardly considered. Business leaders, politicians, communications media commentators, and even government officials competed with one another for opportunities to endorse large-scale increases in government spending during the next fiscal year to counter the yen deflation. An increase in government spending was the one point of the Finance Ministry's May eight-point program to avoid revaluation of the yen upon which it was easy to form a national consensus.

Keidanren, for example, continued to press its position on the subject with the release of the conclusions of a study done by its professional staff of the effects of the yen crisis on Japan's economy during the next few years. Released on December 5, the report estimated that private investment would drop below last year's level during the current fiscal year, and that the economy as a whole would grow during the next year at a rate of only about 4 percent.[15] The significance of the 4 percent growth estimate on Japan in 1971 must be considered in light of the double-digit growth rates to which Japan had become accustomed during the 1960s. The Keidanren staff report concluded that the government should make up for the effect of this decline in private investment with greatly increased government expenditures during the balance of the current fiscal year and the next. The study was discussed with Vice Minister Hosomi when he visited Keidanren the following Tuesday to report on the surprising proceedings of the Group of Ten's ministers' meeting in Rome. Hosomi conveyed Finance Minister Mizuta's intention to discuss the subject himself with Keidanren's international planning group on the 13th of the month, just prior to his departure for Washington and the Smithsonian Conference[16]

In addition to strong support for an expanded, recession-fighting national budget for the next fiscal year (a measure designed to benefit all sectors of the Japanese economy), pressure continued for more specific government compensation from the industrial sectors and corporations that considered themselves especially disadvantaged by the government's decision to allow a change in the parity of the yen. Export-dependent manufacturers whose products required long lead times between agreement upon contract terms and delivery of product, such as the builders of ships and other heavy industrial equipment, fell into this category. Since most of their existing contracts were denominated in dollars—dollars that would buy fewer yen as a result of the up-valuation—they stood to lose substantial sums at product delivery and payment time.

Five years later, Japan's shipping industry was named without hesitation by government officials, politicians, and journalists active during the 1971 yen crisis as the most vigorous private-sector lobbying force. Japan's shipping interests—builders and owners—had urged the government directly and indirectly to stand firm in opposition to a change in the yen's parity even before August. But, anticipating an inevitable change, they also prepared a case for direct government compensation of losses should they fail to accomplish their primary objective.

Renzo Taguchi, then chairman of the Association of Japanese Shipbuilders (Nihon Zosen Kogyokai), was the association's point man on the yen issue. According to his principal association staff assistant, Kazuichi Murai, the shipping industry was concerned with only two aspects of the yen issue: prevention of a change in the parity and government compensation for losses in the event they failed to accomplish their first objective. They were not at all involved in the discussion of how much the yen should be upvalued once the decision was made. Their energies were directed exclusively toward obtaining compensation after the August float announcement.

Murai said that Chairman Taguchi was very active, especially between August and the end of the year, personally visiting government officials in MITI and the Ministry of Finance, members of the various LDP committees with an interest in the subject, Finance Minister Mizuta and MITI Minister Tanaka, and even Prime Minister Sato. Taguchi, usually accompanied by Murai, delivered the same message at each stop: government officials had committed a "*gyosei misu*" (administrative error) by allowing the parity of the yen to change after they had promised never to do so. Taguchi compared the situation of his industry with that of the victim of a traffic accident. All they wanted was compensation for their injuries from the driver of the car. And they weren't satisfied to be told to go away and get better on their own.[17]

To strengthen their compensation argument vis-à-vis a reluctant government and public, the Association of Japanese Shipbuilders invited Japan's major plant exporting companies—a corporate sector also worried about yen-related losses on long-term contracts—to form a more broadly based coalition with Taguchi as chairman. The new group was named the Coalition of Japanese Machine Manufacturers Associations [Nihon Kikai Kogyo Rengokai]. It called a meeting of the board of directors on December 9 to discuss strategy for pursuing the compensation issue.[18] Taguchi and his supporters realized the government was more vulnerable than usual to criticism with the unsettled yen issue hanging over its head, and hoped that sense of vulnerability would make it more willing to listen to compensation arguments.

There were differences of opinion within the new group over

specific objectives, tactics, and priorities. But early December optimism in government, the business community, and the communications media over a "final" yen settlement before year's end prodded the diverse group toward agreement on a program to increase pressure on the government for some public commitment to provide compensation. After the meeting on the 9th, they announced the formation of a special lobbying committee called "Kisei Domei," chaired by Mr. Taguchi, that would hold its first meeting on December 14 at 10:00 A.M. at the Keidanren Kaikan. Taguchi's group announced plans to persuade the government to agree to the following program of compensation:

1. 25 percent of anticipated losses from the revaluation to be covered by loans from the Export-Import Bank for which principle repayment would be suspended for ten years
2. 40 percent of anticipated losses to be declared as a corporate income tax deduction over a ten-year period
3. The remaining 35 percent of anticipated losses to be liquidated at the time of the loss as an income tax credit[19]

Murai recalled that Taguchi and his group were disappointed with the response to their proposal. Even Keidanren and the other business associations refused to endorse the concept of direct compensation, judging it a politically unrealistic objective. Government officials and politicians were personally sympathetic and polite during Taguchi's visits, but even the politicians were skeptical of the shipping industry's claims. The government rejected the industry's basic claim that they had made an "administrative error," and in the end the shipbuilders estimated that only 20 percent of the industry's actual losses were covered by government compensation.[20]

In addition to pressure for direct compensation for losses, at the end of November Keidanren's international monetary committee and its staff were preparing a report that would recommend the government organize a "floating exchange rate-reserve fund." This program avoided the politically difficult question of government compensation for business losses already suffered and concentrated attention on future international monetary problems. With the Y 360 = $1 fixed rate finally broken it was likely that exchange rates would become more flexible in the future. The Keidanren plan called for a government-controlled reserve fund that would help to insulate Japanese corporations from the risks involved in international business in the more flexible exchange rate period.[21] Somehow, members of the Japanese business community seemed to have little confidence in their ability to prosper under an international monetary system with a flexible exchange rate.

Japan's Public Begins to Tire of the Yen Issue. If Japan's communications media with any accuracy determines and fulfills their public's news interests—and the profitability of Japanese media-related corporations suggests that they do—a review of their output for 1971 indicates that by mid-November Japan's public had shown intense interest in the yen revaluation issue for more than nine months. For nearly a whole year Japan consumed the latest yen-related facts and analysis in electronic, newsprint, and paperback formats as soon as they were available. Since May the various media had been competing for the right to distribute the opinions of anyone, domestic or foreign, able to pass under even the dimmest light as an international monetary expert. After Secretary Connally's exciting visit, however, and the notice of yet another round of meetings with foreigners whose names were difficult to pronounce and impossible to remember, the public was ready for some new intellectual entertainment.

The international moneymen's post-August revision of their traditional morbid view of the effect of a parity change on Japan's economy mentioned earlier was supported by the findings of non-government researchers. For example, in early November Professor Masaomi Tatemoto of Kyoto University published his own forecast of the impact of a 1971 yen revaluation occurring between October and December. Even at his highest hypothetical level of up-valuation, 15 percent (a figure that in early November seemed on the high side), he predicted an annual economic growth rate of 5.1 percent for the following year. And on the bright side, Tatemoto's forecast included the prediction that the wholesale price index would be reduced from 2.4 percent to minus 1.9 percent while the otherwise anticipated rise in consumer prices would decline from 7.5 to 5.7 percent if the American 10 percent surcharge were removed at the same time, and all this with a reassuring $4.2 billion surplus in the current account.[22]

In early December the respected Kokumin Keizai Kenkyu Kyokai, headed by Buntaro Tomizuka, published a similar report on the likely impact of the yen's up-valuation on overall Japanese economy. This report, like several others released around the same time, concluded that damage would be minimal if the level of parity change was held within "reasonable" bounds, and if the government responded to the new situation quickly enough with stimulative measures and efficiently adapted Japan's overall economic policies to the new situation. This report too mentioned certain positive consequences of up-valuation, such as a decline in the prices of imported raw materials and stimulation of the increasingly important tertiary sector.[23] Japan's private research organizations were free now to release their benign predictions of the impact of a yen parity change without fear of threatening calls from the MOF.

By early December both the popular and the specialized economic press had reached the general speculative conclusion that the final level of up-valuation, once it was decided, would be about 15 percent, a figure Japan could live with. According to the recollection of one key MOF participant, technical specialists within the ministry had reached the same conclusion in October and had begun to prepare the public for the change by disseminating a government position quite different from that espoused by the MOF for the past twenty years.[24] The Japanese public, like the business community, began to feel more secure with their new international monetary situation, reducing the commercial value of yen-related news. Bookstores continued to devote one or two tables exclusively to yen-related books, but they no longer attracted the crowds of eager readers they had just a month or two before. Books on China began to take up the slack as Japan's 1971 China boom—stimulated by the "Nixon shock"—began to blossom. One Tokyo book storeowner summed up the situation in mid-December: "Everybody understands, more or less, what the new level of the yen will be. And there are a lot of yen-related books that are almost the same."[25]

Although the direct role of the Japanese public in international monetary policy-making is minimal, the decline in public tension described above did have some positive psychological impact on Japan's international policymakers. It made the subject less attractive for Japan's journalists and reduced the space devoted to yen revaluation in all publications. This, in turn, reduced journalists' pressure on policymakers for "inside information" with which to pay for all those past expense-account dinners and "favorable mentions," which made a career-shattering mistake less likely. The obvious decline in public interest also reassured Japan's policymakers by reducing the likelihood that politicians not directly involved with the issue would attempt to exploit it for their own purposes, or that interest groups opposed to a change would find it more difficult to get press attention for their campaigns.

Connally's Rome Conference Surprise

By November senior Nixon administration officials were certain the United States would run the first *trade* deficit of this century during 1971. Since the surplus in the trade account had been relied upon for many years to pull the other deficit-prone balance-of-payments accounts out of the red, they thought it highly unlikely that the American public and the Democrat-controlled Congress would allow such a milestone to pass without severe criticism of their stewardship. The imminent public announcement of the trade deficit increased pressure on the administration to demonstrate near-term foreign economic progress.

Eager to appear up to handling the foreign economic crisis, which the trade deficit had come to symbolize, Secretary Connally maintained his hard-line position on international monetary reform after returning from Tokyo. In a speech to the Economists Club of New York City on November 16, he repeated his contention that the 10 percent surcharge was invoked in defense of the free trade system, rather than against it. The United States, he argued, could not afford to run a serious deficit. So the surcharge would have to stay in force until more appropriate exchange rates could be agreed upon. Equally important for the Europeans, he flatly rejected any consideration of dollar devaluation, insisting the final settlement should represent progress on the "demonitization" of gold.[26] Connally and his Under Secretary, Paul Volcker, reaffirmed the administration's position on the dollar several times prior to the Rome meeting of the Group of Ten.[27]

During November congressional leaders in both houses continued to criticize Connally's stubborn international monetary position, and to express concern about the future of the world trading system. House Speaker Carl Albert described President Nixon's New Economic Policy as a "blunderbuss program" likely to damage our friends as well as our enemies. Albert called for the immediate suspension of the surcharge, suggesting its imposition risked a trade war—strong language on foreign policy in 1971, even coming from the political opposition.[28] House Ways and Means Committee chairman Wilbur Mills agreed, saying dollar devaluation should be considered during the final settlement by the administration, and he went on to suggest that Connally's target for a balance-of-payments turnaround should be adjusted downward from $13 billion to between $7 billion and $10 billion.[29]

Any domestic criticism of the administration's foreign economic negotiating style or position, particularly from politically influential sources on Capitol Hill, was taken far more seriously abroad than at home. While American observers understood such events as predictable moves in the national political game, especially around election time, each late-1971 anti-Connally statement was carefully scrutinized in Tokyo for clues to future U.S. action and for opportunities to influence the American policy process.

The best example of this in late 1971 was the bipartisan bill introduced on November 18 by Senator Jacob Javits and Congressman Henry Reuss that granted President Nixon the authority to devalue the dollar with an increase in the price of gold of up to 10 percent.[30] Two of the most liberal members of congress on international economic issues, Javits and Reuss introduced their bill in part to encourage Connally to compromise on the dollar devaluation issue out of concern for the world economic system, and in part to express dramatically their disapproval of the Nixon administration's handling of overall foreign economic policy for domestic political purposes. In spite of immediate administration statements denying intentions to implement a devaluation, the bill weakened Connally's argument against dollar devaluation on the grounds of congressional disapproval, and gave European and Japanese observers hope that liberal American political forces might achieve what they had failed to accomplish at the international bargaining table.

Not all members of the House and Senate shared the liberal foreign economic views of Reuss and Javits. In fact, the weight of opinion leaned in the opposite direction. With a rising chorus of constituent demands for protection from international competition ringing in their ears, congressmen and senators were becoming less, rather than more, supportive of the traditional American "free trade" ideological substitute for a genuine foreign economic policy.

A relative abundance of resources and opportunity made postwar foreign economic policy less important *economically* for the United States than for other, less advantaged trading nations. Noneconomic (at least, in the short- and medium-term) strategic, or diplo-military, foreign policy objectives, especially the containment of Communism, were judged more important for the American national interest during the late 1940s, 1950s, and even the early half of the 1960s. Under the "free trade" banner, all nations willing to identify themselves as members of the Free World Camp had been allowed to buy and sell freely in the U.S. market, both to strengthen their economies and insure their support for our international ideals. As a result, a pattern of American foreign economic relations evolved in which *strategic*, or diplo-military, advantage accrued to the United States and *economic* advantage accrued to our trading partners. The volume of red ink required to print the 1971 American international balance-of-payments report was dramatic proof the United States could no longer afford the luxury of ignoring the economic implications of its foreign economic relations.

The chairman of the Senate Finance Committee, Russell Long, a powerful Democratic legislator rarely accused of mindless economic internationalism, helped to balance the international perceptions of the American congress. On November 4 his committee voted to give the president the authority to impose a 15 percent surcharge (a 5 percent increase over the currently imposed level) and almost unlimited import quotas when the basic balance of the U.S. balance of payments showed a deficit for four consecutive quarters, or if U.S. international reserves began to decline seriously.[31] The administration was as quick to deny interest in this measure as it had been in the devaluation proposal. But during a press conference the following day, Secretary Connally did say the action was of value as a source of pressure on foreign countries during ongoing international monetary relations.[32]

Taking advantage of the unusual opportunity to combine personal political advantage with support for the administration's international objectives, Senator Long ignored Connally's polite rejection of his legislative initiative earlier in the month and added similar language as an amendment to the tax reduction bill which had to pass through Long's Committee. An important aspect of the New Economic Policy, the tax reduction bill passed through the Finance Committee with a surprisingly large margin, in spite of its tough international economic amendment.[33] Again the administration expressed its lack of interest, and the language was eventually removed from the tax bill. But Long's amendment had exactly the effect desired by its sponsors: to prove to America's trading partners that the administration's tough international economic policy stance had the support of many important members of congress. The legislative wrangling over the bill provided such a boost to the fortunes of Washington lobbyists representing foreign clients that it later was known as the "Lawyers' Relief Act of 1971."

By mid-November dollar devaluation for the Europeans had become an issue upon which compromise would have been a very bitter pill. The economic impact of either a down-valuation of the dollar or the up-valuation of other currencies would have been the same. But after two decades of resentment and complaints about the dollar's "privileged position" within the international monetary system, dollar devaluation had more than economic significance in Europe. By November 1971 it was of even greater concern than the surcharge, since the United States was most unlikely to maintain the surcharge once certain conditions had been met. But, if Connally and Nixon had been sincere in their often-stated absolute opposition to a devaluation, it was quite possible the Europeans and Japanese might in the end be forced to choose between settling accounts through up-valuation of their own currencies or waiting indefinitely to return to fixed rates.

Perhaps because the Europeans were unable to agree among themselves on individual levels of exchange rate adjustment to achieve cross-rates that would avoid disruption of intra-EEC trade patterns and prevent Japan and the Americans from more successfully exploiting their markets, they placed greater emphasis during this phase of the negotiations on the one issue upon which they all could agree: dollar devaluation. There was even European talk of asking the Japanese to join in a "united front" against the United States if Connally should fail to agree to that devaluation.[34]

During the NHK interview aired in Japan early in May 1981 (cited in the previous chapter), Secretary Connally revealed that his oft-repeated refusals to consider dollar devaluation had been a bluff from beginning to end, just one more source of pressure on the Europeans and Japanese to achieve the results he wanted from the final negotiations. The French, in fact, were playing into Connally's hands by making such a fuss over dollar devaluation when, according to Connally's remarks ten years later, the issue had little significance for the Nixon administration. When asked by the interviewer about his real position on devaluation, Connally replied:

Well, I had discussed this with President Nixon again during the late summer and early fall, and I told him that there was no reason for us whether other countries revalued or we devalued—the net effect was the same. But I said the other, the Group of Ten, wanted the U.S. to devalue. They want us to take the affirmative action of humiliation, to devalue our currency. And I said "It doesn't embarrass me. It is overvalued in relation to other currencies, and it should be devalued." But I said "Politically that's a decision that you have to face." He said "I have no problem with it. None whatever. It's not politically embarrassing or harmful to me. If we need to devalue, if you think we need to devalue, devalue it. You are authorized to do whatever you need to do to bring about the change."[35]

Connally added later in the same interview the interesting comment, "I was for floating exchange rates because I thought the economic situation of the world was so volatile that we could not maintain fixed exchange rates over any period of time. But no one would agree with me." His comment implies that he may, in fact, have had some reluctance to return to the fixed rate system—or at least that he was more relaxed about the current float than other participants—because he didn't from the beginning think the new system of fixed rates would work.

On November 18, Secretary Connally officially informed Japan's Embassy in Washington that he intended, as chairman of the Group of Ten, to convene the next meeting in Rome on November 30 and December 1. Since he had decided to cancel the last Group of Ten meeting scheduled for November 24 on the grounds no progress was likely, Connally's announcement raised hopes in Tokyo for a final international monetary settlement by the end of the year.[36] Any movement at this late date would bring the world very close to a new fixed-parity regime.

Other bilateral and multilateral meetings of significance to Japan's planning scheduled in addition to the November 30 ministers' meeting included a November 29 gathering of the Group of Ten's ministers' representatives just prior to the main event, a conference of the EEC finance ministers in Rome on the 30th, talks between West German Prime Minister Brandt and French President Pompidou on December 3–4, a Nixon-Pompidou meeting on December 13–14, and a December 20–21 meeting between Nixon and British Prime Minister Heath.[37] On the trade side, a November 24 meeting of GATT was scheduled for Geneva which both Japan's

EPA Director General Kimura and U.S. Special Trade Representative William Eberle were scheduled to attend.

The Working Party Three (WP-3) of the OECD had previously scheduled a meeting for November 18–19 in Paris to discuss the 1972 OECD economic outlook for member countries and the world economy. Finance Minister Mizuta asked Yusuke Kashiwagi, then vice chairman of the WP-3, to attend himself to update Japan's assessment of the European situation. Kashiwagi was expected to report back to Tokyo on November 22 after a short stopover in Washington. Upon his return to Tokyo, Kashiwagi conveyed the pessimistic tone of the WP-3 meeting to the press, and suggested that remaining points of disagreement between the United States and Europe gave a final settlement by the end of the year only a fifty-fifty chance.[38]

Although Kashiwagi was understandably cautious in his public remarks, in fact he told Mizuta and his colleagues that conversations with Volcker in Washington had convinced him that a final round of negotiations were likely by the end of the year. He later wrote, "In Japan we try to settle all of our debts by the end of the year. The Europeans and the Americans had a similar feeling that they would like to reach some sort of a solution by Christmas. Since it was clear that any final settlement would have to be political there was hope for some real progress during the next Finance Ministers Conference."[39] So by the end of November Japan's international moneymen assumed they had less than a month in which to prepare the country for their final position.

Finance Minister Mizuta, together with Kashiwagi, Takashi Hosomi, Yoshihito Amano, director of the International Organizations Division of the MOF's International Monetary Bureau (Kokusai Kinyu Kyoku, Kokusai Kiko Kacho), and Toyoo Gyohten, Hosomi's office director, were scheduled to leave for Rome on Sunday afternoon, November 28. The upcoming meetings, which had taken on new importance since the beginning of the week, had been discussed at the regular cabinet meeting on Friday, the 26th. MITI Minister Tanaka, in the midst of explaining a new export promotion program under consideration that was designed to counter the depressing effects of revaluation, broadly hinted to reporters assigned to cover the meeting that 15 percent was the top level of yen revaluation the government would be willing to accept.[40] Tanaka later revised his public yen up-valuation projection limit to between 10 and 15 percent during comments to the press on Saturday the 27th, after the final top-level meeting in preparation for the Rome conference attended by Prime Minister Sato, Foreign Minister Fukuda, Finance Minister Mizuta, MITI Minister Tanaka, Chief Cabinet Secretary Noboru Takeshita, and the Bank of Japan's Governor Sasaki.[41] Tanaka's public estimate was surprisingly close to that in the final instructions agreed upon by the international moneymen just prior to their departure for the final Smithsonian Conference in December.

Under the chairmanship of the vice governor of the Bank of Italy, Rinaldo Ossola, the customary preliminary meeting of the representatives of the Group of Ten's finance ministers got under way in Rome on Monday the 29th, at 3:45 P.M. Although all of the representatives realized events had reached a point at which the political actors themselves, rather than their technical representatives, would have to make the remaining decisions, they were still eager to learn exactly how the American side planned to present its case. The U.S. team, led by Treasury Under Secretary Paul Volcker, suggested during the first round of Rome multilateral meetings that the United States would agree to remove the import surcharge in return for an average revaluation of at least 11 percent for all of the other currencies against the dollar, and agreement from the other countries to begin negotiations on trade barriers to American goods and defense burden-sharing. Although the 11 percent average up-valuation figure represented some U.S. compromise, Volcker still opposed dollar devaluation as part of the final settlement.[42] Kashiwagi later recalled that the other participants were particularly suspicious of the American proposal for simultaneous bilateral trade and defense burden-sharing negotiations, fearing they would complicate the settlement on new exchange rates. Volcker assured the group the trade and defense discussions would proceed in parallel, with no direct link to the issue of exchange rates. With that assurance, by the end of the conference the Europeans agreed to trade discussions, and Japan and Canada reaffirmed their continuation.[43]

Tuesday the 30th began with several individual meetings between Secretary Connally and his counterparts and the strategy session planned for the EEC finance ministers, also attended by Great Britain. At 4:00 P.M. (December 1, 12:00 midnight, Japan time), the first session of the long-awaited Group of Ten's finance ministers' meeting was called to order by Chairman Connally at the Palazzo Corsini. As agreed during their morning meeting, the

Europeans demanded immediate suspension of the import surcharge and American agreement to devalue the dollar as part of the final settlement. The American team continued to oppose dollar devaluation—citing firm Republican party opposition—and to press for a comprehensive settlement that would include progress on trade liberalization and defense burden-sharing. After four hours of heated debate the first ministerial session adjourned around 8:00 P.M. to report only modest progress to the expectant press corps.[44]

The following day, December 1, a meeting of the ten finance ministers was scheduled for 10:45 A.M., Rome time. Earlier that morning Under Secretary Volcker was reported to have stunned the whole group by hinting to one of the French participants that the United States might be willing now to consider a revaluation, and asking his opinion of the European reaction should Secretary Connally raise the subject during the next meeting. Volcker's comments inspired a sudden flurry of multilateral and bilateral discussions, including another of the EEC (plus England) at 9:30 A.M., during which everyone tried in light of the new development to achieve consensus on a European response.[45]

The finance ministers' meeting opened later in the morning on schedule, and Connally confirmed Volcker's early-morning hint with the sudden additional request for individual counterproposals to a hypothetical American offer to devalue the dollar by 10 percent. Agreement to discuss dollar devaluation alone had been surprise enough for the group. A devaluation of 10 percent was simply unimaginable. Even after Volcker's bolt the group was taken by surprise, and after several more hours of discussion and separate meetings that day, the Rome meeting of the Group of Ten was adjourned. Connally later described his motives and actions at the Rome Conference:

> Well, it was very very interesting because we had heard from every source, every country "You have to devalue! The Government of U.S. [sic] has to devalue!" Finally this became a great issue in the Rome meeting, and I finally said "Well, if that is necessary in order to bring about a solution to our problems, I'm prepared to tell you that we would devalue the dollar 10%." There was total silence in the room for approximately 40 minutes. No one said anything—they sat there and looked at each other, whispered to each other. Each of us had 4 or 5 people in the room with us, but no one said anything.
>
> Finally after many many many minutes and approximately half an hour, Tony Barber, who was the Chancellor of the Exchequer, spoke

up and said "Oh, we could never agree to your devaluing the dollar that much." And I said "We thought you wanted us to devalue the dollar." "Oh, yes, but not that much." I said "Well, how much?" He said "5%." I said "That will do no good. That makes no sense. We should perhaps devalue it even more than 10%. But I'm trying to work out something if reasonable, and we will devalue it 10%. But if you are only willing to agree to 5%, then there is no way we will ever reach an agreement, and we might as well disband the meeting now, because we will never agree to devalue just 5%." That's the way it happened.[46]

Connally held a press conference just after the December 1 meeting during which he noted that enough progress had been made in Rome to warrant holding the next round of ministerial talks in Washington on December 17–18. He said no specific negotiations were undertaken during the two days of intensive meetings, but he hinted at discussion of a number of "hypothetical situations" which included a devaluation of the dollar.[47] The following day he confirmed the active discussion of dollar devaluation, adding that the United States had retreated from its previous demand of a $13 billion balance-of-payments turnaround to one of only $9 billion, after which he expected appropriate responses from the other countries.[48] All that remained of the dollar devaluation debate was the Nixon-Pompidou meeting in the Azores on December 13 and 14, after which a joint communique would be released announcing Franco-American agreement to cooperate in the resolution of the international monetary problem, which would include devaluation of the dollar and up-valuation of other world currencies. At last the French had achieved what—at least for them—was a significant victory in the international monetary arena.[49]

The optimism of the members of the Japanese delegation after the Rome Conference was obvious in their comments to the press. Their long international monetary nightmare was, at last, drawing to a close. The Americans and Europeans appeared to be well on the road to accommodation, and Japan's most serious remaining problem seemed to be the American insistence on parallel negotiations for trade liberalization. This point was emphasized repeatedly during press interviews by Mizuta and the Bank of Japan's Governor Sasaki.[50]

With the spotlight on Euro-American relations during the Rome meeting, Japan's delegation underestimated the degree to which they eventually would be required to revalue the yen. During an interview five years after the Rome Conference, then Bank of Japan Governor Sasaki recalled asking Secretary Connally how he would respond to a Japanese offer to up-value the yen by 10 percent. Connally replied that Sasaki needn't have bothered to ask. According to Sasaki's recollection, Finance Minister Mizuta and the MOF anticipated an up-valuation of around 10 to 12 percent, and were prepared by mid-December to go as high as 14 percent.[51] Foreign currency speculators, however, were less optimistic. On December 2 and 3 the U.S. dollar was hit with heavy waves of selling pressure, forcing the yen's level of up-valuation during the period of the float from 10.33 percent to 10.4 percent.[52]

9. Negotiating a "Final" Settlement

The 1971 international economic crisis was intensified in mid-August by American efforts to change existing patterns of international economic allocation, in part through re-defining certain accepted patterns of interaction, or "rules of the game" (exchange rates, and to a lesser extent, defense burden-sharing and foreign aid), and in part through insistence upon stricter adherence to other rules ("fair" as well as "free" trade). The Nixon administration from the outset defined its basic objective as correcting the decline in American international economic competitiveness, especially as measured by the balance-of-payments, notably the most politically sensitive trade account.

The economic health of the United States in the long-term was of genuine concern to America's trading partners, including Japan, given the economic and political importance of the United States to the Free World system. But, in 1971 those countries had little incentive to accept the Nixon administration's definitions of America's economic problems, and even less reason to agree to their proposed remedies—at least, not until August 15. The simultaneous suspension of the dollar's convertibility into gold and the imposition of a 10 percent surcharge on all dutiable American imports altered the status quo sufficiently to inspire a more sympathetic review of U.S. proposals. After August 15 the level of dissatisfaction with the status quo declined in Washington and rose in Tokyo, Bonn, London, Paris, and other capitals of the market-economy world. In one day the role of the United States in international economic meetings was transformed from that of complainant to defendant.

From the beginning, Japan's most important immediate objective had been to maintain—and then, after August 15, to reestablish—a stable, fixed-rate international monetary system. For Japan the central 1971 international economic problem was the *en kiriage mondai* (yen revaluation problem); for the United States it was balance-of-payments deficits. This difference in problem perception during the crisis naturally affected the actions of both the United States and Japan and each nation's response to the actions of the other. One significant example on the Japanese side was the tight control exercised over the handling of the issue by those MOF and Bank of Japan officials who were charged with responsibility for Japan's international accounts and preservation of the parity of the yen—the international moneymen. Early on, the Finance Ministry's international team, led by Yusuke Kashiwagi, grasped and held almost exclusive responsibility for the negotiations, arguing that issues that affected the parity of the yen were too sensitive to be handled by other government agency representatives who lacked technical competence. This exclusive attitude generated considerable resentment within the other ministries long before the August 15 "Nixon shock," resentment that was still fresh in the memories of former government officials interviewed five years later.

One former Foreign Ministry bureau director general in early 1976, after explaining at some length the coordinating role the Ministry of Foreign Affairs is supposed to play in Japan's foreign policy, characterized the International Monetary Bureau of the MOF as a "bureau of artisans." He went on to suggest that although the Finance Ministry's international monetary specialists were unquestionably competent in a technical sense, they weren't able to deal with international economic problems in their broader diplomatic context, as could the Foreign Ministry. He also said MOF officials had been much less "exclusive" and more cooperative with the Foreign Ministry and other government agencies on international monetary issues since the negotiations at the Smithsonian, if only to diversify blame should things go wrong.[1]

This overwhelming importance of the yen in Japan's perception of her 1971 economic problems with the United States—contributing to, and then combining with the past exclusivity of the international moneymen—made it more difficult for Japan's negotiators to cope with the nonmonetary aspects of the situation, especially U.S. demands for progress on trade and investment barrier liberalization. The Japanese public understood (and, even more important for government behavior, was believed by the bureaucracy and politicians to understand) this round of negotiations as an international dispute over the vitally important but arcane issue of yen revaluation, which was perceived to be the responsibility of the international monetary "experts" in the Ministry of Finance and Bank of Japan. There was public mention of trade liberalization as well. But on the whole, this was viewed as the Finance Ministry's international struggle to protect the yen. The international moneymen would get the credit for any success, but even more important, only they would be blamed in the event of failure.

Cross-Pressure on Trade Liberalization

During his early November visit to Tokyo, Secretary Connally had reaffirmed his intention to press for trade and investment liberalization as part of the final settlement. He described the overall U.S. objective as a $13 billion turnaround in the balance-of-payments deficit, which he intended to achieve one way or another. Sensing the international moneymen were more concerned about the yen's parity than about trade and investment liberalization measures, Connally warned that a lack of progress on liberalization inevitably would require more U.S. pressure on the yen. It wasn't difficult for the MOF and Bank of Japan to decide that Japan's overall interests were best served through trying to protect the yen by encouraging their counterparts in the other ministries to make more rapid progress on liberalization.

Officials of the other ministries, on the other hand, had little incentive to cooperate with the MOF internationalists. They questioned the extent to which compromise on these difficult liberalization issues was necessary right in the midst of a serious economic slump. They considered the American demands outrageous, especially considering Nixon's recent shocking behavior toward Japan on the yen and China issues, and that alone seemed sufficient reason to resist. MITI and Ministry of Agriculture officials were reluctant to strain their relationships of personal trust and goodwill with client groups, essential within the Japanese context for smooth government-private-sector interaction, by demanding they accept liberalization measures that were bound to increase competition and make business more difficult, all in support of policy objectives defined and controlled by MOF internationalists. Some officials wondered aloud if MOF officials intended to demand commensurate sacrifice from their own client group, Japan's financial institutions? And there was the unspoken question of why officials of other ministries should inconvenience themselves in an effort that, even if successful, would in the end only enhance the reputations of the internationalists in the Ministry of Finance?[2]

Soon after Connally's Tokyo visit Commerce Secretary Maurice Stans sent a letter to MITI Minister Tanaka that included a list of 16 specific items for which the United States was anxious to secure tariff reductions of between 25 and 50 percent by the end of the year. The list, headed by the two most difficult items, computers and agricultural products, included air conditioners, refrigerators, cosmetics, wrist watches, and alcoholic beverages. The letter was promptly leaked to the press.[3]

With settlement of the international monetary instability just a few weeks away (an event that would neutralize the U.S. team's most effective tool of persuasion), American pressure on Japan and the Europeans to engage in simultaneous, "parallel" trade negotiations on trade liberalization increased in early December. In spite of public denial by MITI Minister Tanaka two days earlier that the American side was pursuing a "package deal" settlement strategy which would require trade liberalization and defense spending concessions,[4] on December 9 the government announced its agreement to begin bilateral trade discussions prior to the next—and probably final—round of Group of Ten negotiations, scheduled for Washington on December 17 and 18.[5]

More details were made public the following day after the regular Friday meeting of the cabinet. The discussions were to be held for two days in Honolulu. Japan would be represented by the most senior career officials of the ministries and agency involved, their administrative vice ministers: Hatoyama from Finance, Morozumi from MITI, Morimoto from Agriculture, and Kano from the EPA. MOF Vice Minister for International Monetary Affairs Hosomi would also attend, and the Japanese delegation would be headed by Ambassador to the United States, Nobuhiko Ushiba. The United States delegation, made up of assistant secretaries from Treasury, State, Commerce, and Agriculture, would be headed by President Nixon's Special Trade Representative, William Eberle.[6]

The tone of the announcement and the seniority of Japan's delegation suggested the cabinet had been persuaded—probably by the Ministry of Finance—to take the U.S. demand for negotiations more seriously. But as one of the primary liberalization targets, agricultural interests in Japan strongly opposed the government's agreement to another round of trade negotiations before the yen issue was settled. On Saturday, December 11, the day the negotiations were scheduled to begin, Yutaro Nemoto, chairman of the LDP's Investigative Committee on a Comprehensive Agricultural Policy (Sogo Nosei Chosakai), and Michio Watanabe, chairman of the LDP Agriculture Sub-committee (Norin Bukai), held a joint press conference at the LDP's Nagata-cho headquarters. They denounced the government's decision to discuss further trade liberalization, and said they supported the agricultural community's absolute opposition to any more liberalization of beef or citrus at the Honolulu conference. They announced plans to help agricultural spokesmen lobby the LDP and Ministry of Agriculture in opposition to any last-ditch American demands.[7]

In spite of vigorous private-sector agricultural opposition, the Honolulu conference opened as scheduled at 5:00 P.M. on December 11 at Waikiki's Irikai Hotel. For two days a predictable scenario unfolded: the U.S. demanded Japanese agreement to implement significant trade barrier liberalization prior to the final international monetary negotiations in order to avoid higher yen up-valuation demands; the Japanese explained why such measures would be difficult to implement, but eventually agreed to continue discussions. Eberle insisted trade problems could not be separated from monetary problems, and emphasized the need for immediate liberalization, especially in agriculture where U.S. competitiveness vis-à-vis Japan is strongest. In his public statement, Eberle said he expected the bilateral trade negotiations to continue up to and through the Washington monetary meetings.[8] This was in spite of the announcement in the midst of the conference that the Europeans had declined the American invitation to discuss trade before the Washington conference, and in fairly blunt terms. Saying France was unwilling to negotiate with a "knife at her throat," French Foreign Minister Maurice Schumann estimated January to be the earliest date for the talks.[9]

The U.S.-Japan conference ended in Honolulu on Sunday, December 12, at 4:45 P.M. with Japan's public pledge to implement the eight-point program of liberalization announced earlier in the year—labeled at its inception by its MOF creators as the "eight-point program to avoid yen revaluation"—and the release, after Eberle's departure for New York, of the following joint communique:

Representatives of both countries to the U.S.-Japan trade talks, led by Ambassador Ushiba of Japan and Ambassador Eberle of the United

States, gathered on December 11 and 12 to further discuss trade problems between the two countries.

The conference served to reexamine trade problems remaining between the two countries and to clarify for both countries the understandings arrived at so far in trade negotiations.

The conference showed some progress, and both Japan and the United States each understood their mutual positions on remaining unresolved trade problems. Both Japan and the United States agreed to again open discussions in the near future to examine U.S.-Japan trade problems.[10]

One unusual feature of the December 1971 Honolulu U.S.-Japan trade liberalization talks was the high degree of tension and disagreement within the Japanese team, resulting, in the words of one observer, more in a struggle among the Japanese participants than a scrap with the United States. Battle lines were drawn within the Japanese ranks with the Ministry of Finance on one side, and MITI and Agriculture on the other. The EPA representative was forced into the thankless role of ineffectual mediator. If not in total sympathy, MOF participants were willing to listen, at least, to the American team's list of trade liberalization demands. But MITI and Agriculture were strongly opposed to any significant compromise. They reminded the U.S. side that Japan was already an important market for U.S. agricultural goods, that Japan was already exercising export restraint on a number of products, including textiles, and they charged the United States with use of its antidumping legislation as de facto import-restraint measures.[11]

Several years later two members of Japan's negotiating team reported that the international group in the Ministry of Finance decided, out of frustration with the lack of progress on liberalization, to support American suggestions for parallel trade negotiations. They hoped that direct exposure of their MITI and Ministry of Agriculture colleagues to the intensity of the U.S. demands would encourage them to be more cooperative.[12] Their strategy was nothing new. It had been used a number of times in the postwar period by Japan's central political and bureaucratic authorities to escape domestic political blame for changes in the status quo that the government realized had to be made in the long-term national interest, but that were opposed by business interests whose support was important. If the American side could be encouraged to apply sufficient pressure, to increase the severity of their threats of retaliation to the point the reluctant affected domestic interests would be forced into agreement, then the needed change could be made with little danger of political retribution. The Americans would be blamed, but they didn't seem to mind. They didn't have to stand for election in Japan, and few American politicians have seriously damaged their careers by talking tough to foreigners.

A meeting of the "economic cabinet" was convened after the regular cabinet meeting on Tuesday the 14th. Attending were Prime Minister Sato, Ministers Fukuda, Tanaka, Mizuta, Kimura, Acting Agriculture Minister Yamanaka, and Chief Cabinet Secretary Takeshita. The group was briefed by Foreign Minister Fukuda on the outcome of the Honolulu trade talks. After the meeting the press was told the cabinet considered it inappropriate, under the circumstances, for Japan flatly to refuse to continue bilateral trade negotiations with the United States prior to the final monetary negotiations. EPA Director General Kimura was asked to take responsibility for herding the various interministerial interests into agreement on a package of liberalization measures—heavy on agricultural products—of interest to the United States for presentation during the parallel trade negotiations planned for later in the month in Washington during the Group of Ten's ministers' conference. Kimura was given a deadline of December 16. The cabinet also appointed Ambassador Ushiba as Japan's Chief Trade Negotiator, counterpart to Special Trade Representative Eberle.[13] The press conference ended with comments by the individual cabinet members, including MITI Minister Tanaka, about the need to include trade liberalization concessions in the final settlement because of the U.S. issue-linkage strategy.

The ministries involved began meeting the following day, under the guidance of Director General Kimura, in pursuit of agreement on a more attractive liberalization package. Yet the members of Japan's Honolulu conference negotiating team showed little inclination to compromise in their public comments made upon their return on the evening of the 14th, after the cabinet meeting. Clearly more interested in assuring his domestic constituency that their interests were being protected than in conveying news of Japan's basic cooperative nature to Japanese newspaper readers at the American Embassy in Tokyo, Agriculture Vice Minister Morimoto told a press conference at the airport: "There were strong demands for the promotion of liberalization and tariff reductions from the

U.S. side. But fundamentally we didn't break from the line given to the U.S.-Japan Trade and Economic Conference held in September. Even if a similar sort of conference is held in the near future, we at the Ministry of Agriculture have no intention of opening negotiations concerning the liberalization of agricultural products or tariff reductions."[14]

The Agriculture Ministry's intransigence was supported by Japan's powerful Federation of Agricultural Cooperatives (Zenkoku Nokyo Chuokai). Chairman Miyawaki stated on the 14th that "Since the liberalization of beef, oranges, and citrus juices would damage agriculture, we plan to hold a meeting tomorrow of the heads of the five major agricultural groups at which we will pass a resolution opposing liberalization. This will be sent to the government and to the LDP. If the U.S. continues to insist upon liberalization, Nokyo is considering a suspension of the import of feed-grains that we now buy from the United States."[15] This was the most severe public statement to come from a responsible Japanese spokesman throughout the whole crisis period, and it indicates the degree of tension and resentment the problem had generated in Japan.

Still, in spite of severe domestic opposition and open threats of political retaliation, the liberalization effort continued in Tokyo throughout the week in the hope that something might be agreed upon that would help to reduce pressure on the yen during the final settlement, or at the very least, that would impress the Americans with the sincerity of their effort. On Wednesday, December 15, the Foreign Ministry hosted an afternoon meeting of bureau directors general from the Ministries of Finance, MITI, Foreign Affairs, Agriculture, and the Economic Planning Agency to discuss the situation. They failed to arrive at any specific conclusion, other than to reaffirm that a new proposal should quickly be prepared for the United States.

On Thursday, the day before the Smithsonian Conference was to begin, EPA Director General Kimura was scheduled to convene the vice ministers of the involved ministries to discuss the problem further and to cable news of any progress to Mizuta in Washington. But by Wednesday night the Japanese press was told for publication Thursday morning that the government had given up on any significant agricultural liberalization in the face of extremely hostile farm reaction, but that progress was still possible on increasing the size of existing quotas.[16]

The Nixon administration maintained pressure on the European

Economic Community, Canada, and Japan for participation in meaningful bilateral trade negotiations in parallel with the monetary meetings right up through the Smithsonian meetings. A Department of Treasury spokesman announced on Wednesday the 15th Japan's agreement to hold parallel talks, as an incentive for the Europeans,[17] and hints were made that the surcharge would remain in effect even after fixed parities had been reestablished if no progress was made on trade liberalization and defense burden-sharing.[18] After yet another meeting, this one on bureaucratically "neutral ground" at the Akasaka Tokyu Hotel, Kimura announced Thursday evening that he was hopeful of presenting a liberalization package similar to the measures outlined in the June eight-point program to avoid yen liberalization—a most optimistic estimate considering the circumstances.[19]

After the regular cabinet meeting on Friday the 17th, Prime Minister Sato convened another meeting of "economic cabinet" members to discuss the initial reports received from the delegation in Washington. On the advice of Mizuta and his technical advisers on the scene, the cabinet decided to dispatch a negotiating team of directors general from the Ministries of Agriculture, Foreign Affairs, and International Trade and Industry to take up the trade issue.[20] They were scheduled to leave Tokyo that evening. After strong protests, even refusals to negotiate with "knives at their throats," the Europeans had agreed to begin trade negotiations in Brussels on December 23. The European decision was portrayed in the public announcement as the deciding factor.

The bilateral U.S.-Japan trade talks were scheduled to begin in Washington on Saturday at 1:00 P.M. (3:00 A.M. on the 19th, Japan time) at the Department of State, at the very time that the finance ministers and Secretary Connally would be finalizing an international monetary agreement across town at the Smithsonian's castle on the Mall. Ambassador Ushiba was to head the Japanese team, which included Economic Bureau Director General Hirahara of the Foreign Ministry, MITI's Trade Bureau Director General Yamashita, and others. The American team was to be headed by Special Trade Representative William Eberle.[21] Hard-fought bilateral trade negotiations did begin at the Department of State on Saturday the 18th from 1:00 P.M. For three hours the two sides went over old ground, with the U.S. demanding more import liberalization, larger agricultural quotas, and an overall reduction in Japan's tariff rates. The Japanese side responded with an offer to remove the tariff on soybeans altogether, and to reduce tariffs on thirty other items, including trucks. Also, they suggested increases in the quotas on beef, oranges, turkeys, and assorted beans, and proposed that a certain number of live calves be imported with no tariff.[22]

However, once final international monetary agreement was announced at the Smithsonian's castle on the Mall, the Japanese government instructed its trade negotiating team to "return to white paper," suspend the second trade meeting, and return home. The reason given for this sudden change of plans was that Japan had agreed to immediate bilateral trade negotiations only to avoid a demand from the U.S. side for an unreasonably high level of yen revaluation. Since the exchange rate finally agreed upon was far higher than anticipated—16.88 percent—Japan was not obligated to continue the talks.[23]

The Smithsonian Conference: "Final" Settlement

Wednesday afternoon, December 15, Finance Minister Mizuta boarded a Pan American flight to Washington, bound for an international conference that would assure his place in Japan's postwar diplomatic history. As proposed by Chairman John Connally the previous week, the Group of Ten's ministers were scheduled to meet on the 17th and 18th, their conference to be preceded, as usual, by a preparatory technical advisers' meeting. Mizuta and his colleagues would try one more time to reach agreement on a new set of fixed parities for the world's major currencies, and an end to months—even years—of international monetary anxiety.

Prime Minister Sato and the cabinet had agreed the week before to grant Mizuta full negotiating authority during the conference—a mixed blessing, at best, since such authority carried with it full political responsibility for any errors. Mizuta qualified his mandate during a press conference after the cabinet meeting at which the decision was formalized, stressing his intention to check any final decision on the yen with the prime minister should the level of upvaluation finally demanded exceed his expectations.[24]

Mizuta and his group of technical advisers had good reason to be optimistic about this mid-December conference as they arrived late Wednesday afternoon at the self-consciously luxurious Madison Hotel in downtown Washington. During conversations with the expectant Japanese press corps Mizuta stressed the significance of the American "compromise" on dollar devaluation. The Europeans and Americans at last seemed ready to talk, and it was likely that Japan would be presented with a final demand. When asked his personal assessment of the parallel trade negotiations, especially their probable impact on the final yen settlement, Mizuta reminded the news-hungry press corps of the bilateral summit meeting scheduled for early January, indicating that meeting provided the trade negotiators with a time frame which extended somewhat beyond the Smithsonian conference.[25]

The next day, Thursday the 16th, the senior technical advisers opened their preliminary discussions at IMF headquarters around 11:00 A.M. As expected, their meeting was little more than a reaffirmation of the group's conclusions in Rome—that technical adjustment was impossible, and that only the ministers themselves could make the political decisions necessary to reach a final settlement. That afternoon the technical group met with the IMF's board of directors and prepared a general joint communique that affirmed the importance of Friday and Saturday's political-level talks.[26]

Secretary Connally invited the European and Japanese ministers in for private discussions throughout the day on the 16th while other members of each delegation discussed the upcoming talks with their counterparts, reinforcing their own positions while probing for weakness in the others. As part of that activity, Mizuta and Connally met for two hours on Thursday and Connally described his version of an acceptable settlement.[27] Kashiwagi later wrote that Connally's opening position called for a 9 percent devaluation of the dollar, a 19 percent up-valuation of the yen, a 10 percent up-valuation of the pound and franc, and a 5 percent up-valuation of the mark.[28] In addition to the severe monetary demands, Connally continued to insist that a "package settlement," including Japanese, Canadian, and European trade liberalization, was required to persuade him to remove the import surcharge.

The first day of ministerial meetings began at 11:20 A.M. on Friday the 17th in the Smithsonian's castle. International conferences of such importance become very confusing events if ground rules are not established at the outset which limit the number of staff assistants allowed to participate at one time. During the opening twenty minutes, only the finance ministers and central bank governors were allowed in the conference room. And during the remainder of the conference, only one technical official from each country was allowed in to assist his principal. Yusuke Kashiwagi, of course, was Mizuta's choice as first assistant.

The Smithsonian conferees were faced with the same four points of decision dealt with in Rome:

1. Change in the price of gold, or the level of devaluation of the dollar, and agreement that other countries would not simply devalue in turn to cancel the effects of the change of the dollar devaluation
2. The European cross-rate problem
3. A new exchange rate for Japan's yen
4. The special case of Canada[29]

The meetings continued in strict secrecy throughout the day and evening of Friday the 17th, with only a break for lunch at 1:30 P.M., a coffee break at 5:00 P.M., and a dinner hosted by Connally at 8:00 P.M. As a point upon which to begin discussion, Connally presented his proposal for large-scale up-valuations of each currency against the dollar, and a 9 percent devaluation of the dollar itself. Such large changes, of course, were strongly opposed by the other representatives, and by the end of the day little progress had been made. An aide to Connally complained to the U.S. press about the "snail's pace" of the proceedings, and said any kind of a communiqué at the end of the first day of discussions would be out of the question.[30]

Around 11:00 P.M. Finance Minister Mizuta and Governor Sasaki held a joint press conference at the Madison Hotel during which they did their best to say as little as possible to the Japanese journalists without arousing suspicions that might provoke them into speculating the talks were about to break down. Withholding any specific details, Mizuta said the United States had presented a parity readjustment proposal that would be very difficult for Japan to accept, that the question of whether or not the surcharge would be lifted after currency realignment had been discussed, and that it might take longer than two days for the group to reach final agreement.[31]

During a personal interview five years later, relying only upon memory, Mikio Mizuta recalled the background preparations for the Smithsonian conference. He and the other members of the Japanese team were convinced Connally planned to press for a 20 percent yen up-valuation during the meeting, and that the Europeans and Americans really would not want to settle for anything less than 18 percent. Mizuta said: "The MOF did some calculations prior to the conference and tried to calculate the impact [of yen up-valuation] on the Japanese economy. According to their calculations, the level at which repercussions wouldn't be too severe was 14.3 percent. So, I decided to state at the conference that Japan was willing to go as high as 14 percent. But the others wouldn't even consider that level. Not anyone."[32]

Discussion during the first day of the Smithsonian conference confirmed the Japanese delegation's expectations. After the dinner hosted by Secretary Connally from 8:00 P.M., which Mizuta was unable to attend because of an upset stomach, Yusuke Kashiwagi worked until nearly midnight to further probe U.S. intentions as Minister Mizuta's English-speaking intermediary in private meetings with Secretary Connally, Under Secretary Volcker, and others.[33] Later that night the results of their discussions were transmitted to Tokyo. After receiving the reports from Washington, Prime Minister Sato called a meeting of the "economic cabinet" at 7:00 P.M. Saturday the 18th, Tokyo time (Saturday, 6:00 A.M., Washington time), to discuss the American proposals and the European response. By then it was clear Japan would be forced to accept an up-valuation of more than 15 percent. To reduce the shock potential of the final announcement the cabinet decided to make a preemptive leak of that possibility to the Japanese press. Stories reporting "speculation" from Washington that the up-valution might go even higher than the 15 percent heretofore considered the maximum acceptable rate change appeared in Tokyo's Sunday morning papers.[34]

On Saturday the 18th, the finance ministers and central bank chairmen began the second day of discussions at 10:50 A.M. after conferring with their home governments by cable and telephone. With final instructions in hand, the Europeans met earlier in the morning to work on a solution to their cross-rates problem. Japan too met with representatives of the U.K., West Germany, France, and Italy prior to the meeting, and such bilateral contact continued on through Saturday in the suites occupied by the individual delegations outside the conference hall.

The wrangling that by late Saturday afternoon had produced a new system of fixed exchange rates for the world's major currencies is best summarized by the recollections of the heads of the American and Japanese delegations. First, Secretary Connally:

What happened both in London and in Rome and the meeting at the Smithsonian, we stayed in recess about half of the time in order that the Group of Six—France, Germany, Britain, Italy and so forth—could try to work out their internal relationships. They were more interested in the relationship between the Pound Sterling, the French Franc and the German DM and Italian Lira than they were between those currencies and the dollar or those currencies and the yen. So they met in London, they met in Rome, they met in Washington, the Group of Six trying to agree between themselves what their relative currency values would be.

They finally came to me at the Smithsonian, not the French alone. Giscard d'Estaing, who is now the President of France, he and Karl Schiller who was the Minister of the Treasury, Minister of Finance of Germany, came to me and said in effect "We give up. We cannot agree among ourselves. You are going to have to work it out." I said "all right." This was on Friday before the last day. I said "All right, I'll try and work it out." And then I started, and very quickly (I said) . . . and here were the basic agreements. The French Franc had to be revalued about 10%. But the Germans insisted that they were not going to be revalued more than the French Franc unless the Japanese were revalued more than they were. So I went to Karl Schiller and I said "Now, the French are going to revalue about 10%." He said "Well, what do we have to do?" I said "You have to revalue about 13 or 15%." He said "I won't do that unless I know what the Japanese are going to do" and I said "The Japanese are going to have to revalue 17 or 18%." "Well" he said, "if we can get this kind of an agreement." Then I went back to each one. 10 o'clock Friday night I told Mr. Mizuta, your minister, I told his deputy that they were going to . . . we had been telling the Japanese they had to revalue 10% [sic]. We felt the yen was grossly undervalued. I had told your Prime Minister that I thought the yen should be revalued 25%. But I said "I understand politically you can't do that in one year. So we are going to talk about something less than that for the yen to be revalued," and we had been talking about 19%. About 10 o'clock Friday night I told Minister Mizuta's assistant that he had to agree to 17%. I said we have to reach an agreement. If we can't reach an agreement then we have to break up the conference. But I said "The Germans are going to revalue 13 or 14%, the Japanese have to revalue 17%. This will leave the French at about 10% and so on. And then the Italians and the British were going to revalue about the same." Well, the next morning on Saturday, the last day, the Italians came in and said "We just can't revalue." It's unfair and so forth. And I went back to the French and the Germans and I said "You know, we don't care. The Italian economy is not in good condition, it's not in good shape. It's alright with me if we leave the Lira even with the dollar if it's alright with you." They said okay. That's basically how we got an agreement. I worked it out with all of them, but [sic] all of them agreeing. It wasn't an [sic] unilateral arrangement with the French at all. I negotiated with the French, with the Belgians, with the Italians, with the British, the Germans, and the Japanese—all of them.

[*Interviewer:* Could you remember the final scene of when the Japanese accepted the revaluation?]

They accepted the last day, the Saturday morning. I told them we had to have the final answer by 10 o'clock. 5 minutes before 10 o'clock on Saturday morning the last day, the Japanese accepted.

[*Interviewer:* Who accepted?]

Accepted not 17% but 16.9%.

[*Interviewer:* Why?]

Well, there is a very interesting story. Your representative, and you perhaps have heard the story, I've said 17%. Mr. Mizuta's aid [sic] came in and said he can't accept 17%. I said "Alright, that's fine, and you are going to destroy the whole conference." "Oh, no no" and I turned around and said "We have to have an answer now. You have not said anything for days, and this is your deadline, and if that's your answer, that's your answer," so I turned and walked away. He said "Wait a minute, just a moment." He said "We do not want to accept 17% because in the early 1930s the Japanese yen was revalued 17%. It caused chaos and panic in the money market in Japan, and the Japanese Finance Minister committed suicide because of it. We cannot revalue 17%." and he said "Give me another figure." I said "16.9," he said "okay." That's how you got the 16.9%.[35]

Mikio Mizuta recalled the events at the Smithsonian's castle from his perspective as follows:

Well, the conference was opened, and the session that I didn't attend was held in the morning, but the Japan question was not settled. Everyone was having lunch, and during lunch I left the hotel, went to the room next to the conference and called in Mr. Connally. Here I told Mr. Connally that there was no way that I could accept the demand for an 18% revaluation, and if they persisted in trying to make me accept the demand I would have to leave the conference and return home.

He said that if Japan did such a foolish thing that he would be in trouble. He asked what my reason was for not accepting. But, really, I didn't have any reason. Everyone was insisting that through exhaustive computer analysis they had come to their conclusions, but really it all depends upon how the computers are used as to what rate comes out as the result. I told Connally that since I am coming up all the way from 14.3%, please at least make it under 17%, and after all of the other countries discuss the problem we can come to agreement. Mr. Connally said that without the cooperation of Japan there would be a problem. Canada could do what it likes—cooperate or not—do whatever they like. But, without the cooperation of Japan we will be in trouble. With that, Connally immediately went to talk with the British representative, asking me to wait there for his return. I was asked to wait in that room and he went to negotiate with the others. He convinced the French, talking with Giscard d'Estaing, since the Japanese have been this cooperative let's think over the question of trying to force them up to 18%. After England and France agreed, he went to see the Dutch and Italians, and finally went to the Germans. But, the Germans wouldn't agree.

The reason the Germans wouldn't agree was it would have made the spread between Japan and Germany 5 percent. So, Connally asked them to try to compromise with the French on the spread between the DM and the franc. "If you will go along with what the French are saying about the spread between the franc and the DM for me, I will try to do something for Germany by widening the spread between the DM and the yen." And, apparently, this is what went on in the behind-the-scenes discussions with Mr. Connally intervening. Taking care of the Japanese first, and finally dealing with the Germans. And, according to my wishes the spread between the DM and the yen is more or less 3 percent, isn't it? The Germans didn't like this 3 percent spread. After compromising with both the French and the Japanese it would be tough for the DM. Because there were various meetings in Germany about the problem, and the German president wouldn't agree, the German representatives were in real difficulty, and couldn't make a reply.

Looking at a chart giving the closest even yen rate for 17 percent, or just under 17 percent, we came up with the final rate of 16.88 percent for 308 yen. We couldn't make the rate 308 or 307 and some fraction, in order to make it come out exactly 17 percent. So, when we made it 308 yen it didn't come out even as far as percentages go, but it would have been very difficult to deal with a rate which would have been uneven in terms of yen, and in the end the yen rate which was the closest to 17 percent turned out to be 308 yen, which was 16.88 percent. So, in the end, everyone but the Germans agreed to my wishes.

Mr. Connally and I developed a good relationship. Thinking that there must be good reasons behind my thinking on the 17 percent suggestion, he decided it would be improper to continue to insist upon the 18 percent change. Mr. Connally, having so decided this, he went around to the various countries, convincing them. But, Germany wouldn't go along with him anyway. So, when it came down to what to do with Germany, with Connally's cleverness, he came up with the following idea:

He said that at the beginning of the morning conference he would announce that another conference would follow in the afternoon. He told me that right at the beginning of the conference he would ask me what about Japan? And, I was then to say that we were willing to give up the 14.3 percent proposal that we were hoping on, and have until then insisted upon, and we were willing to compromise up to 16.88 percent. Up until that point it is all right with Japan. He said when I ask you about Japan, please tell me exactly that. Then, right away I will bang the gavel and say thank you, it is decided for Japan. No matter what the outcome is, that is what I will do.

Then I said to Mr. Connally, if Japan right at the beginning plays its final card of 16.88 percent and then, like dickering in the marketplace for bananas, I have to gradually increase, offering various figures, finally settling for the end result of 18 percent it would be unseemly for me. Therefore it would be better for me just to accept the 18 percent figure from the beginning. Mr. Connally replied that there was something to it, and maybe his methods wouldn't work. But there is really nothing to do but to try it.

Then we went in and reopened the conference. We did just as we had previously decided. I said 16.88 percent and Connally replied that the 16.88 percent figure for the yen has been decided. After that Germany began to complain. Then Italy joined in with objections. And the discussion continued on. Then France's Giscard d'Estaing stood up and said let's not bicker over the details and agree at this point.

[laughing heartily] But before coming to a definite conclusion, Connally told us "Mr. Nixon is in the next room, by the way, and he would like to speak to us [go-aisatsu shitai]. So, may I have him come in to extend his greetings?" Well, since the president was in the next room and wanted to greet us, it was impossible for us to refuse. So, then Nixon came in the room and declared "This is not a question of which country won or which country lost. Rather, it is a victory for the free countries of the world over the Communist countries." He went on like that. In other words, he greeted us as if the conference had already come to an end and we had made some sort of outstanding accomplishment upon which he wished to congratulate us.

Then, right away, everyone went to have pictures taken by the various foreign newsmen, and he took everyone with him. But, I didn't go. I was the only one who didn't go. At first the German representative was sitting beside Nixon, and I suppose that if I had gone then I would have had to sit in that place, just next to President Nixon. But I didn't go.

So, the whole thing was handled as if it had already been decided, even though the Japanese and the German situation was still up in the air. Other countries had agreed, but Germany still had reservations. While things were still up in the air, Connally had banged the gavel and Nixon came in and told us that it was a great victory for the Free World over the Communist World, irresponsibly ending the whole thing, bringing the curtain down on the Smithsonian conference. So, at the close the conclusions of the meeting were not summed up and restated as is the custom at such gatherings.[36]

Opinion within Japan's delegation on the final settlement was badly split by the last day of the conference. In spite of four months of international monetary uncertainty and the toll it had taken on the international moneymen's domestic support, in spite of the incredible multilateral pressure Japan's delegation faced during the conference, and in spite of what most observers believed to be a fairly moderate final level of settlement for the yen given current international conditions until the very end, two senior members of the Japanese delegation adamantly opposed Finance Minister Mizuta's acceptance of the 16.88 percent up-valuation figure, considering it outrageously high. They strongly urged him to withdraw from the conference and return home. Their opposition was a source of great concern for the other Japanese delegates, some of whom later complained that it was motivated more by a desire to avoid political retribution once they returned home than by the rational economic arguments they used to support their position.[37]

The concern of the other delegates was understandable. Since Wednesday Mizuta had been telling conference participants, including Connally, that he was most anxious about the domestic reaction to his acceptance of any final international monetary settlement. He referred repeatedly to the February 1932 assassination of Junnosuke Inouye, a prewar Japanese finance minister who fell from public favor over his handling of international monetary problems.[38] Mizuta's preoccupation with the prewar Inouye incident may have been motivated in part by his desire to reduce pressure on the yen by convincing his counterparts of his limited flexibility. Nonetheless, if the group was greeted by severe criticism of their "capitulation" once they returned home, it would be easier to handle the situation if none of the members of the negotiating team opposed the final settlement. Disgruntled team members with inside information could provide their critics with powerful ammunition to use against their colleagues.

Early Saturday morning the Japanese team prepared to convey the terms of the final settlement to Tokyo for confirmation. They assumed their telephone conversations with Tokyo were being monitored by the American intelligence service for quick relay to the American negotiating team. They had more confidence in the security of their embassy's encoded information channels, but decided against using them (according to a Finance Ministry source) during the conference because the embassy took three or four hours each way to encode, send, decode, and distribute messages. The Bank of Japan's communications facilities that the MOF was accustomed to using as an alternative to official embassy channels were another possibility, but they were unavailable at the time in Washington. Since rapid, secure communication was considered essential, it was decided before leaving Tokyo that during the final phase of the negotiation communication between Washington and Tokyo would have to be done over regular telephone lines. For that purpose an elaborate code was created around the metaphor of fishing trips. The places fished and the types and quantities of fish caught represented levels of yen up-valuation and other points of negotiation.

One of the senior Japanese negotiators later recalled calling his superior in Tokyo to discuss the final level of up-valuation. Due to the time difference the official in Tokyo took the call at home—in fact, in his bath, but he had forgotten to bring his copy of the elaborate fishing code home from the office. The two were left with no alternative but to discuss the situation in plain Japanese, believing they were being overheard by the American intelligence community and that their conversation would soon be relayed to the American negotiating team. The source of the story said that neither he nor his superior was too concerned about the security breach, and even hoped the information might help to persuade the Americans of their sincerity.[39]

By late Saturday afternoon the first postwar multilateral readjustment of foreign exchange rates had been completed. The United States agreed to increase the dollar price of gold to $38.00 per ounce (amounting to a 7.89 percent dollar devaluation); the Japanese yen rose 16.88 percent against the dollar. Also, the band of fluctuation allowed under the IMF system was increased to 2.25 percent.[40] This meant that the Japanese yen could fluctuate between Y 314.93 and Y 301.07 to one dollar. The new rates were to go into effect the following Monday, the 20th, but all exchanges were to remain closed for one day as businessmen around the world adjusted to the new situation.

Finance Minister Mizuta, the Bank of Japan's Governor Sasaki, and other members of Japan's Smithsonian delegation arrived together in Tokyo on December 20 at 9:30 P.M. During a stopover in Anchorage, Alaska, they had seen special editions of the major Japanese newspapers printed on the 19th. Although the press was critical of the larger-than-expected concession Japan had been forced to make on the up-valuation, the group was relieved by the overall tone of the coverage. As usual, a quick news conference was held for the returnees in the Haneda Tokyu Hotel around 10:00 P.M. Mizuta defended the level of revaluation to which he had agreed with explanations of the complexity of the international situation. He also added that even though the band of allowable fluctuation had been increased to 2.25 percent, each country was free to do as it wished, and the MOF intended to reduce the actual amount of rate fluctuation.[41]

Prime Minister Sato called a special cabinet session at his official Nagata-cho residence on Sunday morning at 9:20 A.M. to agree to the new exchange rate as required by Japan's foreign exchange law. After the cabinet meeting Sato held a press conference beginning at 10:00 A.M. during which he read a statement welcoming the international agreement on exchange rates as a step toward a more stable international economic system. Sato added that although the up-valuation was larger than expected and would adversely affect the Japanese economy, he was confident the situation would return to normal within a year.[42] Sato's comments were followed by a statement from Mizuta. Anticipating public criticism of the higher-than-expected 16.88 percent up-valuation, Mizuta argued that the final level of up-valuation was appropriate since it reflected the increasing importance of the yen in world affairs, and from that point of view it could even be welcomed.[43]

As planned, interbank foreign currency transactions were suspended for Monday the 20th, and trading began normally on Tuesday the 21st at 9:00 A.M. During the last day of trading on Saturday the 18th, heavy dollar selling had pressed the rate up to Y 320 to $1, or to a level equal approximately to a 12.29 percent up-valuation over the old fixed rate, according to the IMF method of calculation. On Tuesday morning, after the IMF agreement, the yen began trading at about Y 314 to $1, in orderly markets that headed for the newly established "fixed" rate.[44]

The international moneymen were not surprised by immediate opposition party criticism of the large up-valuation. Both the Japan Socialist party and the Komeito issued official statements on Sunday the 19th in which they accused the government of wilting in the face of unfair U.S. demands, and of ignoring Japan's current weakened economic situation.[45] During a plenary session of the Lower House on Tuesday the 21st, Representative Masao Hori, one of the JSP's most knowledgeable economic policy observers, rose to accuse the LDP of "*tsuizui seisaku*" (literally, a policy of following in the wake of another craft) for its capitulation to U.S. pressure. Hori then turned to Foreign Minister Fukuda and said, "When you were Finance Minister you lied, saying you didn't have any thought of a yen revaluation, even in the corner of your mind. Why don't you take responsibility for that!" Fukuda rose, approached the microphone with a twinkle in his eyes, and replied, "It is certainly true that I said there was no thought of a yen revaluation in the corner of my mind. The truth of the matter was that it was right at the center of my mind. However, it is internationally accepted that Finance Ministers needn't tell the truth about international monetary problems. Finance Ministers really have it tough!"[46]

By December 19, 1971, Japan's international moneymen had finally achieved their secondary goal: an orderly settlement of the international monetary crisis with no more disadvantage for Japan than for the other nations. Resolution of the intense crisis had taken just a little over four months, leaving Japan's public and business community throughout uncertain about their future. Japan's political system had survived the crisis. Its overall performance deserved no praise, but public assessment was sufficiently benevolent to avoid either of the two dreaded evils: electoral failure or meaningful bureaucratic reform.

10. Conclusion

The Bretton Woods international monetary system suffered severe strain during the late 1960s and early 1970s, strain to which Japan was related both as victim and perpetrator. As victim, Japan's business community, government, and public felt highly dependent upon that vital link to the world economy for their national well-being, and they suffered economic and emotional stress from the loss of confidence and predictability. Japan's representatives encouraged large member nations, especially the United States, to implement the appropriate domestic and international economic measures necessary to balance their accounts and restabilize the system.

As perpetrator, Japan was one of two countries blamed most often for threatening the system's stability through the accumulation of large foreign currency reserves from trade account surpluses and inflows of speculative foreign capital. Japan also was charged with maintaining protectionist restrictions on imports and foreign investment far longer than justified to assure postwar economic recovery, restrictions that risked retaliatory imitation by her trading partners. Japan's market remained well protected from foreign penetration throughout the period, and by the early 1970s she was the only major IMF member to have avoided exchange rate adjustment in response to postwar reconstruction and economic advancement.[1]

After decades of struggle against foreign exchange scarcity, Japan's international economic situation changed dramatically in 1969. For the first time domestic economic upswing was accompanied not by decline, but by surpluses in her international accounts. Ministry of Finance economists privately agreed with the international community's judgment of fundamental change. But Japan's international monetary officials publicly interpreted this shift of fortune as only a temporary aberration in a long series of balance-of-payments cycles certain soon to return to normal, and they rejected international calls for a fundamental shift in Japan's aggressive foreign economic policy.

Japan's most politically sensitive international economic indexes (the overall trade balance, overall current account balance, total foreign currency reserves, and bilateral U.S.-Japan trade balance) continued their rise throughout 1969 and, after a relatively quiet first nine months of 1970, shot skyward again from the last quarter onward—all within the context of an increasingly shaky, crisis-prone international monetary system. Still Japan stood firm, rejecting pointed U.S. and European demands that she modify her surplus-generating system. MOF officials responded with a series of technical measures designed to slow accumulation of reserves without affecting the economic fundamentals—such as the "yen shift"—and with the flamboyant announcement but leisurely implementation of liberalization measures designed to stall for time and quiet international criticism.

The surprise May 1971 up-valuation of the West German mark and attendant tremors throughout the international monetary system was as much a thunderbolt for Japan as for other IMF nations and even inspired domestic business and communications media pressure for more substantial government efforts to calm the situation. But this combined international and domestic pressure only resulted in the early June release of a comprehensive package of measures, guaranteed difficult if not impossible to implement, labeled the "Eight-Point Program to Avoid Yen Revaluation." Japan's international monetary officials in mid-1971 remained confident they could survive the crisis with a minimum of liberalization supported by vigorous international lobbying and public relations ploys, but by mid-August global conditions were ripe for dramatic change.

President Nixon's August 15, 1971, double-barreled initiative finally persuaded senior MOF officials that something more substantial than international public relations was required to cope with changes in their international economic environment. After nearly two weeks of bitter internal struggle the Ministry of Finance agreed to allow the yen to float upward in response to market pressures, but even then only under highly controlled conditions. The domestic, bilateral, and multilateral tussle continued from the August 27 controlled float to the December 18 "final" international settlement at the Smithsonian's castle on the Mall.

The economic and political costs to Japan of refusing to acknowledge the fundamental change in her relationship with the international economic environment, and then refusing to devise and implement a policy response appropriate to cope with the new situation, were enormous. Economically, failure to face the inevitable prolonged the growth-stifling period of international monetary uncertainty as Japanese business struggled to recover from recession in 1971. The huge exchange-market intervention purchases necessitated by the government's effort to maintain the yen's parity forced Japan to absorb billions of rapidly depreciating American dollars. University of Tokyo economist Takafusa Nakamura has even charged that the government's unwillingness to cope with rising wholesale prices in late 1969 with a moderate exchange rate adjustment rather than credit restraints exacerbated the international trade imbalance problem, unnecessarily prolonged the later periods of recession, and encouraged recession countermeasures which, when overdone, worsened the inflation that wracked Japan later in the decade.

The political cost of Japan's delayed response was even more severe, and more enduring. Lack of response was interpreted in the United States and Europe as evidence of Japan's unwillingness to assume her share of the costs of maintaining the international economic system, even as she prospered mightily from its efficient operation. Japan's inaction eroded much of the international goodwill her government, industry, and private citizens had labored to inspire since 1945. It mattered little that other countries also were guilty of selfish, "free rider" international economic behavior. Japan was the one getting rich, and the one considered the most flagrant case. This, combined with the latent—sometimes overt—racism and resentment remaining from the war, created a hostile atmosphere that would prejudice foreign perceptions of Japan for years to come.

Skeptics may dismiss international goodwill as unrelated to corporate profit-and-loss statements, national employment statistics, or any other imaginable index of Japanese well-being, save possibly the welcome Japan's tourists receive abroad. And in the short run such reservations would appear reasonable. But over the longer term this erosion of international goodwill from the late 1960s onward helped to justify harsh treatment of Japan abroad, with the manner in which the "Nixon shocks" of 1971 were administered a prime example. Japan's stubborn posture strengthened the position of Nixon administration policy participants who argued for "tough," unilateral international economic measures. As Japan's public image deteriorated abroad it became more difficult for foreign economic officials to make cooperative gestures toward Japan, even when so inclined, for fear their domestic political opposition would take advantage of a public backlash against them.

After four months of exhausting bilateral and multilateral negotiation Japan's international monetary officials agreed at the Smithsonian Conference to what later would prove a moderate change in the yen's parity. Years of contrary prediction aside, the change only temporarily sidetracked Japan's upward economic spiral. Business and government adjusted with little difficulty first to a new fixed exchange rate and later even to floating rates. Perceived as only a reluctant ratifier of inevitable change, Japan earned little credit abroad for cooperation in the final international monetary settlement. It was her stalling tactics and clumsy public relations blitzes that remained in the memories of foreign policy-making elites, ready to influence disputes over issues yet to arise. By waiting until forced by the United States to implement measures inevitably required to adapt to changes in her international environment, Japan's policymakers not only intensified anti-Japan sentiment abroad, but also generated antiforeign feeling at home in natural response to the heavy-handed *gai-atsu* that strategy required. Increased resentment at home and abroad further complicated implementation of politically sensitive measures required for Japan to adapt in later years to international environmental change.

The simple explanation of Japan's response to the late 1960s-early 1970s international monetary crisis is that officials in the Ministry of Finance were able to control response to changes in her global economic environment. They opposed any change in the fixed Y 360=$1 parity of the yen, and devoted their considerable talents and influence to its preservation. Explanation of why they were so opposed to a parity change and, more significant, how a small group of highly specialized bureaucrats was able to gain and maintain such effective control for so a long time over an issue with national interest implications for Japan as broad as those faced in 1971 requires more detailed examination of the nature of the particular issue, the individual actors and their interaction in the policy process, and supraministerial policy coordination within Japan's postwar political system.

The Nature of the Issue

The policy processes of any political system are influenced greatly by the nature of the issues they encounter. All policy participants agreed that issues related to Japan's relationship with the international monetary system during the late 1960s and early 1970s were very important, of "general" rather than "specific" significance, highly technical, sensitive, and therefore necessarily secretive.

Importance of the Issue. Japan's primary school children were—and still are—required to memorize detailed global maps that show by country the types and quantities of imports essential for Japan's economic survival. They learn early that Japan's postwar economic miracle and rising living standard depend greatly upon her ability to import raw materials, semimanufactures, and those high technology products not yet available at home, and to export manufactures in quantities adequate to pay for her foreign purchases. The yen's international rate of exchange was and is recognized as a critical factor in Japan's international economic relations, and therefore of great national importance. Government officials for more than twenty years had argued that any change in the fixed Y 360 = $1 rate of exchange would introduce disastrous unpredictability into Japan's domestic economy and repeatedly had justified growth-dampening economic policies as necessary to defend the fixed yen exchange rate. This widespread sense of importance assured a high, if only speculative, level of communications media and public interest in the government's activities, and at least passive interest throughout the national economic bureaucracy.

Of General Rather than Specific Significance. The issue of Japan's relationship to the international monetary system was perceived not only as important, but important to the whole nation rather than to only a specific group or sector. I had anticipated significant differences of opinion on the merits of yen up-valuation, differences determined by the government or corporate respondent's relationship with export- or import-dependent sectors of the economy. Industries such as electronic appliance manufactures, whose profits depended more upon export sales than on the cost (within reason) of imports, would have more reason to oppose up-valuation than industries whose profits depended more on the cost of imported raw materials than export success, such as utility companies or the importers of agricultural products. Manufacturers of goods such as steel or automobiles, for whom both export markets and raw materials costs were important, might stand somewhere in the middle as mediators.

But such different interests had only a slight influence on the policy process. Shipping companies lobbied during early 1971 in support of maintaining the fixed rate, but the MOF at that time hardly needed encouragement. Export-dependent small business owners complained to sympathetic parliamentarians about the adverse impact of the yen float, and they in turn complained to Finance Minister Mizuta. But their impact was marginal, at best, and too late to change the course of events. Before the August "Nixon shock" Japan's business community and public thought of change in the fixed yen rate more in terms of its negative impact on the vigor and stability of the overall Japanese economy than in terms of its likely impact upon their particular economic interests. This more general concern overwhelmed any differences of opinion inspired by varying degrees of export and import dependence.

Thus the yen's parity, much like overall national security, remained a "general" rather than "specific" issue, and as such failed to stimulate conflict among private-sector interest groups with dissimilar interests. Private-sector interests did not appeal to political actors to oppose bureaucratically determined policies. This made the issue less attractive for the support-conscious (campaign funding and votes-oriented) LDP and opposition politicians, and discouraged the political sector from approaching Japan's international monetary affairs critically until it was too late to make any real difference in policy outcomes.

Its Highly Technical Aspect. Issues related to international monetary affairs are perceived by the general public, the communications media, the business community, politicians, and even the rest of the economic bureaucracy, as highly technical and difficult to understand. An objective examination of the principles of international monetary affairs fails to justify that reputation, but whether justified or not, only ordained international monetary specialists in Japan were considered qualified even to discuss the subject. Its mystique, especially within the economic bureaucracy, may have been enhanced by the importance that foreign-language fluency plays in its pursuit.

The highly technical reputation of the issue was mentioned repeatedly by political, bureaucratic, and private-sector interviewees in response to questions about the ability of the international monetary specialists to maintain such enduring and effective control over an issue of such general importance. The experts were able to fend off all but the most determined interloper with technical jargon heavily laced with *gairai-go* (foreign language words used in a Japanese context).

Its Highly Secretive Aspect. The extreme sensitivity of the foreign exchange market under a system of fixed exchange rates and the need for absolute secrecy in the implementation of government market intervention also influenced the policy process, and for good reason. It was well known that a leak of government plans for foreign exchange market operations would be certain to trigger a disastrous avalanche of costly speculative transactions. It also was well known that an individual with direct or indirect access to inside information could profit greatly from improper use of such information. Japan's senior politicians, according to LDP sources, therefore avoided any association with the issue to the extent possible out of fear they might be accused publicly of trying to manipulate the foreign exchange market to their own personal financial advantage, and private-sector representatives stayed clear for the same reason.

Max Weber provides an interesting note of caution on the natural inclination of bureaucrats to protect themselves behind cloaks of secrecy:

> The concept of the "official secret" is the specific invention of bureaucracy, and nothing is so fanatically defended by the bureaucracy as this attitude. . . . In facing a parliament, the bureaucracy, out of a sure power instinct, fights every attempt of the parliament to gain knowledge by means of its own experts or from interest groups. The so-called right of parliamentary investigation is one of the means by which parliament seeks such knowledge. Bureaucracy naturally welcomes a poorly informed and hence a powerless parliament—at least in so far as ignorance somehow agrees with the bureaucracy's interests.[2]

Government officials responsible for Japan's international monetary affairs certainly were justified in their exercise of strict security precautions over foreign exchange market operations. But whether intended or not, the aura of secrecy that gradually enveloped international monetary affairs discouraged critical review of their stewardship by outsiders with broader policy orientations.

Policy Process Participants: Influence, Objectives, and Patterns of Interaction

Policy process participants most influential in determining Japan's response to the 1969–1971 international monetary crisis included: the Ministry of Finance; the remaining ministries and agencies of the national economic bureaucracy; established and ad hoc private-sector business organizations; the communications media and general public; ruling and opposition political parties; and the prime minister and cabinet.

The Ministry of Finance. Japan's international monetary relations remained under the undisputed control of the Ministry of Finance throughout the late 1960s and early 1970s. Officials most important within the MOF up through the 1971 "protracted crisis" were the vice minister for international monetary affairs, the director general and division directors of the International Monetary Bureau, and occasionally, the director of the Office of Research and Planning in the Minister's Secretariat, with the latter confined to ad hoc sensitive research and analysis projects as required. Once Nixon's August 15 announcement upgraded the level of crisis from "protracted" to "intense," the administrative vice minister (MOF's top career official) and the finance minister himself became more directly involved as well.

The unrelenting forward march of Japan's higher civil service promotion and retirement cycle forced Yusuke Kashiwagi to end his regular bureaucratic career as vice minister for international affairs in June of 1971. He immediately moved down the hall to become special adviser to the Minister of Finance, a temporary position from which he continued to exercise great influence over international monetary policy throughout the period of the study. MOF official policy from beginning to end, as enunciated and enforced by Kashiwagi, opposed any change in the fixed Y360 = $1 parity of the yen. Expressions of doubt, such as those in 1969 of Taizo Hayashi, then Director of the Office of Research and Planning in the Minister's Secretariat, and of Economic Planning Agency economists, were dismissed at first as empty academic "theorizing," then were banned absolutely within the MOF, and serious efforts even were made to prevent public discussion of the issue within the business community.[3]

By 1969 this fixed yen exchange rate had become a fundamental, nonnegotiable feature of Japan's international monetary policy. As pressure intensified in the form of sustained surpluses in Japan's four politically critical international economic indicators, heightened foreign criticism, and eventually domestic business and communications media unrest, MOF deliberations focused upon means to shield the fixed parity from their influence. The exchange rate, in essence, became the *object* of Japan's international monetary policy, rather than a policy *instrument* in the service of more general economic objectives. The formulators and implementers of Japan's international monetary policy spent the next two years in pursuit of that basic objective.

Why were Japan's international monetary experts so opposed to change in the parity of the yen in spite of mounting statistical and political pressure? The most frequently mentioned reasons during interviews several years after the event were historical. First, Japan's long experience with domestic growth-dampening international deficits inclined officials to view current surpluses as a temporary embarrassment of riches. Second, the very fact the yen's parity had remained fixed at Y360=$1 for twenty years by 1969—an argument often raised abroad in *support* of change—made it more difficult for MOF bureaucrats to imagine discharging their responsibilities under a different rate. A third factor often mentioned was the Finance Ministry's hesitance to implement measures that would adversely affect recovery from an existing economic downturn, first during late 1969 when belt-tightening measures taken to counter imported inflation began to bite, and later during the more pronounced slump in 1971.

A fourth factor was related to the third. After years of describing even the possibility of an up-valuation of the yen to the business community and public as dangerous and undesirable, MOF officials believed sudden announcement of a parity change would create public panic and economic disorder for which the Ministry of Finance was sure to be blamed. A possible fifth factor not mentioned by any of the interviewees, but likely to have contributed to bureaucratic inertia, was the fear that the MOF would be besieged by budget-breaking demands for compensation from stunned business community representatives, accusing it of being responsible for their foreign exchange-related losses after having promised unequivocally for so long to maintain the fixed exchange rate.

But most important, Kashiwagi and his MOF subordinates simply believed yen up-valuation would permanently reduce the international price competitiveness of Japan's foreign exchange-earning manufactures, and therefore that it went against Japan's basic national interests. They recognized the impact of their "stand fast" posture on the international monetary crisis and its adverse impact on Japan's reputation as an international economic actor. Nonetheless, until news of the Nixon initiative reached Tokyo on the morning of August 16, 1971—indeed, for nearly two weeks thereafter—the MOF specialists believed it was possible for Japan to maintain this important source of foreign trade advantage somewhat longer, by dulling international criticism and stalling for more time through minimal liberalization gestures and international public relations efforts until the global economic environment improved sufficiently to dampen European and American pressure for meaningful change.

Domestically oriented senior MOF officials were the first to realize after Nixon's suspension of the dollar's convertibility and imposition of the 10 percent surcharge on all dutiable American imports in August that Japan's inflexible position was doing more harm than it could possibly be worth. They were no more eager than their international monetary specialist colleagues to surrender the commercial advantages the fixed Y 360 = $1 rate had provided Japan for so long. But unprejudiced assessment of the situation led to the inevitable conclusion that adjustment of the yen's parity represented the lesser of several evils. Kashiwagi opposed the change even after the "Nixon shock," but the wrenching break in the fixed rate and float of the yen was facilitated by the presence of domestically oriented incumbents in the Finance Ministry's key positions of vice minister for international monetary affairs and administrative vice minister.

The Bank of Japan. Other government ministries and agencies had a natural interest in anything as important as Japan's international monetary policy. But throughout the period of the study they remained observers for the most part, and only occasionally served as sources of unwelcome advice. The one exception was the Bank of Japan. But even the role of the Bank of Japan, which coordinated interaction with the banking community, including the delicate and highly secretive foreign exchange market intervention process, was restricted mainly to implementation of policies determined by the Ministry of Finance. This point was made with table-thumping emphasis by Tadashi Sasaki, governor of the Bank of Japan in 1971, during a 1976 personal interview:

> One thing I would like to make clear here is that all matters related to foreign exchange rates in Japan are within the jurisdiction of the Ministry of Finance. And ultimately, whether or not to keep the market open or closed is a decision that has to be made by the Finance Minister. Even in the case of market intervention, that money comes from the Finance Ministry's Foreign Exchange Special Account [Gaikoku Kawase Tokubetsu Kaikei] for the transactions and the Bank of Japan serves as agent *[dairi]*. So, as opposed to the domestic change of the official discount rate, in foreign exchange markets the Ministry of Finance has all the authority, and the Bank of Japan only can act as the representative of the Ministry of Finance. That point should be understood![4]

The opinions of the Bank's governor and senior officials with international monetary responsibility, especially about current market conditions, were conveyed to the MOF, but the Ministry of Finance determined policy. To this extent, Japanese newspaper articles which frequently began stories about international monetary policy with the set phrase "Today Government and Bank of Japan authorities announced *their* decision to . . ." were somewhat misleading. The Ministry of Finance *decided;* the Bank of Japan *implemented.*

Ministry of International Trade and Industry. MITI followed international monetary events with great interest, collecting information at home and abroad, with primary emphasis on how a parity change would affect Japan's commercial competitiveness in international markets. During the "protracted crisis" period before the August "Nixon shock," MITI grew increasingly concerned about the possibility of foreign economic retaliation but agreed with the prevailing opinion that a change in the parity of the yen would be an economic disaster for Japan, that it should be avoided at all—or nearly all—cost, and basically supported the Finance Ministry's "stand fast" position.

Their most direct involvement came through participation in the many interministerial meetings held to coordinate implementation of the liberalization measures detailed in the Finance Ministry's early June "Eight-Point Program to Avoid Yen Revaluation." While opposed to any change in the yen's parity, MITI also resisted some of the more politically significant liberalization measures detailed in the eight-point plan.

Their basic posture changed little after the "Nixon shock." In September the Japanese press carried rumors suggesting that senior MITI officials had urged the Ministry of Finance to accept a substantial unilateral up-valuation of the yen, either instead of the float as a means to persuade Washington to lift the surcharge, or in place of more draconian trade and investment liberalization. I was unable to confirm specific instances of such proposals during interviews five years later. But even if true, such advice from MITI would have had little impact on the Finance Ministry's deliberations. The yen crisis did provide MITI officials with ample opportunity during the late 1971 budget negotiation season to propose costly projects for the next fiscal year under the banner of countering the recessionary impact of the inevitable up-valuation.

Ministry of Agriculture. The Ministry of Agriculture was less internationally oriented than MITI, but played a similar role in the international monetary policy process during the 1969–1971 period. Officials there worried too more about liberalization than about the parity of the yen and exercised no significant influence over the international moneymen's deliberations. Those few Agriculture officials who could be considered "internationalists" were import- rather than export-oriented, and therefore unconcerned about the negative impact of a yen parity change on their private-sector client groups. They too accepted the consensus opinion of the protracted crisis period that yen revaluation should be avoided because it would seriously damage Japan's overall economy.

The import orientation of some of the Ministry of Agriculture's private-sector clientele (grain and other primary food product importing trading companies, etc.) and of the internationalist officials themselves was no match in intraministerial battles for the domestic producer groups supported by the politically powerful agricultural cooperatives. The Agriculture Ministry never encouraged the MOF to consider yen up-valuation with the argument it would reduce the yen cost of Japan's imported food. This critical point did not become part of the private and public yen policy debate until December when Finance Minister Mizuta began to prepare public opinion for the inevitable up-valuation.

Agriculture officials were even more opposed than their MITI colleagues to the liberalization measures the Ministry of Finance proposed as alternatives to a parity change in the interminable interministerial meetings during the latter half of 1971. Backed by noisy and politically potent national farm organizations, they resisted all but the most innocuous proposals to the very end. After the mid-August Nixon announcement, hard-line ministry officials were rumored to sympathize with farm group representatives who told the press they preferred yen up-valuation to the level of agricultural liberalization urged by the MOF to appease Washington. Why, the argument went, should agriculture be asked to sacrifice once again for the sake of the industrial sector as it suffered the consequences of its own excesses? But such comments were less serious policy proposals than defensive grumbles tossed out in the confidence they would be disregarded by the policymakers responsible for the yen. In the face of rather rough treatment by their frustrated MOF colleagues, as at the December bilateral trade negotiations in Hawaii, Agriculture Ministry bureaucrats devoted themselves to maintaining Japan's status as an international economic special case, manipulating their sympathetic minister, Munenori Akagi, as an effective weapon in the domestic battle.

The Economic Planning Agency. The Economic Planning Agency was more interested in the yen's international value throughout the period of the study than either MITI or the Ministry of Agriculture. EPA lacked political clout on most economic issues, but had organized a number of Japan's most able economists into a highly respected professional staff. Given its impressive analytical capabilities, one might expect the EPA to have played an important role in the formulation of Japan's international monetary policy during the late 1960s and early 1970s. But according to the recollections of senior EPA economists, it was isolated almost completely from the policy process. The MOF had no intention of allowing a government organization that lacked even ministerial status to enter its fiefdom, especially one whose officials disagreed with its policy positions.

Dr. Masaru Yoshitomi, assigned in 1971 to IMF headquarters in Washington as assistant to Japan's director, Hideo Suzuki, recalled during an interview in 1976 that many EPA professional staff economists believed the government should take a more flexible attitude toward parity adjustment, but they were prevented from expressing their opinions in public. When asked to assess EPA's role in the policy process, Yoshitomi concluded it was limited because the agency had no authority *(ken'i)* over the yen issue, and because all EPA public statements of opinion had to be cleared by the ministries concerned. He said the question of the government's handling of the yen issue in 1971 remained sensitive even five years after the event, with other ministries insisting that EPA avoid any reference to the yen issue in their publications that might inspire public criticism of their actions.[5]

During a subsequent discussion of the EPA's role in Japan's international monetary policy process during 1971, another senior EPA economist was even more blunt. He said it was common knowledge throughout the 1969–1971 period that EPA economists had concluded from their econometric models that a parity adjustment was needed for Japan to adjust to changes in the world economy. He recalled the painful and frustrating inter-ministerial negotiations required to obtain approval even for the innocuous yen-related portions of the EPA's 1970 and 1971 reports. The MOF flatly refused to approve inclusion of any material that supported the opinion the yen might require a parity adjustment.[6]

Tatsuro Uchino, a senior EPA official during the 1969–1971 period, was more blunt still. He recalled during a 1976 personal interview that the yen parity problem had been an EPA concern since at least the latter half of 1969. After explaining the difficulty of constructing an econometric model of the international monetary situation unambiguous enough to support policy prescriptions, Uchino said that consensus opinion among the agency's economic analysts in 1969 was that Japan required a revaluation of around 6 percent. By 1971 their estimate of the required parity adjustment had risen to 12 percent or more. Uchino characterized the yen issue as "political" rather than "economic," and said "political considerations" prevented the EPA from using its information and expertise to influence the policy process. He bluntly concluded that those responsible for Japan's international monetary affairs in the late 1960s and early 1970s erred seriously by not responding sooner with a parity adjustment.[7]

Ministry of Foreign Affairs. In spite of the international nature of the 1969–1971 yen fracas, and in spite of the fact that Japan's Ministry of Foreign Affairs was best qualified and positioned to assess the direction and intensity of American and European intentions, the Foreign Ministry was allowed to play at best only a peripheral role. While MOF and Ministry of Foreign Affairs informants all endorsed this general assessment, they differed fundamentally over its explanation.

At the best of times, Japan's Foreign Ministry plays with a very high handicap in the international policy arena—at least when the issues involved are considered important by players with more substantial domestic political support. The Foreign Ministry, like its American counterpart, has fallen victim during the 19th and 20th centuries to advances in communications technology and a growing preference among world leaders for more direct interaction that bypasses traditional channels of diplomatic communication, thus weakening first their morale and gradually their effectiveness.

The Foreign Ministry enjoyed a few moments of real influence during the postwar occupation through the fortuitous coincidence of its English-language capability and its reputation for limited political power, which logically excused its personnel from much responsibility for Japan's wartime excesses. Suddenly, dozens of Japan's diplomats were elevated to positions of real influence, serving their non-Japanese-speaking conquerors as links of convenience in the complicated chain of command wrought by the occupation's principle of "indirect" rule. It was a moment from which neither the Foreign Ministry itself nor the ministries over which it temporarily exercised its reflected power have yet to recover.

Foreign Ministry informants emphasized their dual roles of spokesman and coordinator in Japan's relationships with other countries. The substance and significance of the former is obvious. The latter boils down to the Ministry's contention that possessing both foreign language ability and a superior understanding of the international environment enable diplomats to judge more shrewdly the responses required from other ministries to best defend Japan's national interests in the face of foreign threat. More often than not, the Ministry's critics charge, that means sympathizing with foreign demands, especially those from the United States. As a result, even when international compromise is in Japan's best interests, the

Foreign Ministry by so recommending risks accusations from other ministries of weakness in the face of foreign demands.

This history of interministerial animosity made it inevitable from the beginning that Japan would be denied the meaningful participation of her most skilled foreign affairs specialists during the worst international crisis she had faced since the end of World War II. MOF informants admitted and justified their deliberate efforts to exclude them as a defense against the Foreign Ministry's notorious incompetence in economic affairs and traditional weakness vis-à-vis foreigners. Foreign Ministry officials chalked it up to bureaucratic jealousy and MOF embarrassment over its own limited experience with foreign affairs.

The Bureaucratic Actors: Summary. In sum, despite the importance of international monetary policy for Japan's overall national interest, none of the other government ministries or agencies came close to threatening the Finance Ministry's absolute control over its formulation. Only the Bank of Japan was involved significantly even in its implementation, mainly through the monitoring of foreign exchange markets and service as a market intervention agent. MITI, a potential challenger, recognized the signs of crisis but failed to challenge MOF opposition to a change in the parity of the yen. MITI focused on stalling implementation of the liberalization measures proposed in the Finance Ministry's eight-point revaluation-avoidance program and, after the August "Nixon shock," on expansion of its own budget through expensive revaluation-recession countermeasure proposals. Agriculture just wanted to be left alone. Avoidance of agricultural liberalization was the whole issue for that producer- rather than consumer-oriented ministry and its farm clientele.

The Foreign Ministry, considered weak in economic affairs and vulnerable to foreign pressure, was barred from any monetary policy formulation role. Its only significant participation was mobilization of its foreign language ability and familiarity with the United States to coordinate international public relations and lobbying efforts to blunt and delay pressure for trade and investment liberalization. Professional economists on the Economic Planning Agency staff had the expertise required to analyze the complicated foreign exchange issue, and many of them disagreed with the Finance Ministry's yen doctrine. But lack of political influence effectively neutralized their early efforts to change the MOF line, depriving Japan of an important source of policy expertise which, if utilized, could have provided useful counterbalance.

There is nothing unusual about dedicated civil servants concluding after years of service in one position that the national interest depends more than anything else upon the competent discharge of their particular responsibility. While equating personal bureaucratic interest with that of the nation, they can in clear conscience defend their area of authority with canine ferocity from the interference of would-be trespassers who lack their own experience and judgment.

Instances of bureaucratic "dictatorship" are common at all levels in any large administrative system. But in most cases its long-term survival requires that the domain be restricted to relatively obscure areas in which other potentially powerful actors have no particular, or at least, no sustained interest. It is one thing to believe the mission of one's agency is the most important thing in the world; it is quite another to get away for very long with acting out the part, especially when such acting seriously inconveniences other politically powerful policy participants.

International monetary policy in Japan during the 1969–1971 period was an exception. The bureaucrats responsible for this particular aspect of Japan's overall foreign and domestic government policy considered their area of responsibility—maintenance of the fixed Y360 = $1 exchange rate, as they defined it—a vital determinant of Japan's economic prosperity, and considered only themselves qualified to call the shots. The surprising thing was that their claim went for so long unchallenged either by other bureaucratic agencies or by actors with broader economic and political responsibility. In spite of its general importance, in spite of the adverse "spill-over" impact of the MOF position on the other government sectors (stronger demands for liberalization and the threat of a protectionist backlash abroad, for example), and in spite of the widespread government and public interest the subject generated, the Finance Ministry's international moneymen were able to maintain their "stand fast" position until forced to compromise (and even during the float, only slowly and reluctantly) by other MOF officials who were more domestic in perspective.

The Business Community. The direct influence of the members of Japan's business community on the management of international monetary policy, like that of other actors, was limited by their general agreement with the Finance Ministry's "stand fast" position, at least prior to the August 1971 Nixon announcement, when their opposition might have made a difference. Japan's exporting manufacturers had no interest in losing the competitive advantage of an artificially low exchange rate, and nonexporting Japanese business was persuaded of the recessionary impact exchange rate change would have on the whole economy. Business observers had a somewhat more accurate view of the dangerous buildup of anti-Japan pressure abroad than did the government, but they preferred to believe government's claims that they would be able to wait out the storm behind an international public relations screen.

Public expressions of concern from Keizai Doyukai chairman Kikawada and banking spokesman Goro Koyama frightened MOF officials, who moved swiftly and forcefully to squelch them. But these men had little influence on the policy process, and even failed to stimulate additional support within the business community for a reassessment of policy, drawing instead criticism from other businessmen almost as severe as that from the government.

Stung by the double punch of Nixon's August 15 suspension of the dollar's convertibility and imposition of the surcharge, Japan's business community became more willing to criticize the government's international monetary stewardship, but with little effect. Diversity of interests made it difficult to achieve a consensus—even within the separate business organizations—adequate to produce policy proposals on anything but the most general level.[8] Complaints were made through LDP politicians about the speed of the up-valuation under the float, but these were little more than an irritant. Individual industrial sectors, such as shipping and shipbuilding, focused their lobbying efforts with only limited success on the more specific issue of government compensation for losses related to the rate change rather than on international monetary policy itself.

The banking community requires special mention. As a direct result of the Finance Ministry's decision to hold open the foreign exchange market for nearly two weeks after the Nixon announcement, Japan's foreign exchange banks were able to sell off huge amounts of their rapidly depreciating U.S. dollar holdings, vastly improving their balance sheets for that fiscal year. The official government position, as stated during Diet testimony and to the press, was that the banks' potential losses had no influence on the decision to maintain exchange operations, or upon the timing of their eventual suspension. It is a position I find difficult to accept. It was the banking community—the Finance Ministry's own "client industry" (and to a lesser extent, the leads/lags-speculating international traders and manufacturers)—that received special treatment through an amazing opportunity to unload huge quantities of depreciating U.S. dollars in a short period of time at government expense. To that extent the financial sector may have delayed somewhat Japan's response to the August 15 "Nixon shock."

Private Sector International Monetary Experts. The technical nature of the international monetary issue and the astounding volume of material published on the subject led me to assume while planning this study that private-sector experts were closely involved in the policy process. They weren't. Closer examination revealed that much of the published material—books and articles appearing in regular economic, business, and general periodicals—was either too general or too technical to have much influence on the policy process, even if the policymakers were open to external opinions and ideas. And they weren't. The Finance Ministry's international moneymen were confident they knew more about the subject than anyone in the private sector, and therefore felt no need for external advice. Only the problem of managing the float stimulated them to seek advice from outside experts, and almost all of those contacted were retired MOF officials.

The sensitive nature of international monetary affairs also discouraged external participation. When asked during interviews about offering advice even if unsolicited, several respected banking-sector economists recalled that they refrained, assuming that any initiative would have been misinterpreted by touchy MOF officials as an improper effort to "manipulate" the process. They also confirmed that their opinions were not sought by the government. Meetings arranged by the major economic organizations to exchange views between their economists and government officials were described by private-sector participants as ending up to be one-sided explanations by the government of the problems it faced, general outlines of its plans to cope, and calls for public-sector support for its position.

MOF officials by no means ignored the public statements of private-sector international monetary experts. In fact, they went to considerable pains to suppress any criticism of their policies, fearing adverse impact on the foreign exchange market in the short term, and on their control of the situation in longer term. The public statement by the group of 36 respected international economists, headed by Tokyo University professor Ryutaro Komiya, was the most celebrated example. MOF officials ignored the group's technical argument, but concerned about its possible impact on public opinion at home and abroad, they issued a sharp public rebuttal in the next edition of the daily newspapers, while sounding an even sharper private response to individual committee members.

In one sense, the high level of in-house international monetary expertise intensified the Finance Ministry's isolation from sources of alternative interpretation, becoming more of a weakness than a strength. If external sources had been tapped early in the crisis the MOF would have been exposed to a wider range of opinions on issues such as the severity of the Bretton Woods system's structural problems and the intentions of the United States. Such views might well have strengthened the positions of early in-house supporters of exchange rate adjustment. As it turned out, Japan's private-sector international monetary experts were well paid for a year or so to churn out articles and books on their specialty, making the issue more significant for them than they were for it.

The Communications Media and the General Public. International monetary affairs, especially under a system of fixed exchange rates, by its very nature discourages widespread public participation. MOF officials were most concerned about the impact of public opinion on the foreign exchange market, and did what they could to conserve intervention spending by persuading the public through the communications media of the permanence of the status quo—a fixed Y 360=$1 rate before the August float, and only a slow increase during the float—until it became clear even to the Ministry of Finance late in 1971 that a more substantial rate change was required. MOF officials then shifted their domestic public relations theme to instituting a more positive image of the inevitable upvaluation.

The communications media serves as a two-way link between policymakers and the general public. I assumed at the beginning of the study that the government had commissioned opinion polls on international monetary affairs, or at least had included related questions in more general regular government polls. But I could find no evidence of such polls, and interviewees insisted that no polls were commissioned simply because they were "unnecessary." Thus government perceptions of public opinion on this issue came largely from the communications media themselves. Interviews confirmed that supposition. When interview subjects referred to "public opinion" they usually meant communications media reports. The news organizations were well aware of this dual nature of their communications function and sometimes used it to lecture the government on management of the yen issue, as well as one other foreign and domestic issues.

The communications media, especially the large national daily newspapers, raised the level of tension felt by policymakers during the "protracted crisis" period of 1971, increasing their "bunker mentality" through incessant speculation on the likelihood of a change in the yen's parity. Japan's large news organizations had their own international monetary experts, and equally important, their own sources of information about the international environment, which inclined them to doubt the government's ability to "stand fast" forever. The close personal relationships that develop within the context of the press club system between reporter and source were strained to their limits during this period, in some cases beyond the breaking point, by the prolonged period of suspense. In sum, for this issue as for other sensitive and complex international issues, the influence of Japan's public and communications media was more negative than positive, more that of establishing parameters beyond which government's policymakers felt uncomfortable straying, than stimulating action in one direction or another.

The Political Actors. Finance Minister Mizuta, by all accounts, performed admirably the domestic and international role expected of him, as had his predecessor Takeo Fukuda. But then, not much was expected. Only once did Mizuta's participation amount to much more than ratification of decisions predetermined by the international moneymen: his agreement the week after the "Nixon shock" to allow Hosomi and Hatoyama to float the yen in spite of the opposition of his senior international monetary adviser, Yusuke Kashiwagi. And even that was too late to have much effect on the issue's outcome. Prime Minister Sato, at the top of the official responsibility pyramid, served throughout as the ultimate ratifier of decisions made, and supported Mizuta and the international moneymen with public statements when required. But Sato's main contribution was described by policy process participants as his lack of opposition to the level of yen up-valuation required, once it had become inevitable.

The remaining LDP leaders and members were briefed in the Policy Affairs Research Council and during Diet hearings by MOF officials, but they played no direct role until after the August 16 "Nixon shock" announcement. And even then politicians were limited to more private, specific complaints to Mizuta and the MOF on behalf of export-dependent supporters and constituents about the rapidity of the upward movement of the exchange rate under the float. According to Vice Ministers Hosomi and Hatoyama, such complaints made Mizuta more difficult to deal with when his permission for more upward movement was required, but he always agreed in the end.

With ruling party participation so marginal, it was no surprise to learn that Japan's opposition parties had little influence on international monetary affairs between 1969 and 1971. Before the August 1971 Nixon initiative, when they might have exercised at least marginal influence as part of their traditional "gadfly" role, all of the opposition parties supported the Finance Ministry's policy of maintaining the fixed parity and therefore ignored the problem. Once the MOF was forced to abandon the fixed rate, the opposition, like some of the LDP's antimainstream factions, exploited the opportunity to criticize the government's failure to maintain its promise to "stand fast."

Their efforts amounted to little more than incidental irritation and were perceived by the press as unimaginative examples of political opportunism. The opposition failed, for reasons I have yet to determine, to pursue its one big opportunity: to criticize the government's decision to hold open the foreign currency exchange for nearly two weeks after the Nixon announcement. That potentially damaging issue was dropped after several dramatic hearings during which Shiro Inoue of the Bank of Japan became the unfortunate victim of Japan Socialist party member Wada's misdirected attack.

Failure of Supraministerial Policy Coordination

Central political leadership, the prime minister and cabinet, share responsibility for Japan's failure to define and implement policy measures appropriate to respond during the late 1960s and early

1970s to her shift from deficit- to surplus-prone international economic status and an increasingly unstable international monetary system. According to the 1946 Constitution, it is the cabinet collectively that is responsible under the prime minister for the management of national domestic and international affairs, and individually for the supervision of each government ministry and agency. Article 65 of Chapter V states that "Executive power shall be vested in the Cabinet," and subsequent articles confirm that the prime minister, designated by majority vote of the Diet, is expected to play the key role with power to appoint and dismiss members of his cabinet and exercise "control and supervision over various administrative branches."[9]

The cabinet and prime minister long before August 1971 should have recognized signs that the international monetary tail had begun to wag the overall economic dog, that the international monetary officials' resistance to meaningful change had begun to threaten Japan's more general national economic interests, and then to have ordered a reassessment of policy. Had the prime minister or finance minister decided to act, their orders certainly would have been obeyed—perhaps not joyfully, but obeyed. This judgment does not presume a higher level of international monetary expertise among Japan's prime minister and cabinet colleagues than that of their MOF subordinates. Rather, Prime Minister Sato, a former senior civil servant, and other cabinet members should have sensed the dangers of bureaucratic sectionalism early on and developed channels through which dissenting expert opinions expressed throughout the period could have been given more serious consideration from a perspective broader than that of the international monetary officials.

When asked why Japan's central political leadership did not play a more effective coordination role in the policy process, Finance Minister Mizuta and other interviewees in the political sector all mentioned the highly technical, secretive nature of the issue. Generalist politicians necessarily rely on the advice of expert subordinates in charge of particular issues. The more technical the problem the greater their dependence on expert advice. The reputations of Kashiwagi and his MOF international monetary specialists were such, however, that they found it difficult even to imagine going outside that charmed circle for additional opinions. The response to a shift from deficit- to surplus-prone international economic status and the parity of the yen remained for the political actors "technical" issues well within the ken of the bureaucracy, in spite of the considerable national significance these issues had. Neither Mizuta nor any other interviewee in the political sector believed the political actors had failed to discharge their constitutionally defined responsibilities, and all concluded the bureaucrats alone were responsible for any errors of judgment.

One might dismiss the statements of those in the political sector as obvious efforts to avoid blame for past policy errors. But their opinions were confirmed during interviews with opposition politicians, businessmen, journalists, and even the bureaucrats themselves. None of the interviewees, even when nudged, were inclined to blame the key political actors for errors of judgment. They blamed instead the bureaucracy and individual officials, charging that they, with their superior qualifications and experience, should have adapted their "stand fast" position earlier in the game to changing international economic reality. Even interviewees openly hostile to individual politicians involved, to the LDP, or to the political sector in general, declined to settle "blame" on the politicians.

Etiquette requires Japan's civil servants to be deferential—embarrassingly so by American standards—during direct personal contact with politicians. But even greater deference is paid to the principal of "political noninterference" in the work of Japan's bureaucracy. "Political noninterference," often compared favorably with the clumsy amateurism of the American system and its underqualified political appointees, is identified regularly as an important determinant of Japan's economic success, one that discourages the particularistic and self-interested meddling of politicians in the bureaucracy's efforts to promote the national interest through formulation and implementation of "correct" economic policies.[10]

Chalmers Johnson describes this phenomenon in his study of MITI:

> The Japanese bureaucracy jealously guards the practice of making no political appointments below the ministerial level; the bureaucrats believe that this helps establish their claim to be above politics and to speak only for the national interest. One of the bureaucracy's greatest fears is "political interference" in its internal affairs or, worse, a ministry's being made subservient to a party or a politician.[11]

He associates this practice, which has survived the war and postwar constitutional reform, with a "separation between power and authority" rooted in Japan's feudal tradition and the adoption of the Prussian model of the "capitalist developmental state" during the Meiji period. He, like other analysts, emphasizes the positive aspects of this separation of power and authority, or minimization of "political interference," in Japan's economic development, but wisely adds that "One of the most serious consequences for Japan of adopting this system was its decision in 1941 to go to war with the United States and Great Britain—a decision in which neither the monarch nor the parliament participated."[12]

What may be an advantage for the management of specific domestic issues may prove a serious disadvantage when Japan is forced to respond to general international issues. Japan's bureaucrats are at least as vulnerable as their international counterparts to the lapses of judgment symptomatic of the "localitis" and "tunnelvision" associated with long periods of exertion in specific and specialized fields. And in the presence of these maladies, the principle of "political noninterference" has negative as well as positive consequences for the effectiveness of the policy process and for the maintenance of Japan's economic prosperity and political wellbeing.

Japan's national policy system is most effective when implementing universally accepted, clearly defined goals—especially those that fall under the exclusive, or near exclusive, domain of one powerful ministry, or at least those goals that pose little danger of interministerial conflict. When external conditions change, and preservation of Japan's most general, long-term national interests requires a powerful ministry or agency to deviate from established policy on issues it considers important, or when the interests of the client groups of two or more important bureaucracies collide, constitutionally mandated political responsibility for oversight and integration becomes more than an ideological nicety. Here, in the realm of supraministerial policy-making, the performance of Japan's system is less than impressive.

Lacking effective central political coordination of her separate bureaucratic fiefdoms, Japan, in a pattern reminiscent of the occupation period, once again in 1971 substituted the deus ex machina of irresistible American external pressure *(gai-atsu)* for supraministerial political leadership to force the required changes. With the simultaneous suspension of the U.S. dollar's gold convertibility and imposition of the import surcharge, the Nixon administration in one crushing blow turned Japan toward the required adjustments by rendering the status quo so obviously less appealing than the disadvantages anticipated from the necessary change.

The application of *gai-atsu* was successful—at least in the short term. Japan soon agreed to make significant adjustments to adapt to her new international economic status, and Japan's political leaders avoided blame from their business group supporters and the voters for ordering the required changes. American political leaders and bureaucrats involved seemed almost to enjoy the opportunity once again to talk tough to foreigners and certainly suffered no domestic political damage as a result. But the longer term costs both for Japan and the United States were enormous. This episode left the policymakers and publics of both countries more resentful and suspicious of the other, and made the Japanese more inclined to see the United States as an insensitive bully while making Americans more likely to see Japan as the devious, unfair exploiter of an international economic system she was unwilling to support until forced.

Gai-atsu, especially but not exclusively from the United States, has remained a significant and increasingly unwelcome aspect of national politics in Japan since this dramatic episode in late 1971. In the absence of effective central Japanese political leadership, it is still required and continues to create serious problems both for Japan and for her diplomatic partners. Only a dramatic improvement at the supraministerial level, in the policy coordination functions of Japan's prime minister and cabinet, can provide an alternative.[13] And that must await development of political parties and a political party system capable of producing central political leaders with authority adequate to compete with Japan's national bureaucracy as legitimate definers and implementers of Japan's national interest.

Notes

Preface

1. The Group of Ten consists of ten of the largest contributors to the International Monetary Fund—the United States, the United Kingdom, France, West Germany, Belgium, the Netherlands, Italy, Sweden, Canada, and Japan—who entered into the General Agreement to Borrow (GAB) in 1962 to increase IMF resources. The member countries' central bankers, finance ministers and their deputies hold frequent meetings to discuss international monetary policy coordination.

2. I. M. Destler, Haruhiro Fukui, and Hideo Sato, *The Textile Wrangle,* pp. 315–338. Also see Destler's comments on a more similar issue —macroeconomic policy and bilateral trade imbalances—in I. M. Destler, "U.S.-Japanese Relations and the American Trade Initiative of 1977, pp. 210–213, 223–224.

3. See Raymond A. Bauer, "The Study of Policy Formation," pp. 1–2.

4. See Graham T. Allison, *Essence of Decision,* and Morton H. Halperin, Pricilla Clapp, and Arnold Kanter, *Bureaucratic Politics and Foreign Policy,* for pioneering work in bureaucratic politics.

1. The Rise and Decline of the Bretton Woods System

1. For a survey of the traditional interpretation of the gold standard see Michael D. Bordo, "The Gold Standard," pp. 23–113.

2. Richard N. Cooper, "The Gold Standard," p. 19.

3. Ibid., pp. 19–20.

4. See Robert Triffin, *Gold and the Dollar Crisis,* pp. 29–30, for a summary of those factors.

5. See ibid., pp. 21–30, for a more elaborate interpretation of convertibility.

6. League of Nations, *International Currency Experience,* p. 39.

7. Leo Pasvolsky provides details of the 1933 conference in *Current Monetary Issues,* pp. 64–91.

8. W. Funk, *Wirtschaftliche Neuordnung Europas,* cited in Armand Van Dormael, *Bretton Woods,* p. 6.

9. For more detailed discussions of the formation of the international monetary system, see Richard N. Gardner, *Sterling-Dollar Diplomacy,* passim, and J. Keith Horsefield, *The International Monetary Fund: 1945–1965, vol. 1: Chronicle,* pp. 3–118.

10. See Joseph Gold, general counsel and director of the Legal Department of the IMF from 1960 to 1979, "Keynes and the Articles of the Fund," pp. 29–38.

11. Horsefield, *The International Monetary Fund: 1945–65, vol. 3: Documents,* pp. 3–18.

12. Ibid., 3:3.

13. Ibid., 3:83–96.

14. Ibid., 3:81.

15. Ibid., 3:89.

16. Richard N. Gardner, *Sterling Dollar Diplomacy in Current Perspective,* pp. xxxiv-xxxv.

17. Horsefield, *The International Monetary Fund,* 1:54.

18. For some of the formal statements and records of meetings see U.S. Department of State, *Proceedings and Documents of the United Nations Monetary and Financial Conference, Bretton Woods, New Hampshire, July 1–22, 1944* (Washington, D.C.: GPO, 1948).

19. For the text of the Articles see Horsefield, *The International Monetary Fund,* 3:187–214.

20. Ibid., 1:156.

21. Margaret Garritsen de Vries, "The IMF: 40 Years of Challenge and Change," pp. 7–10.

22. Robert Solomon, *The International Monetary System,* pp. 31–32.

23. Robert Triffin, "The International Role and Fate of the Dollar," p. 272.

24. Gold, "Keynes and the Articles of the Fund," p. 41.

25. John Williamson, "On the System in Bretton Woods," p. 74.

26. See Solomon, *The International Monetary System,* pp. 16–20, for details of the Marshall Plan's impact.

27. Ibid., p. 271.

28. See Gardner, pp. 287–347, for a detailed discussion of Great Britain's move to convertibility and its consequences.

29. Not all observers, even in the early 1950s, were as complacent about the long-term impact of the U.S. dollar outflow. See Robert Triffin, *The World Money Maze,* pp. 51–53, for a recollection of his skepticism expressed in 1952 with "extreme forms of the dollar gap theory."

30. Rolfe and Burtle, pp. 76–77.

31. See Robert V. Roosa, *The United States and Japan in the International Monetary System,* p. 6, for details.

32. Horsefield, *The International Monetary Fund,* 1:483.

33. Ibid., 1:510–512.

34. Richard N. Cooper, *The Economics of Interdependence.* pp. 48–49.

35. For additional information on U.S. and international efforts to prop up the system during this period see Rolfe, *Gold and World Power,* pp. 185–187; Solomon, *The International Monetary System,* pp. 37–44; Roosa, *The United States and Japan,* pp. 5–16.

36. See Solomon, *The International Monetary System,* pp. 114–127, for an entertaining summary of the "Great Gold Rush of 1967–68."

37. See de Vries, *The International Monetary Fund,* 1:453–458.

38. Ibid., 1:496–500.

39. For a general discussion of these two proposals, called the "bank" proposal and the "shiftable-parity" proposal, see W. Fellner, "On Limited Exchange Rate Flexibility," pp. 212–222.

40. See de Vries, *The International Monetary Fund,* 1:500–516, for a summary of the debate and the report.

41. Unless otherwise noted, U.S. economic statistics in this section are taken from the *Survey of Current Business,* published monthly by the U.S. Department of Commerce. Where possible, the unrevised figures are used rather than the more accurate revisions since the former are closer to the early estimates that influenced the actions of policymakers at the time of their release.

42. William B. Dale, "Exchange Rate Realignment and Related Matters," January 28, 1971.

43. Ibid.

44. Ibid.

45. George H. Willis, "Financing the 1971 Deficit—and Beyond 1971," February 22, 1971.

46. Michael Bradfield, "Powers of the Secretary of the Treasury—Gold and Foreign Exchange," March 31, 1971.

47. *New York Times,* March 30, 1971, p. 45.

48. Editorial, *New York Times,* April 4, 1971, sec. 3, p. 12.

49. *New York Times,* April 4, 1971, p. 49.

50. *New York Times,* April 28, 1971, p. 63.

51. *New York Times,* April 28, 1971, p. 78.

52. For an explanation of the significance of the May deutsche mark crisis as seen from the IMF staff's point of view see de Vries, *The International Monetary Fund, 1966–1971,* 1:519–524.

53. *New York Times,* May 13, 1971, p. 75.

54. *New York Times,* May 18, 1971.

55. *Nihon Keizai Shimbun,* May 19, 1971. *Nihon Keizai Shimbun* is Japan's major economic newspaper.

56. *Nihon Keizai Shimbun,* May 25, 1971, p. 1.

2. Japan in the Postwar World Economy

1. Jerome B. Cohen has provided one of the more vivid descriptions of the immediate postwar economic situation in *Japan's Postwar Economy*, pp. 14ff. Also see Tatsuro Uchino, *Japan's Postwar Economy*, pp. 13–18, and Keizai Kikakucho (Economic Planning Agency), ed., *Gendai Nihon Keizai no Tenkai*, pp. 18–19, for descriptions of immediate postwar economic conditions as seen from the perspective of official Japan.

2. See ibid., pp. 18–21, for the Economic Planning Agency's own interpretation of the determinants of the early occupation inflation.

3. See Charles L. Kades, deputy chief of SCAP's Government Section (see note 7 below) during the early occupation, "The American Role in Revising Japan's Imperial Constitution," pp. 217–219, for a summary of the occupation's overall social, political, and economic objectives.

4. See Hans H. Baerwald, *The Purge of Japanese Leaders Under the Occupation*, for an early discussion of the objectives and accomplishments of the purge.

5. See Theodore Cohen's informative memoir, *Remaking Japan*, pp. 5–48, for an informative interpretation of the Washington presurrender economic planning process from the perspective of a "New Dealer" participant.

6. Kazuo Kawai describes the impact of the early emergency relief efforts on the Japanese public in *Japan's American Interlude*, pp. 136–138.

7. SCAP (Supreme Commander for the Allied Powers) was an acronym used to identify both General MacArthur and the occupation forces as a whole.

8. See Eleanor M. Hadley, *Antitrust in Japan* (Princeton, N. J.: Princeton University Press, 1970), pp. 115–118, for details of government efforts to cope with war-related financial dislocations and their impact on Japan's corporations.

9. See Uchino, *Japan's Postwar Economy*, pp. 29–32, for details of this program.

10. Ibid., pp. 32–33.

11. See ibid., pp. 34 ff, and Chalmers Johnson, *MITI and the Japanese Miracle*, pp. 180–81, for details of the formation and operation of the Economic Stabilization Board, which Johnson has compared in objective and scope of responsibility to the prewar Cabinet Planning Board established by the Konoye government in 1937.

12. Uchino, *Japan's Postwar Economy*, pp. 37ff. See Keizai Kikaku Cho, *Gendai Nihon Keizai no Tenkai*, pp. 43–49, for a detailed summary of the commodities rationing, price, capital, and foreign trade controls during the 1947–1948 period.

13. Johnson, *MITI and the Japanese Miracle*, p. 188.

14. Details of the "Emergency Economic Policy" are provided in Uchino, *Japan's Postwar Economy*, pp. 38–39. Uchino, a longtime Economic Planning Agency official, defends the work of the ESB in the face of widespread criticism of its inflationary impact. He argues that the decline in inflation and increase in production experienced by the Ashida Cabinet were, in fact, the fruits of the wise policies of the short-lived Katayama Cabinet and the BOT's work rather than any policy changes initiated by Ashida's administration: "The economic policies of the Katayama Cabinet have been highly criticized up to the present. Such criticism ignores the interval between policy and effect and, considering that the Katayama Cabinet was in power for only nine months and held only 58 percent of the seats in the Diet (including those of the two other parties in the coalition), its economic policies were exceptionally effective. This was due in large measure to its reorganization of the Economic Stabilization Board and the degree to which it allowed the board to function as an independent body for economic planning." Ibid., p. 44.

15. For quite a summary of the many interpretations of the nature and origins of the reverse course, see Robert E. Ward, "Conclusion," in *Democratizing Japan: the Allied Occupation*, pp. 405–414.

16. Cohen, *Remaking Japan*, p. 310.

17. Noel Hemmendinger, then a political economist in the Bureau of Far Eastern Affairs, U.S. Department of State, discusses the bilateral debate surrounding the setting of the yen's exchange rate from the Department of State perspective in "Establishment of the Japanese Controlled Single Exchange Rate" (unpublished paper), p. 1.

18. Ibid., pp. 4–5.

19. I am grateful to Rich Thomas of *Newsweek*'s Washington Bureau for sharing information from his interviews with Mr. Young and copies of the relevant documents.

20. Draper to Young, May 14, 1948, Washington, D.C., p. 2.

21. Cohen, *Remaking Japan*, p. 419.

22. "Report of the Special Mission on Yen Foreign Exchange Policy," Tokyo, Japan, 12 June 1948, pp. 4–5.

23. Cohen, *Remaking Japan*, p. 422.

24. See ibid., pp. 429–439, for details of Dodge's remarkable performance reported from the perspective of a skeptical SCAP staff member.

25. Uchino, *Japan's Postwar Economy*, pp. 44–46.

26. Cohen *Remaking Japan*, pp. 427–428.

27. Special procurements so defined include not only direct UN procurement, but also additional yen expenditures of UN military personnel in Japan and the expenditures of the various relief organizations. Uchino, *Japan's Postwar Economy*, p. 57.

28. Keizai Kikakucho, *Gendai Nihon Keizai no Tenkai*, p. 64.

29. Takafusa Nakamura, *The Postwar Japanese Economy,* pp. 43–48.

30. For a detailed discussion of the overloan phenomenon and its impact on the Japanese economy, see Henry C. Wallich and Mable I. Wallich, "Banking and Finance," in Hugh Patrick and Henry Rosovsky, eds., *Asia's New Giant* (Washington, D.C.: Brookings Institution, 1976), pp. 284–290.

31. Johnson, *MITI and the Japanese Miracle,* p. 203.

32. See Edward J. Lincoln, *Japan's Industrial Policies* (Washington, D.C.: Japan Economic Institute of America, 1984), pp. 20–23, for details of the Japan Development Bank's role in Japan's postwar economic growth.

33. Kozo Yamamura, *Economic Policy in Postwar Japan,* pp. 148–149.

34. See Uchino, *Japan's Postwar Economy,* p. 65ff, Nakamura, *The Postwar Japanese Economy,* p. 44, and Johnson, *MITI and the Japanese Miracle,* p. 218 for detailed explanations of this complex legislation and its impact on Japan's postwar industrial development.

35. Warren S. Hunsberger, *Japan and the United States in World Trade,* p. 133.

36. See Nakamura, *The Postwar Japanese Economy,* pp. 74–80, for his assessment of the significance of imported technology for Japan's postwar economic growth.

37. Hunsberger, *Japan and the United States in World Trade,* pp. 170–173.

38. For an early explanation of this phenomenon in English see Hugh T. Patrick, "Cyclical Instability and Fiscal-Monetary Policy in Postwar Japan," pp. 565–566. Nakamura provides a more recent version in *The Postwar Japanese Economy,* pp. 51–53.

39. *New York Times,* April 5, 1959, p. 1.

40. American gold reserves had risen during World War II to an unusual level through transfer of large quantities of European gold to the United States in anticipation of German occupation. The late 1950s "gold flow" was journalistic shorthand for the transfer of U.S. gold stocks abroad to settle balance-of-payment deficits with other countries. For the flavor of the political implications of the issue see the *New York Times* July 1, 1959, p. 20, report on a June 30, 1959, hearing of the Joint Economic Committee of Congress at which administration officials and private economists, including MIT's Charles Kindleberger, discussed the economic and political implications of the issue.

41. See coverage of the American reaction to Japanese cancellation of the Eisenhower visit in the July 4, 1960, issue of *Time,* p. 76.

42. For analysis of the U.S. response to economic Japan see Robert C. Angel, "Beikoku no Sengo Seiji ni Okeru Nihon no Imi" (The Significance of Japan in Postwar American Politics), pp. 18–34.

43. See Anne H. Rightor-Thornton, "An Analysis of the Office of the

Special Representative for Trade Negotiations," pps. 88–104, for a thoughtful treatment of the functions of the STR.

44. For a description of Japan's early liberalization efforts see Alfred K. Ho, *Japan's Trade Liberalization in the 1960s,* passim.

45. Johnson, *MITI and the Japanese Miracle,* pp. 41–45.

46. See Kent Calder, *Crisis and Compensation,* pp. 117–126, for analysis of the role of foreign pressure in Japan's domestic policy processes during the 1970s and 1980s.

47. Edward Lincoln discusses Japan's resistance to inward trade and investment liberalization and the importance of foreign pressure in the liberalization process in *Japan's Unequal Trade,* especially pp. 61–67 and 156–158.

48. For a discussion of the manipulation of foreign pressure in Japan's policy process under the rubric of "imported crisis," see Kent Calder, *Crisis and Compensation,* pp. 121–126.

3. From "Surplus-Prone" Status to "Protracted Crisis" State

1. For summaries of these reports see United States-Japan Trade Council, *Trade Roundup* (March 15, 1968), no. 5:5, and (April 23, 1968), no. 8:7.

2. Interview with Koichi Inamura, Tokyo, June 23, 1976.

3. For a compact description of economic conditions, policy measures, and their impact, see the Organisation for Economic Cooperation and Development, *OECD Economic Survey: Japan* (Paris: OECD, 1969), pp. 6–39.

4. Ibid., p. 5.

5. Ibid.

6. *Japan Times,* January 1, 1969, p. 11.

7. Taizo Hayashi, "En Kiriage Sagyo no Zasetsu kara Furoto Made" ("From the Breakdown of the Yen Revaluation Operation to the Float"), p. 38.

8. T. F. M. Adams and Iwao Hoshii, *A Financial History of the New Japan,* pp. 508–510.

9. *Japan Times,* April 9, 1969, p. 11.

10. *Japan Times,* April 26, 1969, p. 10.

11. *Japan Times,* June 28, 1969, p. 8.

12. *Japan Times,* September 23, 1969, p. 1.

13. See Ho, *Japan's Trade Liberalization,* pp. 15–19, for an assessment of the liberalization effort.

14. *Japan Times* May 19, 1969, p. 11.

15. *Nihon Keizai Shimbun,* "Watashi no Iken," September 29, 1969, p. 1.

16. *Nihon Keizai Shimbun,* October 14, 1969, p. 1.

17. *Nihon Keizai Shimbun,* October 17, 1969, p. 1 (evening edition).

18. For a comprehensive and readable interpretation of Japan's trade barriers from the perspective of an economist, see Edward J. Lincoln, *Japan's Unequal Trade,* especially chapters 2, 3, and 4.

19. For an interpretation of Japan's foreign aid policies during this period see Dennis Yasutomo, *Japan and the Asian Development Bank* (New York: Praeger, 1983).

20. *Japan Times,* April 11, 1969, p. 9.

21. For a U.S. Treasury Department official's evaluation of the late 1960s and early 1970s Japanese foreign aid program as it related to her overall international economic relations, see Wilbur F. Monroe, *Japan,* pp. 194–197.

22. *Japan Times,* June 16, 1969, p. 10.

23. *Nihon Keizai Shimbun,* September 25, 1969. p. 1.

24. *Nihon Keizai Shimbun,* October 1, 1969, p. 1.

25. For an interesting description of the political, bureaucratic, and public interaction preceding changes in the official discount rate, see Edward Lincoln, "Discount Rate Cut Under Consideration," pp. 7–8.

26. See *Nihon Keizai Shimbun,* April 2, 1971 (evening edition), p. 1, for details.

27. See *Nihon Keizai Shimbun* May 1, 1971, p. 5, for public reaction in Japan.

28. *Nihon Keizai Shimbun,* March 3, 1971, p. 2.

29. *Nihon Keizai Shimbun,* March 11, 1971, p. 5.

30. *Nihon Keizai Shimbun,* March 26, 1971, p. 4.

31. See the United States-Japan Trade Council, *Trade Roundup* (April 2, 1971), no 5:5–6, for the specific items reduced and a description of the Export Contribution Corporation.

32. Japan's ambassador to the United States, Nobuhiko Ushiba, provided an example of this effort during a speech in New York City on March 23, 1971 reported in *Nihon Keizai Shimbun,* March 24, 1971, p. 3.

33. *Nihon Keizai Shimbun,* April 13, 1971, p. 5.

34. *Nihon Keizai Shimbun,* April 17, 1971, p. 1.

35. Monroe, *Japan,* pp. 18–24.

36. *Nihon Keizai Shimbun,* April 30, 1971, p. 1.

37. See an article in *Nihon Keizai Shimbun,* March 26, 1971, p. 5, obviously inspired by the shipbuilding industry.

38. *Nihon Keizai Shimbun,* March 24, 1971, p. 9.

39. *Nihon Keizai Shimbu,* March 14, 1971, p. 5.

40. *Nihon Keizai Shimbun,* April 9, 1971 (evening edition), p. 1.

41. Interview with Seiichi Yamashita, Tokyo, July 28, 1976.

42. See *Nihon Keizai Shimbun,* April 15, 1971, pp. 1 and 2, for examples of the government's reaction to the Kikawada statement.

43. Interview with Takashi Hosomi, Tokyo, July 13, 1976.

44. See Taizo Hayashi's statement in *Nihon Keizai Shimbun*, May 7, 1971, p. 3, as the most comprehensive statement of the argument.

45. *Nihon Keizai Shimbun*, May 7, 1971 (evening edition), p. 1.

46. See *Nihon Keizai Shimbun*, May 26, 1971, p. 4, for Keidanren's statement; May 22, 1971, p. 5, for Keizai Doyukai's statement; and May 26, 1971, p. 4, for a report of the speech of Chairman Goro Koyama of the Zenkoku Ginko Taikai.

4. The Eight-Point Program To Avoid Yen Reevaluation

1. For the Japanese reaction to the Reuss proposal see *Nihon Keizai Shimbun*, June 4, 1971 (evening edition), p. 1.

2. See the statement of Goro Koyama, chairman of the National Banking Association (Zenkoku Ginko Kyokai) on June 1 with Prime Minister Sato and several other key cabinet members in attendance during which he requested more specific government action to quiet the international criticism of Japan's foreign economic policies in *Nihon Keizai Shimbun*, June 2, 1971, p. 5.

3. *Nihon Keizai Shimbun*, June 3, 1971, p. 8.

4. Tadashi Takakura, then executive secretary and senior LDP administrative staff person, said during an interview that LDP politicians avoided discussion and involvement in international monetary policy for the same reasons they avoided discussion of changes in the official discount rate—the fear of being accused of trying to profit personally from financial speculation in anticipation of the change. He also said that international monetary policy, when compared with other economic issues, had little appeal for the politicians because it was difficult to relate directly to the interests of their districts. Personal interview with Tadashi Takakura, Tokyo, July 1, 1976.

Zentaro Kosaka, then chairman of the LDP's Policy Affairs Research Council, expressed the same opinion, saying that his group only listened passively to the explanations of the MOF professionals with little reaction. He stressed that the subject was too technical for nonprofessionals like politicians to understand. Interview with Zentaro Kosaka, Tokyo, August 16, 1976.

5. *Nihon Keizai Shimbun*, June 3, 1971, p. 1.

6. From Yusuke Kashiwagi, pp. 192–94.

7. Kashiwagi was modest and vague about the authorship of the plan during a personal interview on May 28, 1976. But other policy participants, including Mikio Mizuta, who became finance minister in July, 1971, Iichiro Hatoyama, director general of the MOF budget bureau and soon to become MOF administrative vice minister, Takashi Hosomi, director general of the MOF tax bureau and soon to be named to succeed Kashiwagi, and Takehiro Sagami, director of the research

and planning division of the Finance Minister's secretariat, all confirmed that the program was Kashiwagi's.

8. Interview with an anonymous senior MOF official involved in the complex effort to create the post of vice minister for international monetary affairs, Washington, D. C. , August 12, 1980.

9. See, for example, *Nihon Keizai Shimbun,* June 16, 1971, p. 1, for an example of their work.

10. *Nihon Keizai Shimbun,* June 19, 1971, p. 1.

11. *Nihon Keizai Shimbun,* June 20, 1971, p. 5.

12. Mizuta mentioned during a August 20, 1976 personal interview that in contrast to Fukuda he had been pressing for a more aggressive economic stimulation policy early in 1971 as a means of coping with the international monetary situation. Interview with Mikio Mizuta, Tokyo, August 20, 1976.

13. See *Nihon Keizai shimbun,* July 5, 1971 (evening edition), pp. 1–3, for the cabinet line-up and initial reaction to the appointments.

14. *Nihon Keizai Shimbun,* July 6, 1971, p. 2.

15. *Nihon Keizai Shimbun,* July 7, 1971, p. 2.

16. *Nihon Keizai Shimbun,* July 9, 1971 (evening edition), p. 1.

17. *Nihon Keizai Shimbun,* July 19, 1971 (evening edition), p. 3.

18. *Nihon Keizai Shimbun,* July 27, 1971, p. 1.

19. *Nihon Keizai Shimbun,* July 30, 1971 (evening edition), p. 1.

20. Among others, Kenjiro Taguchi, then director of the Foreign Exchange Division of MITI's Trade Bureau, (the MITI official most directly concerned with the yen problem after his appointment in June, 1971), mentioned that particular concern as a cross-pressure on the bureaucracy as they worked to implement the agreement. Interview with Kenjiro Taguchi, Tokyo, October 29, 1975.

21. *Nihon Keizai Shimbun,* June 26, 1971, p. 4.

22. *Nihon Keizai Shimbun,* July 21, 1971, p. 3.

23. *Nihon Keizai Shimbun,* June 4, 1971, p. 1.

24. *Nihon Keizai Shimbun,* June 12, 1971, p. 1.

25. *Nihon Keizai Shimbun,* June 25, 1971, p. 1.

26. *Nihon Keizai Shimbun,* July 16, 1971, p. 3.

27. *Nihon Keizai Shimbun,* July 22, 1971, p. 2.

28. *Nihon Keizai Shimbun,* June 23, 1971, p. 1. Supplementary national budgets had been compiled during the second half of the fiscal year since the early 1960s, first in response to tax revenues that exceeded anticipated levels under conditions of rapid economic growth, and later as a counter-cyclical fiscal measure. See Takafusa Nakamura, *The Postwar Japanese Economy,* pp. 130–133, for a discussion of the significance of supplementary budgets in Japanese fiscal policy.

29. *Nihon Keizai Shimbun,* July 27, 1971 (evening edition), p. 1.

30. For a measured international assessment of the impact of the

government's effort to stimulate the economy and its anticipated impact released in late 1971, see The Organisation for Economic Co-Operation and Development, *OECD Economic Outlook,* Number 10, December 1971, pp. 78–82.

31. *Nihon Keizai Shimbun,* June 19, 1971, p. 1.
32. *Nihon Keizai Shimbun,* June 20, 1971, p. 1.
33. *Nihon Keizai Shimbun,* June 26, 1971, p. 1.
34. *Nihon Keizai Shimbun,* June 26, 1971, p. 1.
35. *Nihon Keizai Shimbun,* July 14, 1971, p. 1.
36. *Nihon Keizai Shimbun,* July 23, 1971, p. 1.
37. *Nihon Keizai Shimbun,* July 24, 1971, p. 1.
38. *Nihon Keizai Shimbun* July 29, 1971, p. 1.
39. *Nihon Keizai Shimbun,* June 29, 1971 (evening edition), p. 1.
40. *Nihon Keizai Shimbun,* June 29, 1971, p. 9.
41. *Nihon Keizai Shimbun,* July 30, 1971, p. 1.
42. Kashiwagi, p. 189.
43. *Nihon Keizai Shimbun,* June 19, 1971, p. 5, for a discussion of this problem.
44. *Nihon Keizai Shimbun,* June 17, 1971, p. 1.
45. Interview with an anonymous Keidanren official, June 21, 1976.
46. *Nihon Keizai Shimbun,* July 16, 1971, p. 3.
47. *Nihon Keizai Shimbun,* June 20, 1971, p. 1.
48. Interviews with Mikio Mizuta, Tokyo August 20, 1976; with Iichiro Hatoyama, Tokyo, April 9, 1976; and with Takashi Hosomi, Tokyo, 29 June 1976.
49. *Nihon Keizai Shimbun,* July 23, 1971 (evening edition), p. 1.
50. *Nihon Keizai Shimbun,* June 28, 1971, p. 1.
51. See, for example, a *Tokyo Shimbun* article published the day after the program's release on this point. *Tokyo Shimbun,* June 5, 1971, in U.S. Department of State, "Survey of the Japanese Press."
52. *Nihon Keizai Shimbun,* July 1, 1971, p. 3.
53. *Nihon Keizai Shimbun,* June 19, 1971, p. 5.
54. See, for example, *Nihon Keizai Shimbun,* July 11, 1971, p. 1.
55. *Nihon Keizai Shimbun,* July 11, 1971, p. 1.
56. Kashiwagi made this point during his May 28, 1976 interview, as did all the other major policy participants.
57. *Nihon Keizai Shimbun,* June 8, 1971 (evening edition), p. 1.
58. See U.S.-Japan Trade Council, *Council Report,* (July 13, 1971), no. 42, for a summary of the arguments presented at the hearing.
59. *New York Times,* July 7, 1971, p. 16.
60. *Nihon Keizai Shimbun,* July 16, 1971 (evening edition), p. 1, has initial Japanese reaction to this event.
61. *New York Times,* July 30, 1971, p. 1.
62. *New York Times,* June 17, 1971, p. 53.

63. *New York Times,* July 30, 1971, p. 1.

64. Interview with an anonymous Foreign Ministry official (at that time stationed in Washington), Tokyo, March 15, 1976.

65. The U.S.-Japan Businessmen's Conference had been meeting once a year since 1961 with the U.S. Chamber of Commerce and Keidanren as cosponsors.

66. Interview with John Caldwell, Washington, D. C., February 9, 1982.

67. Interview with an anonymous Japanese industrial organization's staff member, Washington, D. C., 1979.

68. *Nihon Keizai Shimbun,* June 15, 1971, p. 1.

69. See U.S.-Japan Trade Council, *Council Report* (June 25, 1971), no. 35, for the text of the communique and a brief summary of the outcome of the meetings. Also see the *New York Times,* June 19, 1971, p. 33.

70. *Nihon Keizai Shimbun,* June 22, 1971, p. 5.

71. Interview with Hideo Suzuki, Tokyo, July 16, 1976.

72. *Nihon Keizai Shimbun,* July 23, 1971 (evening edition), p. 1.

73. Organisation for Economic Cooperation and Development, *OECD Economic Survey: Japan* (Paris: OECD, 1971), p. 52.

74. *Nihon Keizai Shimbun,* July 28, 1971 (evening edition), p. 1.

75. *New York Times,* June 25, 1971, p. 48.

76. Interviews with Iichiro Hatoyama, Tokyo, April 9, 1976; August 2, 1976; and August 18, 1976.

77. *Nihon Keizai Shimbun,* August 3, 1971, p. 1.

78. *Nihon Keizai Shimbun,* August 1, 1971, p. 1.

79. *Nihon Keizai Shimbun,* August 8, 1971, p. 1 and August 9, 1971, p. 1.

80. *Nihon Keizai Shimbun,* August 12, 1971, p. 1.

81. *Nihon Keizai Shimbun,* August 3, 1971, p. 3 and August 13, 1971 (evening edition), p. 1.

82. *Nihon Keizai Shimbun,* August 11, 1971, p. 1.

83. *Nihon Keizai Shimbun,* August 3, 1971 (evening edition), p. 4.

84. *Nihon Keizai Shimbun,* August 3, 1971 (evening edition), p. 4.

85. *Nihon Keizai Shimbun,* August 5, 1971, p. 5.

86. *Nihon Keizai Shimbun,* August 13, 1971 (evening edition), p. 3.

5. The "Nixon Shock" and the Decision to Float the Yen

1. Lyle Widman, Research Department, International Affairs Division, Department of Treasury, May 8, 1971, pp. 1–2: seven-page confidential memorandum entitled "Contingency: Eyes Only," declassified under the Freedom of Information Act on June 22, 1974.

2. Ibid., p. 4.

3. Transcript, pp. 1–2, of an NHK interview with John Connally dated April 1981 and aired in Japan in May 1981.

4. Ibid., p. 1.

5. For a brief description of the Camp David meeting, in which he makes an effort to absolve the British of guilt for triggering the decision to close the gold window, see Henry Brandon (chief American correspondent for the *Sunday Times*, London), *The Retreat of American Power*, pp. 218–226.

6. Canadian exports to the United States were roughly double Japan's at the time, but 75 percent of these entered duty-free and were therefore excluded from the surcharge, and the Canadian dollar was already floating.

7. Interview with Takehiro Sagami, Tokyo, May 27, 1976.

8. For a U.S. account of the briefing see the *New York Times*, August 16, 1971, p. 1.

9. Interviews with Iichiro Hatoyama, Tokyo, August 27, 1976; Takashi Hosomi, Tokyo, February 13, 1976; Yusuke Kashiwagi, Tokyo, May 28, 1976; and Takehiro Sagami, Tokyo, May 27, 1976.

10. Details of the Monday night meetings are from interviews with Hatoyama, August 27, 1976; Hosomi, February 13, 1976; Kashiwagi, May 28, 1976; Mizuta, August 20, 1976; and, Sagami, May 27, 1976, all in Tokyo.

11. Interview with Mikio Mizuta, Tokyo, August 20, 1976.

12. *Nihon Keizai Shimbun*, August 17, 1971, pp. 1 and 6.

13. Ibid.

14. Yusuke Kashiwagi, *Gekidoki no Tsuka Gaiko*, p. 4; and *Nihon Keizai Shimbun*, August 17, 1971 (evening edition), p. 1.

15. Ibid.

16. Ibid.

17. *Nihon Keizai Shimbun*, August 19, 1971, p. 1.

18. Interview with Yusuke Kashiwagi, Tokyo, May 28, 1976.

19. *Nihon Keizai Shimbun*, August 18, 1971 (evening edition), p. 1.

20. *Nihon Keizai Shimbun*, August 20, 1971 (evening edition), p. 2.

21. *Nihon Keizai Shimbun*, August 17, 1971 (evening edition), p. 1.

22. *Nihon Keizai Shimbun*, August 17, 1971, p. 1.

23. *Nihon Keizai Shimbun*, August 19, 1971, p. 1.

24. Interview with Yusuke Kashiwagi, Tokyo, May 28, 1976.

25. *Nihon Keizai Shimbun*, August 19, 1971, p. 1.

26. Interviews with Nobuhiko Ushiba, Tokyo, March 15, 1976, and August 6, 1976.

27. *New York Times*, August 16, 1971, p. 14.

28. Ibid., p. 26.

29. See *Nihon Keizai Shimbun*, August 18, 1971, p. 3, for the public warning.

30. *Nihon Keizai Shimbun*, August 20, 1971, p. 2.

31. See, for example, Yoshizane Iwasa's public comments after meeting Prime Minister Sato on the 17th in *Nihon Keizai Shimbun*, August 18, 1971, p. 3.
32. *Nihon Keizai Shimbun*, August 19, 1971, p. 3.
33. *Nihon Keizai Shimbun*, August 20, 1971, p. 3.
34. Interview with Takashi Hosomi, Tokyo, June 24, 1976.
35. Interview with Takashi Hosomi, Tokyo, February 13, 1976.
36. *Nihon Keizai Shimbun*, August 19, 1971, p. 3.
37. Ibid, p. 1.
38. See, for example, MITI Minister Tanaka's Tuesday statement in *Nihon Keizai Shimbun*, August 18, 1971, p. 1.
39. His insistence was later confirmed by Mizuta and Hosomi during personal interviews.
40. The details of this call, its background and impact, are taken from a July 16, 1976, interview with Hideo Suzuki and the June 24, 1976, interview in Tokyo with Takashi Hosomi.
41. Interview with Takehiro Sagami, Tokyo, May 27, 1976.
42. Interview with Mikio Mizuta, Tokyo, August 20, 1976.
43. Interview with Takashi Hosomi, Tokyo, June 24, 1976.
44. *Nihon Keizai Shimbun*, August 24, 1971, p. 19.
45. Ibid., p. 1.
46. *Nihon Keizai Shimbun*, August 23, 1971 (evening edition), p. 1.
47. See the statement of Zenkoku Nogyo Chuo-kai President Miyawaki on August 20 in *Nihon Keizai Shimbun*, August 21, 1971, p. 3, and Zenkoku Nomin Sorenmei's statement the following day to Agriculture Minister Akagi in *Nihon Keizai Shimbun*, August 22, 1971, p. 3.
48. *Nihon Keizai Shimbun*, August 24, 1971 (evening edition), p. 1.
49. *Nihon Keizai Shimbun*, August 26, 1971, p. 1.
50. *Nihon Keizai Shimbun*, August 24, 1971, p. 6.
51. *Nihon Keizai Shimbun*, August 21, 1971, p. 3.
52. See *Nihon Keizai Shimbun*, August 26, 1971 (evening edition), p. 1, for a report on the shift.
53. *Nihon Keizai Shimbun*, August 28, 1971, p. 1.
54. *Nihon Keizai Shimbun*, August 28, 1971, p. 1.

6. Hopes Dashed for an Early Settlement

1. *Nihon Keizai Shimbun*, August 28, 1971, p. 2.
2. Interview with Yusuke Kashiwagi, Tokyo, May 28, 1976.
3. See *Nihon Keizai Shimbun*, September 3, 1971 (evening edition), p. 2, for the Japanese view of the meeting's significance.
4. *New York Times*, September 11, 1971, p. 1.

5. *Nihon Keizai Shimbun,* September 14, 1971 (evening edition), p. 1.

6. *Nihon Keizai Shimbun,* August 28, 1971, p. 1.

7. *Nihon Keizai Shimbun,* August 30, 1971 (evening edition), p. 2.

8. *Nihon Keizai Shimbun,* August 31, 1971 (evening edition), p. 1.

9. *Nihon Keizai Shimbun,* September 1, 1971 (evening edition), p. 1.

10. *New York Times,* August 31, 1971, p. 17.

11. See *Nihon Keizai Shimbun,* September 9, 1971, p. 3, for the immediate Japanese reaction to Connally's comments before the committee.

12. See *New York Times,* September 17, 1971, p. 26, for Japan's reaction to Nixon's statement.

13. See the *New York Times,* September 5, 1971, p. 36, for Volcker's statement, and *Nihon Keizai Shimbun,* September 9, 1971 (evening edition), p. 3, for Connally's confirmation.

14. *Nihon Keizai Shimbun,* August 28, 1971, p. 2.

15. Ibid.

16. Ibid.

17. Ibid.

18. *Nihon Keizai Shimbun,* August 31, 1971, p. 2.

19. *Nihon Keizai Shimbun,* September 1, 1971 (evening edition), p. 1.

20. Ibid.

21. *Nihon Keizai Shimbun,* September 2, 1971 (evening edition), p. 1.

22. Ibid.

23. Interviews with Iichiro Hatoyama, Tokyo, August 2, 1976 and Takashi Hosomi, Tokyo, June 24 and 29, 1976.

24. *Nihon Keizai Shimbun,* September 1, 1971, p. 1.

25. *Nihon Keizai Shimbun,* September 6, 1971, p. 1, and September 7, 1971, p. 2.

26. *Nihon Keizai Shimbun,* September 18, 1971, p. 3.

27. *Nihon Keizai Shimbun,* August 28, 1971, p. 1.

28. *Nihon Keizai Shimbun,* August 31, 1971 (evening edition), p. 1.

29. For an explanation of the role supplementary budgets have played in Japan's postwar fiscal policies, see John Creighton Campbell, *Contemporary Japanese Budget Politics,* pp. 201–207.

30. Campbell calls this the floating of "ad balloons." Ibid., pp. 22–23.

31. *Nihon Keizai Shimbun,* August 28, 1971, pp. 2–3.

32. *Nihon Keizai Shimbun,* September 17, 1971, p. 1.

33. Interviews with Kenjiro Taguchi, Tokyo, October 29, 1975, and August 17, 1976.

34. *Nihon Keizai Shimbun,* August 28, 1971, p. 2.

35. *Nihon Keizai Shimbun,* August 28, 1971 (evening edition), p. 1.
36. Interview with Kazuichi Murai, Tokyo, August 16, 1976.
37. *Nihon Keizai Shimbun,* September 2, 1971 (evening edition), p. 3, and September 8, 1971, p. 6.
38. *Nihon Keizai Shimbun,* September 7, 1971, p. 3.
39. *Nihon Keizai Shimbun,* September 17, 1971, p. 3.
40. *Nihon Keizai Shimbun,* September 2, 1971, p. 1.
41. *Nihon Keizai Shimbun,* September 8, 1971, p. 3.
42. *Nihon Keizai Shimbun,* September 12, 1971, p. 4.
43. *Nihon Keizai Shimbun,* September 14, 1971, p. 1.
44. *Nihon Keizai Shimbun,* September 14, 1971, p. 1.
45. *Nihon Keizai Shimbun,* September 14, 1971 (evening edition), p. 2.
46. *Nihon Keizai Shimbun,* September 15, 1971, p. 1.
47. *Nihon Keizai Shimbun,* September 15, 1971, p. 6.
48. See Morozumi's remarks in *Mainichi Shimbun,* August 31, 1971, U.S. Embassy, *Survey of the Japanese Press.*
49. *Nihon Keizai Shimbun,* September 3, 1971, p. 2.
50. *Nihon Keizai Shimbun,* September 7, 1971, p. 2.
51. *NIhon Keizai Shimbun,* September 3, 1971, p. 4.
52. *Nihon Keizai Shimbun,* September 4, 1971 (evening edition), p. 1.
53. *Nihon Keizai Shimbun,* September 3, 1971 (evening edition), p. 1.
54. *Nihon Keizai Shimbun,* September 7, 1971 (evening edition), p. 1.
55. *Nihon Keizai Shimbun,* September 9, 1971 (evening edition), p. 1.
56. *Nihon Keizai Shimbun,* September 10, 1971, pp. 2–3.
57. Interview with Takashi Hosomi, Tokyo, June 29, 1976, and discussions with one of the State Department's language specialists unfortunate enough to have been pressed into service for the meeting.
58. Details of the conversation are taken from unpublished notes of an anonymous Japanese participant.
59. *Nihon Keizai Shimbun,* September 11, 1971, p. 1.
60. *Nihon Keizai Shimbun,* September 11, 1971 (evening edition), p. 1.
61. Recollection of an anonymous Japanese participant during a personal interview.
62. Details of the conversation are from unpublished notes taken by one of ther Japanese participants in the meeting.
63. *Nihon Keizai Shimbun,* September 13, 1971 (evening edition), p. 1.
64. Interview with Toyoo Gyohten, Tokyo, April 12, 1976.

65. *Nihon Keizai Shimbun,* September 14, 1971 (evening edition), p. 2.

66. *Nihon Keizai Shimbun,* September 16, 1971, p. 5. See the *New York Times,* September 12, 1971, p. 37, for Connally's comments.

67. Details of the conversation are from unpublished notes taken by one of the Japanese observers at the meeting.

68. de Vries, *The International Monetary Fund,* vol 1:544.

69. *New York Times,* September 17, 1971, p. 1, and *Nihon Keizai Shimbun,* September 17, 1971, p. 1.

70. *Nihon Keizai Shimbun,* September 17, 1971, p. 1.

71. *New York Times,* September 8, 1971, p. 30.

72. Interviews with Takashi Hosomi, Tokyo, June 29, 1976, and Takehiro Sagami, Tokyo, August 9, 1976.

73. *Nihon Keizai Shimbun,* September 18, 1971 (evening edition), p. 1. The text of Mizuta's statement is on p. 3.

7. *The Waiting Game*

1. *Nihon Keizai Shimbun,* September 26, 1971, p. 1.
2. *New York Times,* October 1, 1971, p. 1.
3. *Nihon Keizai Shimbun,* October 18, 1971, p. 1.
4. *Nihon Keizai Shimbun,* October 11, 1971, p. 2.
5. Personal interview with Mikio Mizuta, Tokyo, August 20, 1971.
6. Personal interview with Takehiro Sagami, Tokyo, August 9, 1976. Sagami stressed that these individuals were consulted as experts, not as representatives of private-sector interests, and their participation reflected that perspective.
7. *Nihon Keizai Shimbun,* October 12, 1971, p. 1.
8. *Nihon Keizai Shimbun,* September 28, 1971, p. 1.
9. *Nihon Keizai Shimbun,* October 15, 1971 (evening edition), p. 1.
10. *Nihon Keizai Shimbun,* October 20, 1971, p. 1.
11. *Nihon Keizai Shimbun,* October 9, 1971 (evening edition), p. 1.
12. *Nihon Keizai Shimbun,* October 18, 1971, p. 2.
13. Personal interview with Kenjiro Taguchi, Tokyo, October 29, 1975.
14. *Nihon Keizai Shimbun,* October 12, 1971 (evening edition), p. 1.
15. *Nihon Keizai Shimbun,* September 12, 1971 (evening edition), p. 2.
16. See Chapter V, pps. 205–207.
17. Personal interview with Yoshizane Iwasa, Tokyo, July 27, 1976.
18. *Nihon Keizai Shimbun,* October 15, 1971, p. 3.
19. *Nihon Keizai Shimbun,* September 20, 1971, p. 1.

20. *Nihon Keizai Shimbun,* October 5, 1971 (evening edition),p. 1.

21. *Nihon Keizai Shimbun,* October 5, 1971, p. 2. For the text of the Horikoshi group's recommendations, see *Keidanren Shuho* (October 21, 1971), no. 1031:1–3.

22. *Nihon Keizai Shimbun,* October 6, 1971, p. 3.

23. *Nihon Keizai Shimbun,* October 12, 1971, p. 4.

24. *Nihon Keizai Shimbun,* October 20, 1971 (evening edition), p. 3.

25. *Nihon Keizai Shimbun,* September 21, 1971, p. 1.

26. *Nihon Keizai Shimbun,* September 22, 1971, p. 1.

27. *Nihon Keizai Shimbun,* October 13, 1971, p. 2.

28. *Nihon Keizai Shimbun,* October 16, 1971, p. 5.

29. *Nihon Keizai Shimbun,* October 18, 1971 (evening edition), p. 1.

30. *Nihon Keizai Shimbun,* September 29, 1971, p. 1.

31. *Nihon Keizai Shimbun,* October 1, 1971, p. 1.

32. *Nihon Keizai Shimbun,* September 27, 1971, p. 2.

33. Personal interview with Masao Hori, then chairman of the Finance Subcommittee (Okura Bukai) of the JSP's Policy Advisory Council (Seisaku Shingikai), Tokyo, August 5, 1976. During the interview Hori said that he personally opposed the concensus of opinion within the party, but as chairman of the group had to go along.

34. *Nihon Keizai Shimbun,* October 1, 1971, p. 23.

35. *Nihon Keizai Shimbun,* October 30, 1971, p. 2.

36. *Nihon Keizai Shimbun,* October 1, 1971, p. 23.

37. *Nihon Keizai Shimbun,* October 4, 1971, p. 23.

38. *Nihon Keizai Shimbun,* October 5, 1971 (evening edition), p. 1.

39. *San Giin Kessan Iinkai, Kaigi-Roku, Dai-4–go* (Upper House Accounts Committee, Proceedings, Number 4), October 5, 1971, pp. 1–11.

40. *Nihon Keizai Shimbun,* September 22, 1971, p. 2.

41. Yusuke Kashiwagi, *Gekidoki no Tsuka Gaiko* (International Monetary Diplomacy in a Period of Turmoil),pp. 141–42.

42. *New York Times,* September 27, 1971, p. 1. See de Vries, *The International Monetary Fund,* 1:545, for a summary of the Group of Ten's meeting.

43. *Nihon Keizai Shimbun,* September 27, 1971 (evening edition), p. 1.

44. *Nihon Keizai Shimbun,* September 29, 1971, p. 1.

45. *New York Times,* September 28, 1971, p. 32.

46. de Vries, *The International Monetary Fund,* 1:331–332.

47. *New York Times,* September 30, 1971, p. 69.

48. *New York Times,* October 1, 1971, p. 1.

49. For the text of the resolution see de Vries, *The International Monetary Fund,* 2:331–332.

50. *Nihon Keizai Shimbun,* October 2, 1971, p. 1.

51. *Nihon Keizai Shimbun,* September 23, 1971, p. 3.

52. See *Nihon Keizai Shimbun,* October 19, 1971 (evening edition),

p. 1, and October 20, 1971, p. 1, for descriptions of the atmosphere of the meeting.

53. *Nihon Keizai Shimbun,* October 21, 1971, p. 5.

54. *Nihon Keizai Shimbun,* October 21, 1971 (evening edition), p. 3.

55. Yusuke Kashiwagi, *Gekidoki no Tsuka Gaiko,* pps. 7–8.

56. See *Nihon Keizai Shimbun,* November 5, 1971 (evening edition), p. 1, for a summary of Mizuta's testimony on this point, and *San Giin Yosan Iinkai, Kaigi-Roku Dai-2–go* (Upper House Budget Committee, Proceedings, no. 2) (November 5, 1971), pp. 1–2, for a transcript of the hearing.

57. *Nihon Keizai Shimbun,* September 25, 1971, p. 1.

58. *Nihon Keizai Shimbun,* September 27, 1971 (evening edition), p. 2.

59. *New York Times,* October 8, 1971, p. 27.

60. *New York Times,* October 9, 1971, pps. 1, 16.

61. *New York Times,* October 18, 1971, p. 1, and *Nihon Keizai Shimbun,* October 18, 1971 (evening edition), p. 2.

62. *Nihon Keizai Shimbun,* October 21, 1971 (evening edition), p. 3.

63. *New York Times,* September 18, 1971, p. 27. See the *Keidanren Shuho* (September 23, 1971), no. 1027:5–6, for the Keidanren summary of McGovern's appearance. According to the Keidanren summary, McGovern also agreed with Connally's opinion that the U.S. Congress would oppose a devaluation of the dollar.

64. The JEC has no legislative authority but often serves as a forum for the discussion of complex economic policy issues for interested members of both chambers.

65. *Nihon Keizai Shimbun,* September 20, 1971 (evening edition), p. 2.

66. *New York Times,* September 29, 1971, p. 15.

67. *New York Times,* September 22, 1971, p. 1.

68. *Nihon Keizai Shimbun,* September 29, 1971, p. 1.

69. *Nihon Keizai Shimbun,* October 1, 1971 (evening edition), p. 1.

70. *New York Times,* October 14, 1971, p. 65.

71. *New York Times,* October 21, 1971, p. 69.

72. *New York Times,* October 26, 1971, p. 59.

73. *New York Times,* September 20, 1971, p. 15.

74. *New York Times,* September 22, 1971, p. 1.

75. *New York Times,* October 9, 1971, p. 41, and October 25, 1971, p. 50.

76. *Nihon Keizai Shimbun,* October 19, 1971 (evening edition), p. 1.

77. *Nihon Keizai Shimbun,* October 23, 1971 (evening edition), p. 1.

78. *Nihon Keizai Shimbun,* October 31, 1971, p. 1.

79. *Nihon Keizai Shimbun,* November 6, 1971, p. 2.

80. *Nihon Keizai Shimbun,* November 6, 1971 (evening edition), p. 1.

81. *New York Times,* November 7, 1971, p. 20.

82. *Nihon Keizai Shimbun,* November 10, 1971, p. 22.

83. *Nihon Keizai Shimbun,* November 10, 1971 (evening edition), p. 1.

84. Personal interviews with Takashi Hosomi, Tokyo, August 10, 1976, and Takehiro Sagami, Tokyo, August 9, 1976.

85. *Nihon Keizai Shimbun,* November 11, 1971, p. 1.

86. *Nihon Keizai Shimbun,* November 11, 1971 (evening edition), p. 2.

87. Ibid., p. 1.

88. For Ambassador Meyer's account of the Connally visit see Armin H. Meyer, *Assignment: Tokyo,* pp. 251–54, in which he mentions that Connally carried a "back channel" message from Nixon to Sato, the content of which Meyer thanks Connally for sharing with him, but which Meyer fails to share with his readers.

89. *Nihon Keizai Shimbun,* November 12, 1971, p. 1.

90. Personal interview with Yusuke Kashiwagi, Tokyo, May 28, 1976.

91. *Nihon Keizai Shimbun,* November 13, 1971, p. 1.

92. *New York Times,* November 11, 1971, p. 71, and *Nihon Keizai Shimbun,* November 12, 1971, p. 3.

8. Japan and the United States face the Inevitability of Meaningful Change

1. These generalizations are based on "off-the-record" expressions of personal opinions of Connally in 1975–1976 personal interviews with Japanese officials who had dealt directly and indirectly with him during the 1971 crisis.

2. *Nihon Keizai Shimbun,* November 15, 1971 (evening edition), p. 1.

3. *Nihon Keizai Shimbun,* November 16, 1971, p. 3.

4. *Nihon Keizai Shimbun,* December 1, 1971, p. 1.

5. *Nihon Keizai Shimbun,* November 27, 1971, p. 9.

6. *Nihon Keizai Shimbun,* November 21, 1971, p. 1.

7. *Nihon Keizai Shimbun,* December 3, 1971, p. 1.

8. *Nihon Keizai Shimbun,* December 7, 1971, p. 1.

9. *Nihon Keizai Shimbun,* November 26, 1971, p. 9.

10. *New York Times,* November 9, 1971, p. 74.

11. *Nihon Keizai Shimbun,* November 27, 1971 (evening edition), p. 1.

12. *Nihon Keizai Shimbun,* November 20, 1971, p. 1.

13. *Nihon Keizai Shimbun,* November 19, 1971, p. 3.

14. Personal interview with Goro Koyama, Tokyo, July 27, 1976.

15. *Nihon Keizai Shimbun,* December 6, 1971, p. 1.

16. *Nihon Keizai Shimbun,* December 9, 1971, p. 2.
17. Personal interview with Kazuichi Murai, Tokyo, August 16, 1976.
18. *Nihon Keizai Shimbun,* December 10, 1971, p. 6.
19. Ibid.
20. Personal interview with Kazuichi Murai, Tokyo, August 16, 1976. For a public statement of the industry's estimates of its losses and government compensation, see *Zosen-Kai* (June 1972), no. 37:60–65.
21. *Nihon Keizai Shimbun,* November 30, 1971, p. 2.
22. *Nihon Keizai Shimbun,* November 3, 1971, p. 3.
23. *Nihon Keizai Shimbun,* December 7, 1971, p. 3.
24. Personal interview with Takehiro Sagami, Tokyo, August 9, 1971.
25. *Nihon Keizai Shimbun,* December 16, 1971, p. 22.
26. *New York Times,* November 17, 1971, p. 65, and *Nihon Keizai Shimbun,* November 17, 1971 (evening edition), p. 1.
27. See, for example, Connally's November 22 speech in the *New York Times,* November 23, 1971, p. 59, and Volcker's assertion that the United States could wait indefinitely for a settlement without compromise, *New York Times,* November 25, 1971, p. 61.
28. *New York Times,* November 16, 1971, p. 65.
29. *New York Times,* November 17, 1971, p. 65.
30. Compare, for example, the *New York Times* coverage on November 19, 1971, p. 1, with that which appeared just hours after the announcement in Tokyo in the *Nihon Keizai Shimbun,* November 19, 1971 (evening edition), p. 1.
31. *New York Times,* November 5, 1971, p. 1.
32. *New York Times,* November 6, 1971, p. 41.
33. *Nihon Keizai Shimbun,* November 17, 1971 (evening edition), p. 1.
34. *New York Times,* November 27, 1971, p. 43.
35. John Connally, transcript of an April 1981 interview (aired in Japan in May) with NHK.
36. *Nihon Keizai Shimbun,* November 19, 1971 (evening edition), p. 1.
37. *Nihon Keizai Shimbun,* November 28, 1971, p. 1.
38. *Nihon Keizai Shimbun,* November 23, 1971, p. 1.
39. Yusuke Kashiwagi, *Gekidoki no Tsuka Gaiko,* pp. 8–9.
40. *Nihon Keizai Shimbun,* November 26, 1971 (evening edition), p. 1.
41. *Nihon Keizai Shimbun,* November 27, 1971 (evening edition), p. 1.
42. See detailed preliminary American and Japanese press reports of the Rome Conference in the *New York Times,* November 30, 1971, p. 1, *Nihon Keizai Shimbun,* November 30, 1971 (evening edition), p. 1, and *Nihon Keizai Shimbun,* December 1, 1971, p. 1.
43. Kashiwagi, *Gekidoki no Tsuka Gaiko,* p. 145.

44. *Nihon Keizai Shimbun,* December 1, 1971 (evening edition), pp. 1–2. One interviewee stated that Connally actually made his dollar devaluation offer during this first session, which was followed by a suddenly arranged meeting of the EEC finance ministers.

45. *Nihon Keizai Shimbun,* December 2, 1971, p. 1

46. John Connally, transcript of an April 1981 television interview with NHK (aired in Japan in May).

47. *New York Times,* December 2, 1971, p. 1.

48. *New York Times,* December 3, 1971, p. 1.

49. See the *New York Times,* December 15, 1971, pp. 1 and 48, for the full text of the joint communique, and *Nihon Keizai Shimbun,* December 15, 1971, p. 1.

50. See *Nihon Keizai Shimbun,* December 2, 1971 (evening edition), p. 1, and a special interview with Governor Sasaki done in Rome by Nikkei Special Correspondent Ichioka (later Nihon Keizai Shimbun's Washington bureau chief) in *Nihon Keizai Shimbun,* December 2, 1971 (evening edition), p. 2.

51. Personal interview with Tadashi Sasaki, Tokyo, August 11, 1971.

52. *Nihon Keizai Shimbun,* December 3, 1971 (evening edition), p. 1.

9. Negotiating a "Final" Settlement

1. Personal interview with anonymous director general, Ministry of Foreign Affairs, Tokyo, February 1976.

2. This is a summary of critical comments made by non-MOF and Bank of Japan former government officials about the behavior of the international moneymen, all given "off-the-record." Five years after the event, even retired officials were surprisingly unwilling to criticize the Ministry of Finance directly for attribution.

3. *Nihon Keizai Shimbun,* November 18, 1971, p. 1.

4. *Nihon Keizai Shimbun,* December 7, 1971 (evening edition), p. 1.

5. *Nihon Keizai Shimbun,* December 12, 1971, p. 1.

6. *Nihon Keizai Shimbun,* December 10, 1971 (evening edition), p. 1.

7. *Nihon Keizai Shimbun,* December 11, 1971 (evening edition), p. 1.

8. *Nihon Keizai Shimbun,* December 13, 1971, pp. 1 and 3.

9. *Nihon Keizai Shimbun,* December 13, 1971 (evening edition), p. 1.

10. Ibid.

11. Recollection of a member of Japan's negotiating team at the Honolulu conference, and *Nihon Keizai Shimbun,* December 13, 1971, pp. 1 and 3.

12. Personal interviews with two members of Japan's negotiating team who wish to remain anonymous on this point.

13. *Nihon Keizai Shimbun*, December 14, 1971 (evening edition), p. 1.

14. *Nihon Keizai Shimbun*, December 15, 1971, p. 1.

15. Ibid., p. 3.

16. *Nihon Keizai Shimbun*, December 16, 1971, p. 2.

17. *New York Times*, December 16, 1971, p. 44.

18. *New York Times*, December 17, 1971, p. 63.

19. *Nihon Keizai Shimbun*, December 17, 1971, p. 1.

20. *Nihon Keizai Shimbun*, December 17, 1971 (evening edition), p. 1.

21. *Nihon Keizai Shimbun*, December 18, 1971 (evening edition), p. 1.

22. *Nihon Keizai Shimbun*, December 20, 1971, p. 2.

23. Ibid.

24. *Nihon Keizai Shimbun*, December 7, 1971 (evening edition), p. 1.

25. *Nihon Keizai Shimbun*, December 16, 1971 (evening edition), p. 1.

26. *Nihon Keizai Shimbun*, December 17, 1971 (evening edition), p. 1.

27. *Nihon Keizai Shimbun*, December 17, 1971, p. 1.

28. Yusuke Kashiwagi, *Gekidoki no Tsuka Gaiko*, p. 149.

29. Ibid., pp. 146–147.

30. *New York Times*, December 18, 1971, p. 45.

31. *Nihon Keizai Shimbun*, December 19, 1971, p. 1.

32. Personal interview with Mikio Mizuta, Tokyo, August 20, 1976.

33. Mizuta later admitted his illness was more diplomatic than gastric. He said he had stayed away from the dinner to avoid being pressed during the dinner discussion to commit Japan to a specific rate of up-valuation, preferring to negotiate further with Connally through Kashiwagi. Personal interview with Mikio Mizuta, Tokyo, August 20, 1976.

34. *Nihon Keizai Shimbun*, December 19, 1971, p. 1.

35. From the transcript of an interview taped with John Connally in April 1981 for broadcast by NHK in May 1981.

36. Personal interview with Mikio Mizuta, Tokyo, August 20, 1976.

37. Interviews with two members of Japan's delegation to the Smithsonian conference who wish to remain anonymous on this particular point.

38. Ibid.

39. Personal interview with a member of Japan's negotiating team who wishes to remain anonymous on this point.

40. *New York Times*, December 19, 1971, p. 1. Also see de Vries, *The*

International Monetary Fund, 1:553–556, for a summary of the full settlement.

41. *Nihon Keizai Shimbun,* December 21, 1971, p. 1.

42. *Nihon Keizai Shimbun,* December 19, 1971 (special edition), p. 1.

43. Ibid.

44. *Nihon Keizai Shimbun,* December 21, 1971 (evening edition), p. 1.

45. See *Nihon Keizai Shimbun,* December 20, 1971, p. 4, for their statements and the lackluster treatment they received in the press.

46. *Nihon Keizai Shimbun,* December 22, 1971, p. 2.

10. Conclusion

1. The United States too had not experienced a postwar exchange rate change, but as the "key currency" nation it was a special case.

2. Max Weber, "Bureaucracy," in *From Max Weber: Essays in Sociology,* pp. 233–234.

3. See Taizo Hayashi, "Arufa Sagyo (En Kiriage Junbi) no Zasetsu [Collapse of the Alpha Operation (Preparation for Yen Revaluation)], *Kinyu Zaisei Jijo,* February 7, 1977, pp. 36–40, for a detailed, almost bitter account of his effort to persuade the MOF leadership to up-value the yen in late 1969.

4. Personal interview with Tadashi Sasaki, Tokyo, August 11, 1976.

5. Personal interview with Dr. Masaru Yoshitomi, Tokyo, August 3, 1976.

6. Personal interview with an anonymous EPA official, Tokyo, August 1976.

7. Personal interview with Tatsuro Uchino, Tokyo, August 16, 1976.

8. On this point see Gerald L. Curtis, "Big Business and Political Influence," pp. 33–70, especially p. 59.

9. Constitution of Japan, Chapter V, Articles 68 and 72.

10. For a balanced view of the positive and negative aspects of the American system of political appointees in the bureaucracy, see Hugh Heclo *A Government of Strangers: Executive Politics in Washington.*

11. Johnson *MITI and the Japanese Miracle,* p. 52.

12. Ibid., p. 36.

13. See Robert C. Angel, "Prime Ministerial Leadership in Japan," pp. 583–602, for details of the Nakasone administration's efforts to create a "presidential" style premiership.

Selected Bibliography

Books, Articles, and Government Documents

Ackley, Gardner and Hiromitsu Ishi. "Fiscal, Monetary, and Related Policies." In *Asia's New Giant: How the Japanese Economy Works,* pp. 153–247. Washington, D.C.: Brookings Institution, 1976.

Adams, T. F. M. and Iwao Hoshii. *A Financial History of the New Japan.* Tokyo: Kodansha International, 1972.

Allison, Graham T. *Essence of Decision: Explaining the Cuban Missile Crisis.* Boston: Little, Brown, 1971.

Angel, Robert C. "Beikoku no Sengo Seiji ni Okeru Nihon no Imi" (The Significance of Japan in Postwar American Politics). In *Kokusai Mondai* (International Affairs) (January 1986), no. 310, pp. 18–34.

Angel, Robert C. "Prime Ministerial Leadership in Japan: Recent Changes in Personal Style and Administrative Organization," *Pacific Affairs* (Winter 1988–89), vol. 61, no. 4.

Asahi Shimbun-sha. *Keizai Seisaku no Butai-ura* (A Behind-the-Scenes Look at Economic Policy). Tokyo: Asahi Shimbun-sha, 1974.

Baerwald, Hans H. *The Purge of Japanese Leaders Under the Occupation.* New York: Columbia University Press, 1959.

Bauer, Raymond A. "The Study of Policy Formation: An Introduction." In Raymond A. Bauer and Kenneth J. Gergen, eds., *The Study of Policy Formation,* pp. 1–26. New York: Free Press, 1968.

Bieda, K. *The Structure and Operation of the Japanese Economy.* New York: Wiley Australasia, 1970.

Bordo, Michael D. "The Gold Standard: The Traditional Approach." In Michael D. Bordo and Anna J. Schwartz, eds., *A Retrospective on the Classical Gold Standard, 1821–1931,* pp. 23–113. Chicago: University of Chicago Press, 1984.

Bradfield, Michael. "Powers of the Secretary of the Treasury—Gold and Foreign Exchange." Office of the General Counsel, U.S. Department of Treasury, (departmental memorandum) March 31, 1971.

Brandon, Henry. *The Retreat of American Power.* New York: Dell, Inc., 1972.

Calder, Kent. *Crisis and Compensation: Public Policy and Political Stability in Japan, 1949–1986*. Princeton, N.J.: Princeton University Press, 1988.

Campbell, John Creighton. *Contemporary Japanese Budget Politics*. Berkeley: University of California Press, 1977.

Cohen, Jerome B. *Japan's Postwar Economy*. Bloomington: Indiana University Press, 1958.

Cohen, Theodore. *Remaking Japan: The American Occupation as New Deal*. New York: Free Press, 1987.

Cooper, Richard N. *The Economics of Interdependence*. New York: McGraw-Hill, 1968.

Cooper, Richard N. "The Gold Standard: Historical Facts and Future Prospects." In *Brookings Papers on Economic Activity* (1982), no. 1.

Curtis, Gerald L. "Big Business and Political Influence." In Ezra F. Vogel, ed., *Modern Japanese Organization and Decision-making*, pp. 33–70. Berkeley: University of California Press, 1975.

Dale, William B. "Exchange Rate Realignment and Related Matters." U.S. Department of Treasury, (departmental memorandum), January 28, 1971.

Destler, I. M. "U.S.-Japanese Relations and the American Trade Initiative of 1977: Was This 'Trip' Necessary?" In William J. Barnds, ed., *Japan and the United States: Challenges and Opportunities*, pp. 190–230. New York: New York University Press, 1979.

Destler, I. M., Haruhiro Fukui, and Hideo Sato. *The Textile Wrangle: Conflict in Japanese-American Relations. 1969–1971*. Ithaca, N.Y.: Cornell University Press, 1979.

de Vries, Margaret Garritsen, "The IMF: 40 Years of Challenge and Change," in *Finance and Development* (1986), vol. 22, no. 3, pp. 7–10.

de Vries, Margaret Garritsen. *The International Monetary Fund: 1966–1971: The System Under Stress*, Vol 1: *Narrative*, Vol 2: *Documents*. Washington, D.C.: IMF, 1976.

Fellner, W. "On Limited Exchange Rate Flexibility." In R. N. Cooper, ed., *International Finance*. pp. 212–222. Harmondsworth, England: Penguin Books, 1969.

Fried, Edward R. and Philip H. Trezise. *Japan's Future Position in the World Economy*. Report no. DCS/XR 320048. Washington, D.C.: National Technical Information Service, 1974.

Fujioka, Masao. *Tenkanki no Kokusai Kinyu* (International Monetary Affairs at a Turning Point). Tokyo: Kinyu Zaisei Jijo Kenkyukai, 1975.

Fukui, Haruhiro. "Policy-Making in the Japanese Foreign Ministry." In Robert A. Scalapino, ed., *The Foreign Economic Policy of Modern Japan*, pp. 3–35. Berkeley: University of California Press, 1977.

Funk, W. *Wirtschaftliche Neuordnung Europas*. Berlin: M. Muller und

Sohn, 1940. Cited in Armand Van Dormael. *Bretton Woods: Birth of a Monetary System.* New York: Holmes & Meier, 1978.

Gardner, Richard N. *Sterling-Dollar Diplomacy.* London: Oxford University Press, 1956.

Gardner, Richard N. *Sterling Dollar Diplomacy in Current Perspective.* New York: Columbia University Press, 1980.

Gold, Joseph, "Keynes and the Articles of the Fund." *Finance and Development* (September, 1981), vol. 18, no. 3, pp. 38–129.

Haitani, Kanji. *The Japanese Economic System: An Institutional Overview.* Lexington, Mass.: Lexington Books, 1976.

Halperin, Morton H., Pricilla Clapp, and Arnold Kanter. *Bureaucratic Politics and Foreign Policy.* Washington, D.C.: Brookings Institution, 1974.

Hayashi, Taizo. " 'En Kiriage Sagyo' no Zasetsu kara Furoto Made" (From the Collapse of the 'Yen Revaluation Operation' to the Float) *Kinyu Zaisei Jijo,* January 31, 1977, to March 3, 1977.

Heclo, Hugh. *A Government of Strangers: Executive Politics in Washington.* Washington, D.C.: Brookings Institution, 1977.

Hemmendinger, Noel. "Establishment of the Japanese Controlled Single Exchange Rate." Paper presented at American University, January 1950.

Ho, Alfred K. *Japan's Trade Liberalization in the 1960s.* White Plains, N.Y.: International Arts and Sciences Press, 1973.

Horsefield, J. Keith. *The International Monetary Fund: 1945–1965.* 3 vols. Washington, D.C.: International Monetary Fund, 1969.

Hunsberger, Warren S. *Japan and the United States in World Trade.* New York: Harper and Row, 1964.

Japan, Kokkai, Sangiin *Kaigiroku.* Dai 66–kai, Dai 1–rui, pt. 14, Kessan Iinkai, October 5, 1971.

Japan, Kokkai, Shugiin, *Kaigiroku.* Dai 66–kai, Dai 1–rui, pt. 5, Okura Iinkai, September 1, 1971.

Japan Culture Institute. "The Bureaucracy: Japan's Pool of Leadership." In Hyoe Murakami and Johannes Hirschmeier, eds., *Politics and Economics in Contemporary Japan.* pp. 79–92. Tokyo: Kodansha International, 1983.

Johnson, Chalmers. *MITI and the Japanese Miracle.* Stanford, Calif.: Stanford University Press, 1982.

Kades, Charles L. "The American Role in Revising Japan's Imperial Constitution." In *Political Science Quarterly* (1989), vol. 104, no. 2, pp. 217–219.

Kashiwagi, Yusuke. *Gekidoki no Tsuka Gaiko* (International Monetary Diplomacy in a Period of Turmoil). Tokyo: Kinyu Zaisei Jijo Kenkyukai, 1972.

Kawai, Kazuo. *Japan's American Interlude.* Chicago: University of Chicago Press, 1960.

Keizai Kikakucho (Economic Planning Agency), ed., *Gendai Nihon Keizai no Tenkai: Keizai Kikakucho 30–Nen Shi* (The Evolution of Japan's Modern Economy: A 30–Year History of the Economic Planning Agency). Tokyo: Keizai Kikakucho, 1976.

League of Nations: Economic, Financial, and Transit Department. *International Currency Experience: Lessons of the Inter-War Period.* Princeton, N.J.: Princeton University Press, 1944.

Lincoln, Edward. "Discount Rate Cut Under Consideration." In *JEI Report* (Washington, D.C.: Japan Economic Institute) (January 16, 1981), no. 2, pp. 7–8.

Lincoln, Edward J. *Japan's Unequal Trade.* Washington, D.C.: Brookings Institution, 1990.

Meier, Gerald M. *Problems of a World Monetary Order.* New York: Oxford University Press, 1974.

Meyer, Armin H. *Assignment: Tokyo.* Indianapolis, Ind.: Bobbs-Merrill, 1974.

Monroe, Wilbur F. *Japan: Financial Markets and the World Economy.* New York: Praeger, 1973.

Nakamura, Takafusa. *The Postwar Japanese Economy: Its Development and Structure.* Translated by Jacqueline Kaminski. Tokyo: University of Tokyo Press, 1981.

Nihon Keizai Chosa Kyogikai. *Kokusai Tsuka oyobi Kokusai Kinyu Mondai* (International Currency and the International Monetary Problem). Tokyo: Nihon Keizai Chosa Kyogikai, 1970.

Organization for Economic Cooperation and Development. *Economic Survey: Japan, 1969.* Paris: OECD, 1969.

Pasvolsky, Leo. *Current Monetary Issues,* pp. 64–91. Washington, D.C.: Brookings Institution, 1933.

Patrick, Hugh T. "Cyclical Instability and Fiscal-Monetary Policy in Postwar Japan." In William W. Lockwood, ed., *The State and Economic Enterprise in Japan,* pp. 565–566. Princeton, N.J.: Princeton University Press, 1965.

Patrick, Hugh T. "The Phoenix Risen from the Ashes: Postwar Japan." In James Crowley, ed., *Modern East Asia: Essays in Interpretation.* New York: Harcourt, Brace Jovanovich, 1970.

Rightor-Thornton, Anne H. "An Analysis of the Office of the Special Representative for Trade Negotiations: The Evolving Role, 1962–1974." Appendix H: *Case Studies on U.S. Foreign Economic Policy: 1965–1974,* pp. 88–104. Report of the Commission on the Organization of the Government for the Conduct of Foreign Policy, 93rd Cong., 2d sess., 1975.

Rolfe, Sidney E. *Gold and World Power.* New York: Harper and Row, 1966.

Rolfe, Sidney E. and James Burtle, *The Great Wheel: The World Monetary System, a Reinterpretation.* New York: Quadrangle Books, 1973.

Roosa, Robert V. *The United States and Japan in the International Monetary System, 1946–1985.* New York: Group of Thirty, 1986.

Saxonhouse, Gary. "The Textile Confrontation." In Jerome B. Cohen, ed., *Pacific Partnership: United States-Japan Trade.* pp. 177–99. Lexington, Mass.: Lexington Books, 1971.

Solomon, Robert. *The International Monetary System, 1945–1976: an Insider's View.* New York: Harper and Row, 1977.

Spindler, J. Andrew. *The Politics of International Credit: Private Finance and Foreign Policy in Germany and Japan.* Washington, D.C.: Brookings Institution, 1984.

Stockwin, J. A. A. *Japan: Divided Politics in a Growth Economy.* New York: W. W. Norton, 1975.

Triffin, Robert. *Gold and the Dollar Crisis,* Rev. ed. New Haven: Yale University Press, 1961.

Triffin, Robert. "The International Role and Fate of the Dollar." *Foreign Affairs* (Winter 1978–79).

Triffin, Robert. *The World Money Maze: National Currencies in International Payments.* New Haven: Yale University Press, 1966.

Uchino, Tatsuro. *Japan's Postwar Economy: An Insider's View of Its History and Its Future.* Tokyo: Kodansha International, 1983.

U.S. Congress, Senate, Finance Committee, *Hearings,* 92nd Cong., 1st Sess., May 18, 1971.

U.S. Department of State, *Proceedings and Documents of the United Nations Monetary and Financial Conference, Bretton Woods, New Hampshire, July 1–22, 1944* (Washington, D.C.: GPO, 1948).

U.S. Department of State. *United States Foreign Policy, 1972.* General Foreign Policy Series, no. 274, pubn. 8699 (1973).

van Wolferen, Karel. *The Enigma of Japanese Power.* New York: Knopf, 1989.

Vogel, Ezra F. *Japan as Number One: Lessons for America.* Cambridge, Mass.: Harvard University Press, 1979.

Ward, Robert E. "Conclusion." In Robert E. Ward and Yoshikazu Sakamoto, eds., *Democratizing Japan: the Allied Occupation,* pp. 405–414. Honolulu: University of Hawaii Press, 1987.

Weber, Max. "Bureaucracy." In H. H. Gerth and C. Wright Mills, eds. and translators, *From Max Weber: Essays in Sociology,* pp. 196–244. New York: Oxford University Press, 1958.

Widman, Lyle. "Contingency: Eyes Only." Research Department, International Affairs Division, U.S. Department of Treasury, (departmental memorandum) May 8, 1971.

Williamson, John. "On the System in Bretton Woods." *American Economic Review* (May 1985), vol. 75, no. 2.

Willis, George. "Financing the 1971 Deficit—and Beyond 1971." International Affairs Division, U.S. Department of Treasury, (departmental memorandum), February 22, 1971.

Yamamura, Kozo. *Economic Policy in Postwar Japan: Growth Versus Economic Democracy*. Berkeley: University of California Press, 1967.

Newspapers

New York Times, 1969–1971.
Nihon Keizai Shimbun, 1969–1971.
American Embassy, Tokyo. *Daily Summary of the Japanese Press*, 1969–1971 (for *Asahi Shimbun*, *Yomiuri Shimbun*, and *Tokyo Shimbun* coverage of Japanese events).

Interviews

Caldwell, John. Former Executive Secretary, U.S. Delegation to the U.S.-Japan Businessmen's Conference. February 9, 1982.
Connally, John. Former Secretary of the Treasury, United States Government. Transcript of an April 1981 television interview with NHK which was aired in Japan in early May 1981.
Escoube, William. Treasury Attache, American Embassy, Tokyo. August 6, 1976.
Gyohten, Toyoo. Former Assistant to the Vice Minister for International Monetary Affairs, Ministry of Finance, Government of Japan. April 12, 1976.
Hara, Yasushi. Member of the Editorial Board, *Asahi Shimbun*, Tokyo. February 2, 1976.
Hatoyama, Iichiro. Former Administrative Vice Minister, Ministry of Finance, Government of Japan. April 9, 1976; August 2, 1976; August 18, 1976; and August 27, 1976.
Hayashi, Taizo. Former Director General, International Monetary Bureau, Ministry of Finance, Government of Japan. February 16, 1976.
Hori, Masao. Japan Socialist Party Member of the Lower House. August 5, 1976.
Hosomi, Takashi. Former Vice Minister for International Monetary Affairs, Ministry of Finance, Government of Japan. February 13, 1976; June 24, 1976; June 29, 1976; July 13, 1976; and August 10, 1976.
Inamura, Koichi. Former Deputy Director General of the International Monetary Bureau, Ministry of Finance, Government of Japan. June 23, 1976, and August 4, 1976.
Iwasa, Yoshizane. Former Chairman of the U.S.-Japan Economic Council and Chairman of Fuji Bank, Tokyo. July 27, 1976.
Kaji, Motoo. Professor of Economics, Tokyo University. February 7, 1976.

Kashiwagi, Yusuke. Former Vice Minister for International Monetary Affairs and Special Adviser to the Minister, Ministry of Finance, Government of Japan. May 28, 1976.

Kosaka, Zentaro. Liberal Democratic Party Member of the Lower House and former Chairman of the LDP Policy Affairs Research Council. August 16, 1976.

Koyama, Goro. Chairman, Mitsui Bank, Tokyo. July 27, 1976.

Mitani, Katsumi. Director of Research, Nihon Keizai Chosa Kyogikai. May 31, 1976.

Miyazaki, Hiromichi. Director General of the Economic Bureau, Ministry of Foreign Affairs, Government of Japan. February 6, 1976.

Miyoshi, Masaya. Former Director of the International Division, Keidanren, Tokyo. June 21, 1976.

Mizuta, Mikio. Liberal Democratic Party Member of the Lower House and former Minister of Finance, Government of Japan. August 20, 1976.

Murai, Kazuichi. Senior Staff Member, Association of Japanese Shipbuilders, Tokyo. August 16, 1976.

Murai, Shichiro. Former Director General, International Monetary Bureau, Ministry of Finance, Government of Japan. August 4, 1976.

Mylnarchik, Roy A. Political Section, American Embassy, Tokyo. April 23, 1976.

Ogata, Shijuro. Chief Representative, Bank of Japan, New York. June 25, 1975.

Oshima, Yoichi. Associate Adviser, Economic Research Department, Bank of Japan, Tokyo. July 19, 1976.

Sagami, Takehiro. Director of Research and Planning, Minister's Secretariat, Ministry of Finance, Government of Japan. May 27, 1976, and August 9, 1976.

Sasaki, Tadashi. Former Governor, Bank of Japan, and Chairman, Keizai Doyukai, Tokyo. August 11, 1976.

Suzuki, Hideo. Former Japanese Representative to the International Monetary Fund, Washington, D.C. July 16, 1976.

Taguchi, Kenjiro. Former Director, Foreign Exchange Division, Trade Bureau, Ministry of International Trade and Industry, Government of Japan. Interviews, October 29, 1975, and August 17, 1976.

Takakura, Tadashi. Senior Researcher, Policy Research Committee and former Executive Secretary, Liberal Democratic Party, Tokyo. July 1, 1976.

Takeuchi, Ichiro. Director of Research, Bank of Tokyo, Tokyo. August 16, 1976.

Takeyama, Yasuo. Managing Editor, *Nihon Keizai Shimbun,* Tokyo. January 12, 1976.

Taki, Takaaki. Secretary General, Tokyo Chamber of Commerce and Industry, Tokyo. July 23, 1976.

Uchino, Tatsuro. Deputy Minister (*Shingikan*), Economic Planning Agency, Government of Japan. August 16, 1976.

Ushiba, Nobuhiko. Former Japanese Ambassador to the United States. March 15, 1976, and August 6, 1976.

Wakao, Masaaki. General Manager, Special Assignment, Executive Office, Sony Corporation, Tokyo. December 9, 1975.

Yamamoto, Mitsuru. Professor of Economics, Seikei University, Tokyo. February 12, 1976.

Yamashita, Seiichi. Executive Director, Keizai Doyukai, Tokyo. July 28, 1976.

Yoda, Susumu. Director of Research Division, Tokyo Denryoku and former aide to Mr. Kikawada, Chairman of Keizai Doyukai, Tokyo. July 28, 1976.

Yoshitomi, Masaru. Senior Economist, Economic Planning Agency, Government of Japan, and former Staff Member of the International Monetary Fund, Washington, D.C. February 12, 1976.

Index

Studies of the East Asian Institute

The Ladder of Success in Imperial China, by Ping-ti Ho. New York: Columbia University Press, 1962.

The Chinese Inflation, 1937–1949, by Shun-hsin Chou. New York: Columbia University Press, 1963.

Reformer In Modern China: Chang Chien, 1853–1926, by Samuel Chu. New York: Columbia University Press, 1965.

Research in Japanese Sources: A Guide, by Herschel Webb with the assistance of Marleigh Ryan. New York: Columbia University Press, 1965.

Society And Education In Japan, by Herbert Passin. New York: Teachers College Press, 1965.

Agricultural Production And Economic Developments In Japan, 1873–1922, by James I. Nakamura. Princeton: Princeton University Press, 1967.

Japan's First Modern Novel: Ukigumo of futabatei Shimei, by Marleigh Ryan. New York: Columbia University Press, 1967.

The Korean Communist Movement, 1918–1948, by Dae-Sook Suh. Princeton: Princeton University Press, 1967.

The First Vietnam Crisis, by Melvin Gurtov. New York: Columbia University Press, 1967.

Cadres, Bureaucracy, and Political Power in Communist China, by A. Doak Barnett. New York: Columbia University Press, 1968.

The Japanese Imperial Institution In the tokugawa Period, by Herschel Webb. New York: Columbia University Press, 1968.

Higher Education And Business Recruitment In Japan, by Koya Azumi. New York: Teachers College Press, 1969.

The Communists And Peasant Rebellions: A Study In the rewriting of Chinese History, by James P. Harrison, Jr. New York: Atheneum, 1969.

How the Conservatives Rule Japan, by Nathaniel B. Thayer. Princeton: Princeton University Press, 1969.

Aspects of Chinese Education, edited by C.T. Hu. New York: Teachers College Press, 1970.

Documents of Korean Communism, 1918–1948, by Dae-Sook Suh. Princeton: Princeton University Press, 1970.

Japanese Education: A Bibliography of Materials in the English Language, by Herbert Passin. New York: Teachers College Press, 1970.

Economic Development and the Labor Market in Japan, by Koji Taira. New York: Columbia University Press, 1970.

The Japanese Oligarchy and the Russo-Japanese War, by Shumpei Okamoto. New York: Columbia University Press, 1970.

Imperial Restoration in Medieval Japan, by H. Paul Varley. New York: Columbia University Press, 1971.

Japan's Postwar Defense Policy, 1947–1968, by Martin E. Weinstein. New York: Columbia University Press, 1971.

Election Campaigning Japanese Style, by Gerald L. Curtis. New York: Columbia University Press, 1971.

China and Russia: the "Great Game," by O. Edmund Clubb. New York: Columbia University Press, 1971.

Money and Monetary Policy in Communist China, by Katharine Huang Hsiao. New York: Columbia University Press, 1971.

The District Magistrate in Late Imperial China, by John R. Watt. New York: Columbia University Press, 1972.

Law and Policy in China's Foreign Relations: A Study of attitude and Practice, by James C. Hsiung. New York: Columbia University Press, 1972.

Pearl Harbor as History: Japanese-American Relations, 1931–1941, edited by Dorothy Borg and Shumpei Okamoto, with the assistance of Dale K. A. Finlayson. New York: Columbia University Press, 1973.

Japanese Culture: A Short History, by H. Paul Varley. New York: Praeger, 1973.

Doctors in Politics: The Political Life of the Japan Medical Association, by William E. Steslicke. New York: Praeger, 1973.

The Japan Teachers Union: A Radical Interest Group in Japanese Politics, by Donald Ray Thurston. Princeton: Princton University Press, 1973.

Japan's Foreign Policy, 1868–1941: A Research Guide, edited by James William Morley. New York: Columbia University Press, 1974.

Palace and Politics in Prewar Japan, by David Anson Titus. New York: Columbia University Press, 1974.

The Idea of china: Essays in Geographic Myth and Theory, by Andrew March. Devon, England: David and Charles, 1974.

Origins of the Cultural Revolution, by Roderick MacFarquhar. New York: Columbia University Press, 1974.

Shiba Kōkan: Artist, Innovator, and Pioneer in the Westernization of Japan, by Calvin L. French. Tokyo: Weatherhill, 1974.

Insei: Abdicated Sovereigns in the Politics of Late Heian Japan, by G. Cameron Hurst. New York: Columbia University Press, 1975.

Embassy at War, by Harold Joyce Noble. Edited with an intro- duction by Frank Baldwin, Jr. Seattle: University of Washington Press, 1975.

Rebels and Bureaucrats: China's December 9ers, by John Israel and Donald W. Klein. Berkeley: University of California Press, 1975.

Deterrent Diplomacy, edited by James William Morley. New York: Columbia University Press, 1976.

House United, House Divided: The Chinese Family in Taiwan, by Myron L. Cohen. New York: Columbia University Press, 1976.

Escape from Predicament: Neo-confucianism and China's Evolving Political Culture, by Thomas A. Metzger. New York: Columbia University Press, 1976.

Cadres, Commanders, and Commissars: The Training of the Chinese Communist Leadership, 1920–45, by Jane L. Price. Boulder, Colo.: Westview Press, 1976.

Sun Yat-Sen: Frustrated Patriot, by C. Martin Wilbur. New York: Columbia University Press, 1977.

Japanese International Negotiating Style, by Michael Blaker. New York: Columbia University Press, 1977.

Contemporary Japanese Budget Politics, by John Creighton Campbell. Berkeley: University of California Press, 1977.

The Medieval Chinese Oligarchy, by David Johnson. Boulder, Colo.: Westview Press, 1977.

The Arms of Kiangnan: Modernization in the Chinese Ordnance Industry, 1860–1895, by Thomas L. Kennedy. Boulder, Colo.: Westview Press, 1978.

Patterns of Japanese Policymaking: Experiences from Higher Education, by T. J. Pempel. Boulder, Colo.: Westview Press, 1978.

The Chinese Connection: Roger S. Greene, Thomas W. Lamont, George E. Sokolsky, and American-East Asian Relations, by Warren I. Cohen. New York: Columbia University Press, 1978.

Militarism in Modern China: The Career of Wu P'ei-fu, 1916–1939, by Odoric Y. K. Wou. Folkestone, England: Dawson, 1978.

A Chinese Pioneer Family: The Lins of Wu-Feng, by Johanna Meskill. Princeton University Press, 1979.

Perspectives On a Changing China, edited by Joshua A. Fogel and William T. Rowe. Boulder, Colo.: Westview Press, 1979.

The Memoirs of Li Tsung-Jen, by T.K. Tong and Li Tsung-jen. Boulder, Colo.: Westview Press, 1979.

Unwelcome Muse: Chinese Literature in Shanghai and Peking, 1937–1945, by Edward Gunn. New York: Columbia University Press, 1979.

Yenan and the Great Powers: The Origins of Chinese Communist Foreign Policy, by James Reardon-Anderson. New York: Columbia University Press, 1980.

Uncertain Years: Chinese-American Relations, 1947–1950, edited by Dorothy Borg and Waldo Heinrichs. New York: Columbia University Press, 1980.

The Fateful Choice: Japan's Advance into Southeast Asia, edited by James William Morley, New York: Columbia University Press, 1980.

Tanaka Giichi and Japan's China Policy, by William F. Morton. Folkestone, England: Dawson, 1980; New York: St. Martin's Press, 1980.

The Origins of the Korean War: Liberation and the Emergence of Separate Regimes, 1945–1947, by Bruce Cumings. Princeton University Press, 1981.

Class Conflict in Chinese Socialism, by Richard Curt Kraus. New York: Columbia University Press, 1981.

Education Under Mao: Class and Competition in Canton Schools, by Jonathan Unger. New York: Columbia University Press, 1982.

Private Academies of Tokugawa Japan, by Richard Rubinger. Princeton: Princeton University Press, 1982.

Japan and the San Francisco Peace Settlement, by Michael M. Yoshitsu. New York: Columbia University Press, 1982.

New Frontiers in American-East Asian Relations: Essays Presented to Dorothy Borg, edited by Warren I. Cohen. New York: Columbia University Press, 1983.

The Origins of the Cultural Revolution: Ii, the Great Leap Forward, 1958–1960, by Roderick MacFarquhar. New York: Columbia University Press, 1983.

The China Quagmire: Japan's Expansion of the Asian Continent, 1933–1941, edited by James William Morley. New York: Columbia University Press, 1983.

Fragments of Rainbows: The Life and Poetry of Saito Mokichi, 1882–1953, by Amy Vladeck Heinrich. New York: Columbia University Press, 1983.

The U.S.-South Korean Alliance: Evolving Patterns of Security Relations, edited by Gerald L. Curtis and Sung-joo Han. Lexington, Mass.: Lexington Books, 1983.

Discovering History in China; American Historical Writing on the Recent Chinese Past, by Paul A. Cohen. New York: Columbia University Press, 1984.

The Foreign Policy of the Republic of Korea, edited by Youngnok Koo and Sungjoo Han. New York: Columbia University Press, 1984.

State and Diplomacy in Early Modern Japan, by Ronald Toby. Princeton: Princeton University Press, 1983.

Japan and the Asian Development Bank, by Dennis Yasutomo. New York: Praeger Publishers, 1983.

Japan Erupts: the London Naval Conference and the Manchurian Incident, edited by James W. Morley. New York: Columbia University Press, 1984.

Japanese Culture, third edition, revised, by Paul Varley. Honolulu: University of Hawaii Press, 1984.

Japan's Modern Myths: Ideology in the Late Meiji Period, by Carol Gluck. Princeton: Princeton University Press, 1985.

Shamans, Housewives, and Other Restless Spirits: Women in Korean Ritual Life, by Laurel Kendell. Honolulu: University of Hawaii Press, 1985.

Human Rights in Contemporary China, by R. Randle Edwards, Louis Henkin, and Andrew J. Nathan. New York: Columbia University Press, 1986.

The Pacific Basin: New Challenges for the United States, edited by James W. Morley. New York: Academy of Political Science, 1986.

The Manner of Giving: Strategic Aid and Japanese Foreign Policy, by Dennis T. Yasutomo. Lexington, Mass.: Lexington Books, 1986.

Security Interdependence in the Asia Pacific Region, James W. Morley, Ed., Lexington, MA-DC: Heath and Co, 1986.

China's Political Economy: The Quest for Development Since 1949, by Carl Riskin. Oxford: Oxford University Press, 1987.

Anvil of Victory: The Communist Revolution in Manchuria, by Steven I. Levine. New York: Columbia University Press, 1987.

Single Sparks: China's Rural Revolutions, edited by Kathleen Hartford and Steven M. Goldstein. Armonk, N.Y.: M.E. Sharpe, 1987.

Urban Japanese Housewives: At Home and in the Community, by Anne E. Imamura. Honolulu: University of Hawaii Press, 1987.

China's Satellite Parties, by James D. Seymour. Armonk, N.Y.: M.E. Sharpe, 1987.

The Japanese Way of Politics, by Gerald. L. Curtis. New York: Columbia University Press, 1988.

Border Crossings: Studies in International History, by Christopher Thorne. Oxford & New York: Basil Blackwell, 1988.

The Indochina Tangle: China's Vietnam Policy, 1975–1979, by Robert S. Ross. New York: Columbia University Press, 1988.

Remaking Japan: the American Occupation as New Deal, by Theodore Cohen, Herbert Passin, ed. New York: The Free Press, 1987.

Kim Il Sung: The North Korean Leader, by Dae-Sook Suh. New York: Columbia University Press, 1988.

Japan and the World, 1853–1952: A Bibliographic Guide to Recent Scholarship in Japanese Foreign Relations, by Sadao Asada. New York: Columbia University Press, 1988.

Contending Approaches to the Political Economy of Taiwan, edited by Edwin A. Winckler and Susan Greenhalgh. Armonk, NY: M. E. Sharpe, 1988.

Aftermath of War: Americans and the Remaking of Japan, 1945–1952, by Howard B. Schonberger. Kent: Kent State University Press, 1989.

Suicidal Narrative in Modern Japan: The Case of Dazai Osamu, by Alan Wolfe. Princeton: Princeton University Press, 1990.

Neighborhood Tokyo, by Theodore C. Bestor. Stanford: Stanford University Press, 1989.

Missionaries of the Revolution: Soviet Advisers and Chinese Nationalism, by C. Martin Wilbur Julie Lien-ying How. Cambridge, MA: Harvard University Press, 1989.

Education in Japan, by Richard Rubinger and Beauchamp. Honolulu: University Hawaii, 1989.

Financial Politics in Contemporary Japan, by Frances Rosenbluth. Ithaca: Cornell University Press, 1989.

Thailand and the United States: Development, Security and Foreign Aid, by Robert Muscat. New York: Columbia University Press, 1990.

State Power, Finance and Industrialization of Korea, by Jung-Eun Woo. New York: Columbia University Press, 1990.

Anarchism and Chinese Political Culture, by Peter Zarrow. New York: Columbia University Press, 1990.

Competitive Ties: Subcontracting in the Japanese Automotive Industry, by Michael Smitka. New York: Columbia University Press, 1990.

China's Crisis: Dilemmas of Reform and Prospects for Democracy, by Andrew J. Nathan. Columbia University Press, 1990.

The Study of Change: Chemistry in China 1840–1949, by James Reardon-Anderson. New York: Cambridge University Press, 1991.

Explaining Economic Policy Failure: Japan and the 1969–1971 International Monetary Crisis, by Robert Angel. New York: Columbia University Press, 1991.

Pacific Basin Industries in Distress: Structural Adjustment and Trade Policy in the Nine Industrialized Economies, edited by Hugh T. Patrick with Larry Meissner. New York: Columbia University Press, 1991.

From Bureaucratic Polity to Liberal Corporatism: Business Associations and the New Political Economy of Thailand, by Anek Laothamatas. Boulder: Westview Press, 1991.

GPSR Authorized Representative: Easy Access System Europe, Mustamäe tee 50, 10621 Tallinn, Estonia, gpsr.requests@easproject.com

www.ingramcontent.com/pod-product-compliance
Ingram Content Group UK Ltd.
Pitfield, Milton Keynes, MK11 3LW, UK
UKHW040737260926
475591UK00003B/40
* 9 7 8 0 2 3 1 0 7 4 4 0 7 *